AT EASE

To the memory of
David Jacob and Ida Stover Eisenhower
John Sheldon Doud and Elivera Carlson Doud
who first made
possible a life for
Mamie and me together.

Now, as we look back, at ease,
they loom larger than ever

AT EASE:
Stories I Tell to Friends

DWIGHT D. EISENHOWER

Eastern Acorn Press

1981

ISBN 0-915992-04-3

Library of Congress Catalog Card Number 67-13781.

Reprinted 1981 with permission of the original publisher—Doubleday & Company, Inc.—by Eastern Acorn Press, the imprint of Eastern National Park & Monument Association.

Eastern National Park & Monument Association promotes and aids the historical, scientific, and educational activities of the National Park Service. As a nonprofit cooperating association authorized by Congress, it makes interpretive material available to park visitors by sale or free distribution. It also supports research, interpretation, and conservation programs of the Service.

Produced by the Publishing Center for Cultural Resources, NYC. Manufactured in the United States of America.

WARNING TO THE READER

I am usually opposed to the author who puts within quotation marks conversations he never heard or who pretends to recollect with absolute fidelity conversations he heard a long time ago. Now, there are a few conversations reported in this book in which I did not take part and others, which I did hear at first hand, took place fifty and even seventy or more years ago. Of the latter, the key phrases are indelibly imprinted in my memory. But I have engaged in some reconstruction. Consequently, I urge the reader to take all the quoted material, particularly that recollected across the decades, with the necessary grain of salt.

D.D.E.

Contents

Book Three
AT WAR

Book Four
AT PEACE

A Man Talking to Himself

TALKING to oneself in Abilene, in the days of my youth, was common enough. Generally speaking, it was a sure sign of senility or of preoccupation with one's worries. Now, it is nationally advertised as the hallmark of the efficient executive.

He dictates to multiply his effectiveness. Human ingenuity has wrought a revolution in human attitudes, transforming the odd into the admirable. These days, as I direct these casual reminiscences to an inanimate electronic machine that faithfully tapes every word, every tone, every mistake, perhaps I should be immersed in wonder at the changes in life since I was a boy. Happily, change has little place in my thoughts at the moment.

Instead of amazement at the new and novel I have lived to see, the preponderant notion in my mind occurs to all those in a certain age bracket when they find themselves meditating on the years, the events, the people of their past. So it was before the first pyramid was built; so it will be when man is an interplanetary commuter. The notion is, of course: Time flies.

There was a period when time behaved differently. In my case, the coming Friday and the weekend respite from school always seemed, on Monday morning, an age away. Holidays, finally reached, passed instantly. But their arrival was a prolonged, tedious, barely perceptible movement of clock and calendar. I can still recall vividly my first formal idea of time and its glacial passage.

Shortly after we moved into a new home on Fourth Street in Abilene, Kansas—I was getting along in years, being by then almost eight years old—I heard for the first time mention made of my mother's age. In conversation with a neighbor, my mother said, as I recall: "I've been married almost fourteen years and I am thirty-six years old."

And, she added, "For the first time we have a home where my children will have room to play. I am most thankful."

Now I was not especially impressed by her remark about the space we would enjoy because I hadn't been conscious of its lack. But I was so intrigued by the figure 36 that I soon worked out the year in which I would attain her venerability. The result was disheartening. Nineteen-twenty-six was ridiculously far off, a whole lifetime in the future.

Possibly, like most boys, I was convinced that life was a flat plateau of assigned tasks, unchanging in monotony and injustice. I suppose, too, that the only peak on my personal horizon would have been something like entering the halls of higher learning (the eighth grade) or bathing in glory (becoming a full-fledged member of the high-school baseball team).

I doubt that I dared search the future beyond that sort of momentous event. I daydreamed now and then about the highest and most remote peaks of all, fantastically difficult even to contemplate scaling: to be an engineer (there was only one kind), racing across the land, arriving in Abilene, steam engine hissing, bell ringing, once again breaking the record from St. Louis or some other distant, mythical place; or to set down the next three batters on nine pitches in the last half of the ninth, with the bases loaded (of course) to the thunderous applause of five hundred spectators. Certainly I never thought of myself or those about me as makers or participants in any other kind of history.

CHAPTER I

To the Point

STARTING off for West Point in June 1911, I traveled light. No boy of my acquaintance had ever been overburdened with an extensive wardrobe. Our needs were met by an odd assortment of work garb, supplemented by one dress-up suit, school clothes, and an overcoat. I had carefully read the instructions sent to prospective cadets and since all civilian clothes were to be sent home or stored, and there would be no vacation for two years, there was no need for more than a single suitcase.

For the trip I planned to take about a week, stopping off first in Chicago to see a girl named Ruby Norman, who was studying violin at the Chicago Conservatory, and in Ann Arbor, to visit my brother Ed.

I was pleased to see Ruby. She and I had been good friends during the final two years of my life in Abilene. I had been saddened when she went off to the city. We spent a couple of evenings going to the movies and to the parks and seeing the sights. The time passed quickly.

At the University of Michigan, Ed was just completing his second year. He had a job waiting on tables in a vast dining hall, which left him little time for athletics. What was worse, he, a natural athlete, had suffered a prolonged bout of appendicitis. As a result of the illness and operation, he had dropped from 170 pounds to 150. He did try track and baseball but he never got to play his natural game, football, during the Michigan years. While he was finishing his final exams, I walked around the campus and was impressed by the elaborate educational institution.

That evening he hired a canoe and we set out on the river—I believe it was the Huron—with a couple of college girls. We took along a phonograph and played the popular songs. Paddling in the moonlight, we passed canoe-loads of other students, enjoying the pleasant June evening. Afterward, we paid for the canoe and walked the girls back to their dormitories. Altogether it was rather different than the trip Ed and I once had spent floating down a "river" at home (the flood-swollen Buckeye Street) singing songs; this was, instead, up to that moment, the most romantic evening I had ever known.

When I resumed the journey, I had a dismaying feeling that perhaps I had made a mistake in changing my mind about joining Ed at Michigan. It looked to me as if he were leading the right life.

The new class of cadet candidates had been instructed to arrive at the Academy before noon on June 14, 1911. Carrying my suitcase, I left the little railway station at West Point and climbed a long hill to the administration building where the initiation process began. My impression of that first day was one of calculated chaos.

Orders were not given with any serious attempt at instruction or intended for easy comprehension. They were a series of shouts and barks.

By the end of the day we were all harassed and, at times, resentful. Here we were, the cream of the crop, shouted at all day long by self-important upperclassmen, telling us to run here and run there; pick up our clothes; bring in that bedding; put our shoulders back, keep our eyes up, and to keep running, running, running. No one was allowed to do anything at ordinary quick-time; everything was on the double. I suppose that if any time had been provided to sit down and think for a moment, most of the 285 of us would have taken the next train out. But no one was given much time to think —and when I did it was always, "Where else could you get a college education without cost?"

Toward evening, all of us were brought together en masse and sworn in as cadets of the United States Military Academy. Whatever had gone before, this was a supreme moment. The day had been one of confusion and a heroic brand of rapid adjustment. But when we raised our right hands and repeated the official oath, there was no confusion. A feeling came over me that the expression "The United States of America" would now and henceforth mean something different than it ever had before. From here on it would be the nation I would be serving, not myself. Suddenly the flag itself meant something. I haven't heard other officers speak of their memories of that moment but mine have never left me. Across half a century, I can look back and see a rawboned, gawky Kansas boy from the farm country, earnestly repeating the words that would make him a cadet.

The first three weeks were spent in what has been called, from time immemorial, Beast Barracks. Roommates were chosen alphabetically and mine was a lad from the same state as myself. Soon I could see that it was exceedingly difficult for him to accept the rather harsh daily routine that ordered our lives.

During the three weeks as a Beast no form of animal life is more obnoxious and pestiferous than the ubiquitous cadet instructor. He —there were many—was all over the place and his only mission, as we saw it, was to torment and persecute Plebes. When we went to the cadet store for supplies, we would be handed a bundle of clothes and bedding that was almost unmanageable. When we went up and down stairs to the bathroom in the basement or Plebe Heaven on the fourth floor, we had to take the steps two at a time. We went back to our rooms at double-time all the time.

Because the summer was a hot one—West Point, New York, could export heat without loss—the experience was strenuous and for some it approached the unendurable. It was hardest on those who were not used to exercise or who had been overindulged. My working experience and age came to my rescue. At times the whole performance would strike me as funny and in the semi-privacy of my room, I could laugh a little at myself and at the system. But whenever an upperclassman saw the sign of a smile, the shouting and nagging started again.

Military drill was a problem. Although my physical condition was excellent, and I had handled guns all my life, I had no training in marching. To keep in step with the music of the band was more than difficult, and the instructors constantly barked at us to get our shoulders back, our heads up, and to *get in step*. For days I was assigned to the Awkward Squad until I could co-ordinate my feet with the beat.

My roommate told me that when he had received his appointment, a celebration had been held in his little town. When he departed, he had been escorted to the train by a band and the entire village. He left the town a hero—and the contrast of Beast Barracks was too much. Part of his difficulty was that he had come to West Point quite young. At the moment, I was nearing twenty-one while he was a month or so past seventeen. He had not had the experience of taking care of himself or earning any part of his living. His lack of self-confidence meant that the Plebe life was much more of a burden on him than on me—I had encountered difficult bosses before.

Trying to lead him into a more optimistic frame of mind, I reminded him several times that thousands of others had preceded us, had undergone the same trials, and that we could do the same. He would reply, often in tears, that "It's easy for you, but you haven't had all the acclaim they gave me. What would my friends say if they could see me now?"

My crude efforts at bucking him up were no help. At the first examinations during our Plebe year, he left the Academy. I liked him and I still think it was only his youth and sheltered existence that defeated him in his chances at a military career.

After the three weeks, we were integrated into the corps of cadets, then living in summer camp, almost on the banks of the Hudson. Life became brighter, although every upperclassman, whether an officer or a plain "Yearling," continued to look upon Plebes as fair game. The yelling went on. The purpose was to get us into the spirit of taking and obeying legitimate orders without hesitation, as well as to straighten out minor idiosyncrasies in our postures and reaction times. The young American is naturally independent, I think, and has been raised to feel entitled to live his own life in his own way. We soon understood that at West Point we were going to do it West Point's way or we were not going to be there at all.

In the first days, when I knew as little as possible about the Army, General Orders had been read and among other instructions we were required to salute all officers. Ten days later, I was double-timing down the street when I heard a band coming. But before it turned the corner, I encountered the most decorated fellow I had ever seen. I hesitated just a second, then snapped to attention and presented arms but he did not return the salute. I did it again and a third time. Realizing that he was not going to return my salute, I made inquiries later and was somewhat mortified to learn I had been saluting not an officer but a drum major.

Beast period over, we were allowed a choice as to tentmates. The choice was limited to men of one's own company, to which assignment had been made according to average height. I was fortunate to find in our company Paul A. Hodgson from Wichita. He had already gone to college for a year or two and was a fine athlete. Paul was a good student and a serious one. I was inclined to be easygoing about studies but he devoted every moment he could during study periods to improving his academic standing. He always urged me to do the same.

One of my reasons for going to West Point was the hope that I could continue an athletic career. It would be difficult to overemphasize the importance that I attached to participation in sports. We were given fixed hours for recreation. We went to the baseball field to work out under the eyes of coaches and we did the same on the football field. Every moment I was allowed on the field I tried to take advantage of the opportunity. At that time my dimensions, as I recall, were five-feet-eleven in height and 152 pounds in weight. I was muscular and strong but very spare. It was dismaying, then, to find that I was too light in comparison to men who were then on the team to be taken seriously. But the only thing to do was keep at it.

Perhaps in baseball I could hold my own. In high school and afterward I had some local reputation as a center fielder. I was good at bat, trained by my coach as a "chop hitter"—to poke the ball, in effect, at selected spots in the infield, rather than swinging away freely. The West Point coach took me aside to say that he thought highly of my fielding. But he could not use me unless I mastered his style of hitting. "Practice hitting my way for a year and you'll be on my squad next spring," he said.

In September, we left summer camp and went back to barracks. "F" Company was housed in what was called New Barracks, close to the gymnasium. There I settled into the regulation world of the Point. The normal life of the cadet has been described many times by numerous and better writers. The most unpleasant phase is the average Plebe's awareness of the conviction that he is awkward, clumsy, and of unequaled stupidity. For some of us, this came to have its amusing aspects.

Once we learned that the punishment meted out by upperclassmen was usually not of great moment, the hardier souls among the Plebes found occasional opportunities to needle their upperclass tormentors. A classmate who lived in "F" Barracks was named Atkins, and we called him, of course, Tommy. He and I were not above (or beneath) bedeviling super-serious upperclassmen in their attempts to make us over. Now and then, Tommy and I got into a situation that brought down upon us the real or spurious wrath of our seniors.

One day, having been found guilty—by a corporal of our division named Adler—of a minor infraction of regulations, we were ordered to report to his room after tattoo in "full-dress coats." This expression signified a complete uniform. Tommy suggested that we obey the literal language of the order.

The full-dress coat is a cutaway with long tails in back, and tailored straight across the waist in front. At the appointed time, each of us donned a full-dress coat and with no other stitch of clothing, marched into the Corporal's room. We saluted and said solemnly, "Sir, Cadets Eisenhower and Atkins report as ordered."

The sound that Corporal Adler let out was the cry of a cougar. While his roommate, a rather easygoing man named Byrne, became convulsed with laughter, the Corporal was transformed into a picture of outraged dignity.

Predictably, all the upperclassmen of the Division, hearing the commotion, rushed into Adler's room to see what was going on. The quick mobilization ended in pandemonium. Some of the upperclassmen, taking their duties as seriously as Corporal Adler, joined him in reading us out as arrogant, unruly Plebes. They forced us to strain our shoulders back, pull in our stomachs, and assume exaggerated positions of attention. Other visitors just howled with glee.

The two jokers, now victims, had to stand silently, doing their best to follow orders, all of which were intended to inflict acute discomfort upon us, and some of which were conflicting. However, as the time approached for taps (always followed by an official inspection) everybody had to rush to his room. As usual, the upperclassman had the last word. Dismissing us, he gave us a new order. "Immediately after taps you will report back to my room in complete uniform including rifles and crossbelts and if you miss a single item I'll have you down here every night for a week." After taps we went back, dressed as instructed, to be braced up against the wall until we left our bodily outlines on it in perspiration. But afterward, we and the other Plebes had a lot of laughs—quiet ones—out of Adler's temporary discomfiture.

Though all Plebes at times felt their life to be miserable, that part of West Point life always provokes more chuckles and amused reminiscence than any other. The discipline was not so much harsh as inexorable. If one was guilty of an offense, report was automatic and the number of demerits to be received was exact. Justice was even-handed, even though at times it seemed too swift.

Offenses were possible everywhere. Dust on the window sills of the room. Improperly folded garments in the clothes locker. A few seconds late for formation. A badly prepared lesson. An unbuttoned jacket. An improper element of the uniform. Negligence of almost any kind. Each had its prescribed demerits and if in any month the total exceeded a certain level, the victim was required to walk the area—an expression used to describe punishment inflicted during free hours.

When the time came to walk a punishment tour, the offender would report to the area and there, under the watchful eye of an officer or the cadet officer of the guard, would march up and down, preserving a soldierly appearance—one hour for each excess demerit. Ultimately, I was discovered in an offense which caused a change in Academy regulations.

After I became an upperclassman, I went to cadet dances only now and then, preferring to devote my time to poker. The financial results of the games were always recorded in books with debts to be paid after graduation. On one of the rare occasions when I did go to a dance, I met a girl, a daughter of one of the professors. We started dancing in a way that the authorities of the time felt was not in accord with the sedate two-step, polka and waltz that made up the repertoire of cadet dance music. This girl and I liked to whirl; to just whirl around the room as rapidly as we could. I suppose the exercise probably showed a little more of the girl's ankles, possibly even her knees, than the sharp-eyed authorities thought was seemly. I was warned not to dance that way any more.

A few months later, it happened that I stopped in at a dance, possibly because it was one of the affairs known as a "Feed Hop" where food was served late in the evening. Often the poker players would take a recess from our Saturday night game, rush over to get a number of sandwiches, a cup of coffee, and go back to play.

I met the same girl again and forgot entirely the warning issued earlier. The exuberant sensation of swinging around the room was too much for me to ignore and so, in due course, I was brought before the Commandant. He informed me that I not only danced improperly, but had done so after a warning. For this offense I was demoted from sergeant to private, was awarded a month on the area with the punishment order reading, as was customary, "and will be confined to the barracks, area of barracks and gymnasium, and will during this period walk punishment tours every Wednesday and Saturday afternoons."

At about the same time, a football injury plagued me and I was put into the hospital for a month, although I was allowed to go to classes on crutches. The result was that while I was confined to my barracks —the hospital—for the month, the injury prevented my walking the area. Confinement meant nothing in these circumstances because I couldn't have left the barracks in any event.

The sharp-eyed Commandant of Cadets realized that I had in effect foiled the purposes of the punishment. Thereafter, orders for punishment of this kind read: "Cadet —— will be confined for one month to the barracks, area of barracks, and gymnasium and will walk twenty-two punishment tours." Even though an offender might have spent the entire month flat on his back, he would still have those twenty-two tours to walk after he left the hospital. This is one of those unwilling contributions to the Academy for which no cadet can thank me.

As has been noted elsewhere, I was, in matters of discipline, far from a good cadet. While each demerit had an effect on class standing, this to me was of small moment. I enjoyed life at the Academy, had a good time with my pals, and was far from disturbed by an additional demerit or two.

After the tiff with the authorities which took my non-commissioned rank, I regained my chevrons, becoming one of the color sergeants for the Corps. No one serving either as commissioned or noncommissioned officer in the Cadet Corps was compelled to walk punishment tours. Instead, he would for each excess demerit be confined to his room for an hour. This, to my mind, was worse than walking tours because it was far from easy to sit in a room on a Saturday afternoon for an hour and contemplate the sin of having had a little extra dust on the shelves of my wall locker or not having folded the blanket correctly on my bed. But I never fully reformed.

Thirty or so years later, when I had become Chief of Staff of the Army—a military post far higher than my loftiest cadet ambitions— an unknown inquirer, unknown at least to me, thought that my West Point years might provide a clue to my later performance. Although an officer's records during his active service are guarded from public scrutiny, somehow or other this researcher managed to get photostats of my disciplinary record. The offenses listed on sheet after sheet, through four years, must have appalled him by their multitude and variety.

Eventually these photostats were sent to the White House after I became President, possibly as evidence, someone suggested charitably, that one cannot always read a man's future in the record of his younger days. The following extract is from my final six months only, when my observance of West Point rules and regulations had improved considerably over earlier times.

Eisenhower	*Reporting Officer*
Jan. 4, 1915 Acting 1st Sergeant at guard mounting, not saluting properly when reporting detail.	Capt. Glade
Jan. 6, 1915 Temperature of room about 70 degrees at a.m. inspection.	Lt. Gregory
Jan. 17, 1915 Smoking in room during call to quarters . . .	Lt. Gregory
Jan. 20, 1915 Falling out of section by permission and going to his room to obtain clothing while section was marching from academic building to gymnasium about 2:45 p.m.	Lt. Gregory
Feb. 1, 1915 Visiting during call to quarters about 9:25 p.m.	Lt. Sayler
Feb. 11, 1915 Hours of instruction not accounting for absence p.m., inspection of Officer of the Guard.	Capt. Walton
Feb. 28, 1915 Hours of instruction not accounting for absence at inspection by 2nd relief.	Col. C. R. Jones
March 19, 1915 Late submitting police report.	Lt. Gregory
April 2, 1915 Hours of instruction not properly posted at inspection of Officer of the Guard.	Lt. Randolph
April 7, 1915 Late at Chapel formation.	Bliss

April 9, 1915
Apparently making no reasonable effort to have his
room properly cleaned at a.m. inspection.   Lt. Wildrick

April 11, 1915
Not wearing gymnasium belt to S. 1.   Lt. Butler

April 15, 1915
Absent from retreat.   Covell

April 22, 1915
Hours of instruction not accounting for absence at p.m.
inspection.   Lt. H. James

April 23, 1915
Late at breakfast.   Ferris

May 13, 1915
Hours of instruction not accounting for absence from
room at inspection, about 9:10 a.m.   Lt. Gregory

May 14, 1915
Officer of the Guard not staying in area between tattoo
and taps as directed.   Eisenhower

May 20, 1915
Not writing two hundred words in Spanish composition
for May 17th, as required.   Lt. Kiehl

(The demerit on May 14th? That was because I was on duty as Officer of the Guard and had to report the infraction myself.)

As I recall, there were about 162 men who finally graduated in my class, and in this list I stood 125th in discipline.

My success in compiling a staggering catalogue of demerits was largely due to a lack of motivation in almost everything other than athletics, except for the simple and stark resolve to get a college education. I didn't think of myself as either a scholar whose position would depend on the knowledge he had acquired in school, or as a military figure whose professional career might be seriously affected by his academic or disciplinary record. I suspect, instead, that I probably looked with distaste on classmates whose days and nights were haunted by fear of demerits and low grades.

The cadets standing high academically were called "tenth-boners." All grades were given in units and tenths thereof. Three units was perfection. Anything above 2.0 was satisfactory while 2.5 was a good grade.

Only a few outstanding athletes were tenth-boners. Most were ranked in the middle section of the class academically and a few were from the bottom. This was a pattern partly of their motivation, to be sure. Most athletes gave their primary energies to perfecting their "arm" or their drive or their hitting. "Hivey" students centered their attention on good grades.

In spite of a passion for athletics, my career as a player was short. Although in those years Plebes were eligible for varsity competition, I was, as mentioned, considered too light to make the football varsity. Although I was promoted briefly to the varsity several times because of my love for hard bodily contact, in my first year I always ended on the scrubs as "too small."

I practiced hitting the way the baseball coach had suggested and during the summer months, whenever I had free time, I worked hard on the running track, practicing fast starts. By fall I had improved my speed considerably. I also set up a severe regimen of gymnastics to strengthen my leg and arm muscles. And I indulged my appetite at the table to the limit.

When the 1912 football season started—I was a player in West Point's first practice game, against a soldier team—I weighed something like 174 extremely solid pounds. No player was more eager to prove himself. To me, that game was as important as the toughest game against a traditional foe. In the second half, partly by good luck and partly because of desire, I showed up quite well. For the first time I attracted attention from the varsity coaches, headed by Captain Ernest Graves.

After completing several post-game laps around the field, I trotted toward the gymnasium, overtaking and passing the group of strolling coaches. I was fifteen or twenty yards beyond when Captain Graves called sharply, "Eisenhower!"

I stopped, ran back, and saluted with a ringing, "Yessir."

"Where did you get those pants?"

They were hanging around my ankles. "From the manager, sir."

"Look at those shoes—can't you get anything better than that?"

I could only reply, "I'm wearing what I was issued."

Turning to the cadet manager, Graves said, "Get this man completely outfitted with new and properly fitting equipment." He went on briefly with other unflattering remarks about my appearance but

I heard hardly a word; I was as high as a kite. This was the first intimation, his way of saying, that I might make the varsity.

Dismissed, I raced to the locker room at a ten-second clip and refused to leave until the manager arrived and had me outfitted for the next day's practice. That encounter with the head coach turned out to be the thrill and the highlight of my football career at West Point.

Thereafter, in no game or practice session could the coaches claim I lacked pugnacity and combativeness, assumed to offset my lack of weight. Although I had put on almost twenty pounds since the previous season, I was still light for line plunging and line backing. But my enthusiasm made up somewhat for my lack of tonnage. In any event, I always played as hard as I knew how, trying to instill the fear of Eisenhower into every opponent. On one occasion, I succeeded beyond my intent; an opposing player made a protest against me. He shouted to the referee "Watch that man!", pointing at me.

The referee with some astonishment asked, "Why? Has he slugged you or roughed you up?"

The man, green and overexcited, replied, "NO! But he's *going* to."

Until my injury, I was used consistently as a varsity player, entitling me to a football letter; and I had every reason to think that I had another two seasons ahead of me with the hope, as weight was added and experience gained, I might make a reputation that would endure for a few years. But in the Tufts game—only a week or so before the Navy contest, the climax of the entire season—I suffered what I thought was a minor injury. I was plunging, having broken through the line, and a man got his hands on my foot. I twisted and threw my weight against it as I turned. Although my knee swelled rapidly, the inflammation was accompanied by little pain. I was hospitalized for two or three days waiting for the swelling to disappear. Then, discharged, with no warning from the medical men that the joint was permanently weakened and with no instructions to be cautious in using it for at least a while, my only worry was the fear that the coaches would keep me benched for the next two weeks, depriving me of any chance for glory against Navy. As it turned out, they had no other option.

A few days after release from the hospital, I reported to the riding hall. While taking part in "monkey drill," I leaped off my horse to vault over him as he jumped a low hurdle. In this fairly easy exercise, the momentum of a trained animal helps pull the rider from the ground as, hand on the neck straps, he levers himself into the air and over the horse. The landing shock to my injured knee was more than it could take. I ended on the ground with my leg twisted behind me. Cartilages and tendons obviously were badly torn.

In the hospital, the doctors spent four days straightening my leg, a process so painful that I scarcely slept during the ordeal. They put the leg in a plaster cast but when later I was again released from the hospital and tried to use it I learned to my dismay that rugged sports were denied to me from then on. To this day I have to be careful in my movements. Periodically in the past half century I have had to spend time in the hospital to recover from careless straining of that injured knee.

Homer and his legendary birthplaces cannot hold a candle to the number of Tufts men who say they caused the original injury. At public dinners and ceremonies, men of my own age have approached me, saying:

"General, I was the man who inflicted that bad knee on you in the Tufts game back in 1912. Wish I hadn't hit you so hard."

Over the years, I must have heard that sort of statement and belated apology two or three dozen times. I wonder how many men Tufs had on the field when I was hurt?

During the Navy game, my leg was encased in the heavy plaster cast. Navy's victory added to my depression. The following year was a different story. Before the game opened, Navy was heavily favored. Had Army played traditional football, the odds-makers might have been proved right. But the Notre Dame game that year had taught us a lesson about the forward pass and option play. Captain Charlie Daly, who had replaced Captain Graves as head coach, changed Army tactics and developed a fine passing combination of "Prichard to Merillat." At half time, Navy was slightly behind.

Nevertheless, such was the general confidence in their team's superiority that a Navy officer, who came over and visited a group of cadets with whom I was sitting, said he wanted to bet even money on Navy. Among a dozen or so of us we collected $65. He took out an equal amount and left it with us saying, "If I win, I'll be back for the money. If you win, keep it." We never saw him again. Army went on to win by 22 to 9. I think it was the first Army victory in something like four years and the scene among the cadets when we finally got back to West Point was an early forerunner of V-E Day.

I found emotional and financial satisfaction in the drubbing the sailors took.

Thirty years afterward, I found myself in the midst of war. I had occasion to be on the constant lookout for natural leaders. Athletes take a certain amount of kidding, especially from those who think it is always brawn versus brains. But I noted with real satisfaction how well ex-footballers seemed to have leadership qualifications and it wasn't sentiment that made it seem so—not with names that turned out to be Bradley, Keyes, Patton, Simpson, Van Fleet, Harmon, Hobbs, Jouett, Patch, and Prichard. Among many others, they measured up. I think this was more than coincidence. I believe that football, perhaps more than any other sport, tends to instill in men the feeling that victory comes through hard—almost slavish—work, team play, self-confidence, and an enthusiasm that amounts to dedication.

The end of my career as an active football player had a profound effect on me. While I did not wholly give up exercise, my activities were now limited to simple gymnastics, walking, and calisthenics. I found that I had to give up boxing, for while my ability to hit was unaffected I could not move laterally on my feet with any speed without renewed injury. But I did sustain and increase my arm and shoulder muscles, by work on the horizontal and parallel bars and on the rowing machines.

I have often wondered why, at that moment, I did not give increased attention to studies. Instead, as the academic record attests, I gave less. I was almost despondent and several times had to be prevented from resigning by the persuasive efforts of classmates. Life seemed to have little meaning; a need to excel was almost gone.

As the disciplinary record shows, I learned to smoke. Even in this, which was sanctioned to an extent, I managed to be rebellious. Regulations allowed cadets to smoke in their rooms, during study periods, if they used pipes or cigars. Cigarette smoking, if discovered, brought serious penalties. So I started smoking cigarettes. These could not be purchased at the cadet store but loose Bull Durham tobacco was available and I became a "roll your own" smoker.

During the short interval between supper and Call to Quarters for study, I was asked by one of the better students in the class to come to his room. He wanted to talk over some piece of business —I've forgotten the subject. When I arrived, he was properly uniformed, deep in study of one of his textbooks. I lounged in, sat down, and reaching into a pocket, produced tobacco and papers to roll a cigarette.

I happened to look up and saw a horror-stricken face. "What's the matter with you?" I asked.

"Please, Ike, if you must smoke, take that cigarette out into the hall and I'll talk to you through the door."

"Well, I didn't *ask* to come here. You wanted to see me. Do you or don't you?"

"Oh yes," he said in distress, "but don't you see if the Tac [the tactical officer in charge of a company] finds ashes or tobacco on the floor, I'll get a demerit for untidiness. This could cost me a file in my class standing. I can't afford it." (A man's initial seniority in the Army follows his class standing at the time of commission.)

Well, I obliged by stepping outside his room and after listening to what he had to say, left. I wanted to avoid embarrassing him, but I was so engrossed in thinking about his anxiety to avoid a single demerit, that I carelessly walked out of the barracks with the cigarette lighted. It was a shock, then, to hear the Tac's voice say, "Mr. Eisenhower, put out that cigarette."

"Yes, Sir," I answered ruefully. This was a multiple demerit offense and I would pay the penalty not only in academic standing but in serving a number of hours in room confinement. Somehow or other, I had come out of the small end of the horn.

Things continued to run downhill. An incident—indeed a lesson—that is vivid in my mind is one in which I learned the wickedness of arrogance and the embarrassment that can come about by the lack of consideration for others.

There's probably no individual in the world more serenely arrogant than the cadet who has just left the ranks of Plebes to become a lordly "Yearling." For a long year, he has been dirt under the feet of every upperclassman. With the year completed, *he* now joins the ranks of upperclassman and has the right to inflict on the incoming Plebes the same kind of verbal abuse that he has so much resented in the twelve months just past. Every Yearling feels it is his bounden duty to make certain that the new class is properly instructed. There is little communication between the Plebe and the upperclassman except in official, traditional language. The Plebe is constantly addressed as Mr. Ducrot, Mr. Dumgard, or, once in a while, Mr. Smith or Mr. Jones if it becomes imperative to use the man's name.

Like other Yearlings, I did my part to see that the Plebes appreciated the superior quality of upperclassmen—particularly of corporals, which lofty position I now held. In order to deflate the already downtrodden and lonely Plebes, there were a number of standard questions which, voiced as roughly as possible, were intended to crush him even more deeply into the mire of inferiority. One was, "Mister, what's your P.C.S.?" (Translation: "Previous Condition of Servitude" or, in clearer language, "What did you do before you came to West Point?")

I ran into a Plebe from my own state. Or, to be more precise, this young fellow, running down the street to carry out the orders he had received from a cadet officer, ran into me. He was knocked down. I reacted with a bellow of astonishment and mock indignation. Noting that he looked rather defeated, I demanded, with all the sarcasm and scorn I could muster in my voice, "Mr. Dumgard, what is your P.C.S.?" And added, "You look like a barber."

He stood up, said softly, "I was a barber, Sir."

I didn't have enough sense to apologize to him on the spot and make a joke of the whole thing. I just turned my head and went to my tent where my roommate, P. A. Hodgson, was sitting. I looked at him and said, "P.A., I'm never going to crawl another Plebe as long as I live. As a matter of fact, they'll have to run over and knock me out of the company street before I'll make any attempt again. I've just done something that was stupid and unforgivable. I managed to make a man ashamed of the work he did to earn a living."

And never again, during the remaining three years at the U.S.M.A., did I take it upon myself to crawl (correct harshly) a Plebe.

About midway in our West Point course we began the study of integral calculus. The subject was interesting but the problems could be intricate. One morning after recitations the instructor said that on the following day the problem would be one of the most difficult of all. Because of this he was giving us, on the orders of the head of the Mathematics Department, an explanation of the approach to the problem and the answer.

The explanation was long and involved. It was clear that he was doing his task completely by rote and without any real understanding of what he was talking about. Because I was a lazy student, with considerable faith in my luck, I decided there was little use in trying to understand the solution. After all, with twelve students in the section, only one of us would get this problem to solve, the odds were eleven to one that I would not be tapped.

The following morning I was chosen. Going to the board, on which I was required to produce the solution, and then explain it to the instructor, I had not the foggiest notion of how to begin. I did remember the answer given by the instructor and wrote it in the corner of the board.

I set to work. I had to make at least a good start on the problem, show *something* or receive a zero which would do nothing for me in a course where my grades were far from high. Moreover, I could be reported to the disciplinary department for neglect of duty in that I had deliberately ignored the long explanation. With this in the back of my mind I sought in every possible way to jog my memory. I had forty-five or fifty minutes to solve the problem and I really concentrated.

After trying several solutions that seemed to relate, at least remotely, to the one I dimly remembered from the morning before, I encountered nothing but failure. Finally, with only minutes remaining, I worked out one approach that looked fairly reasonable. No one could have been more amazed than I when this line of action agreed exactly with the answer already written on the board. I carefully went over the work, sat down, and awaited my turn to recite. I was the last man in the section to be called upon.

With some trepidation I started in. It took me a short time to explain my simple solution—indeed it had to be simple or I never would have stumbled upon it. At the end, the instructor turned on me angrily and said, "Mr. Eisenhower, it is obvious that you know nothing whatsoever about this problem. You memorized the answer, put down a lot of figures and steps that have no meaning whatsoever, and then wrote out the answer in the hope of fooling the instructor."

I hadn't been well prepared but this was tantamount to calling me a cheat, something that no cadet could be expected to take calmly. I reacted heatedly and started to protest. Just then I heard Major Bell, the Associate Professor of Mathematics (whom we called "Poopy," a name that was always applied to anyone at West Point who was above average in academic attainments) who had entered the room for one of his occasional inspections, interrupting. "Just a minute, Captain."

Of course, I recognized the voice of authority and shut up, although according to my classmates' description that night I was not only red-necked and angry but ready to fight the entire academic department. I would have been kicked out on a charge of insubordination if I had not been stopped.

Major Bell spoke to the instructor, "Captain, please have Mr. Eisenhower go through that solution again."

I did so but in such an emotional state that it is a wonder that I could track it through. The long search for a solution and its eventual simplicity stood me in good stead.

Major Bell heard it out and then said, "Captain, Mr. Eisenhower's solution is more logical and easier than the one we've been using. I'm surprised that none of us, supposedly good mathematicians, has stumbled on it. It will be incorporated in our procedures from now on."

This was a blessing. A moment before, I had an excellent chance of being expelled in disgrace from the Academy. Now, at least with one officer, I was sitting on top of the world. This did nothing to endear me to the Captain. I never again got a good grade from him. That instructor was the only man I met at West Point for whom I ever developed any lasting resentment. But from that day on, I've tried always to remember in my prayers of thankfulness one major called Poopy Bell.

It is easy to understand how eagerly every cadet looked forward to the few furloughs authorized for the four-year course. Neither in frequency nor in duration did the Academy system provide the escape from courses and regulations enjoyed by students in other colleges. All things are relative, however. To us at West Point, every academic pressure, every restriction of our use of time and conduct, seemed a little more tolerable because months ahead would come a period when, leaving instructors and Tac officers behind, we would savor the pleasures of the carefree life we knew before arriving on the Hudson.

Every cadet, except the Plebe, was allowed a few days of Christmas leave, if he was not undergoing any punishment tours, if he was completely proficient in his studies and physically fit. In my second, or Yearling, year, there were two small matters that prevented my taking advantage of the privilege. I was in the hospital with an injured knee. And my disciplinary record was not up to standard.

In 1913 and 1914 I was able to spend the eight-day Christmas leave away from West Point. In so short a time, it was impossible for me to go all the way home and back and enjoy a satisfactory visit. One year I went to Buffalo with a friend of mine named Byrne, a rollicking and likeable fellow (Corporal Adler's room-mate). His family was not rich but his mother, a widow, was the essence of hospitality.

My other Christmas leave was spent in New York City. I had not seen the big town on my trip in from Kansas and the cost of such a leave was more than I could afford. Fortunately, the Hotel Astor, then owned by the Muschenheim brothers, was the New York home of the Cadet Corps; the Astor carried all bills until graduation day for those who could not pay cash. And when payment was made, each of us got a 25 per cent discount, excepting only for actual money advanced to us by the hotel cashier.

During this leave, I realized that I needed a few ties more pre-sentable than those I was wearing with my old, comfortable civilian clothes. There was a haberdashery near the hotel. After much screen-ing and sorting, I found two that I liked and had them wrapped.

Making allowances for the high prices of New York City, I was under the impression that these would be expensive and would probably cost about $1.50 each. The salesman proffered the package and said, calmly, "That will be twenty-four dollars."

False pride would not let me say, "I can't afford them." The pur-chase took just about the last cent I had and there was nothing to do but go back to the hotel. From then on, I took all my meals in its dining room where I could sign the bill.

At the end of the second year, West Pointers were given a furlough —about two and a half months. This aroused as much enthusiasm in us as the prospect of graduation. I looked forward to it and when the time arrived went back to Abilene to see my family and renew friendships in the little town to which I still felt very close.

In the early months at West Point, I had visualized myself re-joining old companions on the baseball field and dazzling spectators at every game. This dream was left behind. The leg injury was so severe that I couldn't play in the informal baseball league made up of such towns as Chapman, Herington, Junction City, and Salina. Abilene did ask me to umpire and this chore I could perform without injury to myself, no matter what my decisions and calls may have done to others. In fact, the team was good enough to pay me $15 a game. The arrangement was a windfall for a cadet who was always short of money but who could not decently displace some other young man in a job at the ice plant or elsewhere.*

Although I umpired all home games, there was nothing to do when the team was in another town where a local man always officiated. After the Abilene players had gone off to play Chapman one morning, I had a telephone call from the Chapman manager. They wanted me to come over and umpire. "That's odd," I said. "You're playing Abilene and I live in Abilene." The manager said that made no difference, they knew I'd be fair, and he sent a Model T Ford to pick me up. My own team was so surprised when I showed up to call out "Play ball!" that it took them a few innings to hit their stride.

My own surprise in a little incident earlier that day was, for some peculiar and unexplained reason, extremely unsettling. While waiting for game time, I had a bite of lunch downtown and, wandering around, saw a shooting gallery. I thought it would be fun to try a few shots at the moving targets. As a complete stranger in Chapman, and dressed in ordinary clothes, I could hardly believe my ears when I picked up a rifle and heard a man standing nearby say to another:

"Okay, now, Mister, you've been bragging about your shooting. I just happened to see this soldier boy come in here and I'll bet you ten dollars that he can beat you on any target and in any kind of shooting you want."

Although nothing had been addressed directly to me, when I heard this astonishing statement—nothing I was wearing identified me as a cadet or soldier—unaccountably, and for the first time in my life, a fit of trembling overcame me. My hands shook. Without a word, I laid down the rifle, having already paid for the shells, and left the place without a backward glance.

Never before or since have I experienced the same kind of attack, even though today people somehow manage to call out, "Hey, Ike!" when I think I'm hidden incognito in an unmarked automobile. I think it was such complete surprise to be revealed as a soldier, even without a uniform, that upset me. I wonder how the argument came out and how long it took my unsolicited sponsor to notice that the soldier boy was no longer present.

* The same request to umpire was made during my graduation leave in 1915. The pay was even more acceptable because I received no income from the Army until the President could get around to signing my commission in September of that year. I probably wondered what kept President Wilson so busy that he couldn't sign and get it over with.

The knee that kept me from small-town baseball and big-league football eventually came close to changing my life more drastically. During the year following my injury the football and medical authorities tried every experiment and exercise they could think of to get me back into condition. My principal exercises were distance running and using the rowing machine in the gymnasium. They sent for all sorts of braces. I think they tried a dozen types during the year. None helped enough. While exercise was of value, nothing kept my knee from becoming dislocated under strain.

Once they knew the struggle was hopeless, Captain Dailey, who had become the new coach, suggested that I could keep up my interest in football by coaching the Junior Varsity, or the squad we called Cullum Hall. This was made up of men of all classes who were, because of lack of speed or size or agility, not quite good enough to make the first team. I got interested in this coaching idea and tried it. Because we used all the formations and signals of the varsity, I was able to send on to the squad a few performers who made the grade. My work was done under the supervision of an officer but he knew little of the game and when he did step in to coach, his actions were so resisted or misinterpreted by the squad that the head coach suggested that he give me considerable leeway.

The squad began doing so well that we attracted crowds of good size, although they were made up mostly of cadets. We played important secondary schools, like East Orange, and the New York Military Academy.

At the end of my final season with Cullum Hall, the squad decided to give me a present. They gave me no warning and on a Sunday afternoon, when I was engaged in my favorite indoor sport, .the captain of the team, Johnny Wogan, and two or three of the best players came to the poker table where a game was in progress. They handed me the gift, a set of mother-of-pearl cuff links and studs for white tie occasions. I stood up and expressed my surprise and gratitude but the ceremony having been completely informal, I was soon back at the poker game. Since then I have always regretted that I wasn't more deliberate and formal in expressing my appreciation because I was truly touched. It was probably more embarrassment than indifference that led me into such an exhibition of bad manners.

As the time neared for graduation, I was called to the office of Colonel Shaw, who was head of the medical department. He had just completed a review of my medical history at West Point. This consisted almost exclusively of my torn-up knee and subsequent recurrences, which had me in the hospital from time to time. He said that he might find it necessary to recommend that while I be graduated and receive a diploma, I not be commissioned in the Army.

This was a time when the Army was small. Its total strength in the spring of 1915 was approximately 120,000. The graduating class at West Point more than supplied the immediate demand for second lieutenants. Some of those low in the class were taken in with the second-class status of "additional second lieutenants" of the Army. The authorities were very careful not to commission anyone who had a serious physical difficulty, one that might cause his early retirement and make him a drain on the government throughout his life because of disability pension.

When Colonel Shaw had finished, I said that this was all right with me. I remarked that I had always had a curious ambition to go to the Argentine (as a reader of geographies, I was curious about the gauchos and Argentina sounded to me a little like the Old West), and I might go there and see the place, maybe even live there for two or three years.

He was obviously surprised that anyone so close to commission as a second lieutenant would take the news so equably. I may have been the first in his experience who was not seriously upset by the possible termination of all military ambitions. He said he would think the matter over.

Within a few days he sent for me again. "I think, Mr. Eisenhower," he said, "that if you'd apply for service in the Coast Artillery, I would be justified in recommending your commission."

To which I replied: "Colonel, I do not want a commission in the Coast Artillery."

The Coast Artillery of those days had no duty with the mobile Army. Except for such staff work as its officers might be called on to do, they worked exclusively with the handling of coastal defenses, mostly big guns. These monsters of heavy ordnance, ranging up to sixteen inches in caliber and hidden in deep pits under thick fortifications, had never been fired against an invading force. For that matter, they were seldom fired in practice for the cost of a large shell was a small fortune in the eyes of an army long accustomed to frugal, if not pinch-penny appropriations. Beyond keeping their equipment in readiness, oiling and greasing the ponderous machinery that elevated the guns for firing, and engaging in firing practice with dummy ammunition, a Coast Artillery Corps career—to those outside it—provided a numbing series of routine chores and a minimum of excitement. It was a sedentary, immobile sort of life, and other arms of the service—sometimes out of envy—referred to Coast Artillery posts as "cottages by the sea."

Colonel Shaw seemed disturbed at my abrupt refusal of his suggestion, perhaps because, as it turned out, he had served with the Coast Artillery himself. He brought the interview to an end, and I thought, "Well, that's that."

Although I must have made an unfavorable impression on the Colonel by the seeming nonchalance with which I had gone through the interview, an interview that had undoubtedly caused him a certain amount of thought, I meant only to react in the formal way expected of a cadet when in the presence of an officer. I didn't think he wanted to discuss things; I thought he wanted to tell me what he had decided. Now I began seriously to consider a trip to South America. I wrote for travel literature and costs.

Once more I was called back by Colonel Shaw. He had been going over my entire record, he said, and found that my most serious injury had been aggravated by a riding accident. I confirmed this. He said, "Mr. Eisenhower, if you will not submit any requests for mounted service on your preference card, I will recommend to the Academic Board that you be commissioned."

The preference card given to each cadet before his graduation required him to put down his choices for the several services of the Army he would like to join. Top-ranking students asked for the Engineers for in that branch promotion was faster than in the others. Next in preferred priority was the Field Artillery. The Infantry, Coast Artillery, and the Cavalry were available to the lower two-thirds of the class. Each branch had its adherents.

Although I liked horses, the horse cavalry was out and I didn't want to try for the Field Artillery. So I told Colonel Shaw that my ambition was to go to the Infantry. To which he said, "All right, I'll recommend you for a commission, but with the stipulation that you will ask for no other service in the Army."

When the time came for me to submit my preference card I put down *Infantry* first, *Infantry* second, and *Infantry* third.

In defense of Colonel Shaw and other officers who decided to recommend me for commission, I should put in that my West Point record was not all bad. Perhaps I have overstressed my slight differences with the disciplinary code and the academic life. If my nonchalance was a bit offensive, they probably also recognized it as being defensive as well. I had been a coach, a cheerleader, I gave talks to the Corps before games. One report on my early performance even said—it was shown to me years later—that I was "born to command." The man who wrote that was either a reckless prophet or he had relaxed his standards.

From the first day at West Point, and any number of times thereafter, I often asked myself: What am I doing here? Like the other young men, I sometimes wondered—where did I come from, by what route and why; by what chance arrangement of fate did I come by this uniform?

Book One

THE ABILENE YEARS

CHAPTER II

Sauce for the Gander

My EARLIEST memory involves an incident that occurred two or three months before my fifth birthday. I took a long trip to a strange and far-off place—Topeka—for a tough and prolonged war.

My mother's sister, Aunt Minnie, was visiting us. We lived in a little cottage on Second Street in Abilene. It was decided that I would return with her to Topeka where a considerable number of Mother's relatives lived.

It was a day trip and during the course of the morning the heat of the railroad car and the monotony of the noise made me very sleepy. "Does this train have a sleeping car?" I asked her, using a scrap of worldly knowledge I had presumably picked up while listening to a family conversation. "It's not really necessary to go to a sleeping car," my aunt replied. "Just lie down on the seat and I'll make sure you have a good nap." I did and she was right.

After leaving the train, we next had to take a long ride by horse and buggy to my relatives' farm out beyond the northern outskirts of Topeka. I can remember looking down through the floorboards, watching the ground rush past and the horses' feet, which seemed to slide. When we arrived, life became even more confusing. It was peculiar to be surrounded by so many strangers. It seemed to me that there were dozens or hundreds of people—all grownups—in the house. Even though they were, somehow, my family, I felt lonesome and lost among them.

I began to wander around outside. In the rear of the house was an old-fashioned well, very deep, with a wooden bucket and a long rope threaded through a pulley. My uncle Luther found me, fascinated by the well, and he offered a long story about what would happen to me if I fell in. He spoke in such horrible terms that I soon lost any ambition to look over the fearful edge into the abyss below. Looking around for less dreadful diversion, I noticed a pair of barnyard geese. The male resented my intrusion from our first meeting and each time thereafter he would push along toward me aggressively and with hideous hissing noises so threatening my security that five-year-old courage could not stand the strain. I would race for the back door of the house, burst into the kitchen, and tell any available elder about this awful old gander.

Thus the war began. In the early parts of the campaign, I lost a skirmish every half hour and invariably had to flee ignominiously and weeping from the battlefield. Without support, and lacking arms of any kind, it was only by recourse to distressing retreat after retreat to the kitchen door that I kept myself from disaster.

My enemy was that bad-tempered and aggressive gander. I was a little boy, not yet five years old, who was intensely curious about the new environment into which he was thrust and determined to explore its every corner. But the gander constantly balked me. He obviously looked upon me as a helpless and harmless nuisance. He had no intention of permitting anyone to penetrate his domain. Always hopeful that he would finally abandon his threatened attacks on my person, I'd try again and again, always with the same result.

Uncle Luther decided that something had to be done. He took a worn-out broom and cut off all the straw except for a short hard knob which he probably left so that in my zeal, if I developed any, I might not hurt my odd adversary. With the weapon all set, he took me out into the yard. He showed me how I was to swing and then announced that I was on my own.

The gander remained aggressive in his actions, and I was not at all sure that my uncle was very smart. More frightened at the moment of his possible scolding than I was of aggression, I took what was meant to be a firm, but was really a trembling, stand the next time the fowl came close. Then I let out a yell and rushed toward him, swinging the club as fast as I could. He turned and I gave him a satisfying smack right in the fanny. He let out a most satisfactory squawk and ran off. This was my signal to chase him, which I did.

From then on, he would continue his belligerent noises whenever he saw me (and the stick). He kept his distance and I was the proud boss of the back yard. I never make the mistake of being caught without the weapon. This all turned out to be a rather good lesson for me because I quickly learned never to negotiate with an adversary except from a position of strength.

☆   ☆   ☆   ☆   ☆

Mother and Father maintained a genuine partnership in raising their six sons. Father was the breadwinner, Supreme Court, and Lord High Executioner. Mother was tutor and manager of our household. Their partnership was ideal. This may sound unbelievable, and only recollected in tranquillity, but I never heard a cross word pass between them. Never did I hear them disagree on a value judgment in family, social, or economic affairs—not that there weren't sufficient causes. I never had any indication that they were annoyed with each other. Before their children, they were not demonstrative in their love for each other, but a quiet, mutual devotion permeated our home. This had its lasting effect on all the boys.

Normally, Father worked six days a week. He usually left the house about 6:30 and came home about 5:00. Family life revolved around him. School, chores, meals, and all other activities—winter and summer—had to be adjusted to meet his requirements. His work was hard and the pay was meager. Because of an early experience— two or three years after he married, a general store in the town of Hope, Kansas, in which he was a partner, went bankrupt—he had an obsession against ever owing anyone a nickel. He would not allow any of us a charge account—not that they were so common then. But either cash was paid or nothing was bought.

That early economic catastrophe left its mark. Father had been given a sizable farm as a wedding present by his father but he so disliked farming that he sold it to form the partnership in the store. For a time, all went well but drought and an invasion of grasshoppers one year—I think it was 1887—ruined the crops of Dickinson County. Father continued to extend credit; he carried the farmers to the end. Then his partner proved too weak to go through the ordeal of facing up to the store's own creditors. Taking what little cash was left, the partner departed one night for parts unknown.

My parents never heard from him again. Although Father's pride was hurt, he set out at once to find any kind of job and patiently started to pay off his former suppliers.

He accomplished this in a relatively few years.

His first job was in Denison, Texas, where I was born. My older and younger brothers were all born in Dickinson County, Kansas; we returned to Kansas when I was less than two years old. There,

Father was an engineer in a creamery, later a manager of a gas plant, and finally director of employee savings for a group of public utilities.

My mother, for all her gentleness, was outraged by the injustice of my father's early business venture, specifically at the other partner's disappearance. She began to study law at home. For some years she read legal books, hoping that someday, somewhere, they would meet up with the absconder—fully prepared to take legal action against him. Throughout the years that her sons continued to live under the same roof, this warm, pleasant, mild-mannered woman never ceased to warn them against thieves, embezzlers, chiselers, and all kinds of crooks.

Her household problems were, I realize now, monumental. The least of them was to provide comfortable beds for six boys in three rooms. She skillfully assigned us to beds in such a pattern as to minimize the incidence of nightly fights. She rotated our duties; helping with the cooking, dishwashing, laundry (she never had reason to miss the assistance usually provided by daughters); pruning the orchard, harvesting the fruit and storing it for the winter; hoeing the corn and weeding the vegetable garden; putting up the hay in our immense barn; feeding the chickens and milking the cow. By rotating chores weekly, each son learned all the responsibilities of running the house and none felt discriminated against. The total task of making life happy and meaningful for a family of eight took insight, imagination, and managerial skill.

Mother rarely resorted to corporal punishment and when she did it was a slap on the hand with a ruler or anything handy and lightweight. Instead, she deeply believed in self-discipline and she preached it constantly. According to her, each of us should behave properly not because of the fear of punishment but because it was the right thing to do. Such a philosophy was a trifle idealistic for a platoon of growing boys but in later years we came to understand her ideas better.

Mother took care of minor infractions during the day but anything serious was passed along to Father for settlement. With his family of hearty, active boys, I'm sure that strict discipline was necessary for survival. He certainly was never one for spoiling any child by sparing the rod. If the evidence showed that the culprit had offended deliberately, the application of stick to skin was a routine affair.

Father had quick judicial instincts. Mother had, like a psychologist, insight into the fact that each son was a unique personality and she adapted her methods to each.

Arthur, the first born, gave my parents little trouble. He was studious and ambitious. From my perspective, four years younger, he seemed a man about town. While he had his share of tussles with the rest of us, it is my impression that he was the best behaved. He was not much interested in athletics and still less in fisticuffs with lesser mortals around the house.

Edgar, second in line, was a natural athlete, strong, agile, two years older than I and yet for years we were almost the same size. His superior qualities always made him the victor in our inevitable personal battles. While these never had the ferocity of our fights with other boys—in those cases you stood up and slugged until one gave way—our encounters usually ended up in a highly unscientific wrestling match, with Ed on top.

Being a stubborn sort myself, I found his arm twisting and toe holds not only painful but mortifying. They built up in me a definite intention to get even when I matured enough to battle him on an equal footing. That time was long in coming. Not until I returned from West Point for a vacation in 1913 did I send him an all inclusive challenge—anything he wanted, wrestling, boxing, bare-fisted or with gloves—or plain rough and tumble. Even then he got the best of me. In his reply from wherever his summer job had taken him, he wrote, "I would be glad to meet you with boxing gloves at forty paces." And he did not come home that season so I was robbed of sweet revenge.*

One circumstance that helped our character development: we were needed. I often think today of what an impact could be made if children believed they were *contributing* to a family's essential survival and happiness. In the transformation from a rural to an urban society, children are—though they might not agree—robbed of the opportunity to do genuinely responsible work.

* I suppose those qualities of Ed's that I admired most were shown when we were digging a cistern together one day. He was using an adz and I a shovel. We had just struck a clay formation. I was tired of the shovel, and, giving way to my insistence, we traded tools. I raised the adz and swung, bringing it down neatly through the side of his foot. It had to hurt but Ed's shouted exclamation was, "Oh Dwight! Clean through my new twenty-five-cent socks!"

Roy, like Arthur, had no interest in going to college. He wanted to make money. Arthur, following high school, took a course in a local business college, became a competent secretary, and then went on to a career as a well-known and successful banker in Kansas City. Because Ed and I were constantly paired off, and Earl and Milton were much younger than he, Roy was a bit of a lone wolf. (Another brother, Paul, born in 1894, died in infancy of diphtheria. There was an age gap, then, of six years between Roy and Earl.) Roy began working in a drug store even before he entered high school. He was soon the youngest registered pharmacist in Kansas. Eventually he purchased a drug store in Junction City and did a thriving business.

Earl and Milton, who were born only eighteen months apart, became the other set of natural partners. There were few quarrels between them. Earl, because of blindness in his left eye caused in an accident at the age of four, and Milton, who during infancy had undergone an attack of scarlet fever which left him weakened, did not have as robust and disreputable a boyhood as Ed and I enjoyed. Milton turned his energies more to studies and to the arts, particularly the piano. He became good enough to give an occasional recital in school and later organized a dance band which helped provide him with funds for college education. One or two of his teachers tried to induce him to take further training for the concert stage, but another diverted him to newspaper work, which eventually led him to careers in government and higher education.

In appearance, we shared strong family characteristics but there were notable sources for differences. My father was dark and swarthy; my mother a golden blond. The six boys, therefore, were a predictable mixture. Arthur, resembling my father, was dark. Ed's hair was a chestnut color. I was so light that I was often dubbed "The Swede" by opponents in intercity athletics. Roy, like Arthur, was dark, while Earl was a fiery redhead (a contribution from my paternal grandfather). Milton's coloration was more like Ed's. In our late teens, Ed and I were often thought to be twins.

In this position, Ed, Earl, and I were the hot-tempered and quarrelsome element, while Arthur, Roy, and Milton were always credited with more tractable natures.

There was no shortage of causes for friction. Each week, a nickel magazine, *The Saturday Evening Post*, came into the household and each of us asserted our right to have it first. Mother laid down priorities. Anything scarce around the house, especially any favorite food, was much valued and before the argument was finished, over-valued. Ed and I liked to eat between meals. Frequently Mother issued the classic warning, "Now don't be eating so much or you'll spoil your supper." To satisfy our unreasonable appetites but still determined to avoid overindulgence, she would give us an apple, a pear, or now and then a piece of pie or cake. "Now one of you is to divide it," she said, "and the other is to get first choice." This insured fair play but put an almost intolerable burden on the divider.

Both parents were against quarreling and fighting. They deplored bad manners. I did discover one day that my father was far from being a turn-the-other-cheek type. He arrived home early one after-noon as I came in from the school grounds on the run, chased by a belligerent boy of about my own size. Seeing this, my father called: "Why do you let that boy run you around like that?"

Instantly I shouted back, "Because if I fight him, you'll give me a whipping, whether I win or lose!"

"Chase that boy out of here."

This was enough for me. I turned around and it was the sudden-ness of my counterattack, rather than any fighting prowess, that star-tled my tormentor, who took off at a rapid pace. I, being faster, was more than overjoyed when I caught him, threw him down to the ground, and voiced threats of violence. He seemed to take these most seriously. In fact, I promised to give him a thrashing every day unless he let me alone. I was rapidly learning that domination of others in this world often comes about or is sought through bluff. But it took me some years to learn that pounding from an opponent is not to be dreaded as much as constantly living in fear of another.

Not that I didn't need allies, even then. On my first day of school, Arthur kept an eye on me as I explored the playground. It was not long before a bigger boy, one who seemed to me almost as big as my father, began to chase me, making noises about biting off my ears. I felt toward him much as I had felt toward the gander, but in this case I had no big stick.

Or thought I did not anyhow. Arthur was as big as my tormentor and after this fellow had chased me around the play yard for what seemed an interminable time, Arthur stepped in and said: "That'll be enough of that. Let him alone."

The boy protested that he was just having fun, and Arthur said sharply, "Have your fun with someone else."

I had found a surprising means of protection—my big brothers.

The two of them continued to stand between me and what in those early days was clearly a world of enemies. Most of the enemies, of course, were only teasing. But from the standpoint of a little boy, they were not only tormentors; they represented sheer terror.

In spite of boyish frictions the household and even life outside was exceptionally happy. Though our family was far from affluent, I never heard a word even distantly related to self-pity. If we were poor—and I'm not sure that we were by the standards of the day—we were unaware of it. We were always well fed, adequately clothed and housed. Each boy was permitted to earn his own money and to spend it according to his taste and best judgment. One way to obtain cash was raising and selling vegetables. Another was to get a summer job, or to work in a store after school.

From the beginning of our schooling, Mother and Father encouraged us to go to college. They said constantly, "Anyone who really wants an education can get it." But my father, remembering that he didn't become a farmer as his father had hoped, scrupulously refrained from suggesting courses of study.

His insistence that we go through college recalls one incident that I then looked on as almost tragic. Edgar had decided, early in his high-school days, to follow Arthur's example and earn money for himself rather than go on further in school. For some months he pretended he was going to school while he worked, instead, for the town doctor. One day his continued absence was reported to Father. I never before or after saw him so angry.

At noontime that day, Edgar and I had come home for lunch and Father, in a surprise visit from the creamery, found us in the barn. His face was black as thunder. With no pause for argument, he reached for a piece of harness, a tug it was called, at the same time grabbing Ed by the collar. He started in.

A little over twelve years old at the time, I began to shout to my father to stop. Finally I began to cry as loudly as I could, possibly hoping that Mother would arrive on the scene.

Father stopped his thrashing and then turned on me because I had come up behind him and tried to catch hold of his arms. "Oh, do you want some of the same. What's the matter with you, anyway?"

"I don't think anyone ought to be whipped like that," I said, "not even a dog." Whatever his reason, I suffered no punishment.

Now I know, and I am sure Ed does too, that only through instant and drastic action when he learned about the truancy could my father have persuaded him, a headstrong fellow, to change his attitude toward school. Had it not been for the application of leather, prolonged and unforgettable, my brother might well have become an unhappy handyman in Kansas with no scope for the wide exposition of his economic and political views. Undoubtedly fear that his boy would seriously damage all the years of life ahead provoked my father to a violent display of temper and temporary damage.

Usually, Father was quiet and reserved. Mother was by far the greatest personal influence in our lives. She spent many hours a day with us, while Father's time with us was largely at supper and in the evening. In the end, his desire for his sons' education was fulfilled by four of them. Father secretly hoped Ed would become a doctor. He didn't express this and when Ed decided to go to Michigan to study law, Father approved. All the younger brothers sent Edgar funds on occasion but he worked at the University and essentially financed his own education. My appointment to West Point assured an education for me with no drain on household finances. Ed, remembering the help he received, financed Earl's education at the University of Washington. Milton, by writing for magazines, correcting English papers, and, as I said, playing in a dance band, was able to pay his costs at Kansas State University and later, as the American Vice-Consul at Edinburgh, Scotland, he was able to undertake graduate work there at the University.

This willingness of brothers to aid each other was one consequence of the guidance we received as youngsters. Years later, when Arthur was an authority on grain marketing finance and banking, Edgar a successful lawyer and director of industrial companies, Earl a radio station owner and public relations director of the community newspaper, Milton President of Johns Hopkins University, and I a first administration Republican President, friends often asked why there had not been a black sheep in the family.

I have often thought about this. The answer lies, I think, in the fact that our family life was free from parental quarreling and filled with genuine, if not demonstrated love. I never knew anyone from a divorced family until I went to West Point. Responsibility was a part of maturing. Concern for others was natural in our small community. And ambition without arrogance was quietly instilled in us by both parents. Part of that ambition was self-dependence. My mother could recite from memory long passages of the Bible (family tradition has it that she once won first prize in her church, as a child in Virginia, by memorizing 1365 verses in a six-month period). But these were not her only admonitions. Whenever any of us expressed a wish for something that seemed far beyond our reach, my mother often said, "Sink or swim," or "Survive or perish."

I have started to sketch the people who were David and Ida Eisenhower and the Eisenhower boys in Abilene. Like anyone else who searches the corners of his mind, names and faces and places come crowding across my memory. Having set the stage of personalities, so to speak, I would like to tell a few more stories, describe the town of Abilene, and mention others who were a part of it.

CHAPTER III

The Key to the Closet

MY FIRST READING LOVE was ancient history. At an early age, I developed an interest in the human record and I became particularly fond of Greek and Roman accounts. These subjects were so engrossing that I frequently was guilty of neglecting all others. My mother's annoyance at this indifference to the mundane life of chores and assigned homework grew until, despite her reverence for books, she took my volumes of history away and locked them in a closet.

This had the desired effect for a while. I suppose I gave a little more attention to arithmetic, spelling, and geography. But one day I found the key to that closet. Whenever Mother went to town to shop or was out working in her flower garden I would sneak out the books.

Out of that closet and out of those books has come an odd result. Even to this day, there are many unrelated bits of information about Greece and Rome that stick in my memory. Some are dates. I have a sort of fixation that causes me to interrupt a conversation when the speaker is one year off, or a hundred, in dating an event like Arbela; and often I put aside a book, until then interesting enough, when the author is less than scrupulous about chronology.

In any case, the battles of Marathon, Zama, Salamis, and Cannae became as familiar to me as the games (and battles) I enjoyed with my brothers and friends in the school yard. In later years, the movies taught children that the bad guy was the one in the black hat. Such people as Hannibal, Caesar, Pericles, Socrates, Themistocles, Miltiades, and Leonidas were my white hats, my heroes. Xerxes, Darius, Alcibiades, Brutus, and Nero wore black ones. White or black, their names and those battles were fresh news as far as I was concerned for I could never seem to get it into my head that all these things had happened two thousand years earlier—or that possibly I would be better advised to pay at least a little attention to current, rather than ancient, affairs. Among all the figures of antiquity, Hannibal was my favorite.

This bias came about because I read one day that no account of Carthaginian history was ever written by a friendly hand. Everything we know about Carthage, about Hamilcar and his lion's brood —of which Hannibal was one—was written by an enemy. For a great man to come down through history with his only biographers in the opposite camp is a considerable achievement. Moreover, Hannibal always seemed to be an underdog, neglected by his government, and fighting during most of his active years in the territory of his deadly and powerful enemy. Though I later came to recognize that unless Rome had survived the Punic Wars, Western civilization might easily have disappeared from the earth, my initial championship of Hannibal continued throughout my youth.

In this I was, undoubtedly, much like the young people of all times. Lost causes arouse their sympathy more intensely than overwhelming success begets their admiration. Because they are soon the chief customers in the literary market, and sometimes the chief contributors to it, this youthful attitude, always for the underdog, may very well affect the writing of history both in quantity and in tone.

In the literature of our own Civil War, Lee, for example, bulks larger in the sympathy and even veneration accorded him than Grant, the ultimate victor. Jeb Stuart, who died in battle, outshines Phil Sheridan, who, just as daring, suffered no serious wound. And Lincoln, struck down when his hardest challenge was still before him, has always excited more study and more books than Washington, who could validly claim that all his public responsibilities had been met and fully discharged.

Since those early years, history of all kinds, and certainly political and military, has always intrigued me mightily. When a historical novel is well written and documented, I am apt to spend the whole evening in its reading. The campaigns of the more modern leaders— Frederick, Napoleon, Gustavus Adolphus, and all of our prominent American soldiers and statesmen—I found absorbing.

When I got around to the Americans, Washington was my hero. I never tired of reading about his exploits at Princeton, at Trenton, and particularly in Valley Forge. I conceived almost a violent hatred of Conway and his cabal and could not imagine anyone so stupid and so unpatriotic as to have wanted to remove Washington from command of the American Army. The qualities that excited my admiration were Washington's stamina and patience in adversity, first, and then his indomitable courage, daring, and capacity for self-sacrifice.

The beauty of his character always impressed me. While the cherry tree story may be pure legend, his Farewell Address, his counsels to his countrymen, on the occasions such as his speech at Newburgh to the rebellious officers of his Army, exemplified the human qualities I frankly idolized.

If, in Abilene, I never became as involved in the Civil War, this was because it was relatively recent. After all, when Abilene's men and women, and boys for that matter, talked about "the war," they meant the struggle between North and South, that had ended only twenty-five years before I was born. There were hundreds in the town who remembered the war's beginning; its major campaigns and crises and figures; the ebb and flow of battle that had reached from the Atlantic into our state; the downfall of the Confederacy; the assassination of Lincoln. For them, these events were not yet history. In Abilene as in other American towns of that time, scores of men still in their fifties and early sixties who ran local businesses, worked nearby farms, or practiced the professions, were veterans of the war. Closeness to it in time made that war appear commonplace to me; in any event romance, adventure, and chivalry seemed characteristic of the conflicts of earlier centuries.

Looking back I realize that in reading about Egypt, Assyria, Persia, Greece, Rome, and, later, about the British and French, I was dealing largely with conquerors, battles, and dramatic events. Of course, I could read also about scholars and philosophers, but they seldom loomed so large in my mind as warriors and monarchs. Yet history is not made merely by big names or by startling actions, but also by the slow progress of millions and millions of people. They contribute to the creation of reputations and to the moments of history itself.

Hannibal and Caesar and Scipio would have been nothing except for loyal soldiers who marched and sweated and died to carry out the will of their masters. Plato and Aristotle would have spoken in futility to the breezes sweeping off the Aegean, had not their teachings slowly, almost imperceptibly, been incorporated into the texture of Western thought, and taken for granted (as it were) by people who never read them, possibly never heard of them.

I know now that as a youngster I was concerned almost exclusively with the peaks and promontories—the dramatic features—of the historical terrain. Today, I am interested too in the great valleys within which people, by their work, their zeal, and their persistence, have transformed a savage and crude environment into an industrial complex so that in the 1960s one man in the field can provide the food and fiber for twenty others.

Even as late as our own Revolutionary time 95 per cent or so of our population was rural. It is a far cry from the days, still fairly recent, when the pioneer housewife, getting lye water from boiling wood ashes, and fat from the fall butchering of the hogs, combined the two to make a crude soap to keep her house, her children, and her dishes clean. At the moment, a thousand advertised products guarantee to make her work a pleasure rather than drudgery.

And the oldest problem of the human male, what to do about his beard, once a choice between its painful extraction hair by hair or a dangerous adventure with lethally sharp and unguarded steel (the common-sense nineteenth-century man just let it grow and made the beard into a status symbol), is now a minor task of a few minutes' duration. A man, confronting his morning face in his mirror, shaves either with an electrical contrivance or dabs on lather canned in a far-off factory and then removes it and beard with a device ingeniously designed to protect the face against the careless or shaky hand. A minor achievement, one might say; but not so minor to a man who avoids cutting his own throat.

People from age to age have brought all of this about by their dissatisfaction with the inadequate, a dissatisfaction that moved others to inventiveness, and by their acceptance of new and better ways to accelerate the spiral of change.

As to the future, any predictions of mine might be as wrong as Cecilia Curry's, who wrote the class prophecy about her fellow Abilene High School graduates of 1909. In the yearbook, *The Helianthus* (we might have used plain English and called it The Sunflower, but Latin added a touch of culture), my brother Edgar is described as ". . . the greatest football player of the class." I am described as "our best historian and mathematician." As Cecilia took crystal ball in hand to read the future of us all, she recorded her findings in the form of an undated future letter. It was as if written around 1940 or 1944 during a stop she has made in Cleveland on a dream trip to New York. There, according to her, in the library of a college run by Bessie DeWolf and Winnie Williams of our class, she reads in the political section of a local newspaper that Edgar Eisenhower, finishing his second term as President of the United States, might be elected to a third term. "Then I sat wondering if Edgar really would take the chair the third time."

After a spell, Cecilia turns to Miss DeWolf and asks:

"Say, Bess, do you know what has become of Dwight?"

"Why, yes! I hear about all the great men of the world. He is professor of history at Yale. . . ."

In recalling Cecilia's cloudy reading of the Eisenhower boys' futures, I should learn better than to attempt forecasts of what will come to pass; certainly not in specific terms. In my early years at least, I was content to let well enough alone and read what others had recorded. As a boy, I never played the prophet.

For me, the reading of history was an end in itself, not a source of lessons to guide us in the present or to prepare me for the future. Nor did I become at all aware that the richness and variety of opportunity in this country would give me, like all of us, a chance to be joined, intimately and productively, with both the past and future of the Republic. I did not know what opportunities were there for the learning. I read history for history's sake, for myself alone. Sufficient unto the day was the evil thereof—and good, too—in my thinking.

Had one of our Civil War veterans, for instance, suggested that not many years later, I would visit Gettysburg to study the tactics of the great battlefield where he had fought, my reaction would have been—"Me?"

What would have been incredible to me in 1900 did come to pass in 1915. And then three years later I was to be back in Gettysburg again, as the commander of an Army camp. In 1950 I would buy property next to the fields where Pickett's men had assembled for the assault on Cemetery Ridge.

As I drive between farm and office, as I sit here at my desk overlooking the road where thousands of retreating and pursuing troops poured through on a July afternoon in 1863, all about me are physical reminders that the history made here was an accumulation of little incidents, small contributions, minor braveries, and forgotten heroisms. I am in the path of the disordered Union troops of Howard's XI Corps, driven back by Ewell's Confederates coming in from north and east. In mind's eye, I can see the blue uniforms as they turned again and again in brief stands against the Confederates, many of them making good their escape to Cemetery Hill, a few hundred yards to the south, where two days later the Confederate tide would begin its long, protracted ebb into Lee's surrender at Appomattox and Johnston's at Durham's Station.

To the rapid reader or to the hasty visitor, Gettysburg is Pickett's Charge, Little Round Top, and Devil's Den, the Wheatfield and the Peach Orchard, plus a few names in high command. Everything else is a blur. This is understandable. To tell the whole story, in detail, has required enough books to fill a small library. To read them would require a graduate degree. And the student might soon lose sight of the field in the tangles and brush of the forest.

Nearly 170,000 men were engaged, most of them in peril of their lives. Scores of regiments were given, in the course of three days, an opening for a decisive thrust. Of course, major decisions were the responsibility of a few. But their execution depended on the initiative, the fidelity, the strength of many thousands of individuals, known only to their immediate comrades in the battle, their names forgotten today. Gettysburg, in fact, was a demonstration of what a tiny portion of a nation's number can accomplish in the shaping and the making of history.

That many visitors to Gettysburg are satisfied with a fast review of the scene and a sketchy knowledge of the battle's high points seems to me a pity. Were they to delve a little deeper into the record of those who fought here, they would find lessons and inspirations beyond price. The battle was not just a contest of armed muscle. On the field, men found in themselves resources of courage, of leadership, of greatness they had not known before. Nor were they men of only physical courage. High moral courage marked them, too. Take one example.

George Gordon Meade was assigned command of the Army of the Potomac only three days before the Battle of Gettysburg commenced. No other officer through the war was given so little time to prepare himself and his troops for such a climactic engagement. Moreover, command of the Army of the Potomac through a year and a half had been an avenue to military disgrace; Meade's appointment was only one in a long succession of changes in its chief leadership since McClellan took over two years earlier. To command it seemed to invite the enmity of all the politicians in Washington who knew exactly how the war should be conducted. The Army's commander was seldom permitted the luxury of devoting himself totally to purely military problems.

As he rode toward the battle on July 1, receiving reports throughout the afternoon and evening that his I Corps had been forced back, its commanding general killed on the field, the XI Corps disastrously routed and thousands of its men taken prisoner, Meade's mind must have been torn with anxiety about the future of his army and—for he was only human—occasionally worried about his own fate as its commander.

When he reached the field after midnight, on the eve of the second day of battle, he pushed himself and his horse through hours of inspection. In the darkness, the prospect was far from heartening, for the Confederates—except on the south—were ringing the Union lines and all reports indicated that Lee, reinforced from east, north, and west, would be ready in the morning for a heavy assault on the Union position. It might be late in the day before Meade would have enough troops on the field to balance Confederate strength.

The morning of July 2, after hardly more than a few hours' sleep, he was back on the lines, accompanied only by a staff officer and an orderly. According to one observer, "The spectacles on his nose gave him a somewhat magisterial look . . . nothing of pose, nothing stagey about him. His mind was evidently absorbed by a hard problem. But this simple, cold, serious soldier with his businesslike air did inspire confidence . . ."

In complete silence through the minutes, as he scrutinized from a position on Cemetery Hill the surrounding town and terrain occupied by the enemy, he evidently considered all the elements of the situation; pondering the possibilities of disaster and the probabilities of defeat; weighing the defensive value of the ridges held by his men against the offensive capacity of Lee's victory-heartened veterans; calculating the hours required for the movement of his reserves up the Taneytown Road, Emmitsburg and Baltimore pikes; formulating in his mind moves that might counter or thwart the plans of Lee.

For Meade, this was the moment of truth when all within him, particularly his moral courage, had to bear tough and strong on the problem ahead. No council of war could be called. No delay for leisurely study would be permitted by Lee. The decision had to be made. And the decision was solely Meade's responsibility. As he turned his horse, he is quoted as saying, almost to himself: "We may fight it out here just as well as anywhere else." Then he quietly rode away to issue the orders that would make his decision operative.

In all this, there is neither visible drama nor glamour; only the loneliness of one man on whose mind weighed the fate of ninety thousand comrades and of the Republic they served. Meade's claim to greatness in that moment may very well be best evidenced by the total absence of the theatrical. When thousands of lives were at stake there was no time for postures or declamations.

In the Confederate assault, George Pickett was not the only major-general. Over to the left of the line, Isaac Trimble, three months junior to Pickett in rank but twenty-two years his senior in age, an old man by both Union and Confederate standards for he was then approaching sixty-two, commanded the Confederate division which had the farthest to march under the fire of the Union guns. Wounded in the leg as he led his troops over the fence that lined the Emmitsburg Road on its east side, he was taken prisoner and his leg amputated.

As I walk in the back door of my office or leave by it, I pass a memento of his stoicism in pain and in defeat and of his concern that the record of history be kept straight. This is a hand-drawn map of the battle and its various lines through three days, evidently made by a junior Union officer. The map, given to me by my friend Jock Whitney, Ambassador to the Court of Saint James when I was President, bears in the lower right-hand corner the inscription, "Remarks by Gen. Trimble." Thereafter these words appear:

Two of Hill's Divisions, assisted by Rhode's Div. of Ewell's Corps on the left (on Carlisle road) attacked two Divisions of Federal troops on Wednesday July 1st.

Johnston's & Early's Div's. attacked at night (July 2nd.) Federal right on Cemetery & Wolf Hills.

July 2nd. Confederate Breast Works thrown up forward to B along woody (Seminary) ridge.

July 1st Federal's driven back to (through) Gettysburg. (to Cemetery Hill).

July 3d Confederates driven back to Gettysburg.

Early's Div. came up July 1st & Johnston's 2d July.

July 2d Federal troops all came up & fortified the line.

July 3d Longstreet's Corps pressed back the Federal left to Round Top Hill.

One can picture to himself, Trimble, who had graduated from West Point in the Class of 1822, calm and philosophic despite the loss of a leg, talking to the young man who probably had not been born until Trimble had been more than ten years a Regular Army officer. One must admire this aging man, in such desperate plight, who patiently went over the details of a battle lost so that the record might be correct. Nor can one think without pity of one who, forty years after he received his commission at the United States Military Academy, now stoically faced the end of a soldier's career. But it is good to realize that through another quarter century, outliving most of those who were with him on either side as general officers at Gettysburg, Isaac Trimble was the hero of Maryland and, eventually, revered by many Americans. Here, indeed, is a lesson against collapse into despair because all things seem lost.

For one final example of an individual's role at Gettysburg, consider a man, Frank Haskell, whose place in our history is assured by a brief quarter hour of his life. He was a Wisconsin lawyer who had volunteered in 1861. On the third day of the battle, he was still a first lieutenant. But for fifteen minutes that afternoon, as the waves of Confederate infantry advanced toward Cemetery Ridge, he—one man—focused the strength of the Union defenders on the narrow front that was Lee's chosen target. There, the Union generals had been wounded; the Union regiments had been badly battered and some were in serious disarray; the Union batteries had been crippled. The odds on this part of the front were against the Union troops; before the canister hit the three Confederate divisions at short range, they outnumbered the Union brigades by something like three to one.

Haskell, through a quarter of an hour, on his own, without orders, without heed to the rules of seniority, rallied Union colonels and privates alike to plug gaps in the line; galloped along the front moving guns and muskets to the point of crisis; provided an abundance of leadership, where, without him, confusion and chaos would have ruled. Had he not been there, the Confederate tide could hardly have failed to make a serious breakthrough. But he *was* there. And, in fifteen minutes, he shaped history.

Men such as these are worthy of every American's study. They should not be lost to memory under the tags and labels of quick description that for most of us capsule our history into a few names and a few events. Of course, I realize that too close a reading of even one major event can deteriorate into a dreary examination of detail and statistic, in the long run of little meaning.

I plead only for realization that the handful of heroes on a field such as Gettysburg merely symbolize the courage or the daring or the high-spirited initiative of a multitude of men. And we should try to learn more of the sort of men that some of this multitude were, remembering always that thousands upon thousands of their dead and wounded and unharmed comrades, totally unknown to formal history, performed as gloriously.

Yes, history is far more than the excitement of battle, the flags and guns and desperate assaults. In a place like Gettysburg, the visitor—the native for that matter—may easily become absorbed in the three days of conflict, forgetting that history was also made here in quiet lives, on farm and village street, through a century before the battle, through a century after it.

For each of us, among these men and women who never experienced the fury of war, there may well be individuals who, unobtrusively but effectively, lived their lives so that we must acknowledge a direct indebtedness to them. Again, on the staircase of my office, where I pass it at least four times a day, is a useful reminder.

This is Robert McMurdie's original deed to the farm my wife and I now own and the survey made of the land. The face of the upper document is an official notice to John Lukens, Surveyor General of Pennsylvania, signed on September 10, 1762, by James Hamilton, agent for the Penn Family.*

---

* In part it reads:

BY THE PROPRIETARIES

Pennsylvania, SS, WHEREAS *Robert McMurdie* of the County of *York* hath requested that we would allow *him* to take up *Two hundred and fifty* Acres of Land *adjoining John McKane, Joseph Wilson, James Murphey, Charles Morris, John Morrison, and Thomas Martin in Cumberland Township* in the County of *York* for which *he* agrees to pay to our Use in the Term of six Months from the date hereof at the Rate of Fifteen Pounds Ten Shillings current Money of this Province, for every Hundred Acres, and also to pay the yearly Quit-Rent of One

On the side is this endorsement, signed by Jn. Lukens, S.G.:

To Thomas Armor Deputy Surveyor, Execute this Warrant and make Return thereof in my Office.

Although Robert McMurdie and his neighbors are unknown to formally written history, they are incalculably important to me because on the same ground where we live today these men lived and worked before us. The ground on which my house stands is a tie that binds me to their memory. I cannot visualize their appearance. I have not a word that they have left in the form of story. But I feel a kinship to them that is very real and has excited my curiosity to learn more about them.

I suspect that, in our Gettysburg home, Mamie and I have managed to preserve some relics of Mr. McMurdie's first home, built less than eight years after Braddock's defeat by the French and Indians. When we bought the place in 1950, local tradition said that the house had been built a hundred years or so earlier. When we began rebuilding in 1953, we found that the brick home was actually a brick veneer around a log cabin. The original logs, most of them crumbling into decay, probably antedated the brickwork by a century. Only a few were sound enough for use in the rebuilt house and those we incorporated into the ceiling and wall of my study. Consequently, two centuries after he built his home, I have tangible association through them with Robert McMurdie.

And even though I cannot put a face on him, I can see back to that April day more than two hundred years ago when Thomas Armor, the surveyor, sighted through his primitive transit and theodolite. He jots down the triangulation of the zigzag boundary while the rod boy moves to the next point, basing his calculations on an immense sugar tree that is noted on his plat, and very likely he frets that the boundaries of the adjoining farms already surveyed do not run due north and south, east and west.

Surely, as he went about his work, he must have paused often

---

half-penny Sterling for every Acre thereof, to us, our Heirs and Assigns forever. THESE are therefore to authorize and require You, to survey or cause to be surveyed unto the said *Robert McMurdie* at the Place aforesaid, according to the Method of Townships appointed, the said Quantity of *Two hundred and fifty* Acres, if not already surveyed or appropriated . . .
[Italicized words are handwritten.]

that day when the trees were turning green and the little brook—
now dry—just south of the home where Mamie and I now live, was
gurgling with runoff from the land, to think that at long last winter
had come to an end, that spring had arrived to stay and that this
might very well be the best crop year Cumberland Township had yet
known.

On that day so long ago, he had reason to stop more than once
to gaze westerly at the ridge of South Mountain, clear on the horizon,
thinking of the Indians who still walked in the distant forest, wondering about the fertility of the valleys that lay between him and
the Ohio, dreaming of surveys in that vast territory to be made by
him or, possibly, by a surveyor son.

In such things, human nature changes little in two centuries. One
more slight coincidence, the happenstance of human history, joins
me with Mr. Armor. His survey (given me by The Historical Society
of York County in 1961) is framed in a souvenir of the Conway
plot which had so outraged me when reading about it as a boy in
Abilene. According to the final paragraph in the Certification of
Authenticity the wood frame comes from the residence of General
Horatio Gates. The paragraph continues:

In this York House, at a banquet believed to have been given by Gates,
the Marquis de Lafayette thwarted the Conway Cabal to remove Washington from command of the Continental Army.

CHAPTER IV

Those I Came From

IF I CAN to some extent identify myself with the original family who lived on my farm, I think I may also guess a little about the austerity of life within the primitive cabins that lay in the valley of Marsh Creek. Yet to those of us in a supermarket and jet-powered age, the hazard and harshness of their daily living must remain beyond comprehension.

But I would imagine that the relationship between parents and children, at least, differed little from our lives in Abilene. In their simple faith, in their reliance on a guiding providence, the parents of that distant day could have differed little from my own. Surely, more than one little boy in those rude houses of hewn log remembered all his life and tried to abide by a few familiar words of his father or mother, gently spoken yet as deeply felt as the mountains are rooted in the earth's rocks. With them I am close kin, for just that happened to me.

☆   ☆   ☆   ☆   ☆

The year when I was ten, my mother gave permission to Arthur and Edgar, the two older Eisenhower boys, to go out with a group for Halloween "trick or treating." It was upsetting when my father and mother said I was too young to go along. I argued and pleaded until the last minute. Finally, the two boys took off.

I have no exact memory of what happened immediately afterward, but I was completely beside myself. Suddenly my father grabbed my shoulders to shock me back into consciousness. What I had been doing was standing by an old apple tree trunk and pounding it with my bleeding fists, expressing resentment in rage. My father legislated the matter with the traditional hickory switch and sent me off to bed.

Perhaps an hour later, my mother came into the room. I was still sobbing into the pillow, my feelings—among other things—hurt, completely abused and at odds with the entire world. Mother sat in the rocking chair by the bed and said nothing for a long time. Then she began to talk about temper and controlling it. Eventually, as she often did, she drew on the Bible, paraphrasing it, I suppose. This time she said:

"He that conquereth his own soul is greater than he who taketh a city."

Hatred was a futile sort of thing, she said, because hating anyone or anything meant that there was little to be gained. The person who had incurred my displeasure probably didn't care, possibly didn't even know, and the only person injured was myself. This was soothing, although she added that among all her boys, I was the one who had most to learn.

In the meantime, she had set about putting salve on my injured hands and bandaging the worst places, not failing to make the point that I had expressed resentment and only damaged myself.

I have always looked back on that conversation as one of the most valuable moments of my life. To my youthful mind, it seemed to me that she talked for hours but I suppose the affair was ended in fifteen or twenty minutes. At least she got me to acknowledge that I was wrong and I felt enough ease in my mind to fall off to sleep. The incident was never mentioned again. But to this day I make it a practice to avoid hating anyone. If someone's been guilty of despicable actions, especially toward me, I try to forget him. I used to follow a practice—somewhat contrived, I admit—to write the man's name on a piece of scrap paper, drop it into the lowest drawer of my desk, and say to myself: "That finishes the incident, and so far as I'm concerned, that fellow."

The drawer became over the years a sort of private wastebasket for crumbled-up spite and discarded personalities. Besides, it seemed to be effective and helped me avoid harboring useless black feelings. This device applied, of course, to things purely personal. During World War II, there was no question of the deep-seated hatred I felt for Hitler and all that he stood for. But there were ways to deal with him other than the drawer.

Eventually, out of my mother's talk, grew my habit of not mentioning in public anybody's name with whose actions or words I took violent exception. In private, of course, I have not always exercised tight control on temper or tongue—my staff, at least, has always held up under these bursts with an attitude of cheerful resignation. A quick explosion, as quickly forgotten, can sometimes be a necessary safety valve. I think my mother might have agreed.

Earlier, I said that I had been struck with the notion that time flies. But now, that second idea persists in my mind—that the making of history, the shaping of human lives, is more a matter of brief incidents, quiet talks, chance encounters, sudden flashes of leadership or inspiration, and sometimes simple routine than it is of heroes, headlines, grand pronouncements, or widely heralded decisions.

Great concepts, great ideals, great decisions, can be the engines which move men to greatness themselves. But the documents which express them are sometimes sterile things unless there are people to cause inspiration to flow from them. My good fortune has been a lifetime of continuous association with men and women, widely different, who sometimes in a few minutes by word of mouth, or sometimes over the years by their example, gave others inspiration and guidance. They gave me encouragement or helped me to prepare. My parents were first among them.

During my time at Columbia University, whenever I drove around Manhattan Island, through the busy and narrow streets, past the buildings jammed close together and crowding the curbstones, in the noise and fumes of traffic, the lack of blue sky and elbow room sharply contrasted with all I had known as a boy. New York, as a place to live, seemed to me an environment out of which, only with difficulty and exceptional effort, much good could come. The realization that this city was first in the nation in population and in prestige as a center of business, education, science, culture, and wealth had more than one disheartening moment when one saw the blight in so many neighborhoods.

But behind the dingy walls, inside cramped and airless rooms, there were thousands of homes in which parental love and care burned as brightly, as intensely, as in the homes of Abilene. Clearly, delinquency is a social problem, responsive to environment, but subject to remedy and not a hopelessly fixed pattern.

Hemmed in by masonry walls, confined to thin streets, boys in New York even as in Kansas have found ways to enjoy themselves without hurt to property or to their elders. Stick ball—that peculiarly big-city game whose rules change from block to block, whose strategy and tactics depend on the amount of space a group can find to play, whose unwritten standards demand of the players a lightning agility both in following the ball and avoiding trucks and cars—is evidence that farm boy and tenement boy are one at heart. Given competitive challenges, both can lose themselves in the clean excitement of a hard-fought game. Neither has time to discuss whether he is underprivileged or is leading the good and full life. In some respects, the tenement boy may have it the better of the two. Stick ball, as I understand it, is played without an umpire. Disputes are settled, usually amicably if loudly, by the players themselves. Here is evidence of the fundamental good will for his fellow boy that did not characterize our boyhood games in Abilene. In those days, we had to have an umpire.

We worry much, these days, about our youngsters—possibly over-much. Often they seem to live in a world of their own, far more distant from ours than a difference in decades would justify. They hear talk of peace and they know of three—now four—wars within a span of a half-century. The bomb hangs over their heads and the earth shifts before their eyes. They are exhorted to work hard and yet they see an existence on the dole presented not only as a possibility, but as a respectable way of life. They have seen legal group protests confused with illegal destructive riots; they read about depressions of the past and runaway inflation in the future; they have grown so sophisticated that they are embarrassed by their parents' ignorance about the birds and the bees; they tend to welcome change whether it means progress or retrogression in education, industry, morals, clothes, or the dance. Of course they live apart from us. At least, praise be to the Lord, they have not wholly lost their sense of humor.

A boy came home from school one evening recently, I'm told, and handed to his father this printed notice devised by one of his fellow students:

"In the event of atomic attack, the law prohibiting prayer in this school will be temporarily suspended."

My confidence in young people has been justified many times in war and peace. That does not mean that we can forget about the unfortunate circumstances in which many young people still grow up, trusting that good will flower out of evil. Such a course would be cruelly irresponsible.

When I rode around New York in those Columbia years, looking out the car windows, I found that for long stretches of time I dropped into what used to be called a brown study. Oblivious to sound, my mood was questioning. How could these men and women be moved in unison to channel some portion of their energies and talents to assure their children and grandchildren an even richer heritage? It would not be by the regimentation of the master-planned society. It could be done by enlarging the opportunity and the capacity and the will of the individual.

I grant that such thoughts may very well be a heritage from my ancestors. When they made up their minds to leave Europe for what is now Pennsylvania, life might have been somewhat less complex than it is now—freer from traffic jams, from computer-produced schedules, from keeping up with the neighbors down the block or around the globe.

But the individual—then as now—confronted by elemental forces or human tyrannies, must have thought himself fairly insignificant. We talk much and worry, with reason, about the terrors of nuclear war. To our forebears, the North Atlantic must have been equally terrifying.

To cross its three thousand miles, they depended on a timber vessel of a few hundred tons. They were dependent, too, on the vagaries of weather and of the unknown men, foreign to them in all their practices and ways, who manned the ships. The mariners, indeed, may have seemed as frightful a menace as the ocean itself. Seamen, to plain, devout country folk from a peaceful mountain valley, were profligate and boisterous, given to profanity and wildness at sea, to lewdness and riotous living ashore. More often men of the devil than men of grace, they could turn a ship into a hell on earth.

In such ungodly company, in stormy passages of three or four or five months, hundreds of thousands of them made the attempt. They were convinced that they, under God, could surmount fear and survive terror.

☆   ☆   ☆   ☆   ☆

Of the Eisenhowers* who sailed to this country in the good ship
Europa back in 1741, there was little talk in my boyhood. My
father and mother were not heedless of the past, to be sure. But
they were principally concerned with present responsibilities and
their children's futures. The boys considered the Martin Luther Bible
in the front room, with its antique Fraktur type and its inked record
of births, marriages, and deaths, incontrovertible evidence of the long
family lineage. We were not overwhelmingly accurate. For one
thing, we discussed with pride that fact that our ancestors had begun
their lives as Americans in the same year that George Washington
began his life. This hasty arithmetic brought the Eisenhowers to this
country nine years before their actual arrival. Our mistake did give
me a faint sense of association with the father of our country.
Family trees seem stuffy, although in the last decade I have given
a few hours to the reading of charts and books about the Eisenhowers and the Stovers.

Not long ago, for instance, I was briefed on the distinguished
background of a man who would shortly visit my office. One of
my associates stressed the positions and notable careers of the man's
forebears. Among them, he said, were Dutch patroons and royal
governors in colonial times, generals in all our wars, governors,
senators, famous scholars and lawyers and bankers. His intention
was not to impress me; it was to prepare me for any names which
might be dropped during the visit. I listened attentively to his
genealogical survey and thought: Heaven help the poor man carry
so heavy a burden.

This reaction, though silent, was unkind; I feared that a man so
endowed with family distinction would turn out to be a pompous

---

* The name Eisenhower translates roughly as "iron" and "hewer." To further refine
the original German, I'm told, one should know that *eisenschmidt* would mean
blacksmith, while an *eisenhower* was something of an artist in iron, a man who
literally hewed metal into useful and ornamental shapes, such as armor, weapons,
etc. At various times, friendly people have shown me or presented me with swords,
stamped *Eisenhower*, which they thought my relatives had lost. Now and then I
have explained that the designation was only the mark of a man's trade, not his
name. But I do not always trouble the happy owners by pointing this out.

bore. He was not. Instead, his familiarity with his own and the nation's history gave me a fresh perspective on a crisis or two that was on my desk that afternoon.

At the risk of pompous boredom myself, a few notes on families may be in order.

In 1956, a distant relative, Fannie Bell Taylor-Richardson, of Greenwood, Indiana, began to publish a series of family history bulletins. These covered ten generations and 264 years. Bound together, they make a massive volume, nearly the size of a major city's telephone directory.

Mrs. Richardson had scrupulously searched out all the records of those descended from my great-great-great-grandfather, Hans Nicholas Eisenhauer. He was born in the Palatinate in 1691, came to this country in 1741 with three sons.* Hans and his boys reached Philadelphia on November 17, 1741. Peter was twenty-five, John was born June 24, 1727, and Martin was in his early teens. There, Hans and the two older sons took an Oath to the Government three days later. The father settled in what is now Bethel Township, Lebanon County, Pennsylvania, where he farmed for the next twenty years. Perhaps he started out as a tenant farmer. Mrs. Richardson reports that the first land record in his name is dated January 20, 1753. (And for the collector of coincidences, she points out that this was exactly two hundred years to the day before I was inaugurated President.)

According to Mrs. Richardson, my family must have lived in the thick of Indian troubles. The Pennsylvania *Gazette* of August 12, 1756 reports a letter from Fort Henry advising that Indians were in the neighborhood and that they had burned the house of Hans Nicholas. A year later, she writes, they carried off five children of Peter Wampler, who had accompanied my family on the *Europa*.

During the Revolutionary War, the Susquehanna River territory where the Eisenhowers lived was relatively free from the impact of armed conflict. Undoubtedly, foraging parties from the opposing armies frequently levied requisitions on the larders and barns of the farmers. Food for the troops and fodder for the horses, on the

---

* Another book, *The Eisenhower Family in Germany,* was published in Germany and deals with earlier generations.

American side at least, often worried commanders more than the presence of the enemy. There is a small family sidelight on the supply problem. According to the New York Sons of the Revolution, two of the Eisenhowers, coming to camp to enlist, got special mention in a report because they brought with them "a supply of food." More than likely the family pantry had been raided by the soldiers-to-be because the boys, even then, were dubious about the quality of an Army mess.

I am not sure of the kind of service discharged by the early Eisenhowers during the war. At that time the Army had not made a mammoth enterprise of paper work, covering every detail in a soldier's career from the recruit's first shots to the veteran's final waiver of any claim against the government. On the other hand, we must give credit to paper work for the exactness with which we can now trace a man's service. Except for senior officers, the comings and goings of Revolutionary War soldiers were usually lost to knowledge—as the veterans of that war discovered to their distress when they sought pensions. The support of a claim might require months and even years. Modern veterans, however much they weary of the ever-present mimeograph, can be grateful that the armed services finally discovered the use of paper. Because Hans Nicholas' descendants also kept records, I am on surer grounds after his death.

Of his sons, I am directly descended from Peter, the oldest, who died near Harrisburg, the Pennsylvania capital, in 1802. Peter seems to have been successful in many pursuits. He was the father of seventeen children. A farmer, engaged in many land deals, he was also a blacksmith, a gunsmith, a merchant, and, for a time, at least, a constable. The raising of a large family, I suppose, required of him unusual efforts in money-making. The will he made, on October 3, 1795, orders all his debts and funeral charges to be paid, then continues: "I will and bequeath to my Beloved wife Ann hir bed and furniture thereto belonging with the Dresser and all the furniture theretoo belonging and two milch cows hir choice of all my cows and the interest or benefit of two hundred pounds yearly paid hir while she remains my Widdow . . ."

There was, however, a rider. ". . . but if she marries again," Peter specified, "she is to have only the Intrest of one hundred pounds yearly paid to hir with all the other Specified bequeathment mentioned to hir and this be in lieu of all Dower . . ."

Presumably the dresser mentioned in the will contained linens and china, silver and cutlery.*

Peter's youngest son, Frederick, was my great-grandfather. He lived until 1884 and was the senior Eisenhower in the move from Pennsylvania to Kansas. Frederick was a farmer and weaver and he lived most of his life near Elizabethville where my grandfather, Jacob Frederick Eisenhower, was born September 19, 1826. In Jacob's person—he lived with us in Abilene from the time I was ten until I neared sixteen—the long past of my family drew closer.

By the time Jacob began to grow up, the descendants of Hans Nicholas had already begun to scatter. Some had gone north to Canada; others into the Virginia valleys. A few, apparently, had reached the Cherokee lands in the Carolinas. Jacob may have thought his part of the family a little stick-in-the-mud. Almost a century after his grandfather's arrival in America, the family still lived close to the first Eisenhower farm.

That eventually he was to lead a migration across half a continent, the boy could not foresee.

I never knew Rebecca Matter, my grandmother. Born March 18, 1825, she was the great-granddaughter of a Revolutionary War soldier and the daughter of a War of 1812 captain. She died four months before I was born.†

She and my grandfather had fourteen children. The first twenty years of their married life was marked by sorrow. Of the eight boys and six girls given to them between their marriage on February 25, 1847 and July 30, 1867, when twin boys were born, five sons and one daughter died in infancy or childhood. A second daughter, who would have been my Aunt Lydia, was a little over seventeen when death took her. My grandparents' faith, in the face of repeated personal tragedy, is evident on the limestone marker they placed at the head of Lydia's grave. Still easily read is this inscription:

* In a codicil to his will on June 4, 1801, Peter is more emphatic: "I give and bequeath to my Beloved wife Ann Every Article as is before mentioned in my Wil and that there shall not be any thing not even the value of a spoon disturb or taken from her as long as she remains my Widow . . ." In his last years, he seems to have worried that daughters-in-law might descend on the house and remove some articles of value to women!

† Both Great-grandfather Frederick, and Grandfather and Grandmother Eisenhower —as well as my brother Paul who died in infancy—are buried in Belle Springs, a River Brethren cemetery, that lies twelve miles south of Abilene.

LYDIA A.
DAUGHTER OF
JACOB F. AND REBECCA
EISENHOWER
BORN AUG. 27, 1857
DIED NOV. 15, 1874
AGED 17 YRS. 2 MO. &
19 DAYS

She gave her heart to Jesus
Who took her stains away
And now in Christ Believ
ing, the Father too can say

I'm going home to glory
A golden crown to wear
O meet me meet me over there

Everything I ever heard about them corroborates the sincerity of these chiseled words. The future life was of paramount importance. It *was* going home to glory. This life was only a preparation; the earth a place where heavenly reward might be earned and justified. Undoubtedly frugal in worldly things, a minister who gave more than a tithe to the church, my grandfather nevertheless did not seem to have lost his touch for the practical. He was a good and farsighted steward of the land and the valley farm he bought on the edge of Elizabethville in Pennsylvania's Lykens Valley was ideally situated for a thrifty farmer.

Protected by ridges in all directions, a snug place in winter, the fields running east and west got the full benefit of summer sun. Harvests there are still bountiful, for the loam is deep, and those who followed were good land stewards, too. On that farm, when he was twenty-eight years old, my grandfather built a home. Built more than one hundred ten years ago, the house still stands, four-square and straight, for he built honestly and well. In 1950 Mamie and I made a pilgrimage and were shown the house from cellar to ridgepole by Mrs. Lee Phillips, wife of the present owner. Our reaction was a hope —that if we ever built a place of our own we might do as well in the integrity of workmanship.

Among the Plain People of Pennsylvania, a strong prejudice existed against any practice that implied a lack of trust in God. According to one book I have read, insurance was barred among them. Grandfather, for his own reasons, evidently did not consider an insurance policy a reflection on providence. Within a few weeks of completing his home, he had it insured for $1367 (against an appraised value of $2050) and he paid a premium of $82.02 to the Lykens Valley Mutual Fire Insurance Company. Still, Jacob Eisenhower was a cautious man. His was the forty-eighth policy issued by that company. He waited until the founder and the president of the company took out, respectively, policies forty-six and forty-seven.

In the house they built, my grandparents lived almost a quarter of a century. There my father was born and lived until he was fifteen. And—despite the attractiveness of the homestead and prosperity they enjoyed—he grew up to detest farming.

For the time and place, and despite all the hours given to church work, Grandfather prospered. By 1870, his farm was appraised at $13,000 and his personal property, including savings, at $6000.

In such circumstances, he could easily have spent his declining years in that comfortable house in the valley he knew so well. In the seventies, however, among the River Brethren in the Susquehanna Valley, tales were told of the richness of Kansas lands, of its bountiful wheat crops, of good acreage that could be bought at fairly low prices on the open market. Within the community, there was talk of moving in a body to the Plains.

Letters from those who had gone out there were eagerly passed from hand to hand. Around 1877, some members of the community went out to inspect the prospects, in Dickinson County, whose county seat is Abilene. They arrived there in the peak of wheat-growing excitement when each year the harvest surpassed the previous year.

Pennsylvania newspapers were full of stories about the success of Pennsylvanians who had gone west. The railroad vigorously pushed travel to Kansas by running excursion trains and cutting fares.

In the *Daily New Era* of Lancaster, Pennsylvania, a newspaper that circulated widely among the River Brethren in the Susquehanna Valley, the following notice appears in the March 19, 1878 issue:

The next excursion for Kansas will leave Lancaster and all points on the Pennsylvania Railroad on March 26 and April 2 and 9. The rate of fare to Kansas is $20.05 . . .

My family took the April 9 train and arrived in Abilene on April 12. There, while Grandfather examined the land for sale, they lived in the Emigrant House on the edge of town. This was a large frame building, built during the previous fall and winter by an advance guard of River Brethren to shelter newcomers. Under its roof, scores of families lived as a single community until homesites were bought and dwellings erected.

The land Grandfather bought was priced at $1200 a quarter section, or $7.50 an acre. (In Pennsylvania, his farm had sold for close to $175 an acre.) How much he took up, I do not know. It must have been a substantial amount because his customary wedding gift to his children was a quarter section from the land he owned and $2000 in cash. He himself, a year after arriving in Kansas, was farming 160 acres. The statistics on this first Eisenhower homestead in Kansas are, of course, interesting to me, a member of the family, but I quote them below, from the 1880 census, to suggest what a man would accomplish within a year of his arrival on the Plains.*

That was a bad crop year in Kansas, and worse were to come. Moreover, Grandfather had not yet learned the new methods of cultivation needed in soil so different from the limestone valley he had known in Pennsylvania. But, unlike most of his neighbors, he had two strings to his farming bow—and the second was a dairy herd and poultry.

In 1879, his butter production was a full thousand pounds, more than six times the Dickinson County average. And Grandmother that year had gathered 300 dozen eggs, twice the average of the county's farms. The estimated value of all production was $400, $85 less than average farm income in the county. But most of Grandfather's neighbors had already been on their land five or six years.

In my memory, he is a patriarchal figure, dressed in black, wearing an underbeard with upper lip shaved clean. When I first knew him he was retired and lived across the alley from our home. He kept a horse and buggy which, on occasion, he shared with us boys. His importance, in my mind then, rested on the beard and the buggy and

* According to the record, the entire 160 acres was improved land, although the average Dickinson County farm acreage was less than two-thirds improved. Half of his acreage was tilled; the other half was in permanent meadow, pasture, and orchard. The farm and its buildings were valued at $5000; the implements and machinery at $600 and the livestock at $750. Forty acres were in corn, yielding 800 bushels, and forty acres in wheat, yielding only 170 bushels.

the horse; not on his success as a farmer, or as leader of the family migration. Now I know otherwise.

My grandfather was more than fifty years old when he determined to take his family and leave the pleasant valley where he had lived a half century. This was, I would guess, the great adventure of his life— to risk his possessions and his comforts, to go from the home country where his fathers had lived from the time they settled in America, to start a new life on a new kind of ground.

For all his vision, he had no reason to think that a century and a quarter after he himself was born, his grandson would return to the Susquehanna River area, hoping to end his days on a Pennsylvania farm. Just that has come to pass. Little more than a few score miles, even as the roads here wind and dip, separates my barn from my grandfather's, still standing in the Lykens Valley. In a sense, and not only geographical, I have returned to the home country my grandparents left.

For him to go took courage. And there is a monument to his memory, on the lawn before the house, his Elizabethville home, just off the highway. It was dedicated while I was President by my brother Milton. My name is in the center of the plaque. This is a compliment I appreciate but I think Jacob Eisenhower's worth rests far more on his own deeds, on the family he raised and the spiritual heritage he left them, than on one grandson.

CHAPTER V

The "Gem" on the Plains

As it must to all small boys, there came a time when we began to comprehend that home was more than just our house and backyard. Once in a while, news of the outside world crept in—a world beyond the limits of Kansas, even.

During the Spanish-American War, when I was seven, my uncle Abraham Lincoln Eisenhower was an avid seeker of news. Because he was busy in his veterinary practice, my job, at a penny a day, was to run uptown and get him the local paper, hot off the press. I can never forget his glee when the news came of Dewey's May Day victory over the Spanish Fleet at Manila Bay. I do not know just what day we got the news in Abilene but the smell of gunpowder and victory was in Uncle Abe's nostrils.

Then came the operations in Cuba. My uncle was much interested in the Spanish Fleet, blockaded in the harbor at Santiago, where Admirals William Sampson and Winfield Schley were watching for it to come out. After the battle a public argument developed between those who took Admiral Sampson as their hero and those who thought Admiral Schley should be given credit for the victory. My uncle was a Schley man because at the time of the battle Sampson, who was the senior, had gone up the coast a few miles to confer with the Army commander. But an equal number regarded Sampson as the principal victor, or at least equal in glory with Schley, and I was one of them. It was only by a chance, and while doing his duty, that Sampson was off the scene when the fighting started. In any case, my uncle was overjoyed and fairly danced with pleasure when the news came that the Spanish Fleet, trying to escape, had been sunk to the last vessel—a somewhat misleading, bloodthirsty reaction for a man who would later become a minister.

But before I paid much attention to that distant, outside world, there was a lot to see and learn in the small world around me. The community gradually showed itself as a complex of streets and neighborhoods, each with a personality and identity of its own. Some neighborhoods I knew well. Others were off limits to boys.

Visually, Abilene was in those days just another rural town, undistinguishable from scores of others dotting the plains. It looked peaceful, pastoral, and was, at least in my childhood, happy. After all, the splendiferous C. W. Parker Circus, full of the glittering performers and the dusty glamour of far-off places, made Abilene its home base. Merry-go-rounds were *built* there. Three decades earlier, when founded by a man named McCoy, the town had been rather different.

It was then called the Cow Capital of the World. For a time it maintained its reputation as the toughest, meanest, most murderous town of the territory.

It was the terminus of the Kansas Pacific (later the Union Pacific) Railway. Texas cattlemen, after the Civil War, sought eastern markets. In 1869, they started to drive their herds into Abilene, the nearest railhead. Our national folk heroes were a fairly riotous breed even in the best of times and cowboys coming in off the long, lonely trails were starved for home-cooked food, and more especially for drink, for excitement and amusement. It has been written that early Abilene's infamous Texas Street was "a glowing thoroughfare which led from the dreariness of the open prairies into the delight of hell itself." Whether or not the local hell was an unqualified delight, when the railroad moved on westward, along about 1872, the citizens, or at least the permanent residents, were pleased. They might have missed their chance at developing a metropolitan Sodom, but the people settled down into occupations that made for a slower but steadier growth.

Civic pride, in many American towns of that period, was the most flourishing local industry. When my dad and mother arrived, Abilene was enthusiastic about its future. Some of the dreams of what might lie ahead—the transfer of the state capital to the town, for example —were never realized. But samples of that effervescent optimism may still be read in yellowing advertising literature and real estate prospectuses. On my desk at the moment lies a booklet, printed in 1887, that eighty years later gives us insight into the booster's spirit. The title page proclaims Abilene, modestly,

A GEM

"The City of the Plains"

THE CENTER OF THE "GOLDEN BELT"

The unknown author writes in bountiful and emphatic language about the wonders of Kansas, of the county, and of the town—pardon me, city—itself. On page 55, that the reader may not think him extravagant about his appraisal of the county seat, he submits in corroboration an extract from the Kansas City *Journal*:

But whence this wealth that makes all this possible? Did the birds of the air carry it to them? Did the winds from the prairies waft it to them? Did the waters of the Smoky Hill, with its source in what used to be called the great American desert, bear it to their feet? No. They have never been enriched by any phenomenal act of nature. Then whence these farms in Dickinson County, worth $10,000,000, and wealth in stock, factories, business blocks, homes, railroads, salt wells, gypsum beds, etc., to the amount of $15,000,000—nearly $1,000 for every man, woman and child in the county? The answer is easy and sufficient. They have industriously tilled this great garden of nature, containing 851 square miles—more than half a million acres and its enormous product has been most widely disposed of by a progressive people.

Then the author, surely one of the progressive people to whom he refers, adds a paragraph to nail it all down. This asserts that Abilene is "not only great in its future but in its present. It has all the stuff," he says, of which large cities are made and "this material is in the hands of a citizenship already noted for [its] public spirit, push, intelligence, and business foresight." For any readers not familiar with ancient American jargon, I should translate *push* as being exactly the sort of intemperate energy and drive displayed by the booklet's author.

On this note, he could have—and should have—ended his case. But promotional writers were not paid for understatement. He went on to point out that Abilene had no debt, that her streets and improvements were well perfected, and that she was growing—as he wrote, in a temporary lapse into reality, "not booming, but growing steadily and healthily."

In summary, he rose to new heights of verbosity. One sample of civic puffery would not be seen again in such pure form until the novels of Sinclair Lewis. "We surely need not elaborate," he elaborated: "The foregoing features of attraction are sufficient to commend the country, city, and people as in every way the most desirable." He called for ten thousand more citizens, mechanics, professional men, etc., and pointed to a committee with $100,000 in available cash which would go to manufacturers who would locate there. Abilene, he concluded, "is ready for any class of enterprising people to reap a rich reward from . . . a land favored of heaven and embellished by art."

Whatever its endowments from heaven, and whatever its cultural wonders, Abilene did not get ten thousand more citizens. The boiling expansion of the eighties that transformed many small cities between Pittsburgh and Denver slowed to a simmer in the nineties. Through my boyhood, Abilene was reasonably prosperous but it grew little in population.

The town itself was located a mile or two to the north of the Smoky Hill River and lay largely east of a stream which meandered its way through the flat alluvial plain. On a real estate developer's map, the little waterway is entitled "Serpentine Creek"; we, who knew its true character, called it Mud Creek. Slow-moving streams were always muddy. Boys searching for fishing holes had to be content with a mud cat or an occasional channel cat, the latter always a prize.

Almost as a reaction to the violent earlier days, the town usually seemed extraordinarily peaceful and quiet. To be sure, there were, southwest of the Union Pacific depot, two or three surviving establishments where liquor was sold illegally. (Kansas was a dry state in more than one respect.)

At a place north of town called "The Herd," non-churchgoers gathered of a Sunday, having sent to Kansas City for a keg of beer, and drank it dry as they shot craps for an afternoon's sport. We stayed away from there, naturally, by parental directive, and this sharpened our wonder at what wild things might be going on at The Herd.

Despite Abilene's early reputation, I was nearly fifteen before I saw my first shooting scrape. No one was even slightly wounded. The shooter was standing on a walk, taking pot shots at a man who was setting a new sprint record from a point thirty yards away. The pistol looked very dangerous. Now I know that the little nickel-plated, snub-nosed weapon would have been harmful only in the case of a miraculous shot.

Our major amusements were baseball and football. In the back of a print shop, when I grew older, we had a boxing club. We had no well-organized gymnasiums. Winter sports were skating and hooking a sled behind a horse; the rider, lying flat on his belly, took a fair amount of snow from the horses' hoofs. I remember seeing a tennis court but I do not remember ever seeing anyone play. I had never heard of golf.

The schools were three in number; churches abounded. From memory alone I can identify seven and everybody I knew went to church. (The only exception were people we thought of as the toughs —poolroom sharks, we called them.) Social life was centered around the churches. Church picnics, usually held on the riverbank, were an opportunity to gorge on fried chicken, potato salad, and apple pie. The men pitched horseshoes, the women knitted and talked, the youngsters fished, and everyone recovered from the meal.

High-school students formed little clubs, most with rather pretentious names. Ed and I never joined. By the time I was old enough to be a member, I was gangly and awkward, with few of the social graces. Probably I was more than happy that I was never invited to membership. My brother and I referred with immense disdain to boys and girls who did belong.

It was definitely a small town. Paving was unknown to me for a long time. Crossings of scattered stone were provided at each corner but after a heavy summer rain the streets became almost impassable because of mud. Rubber boots were standard equipment for almost everyone. In winter, snow could practically immobilize the community. I cannot recall when hard pavement was started in town but it was not earlier than 1904 or '05, I think. Even after the streets were paved, sidewalks were still made of lumber, for the most part, and the summer storms would wash the sidewalks out until they were dragged back in place.

The police force was one man, Henny Engle. He could not patrol the streets adequately, of course, so he spent the night watching trains go by or come in, inspecting the arriving passengers for dubious characters. He did walk around to make sure that all the stores were locked up. There was also a town marshal, a daytime man. I never saw him do anything except chase truant boys.

Shopping was not the recreation that it has since become for me.

We had to content ourselves with small shops—grocery stores, meat markets, "notion" stores, drug stores, and barber shops. Modern salesmanship would have been entirely out of order. Shopkeepers assumed that customers came to buy only what was needed. No special effort was made to sell them what they might need, or what they did not need.

Window displays were amateurish. Goods were stored on shelves, protected from prying hands by counters that ran the length of the shop. Nothing was done to encourage the casual browser, the one who, just looking around these days, leaves a store freighted with products he had no intention of buying when he entered. That is just the sort of shopper I am, made for twentieth-century merchandising techniques.

For me, a supermarket is an oriental bazaar. It is a wonderland of bargains, of foods I *must* try, of new specialties I cannot pass by. This may be a reaction to the guarded and sparsely stocked shelves of my boyhood. But it makes me the despair of Sergeant and Delores Moaney, the Sergeant my companion of twenty-five years, who have to find storage space for my latest purchases. And some of these "buys" must bewilder my wife when she tries to fit them into a menu; certain items I have acquired were never designed for making a meal, if they were designed for human consumption at all.

My underground global reputation, I understand, is for the enthusiasm with which I storm a market. A few years ago when Mamie and I were at Culzean Castle, Scotland, with friends, Freeman Gosden and I visited a clothing shop in Ayr. After we left, loaded down, a clerk went up to the proprietor. "You mean to tell me," he said, "that he was the man who used to be the American President? Why, mon, he acted like a lad from the hills!"

And then he added, uttering under his breath, although without distress: "He's no a hard one to sell, that one. . . ." Which may well be one of the better compliments paid me in recent years.

No Abilene clerk or store owner would have radiated such pleasure when speaking of any of the Eisenhower boys. In our personal shopping, when it meant handing over hard-earned spending money, the canny Scots of Ayr could not hold a candle to us in our painstakingly critical scrutiny of goods and prices. As the old expression went, the

Indian on our penny would have screamed if we could possibly have held it tighter.

Not that we were taught to love money; far from it. But all the facts of life taught us a firm respect for it as a commodity hard to come by and quick to vanish unless one exercised vigilant care. Prices were low but not low enough to suit us. The Abilene paper published the day I was born, October 14, 1890, offers a sample of the price structure. Eggs were five cents a dozen. Bread was three cents a loaf. A man could buy a suit of clothing for a few dollars. Boys' requirements were of an entirely different order, however. They were bats and balls and mitts; powder and shot for our obsolete, muzzle-loading guns; footballs and helmets; and there was no money earmarked for these. My father never knew a day of unemployment after his return to Abilene but feeding and clothing his small army of boys required almost every penny. Hand-me-down clothing was an insitution, although not much of our clothing survived the original owner.

We manufactured holes in shoes and stockings, in the elbows of our coats and the knees of our pants. It must have seemed to my parents a conspiracy against the family purse.

Father understood our wants, in fact our desperate need for playtime's implements and accessories. He allotted each boy a bit of ground out of the land surrounding our house. Each was privileged to raise any kind of vegetables he chose and to sell them, if possible, to the neighbors for a profit. (The main garden was devoted to raising vegetables and fruits for immediate family consumption and for canning for the winter.) For my plot, I chose to grow sweet corn and cucumbers. I had made inquiries and decided that these were the most popular vegetables. I liked the thought that I was earning something on my own—and could keep it or spend it on myself.

Ed hated the whole thing. My older brother thought his prospective purchasers always acted superior when he offered his wares for sale. They would search through his whole pack of vegetables to find the best, meanwhile disparaging the quality of the lot—to beat down his price, Ed thought.

I never suffered this way. For one thing, I set the price fairly low to start with.

It was twenty-five cents a dozen for the earliest corn. As the season advanced, the price per ear went down. I always made it a point to be first if I could, when buyers were eager. Having fixed my price, I would show the corn. If customers said the price was too high, I would pick up my pack and go on my way.

During the time our parents lived in Texas, Mother had learned to make Mexican hot tamales. They were delicious and this gave me an idea. I badgered Mother until she demonstrated the whole process, step by step. After I learned, I started making and selling them. My price was five cents for three tamales. This little enterprise did not make me rich but Eisenhower tamales were fun to make and a good off-season sales idea. If there were leftovers, my brothers and I could consume them without strain. It was, inevitably, a case of being able to sell tamales and eat them too.

These money-making ventures began not when we lived on Second Street but only after we had moved to a new, permanent home on Fourth Street. On Second Street, both house and lot were far too small for a cooking business in the kitchen or gardening ventures outside. Even in a town like Abilene where, in its first platting, open land stretched to the horizon, residential lots were just as narrow and shallow as in the older cities of the East. Our Second Street home was tiny. The front yard was a patch. The back yard, with wooden fences on each side and a coal and wood shed not far from the back of the house, was large enough to swing a cat in, if it were a small one.

Mother must have wanted a house with more room inside and out. If ever she gave in to envy, she could have been inspired to it as she looked two streets away to the home of my uncle Abraham, whose veterinary practice required a large barn and open acres around it.

In his boyhood on the family farm in Pennsylvania, Uncle Abe had loved horses more than the land. After his marriage, he had opened up a veterinary office in Father's general store and hung out a shingle that read *A. L. Eisenhower, D.V.S.* So far as anyone knows, he had no serious training in veterinary medicine, although he did take the precaution of serving a slight apprenticeship to a regular vet. The three letters after his name were probably self-conferred. If he lacked a degree, he made up for it in boundless energy and showmanship.

Whenever his time was not occupied by animal care or tending the store, he would hitch up his horse to a two-wheeled gig and drive hurriedly around the countryside, giving the farmers who saw him, trailing a cloud of dust, the strong impression that he was rushing off to answer another emergency call. His practice increased gratifyingly. In fact, the Hope *Herald* reported on April 14, 1887:

A. L. Eisenhower has had extraordinary luck in his veterinary practice. All cases that have come under his care have been fully restored to perfect soundness.

He came to be known as the "genial veterinarian." After Father's partner had absconded, Abraham joined the store formally, making it the Eisenhower Brothers until it was sold the following year. Deciding that his luck with animals might run out, he did a short tour at a Veterinary College in Chicago, at which point, having become legitimate, he started to lose interest in his practice and decided instead to follow the example of his father and grandfather and to be a preacher of the gospel.

Fortunately for us, Uncle Abe now was more concerned with souls than with animals. In 1898 he made up his mind to go West. Father, undoubtedly prompted by Mother, offered to buy his house. And did.

The move from the little cottage on Second to the new house was a step up in the world! A two-story step, for the new house seemed a mansion with its upstairs bedrooms. There were two fairly large bedrooms, with a miniature bedroom at the end of the hall. The first of the large ones was occupied by Father and Mother with the baby, Earl, in a cradle. Three boys slept in the adjoining room, Roy and I in one bed, Edgar in the other. Arthur, the eldest, was awarded the little room at the end of the hall. Its dimensions were 6½ feet by 6½ feet. Whether considered as an underdeveloped bedroom or a generous closet, the rest of us envied his splendid isolation. He was the only person in the house with a room of his own. He soon lost the distinction.

Mother brought in a girl to help with the housework. As I remember, Florence Sexton also attended high school and received as wages $2.00 per week. The best of her emoluments, we thought, was that, as the only girl on the premises, she was given the small room and Arthur had to come in with the rest of us. Two boys then slept in each of two double beds, which together covered almost the entire floor.

I don't know yet how my mother jammed us all in. A quick calculation on a scratch pad reveals that her domain—for living, sleeping, working—totaled 818 square feet for a household of eight. Yet she not only managed to fit us all in, she used the space beautifully.

Since I left Abilene, and whenever I've been given any choice of working quarters, my usual preference as to their size may reflect a subconscious effort to test my own capacity for the use of space against my mother's. I haven't always been a free agent and in the passage of years, my offices got bigger and bigger. After returning from Europe at the end of World War II, for instance, I found that as Chief of Staff my office in the Pentagon was larger than our entire Abilene home. At Columbia University, the President's office is not as large but the lack of floor area is more than offset by the cubic space, for the ceiling is beyond the reach of even a tall ladder. At SHAPE, I was originally assigned to an imperial sort of room overlooking the Champs-Elysées which had been, I was told, originally designed (in secret, to be sure) for the Kaiser when he came to Paris— to watch his victorious troops march up the avenue to the Arc de Triomphe. A few months later, when we moved to Rocquencourt, the French architects had designed for me a handsome and spacious room, even though the new headquarters was allegedly only temporary.

In my next job, I had absolutely no choice whatsoever in the selection of office.

I must confess that no matter what importance the outside world might assign to the business crossing my desk, I never had to contend with the same sort of demands as Mother. And removal to a larger house did not exactly make things easier for her, as she and countless other wives and mothers have discovered. It was no lark for her sons, either.

A large barn and acreage enabled us to keep animals. Now, each morning before school, there were new items on the agenda—milking cows, feeding chickens and horses, putting the stalls and chicken house shipshape. The legend spread in later years was that I was always the last from bed. This may be true but I doubt it. Extra winks would not reduce the amount of work to be done. Mother, and above all my brothers, would not tolerate such escape from full employment.

Some mornings were worse than others. On washdays, all white clothes were boiled to kill germs. While one of us turned the washing machine, the others brought in water for heating in the reservoir, a tank holding five gallons, built as an integral part of a cookstove.

No burden weighs more than a bucket of water on a boy's arm, unless he is carrying one in each hand. If he attempts to cut down the number of buckets by filling each to the brim, splashing and slopping mean mopping up floors. Nor does a bucket brigade, which we tried, in the manner of colonial fire departments, help much when it is made up of boys in a hurry. The vigor with which they swing buckets means empty containers at the end of the chain.

Before running water arrived, the house had to expand. Jacob Eisenhower, my grandfather, lost his housekeeper of many years and came to live with us. The first addition to the house was a two-room wing. This provided a downstairs bedroom for my parents while Grandfather had the other. With his arrival, and without counting the newest baby, Milton, Mother never had less than eight people for breakfast and supper.

Dad carried his lunch or one of us took it to him so that he could have a hot midday meal. The creamery was far enough away to make it worthwhile to hitch old Dick to the buggy or ride him bareback. Either way, and for good reason, dispatch and promptness marked the deliveries. One day Ed, going alone, had dismounted to play a little baseball. In following the hot action on the diamond, he forgot the movement of the clock and Father had to wait until the lunch-hour was past for his lukewarm meal. Edgar did not have to wait as long to get a very distinct physical reaction to remind him of his indifference.

All in all, we were a cheerful and a vital family. Our pleasures were simple—they included survival—but we had plenty of fresh air, exercise, and companionship. We would have been insulted had anyone offered us charity; instead my mother was always ready to take some of her home remedies or food and start out to help anyone who was sick or suffering. The daily prayers of my parents did not fail to include a plea for the hungry, the weary, and the unfortunates of the world.

Somewhere back in that golden time, I had my first experience in a political campaign. I know that some people have always thought that I was not much interested in politics but my debut took place in the fall of 1896, after my entry into grade school. Everybody in school had a button. McKinley buttons, bright yellow, predominated because there were few Democrats in the region. Such Bryan buttons one saw featured the candidate and the figures 16–1.

Excitement in the town grew rapidly. Many people were concerned about what they called The Gold Standard. Of course this meant nothing to me; I had neither gold nor much concern about it. But it seemed to mean a lot to my elders. Though most of them were of the same party, discussions were both continuous and heated. One evening we learned that a big torchlight parade was to take place.

Because I was only six, my mother was loath for me to go uptown to see the parade. Assured by Arthur, now a lordly ten, and Ed, a self-assured eight, that they would take care of me, we started off in the dusk. We were not satisfied to take a place in the middle of the town where the parade would pass. We insisted on going up Buckeye Avenue and into the north end, where it was to start.

The torches were intriguing. They seemed to be nothing but a rod, and a can of liquid at the end with a wick sticking out. As these were lighted, they threw a smoky flame into the evening air. One was to be carried by each person in the parade, then mustering in a column of fours facing the town. As each torch-lighting took place, it soon became clear that there were more torches than bearers.

Spying a group of boys standing wide-eyed on the edge of the formation, the parade managers commanded us to come over. We offered no resistance. Each of us was handed a torch and mine was exactly my own height. We were told to shoulder torches, somewhat like shouldering arms. Off we went.

The town band of a dozen pieces at the head of the procession was supposed to keep us all looking soldierly and marching in cadence. But my short legs presented a problem and the group at the end of the parade was more like a cavorting crowd of lambs. There was a certain amount of disrespectful laughter but we got through the parade in our fashion, with no singed hair and without undoing McKinley. The torches were gathered for return to wherever they had been rented. But my parents missed not only my first appearance in parade formation but my first successful venture into politics. They were among those who were not impressed by the importance of the affair. At least they hadn't taken the trouble to walk the three or four blocks to the parade. It was just as well. There was a tiresome speech under way when my brothers and I took off for home. We wanted to get there before it was too late, for we needed no speeches upon our arrival. Safely concluded, that was one of my few brushes with political life until I found myself drawn into another campaign, half a century later.

CHAPTER VI

Life with Mother

It is clear now that if I were to search out the main faces and forces that shaped me in the early years, these must include my father, my brothers, my town, and, surely not least, my mother. If I devote undue space to town and family, it is not because there is any importance in replaying my life. But Abilene was a microcosm of rural life at that time. And knowing something of how one family lived may give you an inkling of how your grandparents may have lived.

Of my mother's family, I know less than of my father's.* If the Stover most important to me—my mother—was representative of them all, they were a remarkable people.

I may exhibit a son's prejudice. But my feeling reflects the affection and respect of all who knew her. Her serenity, her open smile, her gentleness with all and her tolerance of their ways, despite an inflexible loyalty to her religious convictions and her own strict pattern of personal conduct, made even a brief visit with Ida Eisenhower memorable for a stranger. And for her sons, privileged to spend a boyhood in her company, the memories are indelible.

All her life a woman of peace, my mother was born close to war and the clamor of battle. Growing up, she could see its ravages in a devastated land and in broken bodies. If her hatred of war arose out of childhood memories, she had justification. War's tragedy, inescapable in its waging and in its aftermath, was no tale she had read or heard. She knew it of her own seeing and pondering.

Mother was born May 1, 1862, at Mount Sidney, Virginia, ten miles or so from Staunton in the Shenandoah Valley. That week, Stonewall Jackson and his Confederates were at Port Republic, three or four miles down the road, at the headwaters of the south fork of the Shenandoah River. Defeated six weeks earlier at the north end

---

* In spite of information given in the "Book of Links," written in 1950 by Paxon Link. (My grandmother was a Link.)

of the valley, he was now planning the whirlwind campaign that would become a classic in military tactics.

During her first few weeks, the road outside my mother's home, leading down to Staunton, Jackson's base, must have carried the turmoil and noise of military movement as Jackson gathered all the troops and guns he could rally for the battles that shortly would wreck the Union strategy for the taking of Richmond. They would, too, for the second time in a year, terrify Washington by the threat of a Confederate army crossing the Long Bridge from Virginia into the District of Columbia. To her infant ears, as she lay in her crib in the second month of her life, the winds may very well have carried the sound of artillery fire at Cross Keys and Port Republic where Jackson met the divided Union forces and defeated them. But the worst of war was still two years off.

Through the first three years of the Civil War, the valley above and below Mount Sidney was a secure highway for the movement of Confederate troops and supplies. The valley, too, was the rich granary that supported the armies of Lee. To end all this became a fundamental purpose in Washington. And, in the late summer of 1864, when my mother was well into her third year, Phil Sheridan, detached for the purpose from Grant's forces near Richmond, waged in the valley with fire and sword a campaign so devastating that "a crow flying over it would have to carry its own rations."

For years thereafter, the charred ruins of homes and barns, the blackened soil where straw and haystacks had burned, the decaying trees of uprooted orchards, the wrecked bridges and railways testified that not even in Sherman's march through the deep South had war been more cruel than in this valley of small farms.

My grandmother died when Mother was not quite five. Her father, unable to cope with eleven children ranging in age from seventeen to less than three years, housed them with relatives who were numerous around Mount Sidney. Mother grew up to young womanhood in the home of her maternal grandfather, William Link, who became her legal guardian upon the death of her father, Simon Stover, in 1873. Shortly thereafter, two of her older brothers moved to Kansas. At that time, when she was fourteen or fifteen, she seems to have decided that eventually she would join them there.

In an age when, far more than now, most girls looked forward to careers as housewives, Mother was determined to get a good education before all else. This she did and very much on her own, using a small inheritance from her parents and grandfather, William, to see her through high school. To earn money for college she taught the 1882 school year at Limestone near Mount Sidney. In 1883 she left Virginia for Lecompton, Kansas, where she enrolled at Lane University.

Lane had several advantages. It was fairly new. It was lively. It had certain endowments.* And, though she didn't know it, the man who was to be my father was enrolled there.

I should imagine that out of their two college years, my parents profited more from their association with people than with books or with expensive laboratory equipment. For one thing, the library must have been minuscule and the laboratory simple, if not primitive. The curriculum was a curious mixture of classical and vocational. My father, for example, studied mechanics and Greek. Later he often read from the Greek Bible; other translations made him nervous.

But Lane's people, the elders marked by a dedication to their mission and the students by an optimistic conviction that education was worth sacrifice, created on the campus an atmosphere that fed the traits of self-reliance, of intellectual independence, of faith in God and in oneself. Lane, of course, was most important in my parents' lives because it provided the setting for their first meeting. Their courtship ended on September 23, 1885 when they were married in the campus chapel by Rev. E. D. Slade, the college pastor.

Their wedding photograph hangs beside my desk here in Gettysburg. Others, analyzing their photograph, have tried to analyze their characters. The analyses have sometimes seemed farfetched, even preposterous, to those of us who knew them in daily life. I'm not much of a hand at that sort of thing myself, although as I look at them on the wall almost eighty years later they seem to me what others find paradoxical: both very sober and very happy.

☆　　☆　　☆　　☆　　☆

It is fatuous to remark that a man's hometown has changed since he was a boy. But in later visits to Abilene, I cannot help but notice that the nights, once so quiet that the whistle and rumble of a train

* See Note 1.

could be heard rising and falling away across miles of country, are now disturbed by town noises. Something is missing. What is it?

Well, of course, it is my family. We are gone, scattered, and we can never put the pieces together again.

There are other, more subtle, disappearances. The horse, which once provided transport and power and whose presence was signed on every street, is gone. And with it the hitching rails and posts, the watering troughs and the livery stables with the towering manure heap in the rear and the fringe of loiterers in the front.

Attitudes have gone also—or at least changed. There is a fundamental change, I think, in the attitude toward the temporal role of man.

That role was once expressed in a single word: Work.

The attitude toward the church and toward education was significant. Most houses of worship were plain frame buildings, without adornment of steeple and tower. The River Brethren Church was one of these. There were only a few expensive structures and they constituted the architectural showplaces of the town. The schools, too, were functional, square, two-story buildings without ornament, each with its bell housed in a cupola on the roof.*

Kansans, except for the surviving Indians, were largely literate. On the other hand, few, other than lawyers or physicians, had even a four-year high-school background. The dropout problem, which bothers us so much, was in my boyhood an accepted phenomenon. The boy who left the fifth or sixth grade was not considered a derelict or a burden on society. Ed, who dropped out after completing eighth grade, was exceptional, because having worked for two years, he returned to school among younger people.

Of the two hundred children who entered first grade at Lincoln and Garfield schools in 1897, only sixty-seven entered the Abilene High School eight years later. Of them, only thirty-one graduated—and that was the largest class in the history of the school.

Education, in the small-town view, was intended to produce citizens who could inform themselves on civic problems. Beyond that, schools served to prepare the student for little more than the ordinary round of jobs.

* One of them, however, in early days of Abilene, was the most impressive building there. This was the Garfield School, built before I was born on the higher ground on the north side of the head of Broadway, where it was the focal point for all visitors who arrived by train.

Physical work was done by almost every male. The capitalists of town were no less immune than the poorest. They spent hours each week in currying horses or greasing the axles of a buggy, in managing a base-burner and sifting unburned coal from its ashes. In fact, the last-named task was the mark of the man who knew the value of money. "Waste not, want not" and "A penny saved is a penny earned" were the rule of life.

Because everyone had to put his shoulder to it, there was little social stratification because of a man's job. Bank clerks and others who dealt with paper and pen, professional men, perhaps, may have enjoyed a certain distinction. If so, there were not many of them in a town like mine in the early part of the century. One of our barbers was the social lion of the town. Another man, a telegrapher, because he was in touch with distant places, enjoyed unique esteem. He was the radio and television of our day.

Of Cecil Brooks, the telegrapher in the stock exchange office—we called it a bucket shop—rumor had it that he received a legendary salary—$125 a month. If that helped to set him apart from most men, he was even more notable because during a World Series, he kept his wire open to the East until the games had ended. Nearby, in the "Smoke House," a pool room, the scoreboard was set up and he relayed the results to the board at the end of each half inning. Those of us who crowded around him in his office could get even quicker results. In the 1906 series of hitless wonders, I remember that truancy rose to unusual peaks. Few of us felt the classroom as important a center of learning as was Cecil Brooks' telegraph key.

Baseball players occupied a niche apart from all other human beings. For half the year their names were featured in the daily paper. They made immense sums of money—three, four, *five* thousand dollars, and all for doing what was fun.

To prepare for a career as glamorous and as well paid as a telegraph operator, to become a proficient stenographer, or, like my father, to become a certified engineer was not then considered a job for public education. These heights were scaled only through the graduate's own efforts and at his own expense. My father, after what would be called on-the-job training, mastered engineering through a course from a correspondence school in Scranton. One of the creamery's founders had decided to expand it into the manufacture of ice and ice cream and in cold storage facilities. Father, knowing that the new machines would be far more complicated than the old, enrolled in an ICS course in refrigeration engineering.

Because he had little free time on the job, his studies had to be done at home of an evening under the light of the kerosene lamp on the dining-room table. By then he was approaching forty years of age. But no eager beaver I have ever encountered was more diligent.

Abilene folk believed in education and its value. But for many, I'm afraid, it became beyond a certain point fancies and frills. Remember that most of them were born around the time of the Civil War when few thought it extraordinary that the President of the United States had less than a year's formal schooling. George Washington, after all, had not enjoyed any more; neither had Andrew Jackson, or Lincoln. Then, at least west of the Alleghenies, the well-educated man was more likely to be a well-read man than a much schooled man. Thirty years after Lincoln, to write a good, clear hand, to spell fairly well, to be able to read fine print and long words, to "cipher" accurately was still enough to go with native intelligence and a willingness to work hard. Given those qualities, Abilene thought that most anyone could succeed in the American environment.

In the fall of 1896, I entered the Lincoln School, little aware that I was starting on a road in formal education which would not terminate until 1929 when I finished courses at the Army's War College in Washington, D.C. What I learned at the start would not remain static. In the third of a century between my first and last school was compressed a series of revolutions—political and economic, social and scientific—which were to transform the human environment of the entire globe.

Had I been warned, I doubt that it would have meant much to me. After all, nothing could be more revolutionary, and in a way more revolting to me, than this new experience.

Here I was, transported from the family circle of a small frame house where every figure was familiar, into an immense brick building populated by strangers of varying ages. This upheaval in *my* way of life, had I been able to make the comparison, was far more cataclysmic than any changes to follow.

They used a drum to rally us in ranks for re-entering the school after playtime. The drummer could turn the tumult of a recess crowd into some semblance of quiet, orderly movement. I've always admired the drum since and despised the siren. The drum communicates a message and calms as it warns. The siren is an assault on the senses. In later years, when well-intentioned escorts elected to use a siren on my behalf, I asked—or ordered—that it be stopped.

The automobile and the airplane were, to be sure, two of the transforming instruments. Long before I saw my first automobile, and before I'd ever heard of an airplane, the "airship" was known to me as a vehicle for transporting men and bombs. During the Spanish-American War, there must have been talk about the possibility of the enemy bombarding American cities from the air. At a school recess one morning, a rumor spread that a Spanish airship was over Abilene. All the boys rushed uptown to see the sight, never questioning its feasibility, and classes went to pot. We quieted down when the object high in the sky proved to be a huge box kite, used by merchants who advertised a correspondingly huge sale of straw hats.

Memory is a blur of grades entered and grades passed. At one point a suggestion was made that I should "skip" a grade. This is not tribute to my academic mastery. I suspect that it was simply recognition that I lived in a home where learning was put into practice. The ability to read in a good clear voice and correctly, for example, was necessary if each of us was to maintain his self-respect in a daily family rite. The reading of the Bible, although principally done by our parents, was shared with the boys. A simple rule applied when one of us took over: The honor ended if a mistake were made. This put each of us on his mettle. Undoubtedly, too, it simplified our classroom task of reading aloud. The words in our school readers were in far larger print than the family Bible and were not so polysyllabic. So, I may well have had some advantage over my classmates. The suggestion that I skip a grade was never put into effect. My conduct was not the equal of my reading ability.

Whatever the school thought, I was not without ingenuity. When Earl was several months old, my mother wanted him taken out in the baby carriage and wheeled around. Saddled with the chore, I discovered that I could lie down on the lawn on the front yard and draw the carriage back and forth lengthwise by catching the front axle with my fingers, bringing it back down toward my toes, and then catching the rear axle with my toes and bringing it back the same way. This gave me a perfectly lazy time in the sunlight and kept Earl sufficiently happy so that each time, he finally went to sleep.

A neighbor, Mrs. Brown, thought this was the funniest thing she had ever seen and she regaled my mother with all its details. Mother worried that my new technique might tip the buggy so she asked me for a demonstration. Fortunately, she approved. But despite her care, accidents did happen.

When Earl was about three years old and I was nine or ten, he and I were playing in a workshop attached to the big barn behind our home. He crawled up on a box near a window, unnoticed by me. On the window sill was a knife which I had carefully placed out of his reach when we first arrived. I was busy playing when he, with the knife in his hand, jumped off the box. I heard a scream. Looking around, I saw that his hand had flown up to his face. The blade had punctured his eyeball.

The eye was thought to be the most delicate part of the body and surgery, in small towns at least, was seldom attempted. An injury to the eye was usually irreparable unless nature affected a cure. The doctor believed that Earl's accident would not blind him but we were exceedingly worried and our whole family lived in anxiety as the wound began to heal. Then a second accident occurred.

Milton and Earl were playing a game called "Crokinole." This involved a sizable board of considerable weight. As they went at it, with Earl amusing Milton who was not much older than a baby, the board was accidentally tipped over and the corner of it struck Earl's injured eye. This doomed our hope for his complete recovery. The doctor said nothing could be done.

From then on, of course, everyone in the family was especially sensitive to any possibility of accident where a child's eye could be hurt. Earl went on to be graduated as an engineer, was in newspaper work, and even though retired from industry he has recently been engaged in Illinois politics. Apparently his eye has not bothered him much; but it has always bothered me. I was with him when the first accident occurred and if I had been more alert, it would not have happened. My feeling of regret is heightened by a sense of guilt, even though my parents never charged me with any blame. To this day I think that nothing troubles me more than to see my grandchildren playing with anything which might cause eye injury.

Bruises and emergencies were normal in a household of six boys who were convinced that they could outwit such small considerations as the law of gravity. In the barn we practiced acrobatics and balancing acts. Mother had to keep herself supplied with liniments, poultices, bandages, and disinfectants. Calmness was even more necessary; she could not know in which direction her first-aid skills would be required next. The simplest chore might produce crisis.

Cleaning the stable was Arthur and Ed's task. They became expert at it and, as premature experts will, they also became careless. Ed raked out the stall one day without troubling to take Dick outside and tie him up. In raking, he accidentally struck Dick on the hock. This was too much for the horse. He let fly with both heels, scored a direct hit, and Edgar landed in a heap at the far end of the stable. Arthur rushed to get Mother. She came quickly, and the two of them picked up Ed, whose face was a sorry-looking mess, and carried him to the house.

While Arthur went for the doctor, Mother began washing Ed's face. One eye was blackened, his nose was largely flattened, and both lips hung down until he resembled a human being in only dim particulars. The doctor could not be located right away so Mother fed him a peeled apple to keep him happy. After a while, I eased myself into the living room where the body was installed and soon was arguing with him about a share of the apple.

Ed's accident could have been serious. As it happened, he was at the end of the trajectory of Dick's heels. Had he been two inches closer to the horse's hoofs, he might have had his skull crushed. Soon he was completely restored to respectable visage. But Mother must have taken longer to recover from the shock of seeing still another son bloodied, battered, and bemired.

Ed could have claimed injury in the line of duty. Three years later, he and I risked our lives without any excuse for shattering Mother's peace of mind.

In May 1903, heavy rains throughout the Plains and a slow run-off through the winding Mud Creek and Smoky Hill River caused the lower part of town to be covered with water. When the flood was at its height, Ed and I set out to explore. Buckeye, the main north-and-south street, had turned into a torrent. We found a piece of floating sidewalk to use as a raft. Accumulating several friends, we started off on a ride down Buckeye toward the river. It was great fun and as we went racing along, it turned out to be a wild ride. There seemed to be no reason for not staying with it as long as possible.

We got to singing songs, "Marching Through Georgia" for one, and as we floated fast toward Georgia, neither common sense nor timidity warned us that we were approaching a point of no return. Not for a minute did it occur to us that we might end up in the truly raging currents of the main river. None of us had ever seen so much and such fast water, stretching on either side almost as far as we could see.

The swollen river ahead would have ended voyaging for this group of midwestern boys for all time.

Along the edge of the water, a man on horseback was trying to make his way into Abilene. He came out to us. The water was belly-deep on the horse but the rider made us get down off the board-walk-raft. We were reluctant but he was stern and because he was big and we were small we obeyed. We had to find our footing in water that was more than waist-deep for most of us. The horseman herded us back toward town. It was about a half mile south of Abilene when we first met him and it wasn't until we were near our home that the water was shallow enough to wade.

Ed and I made our way home to find ourselves out of deep water and into deep trouble. Occupied with the gang and having so much fun, we had not only spent the entire morning on the water, but it was after lunch. Mother, exceedingly worried, had sent out one or two neighbors who had saddle horses as searching parties. As soon as we got in the house, and a brief moment of welcome and relief was evident, the real storm broke. Mother had also sent for Father.

We were sent to bed, etc. By early morning, the waters had receded, leaving a sea of mud. Ed and I were put to work digging out our house and yard. This was back-breaking. Once the walks and yard were cleaned up, we had to pump the water out of the cellar. Father had installed a large pump at the cellar window. If the earlier task had been tiring, this was boring. We took turns working the pump wheel. Water poured out of the hose at a great rate but every time we checked the water level in the cellar we could see no sign of its lowering.

I don't remember how long it took but it was several days before we got down to the mud that the pumped-out water had left. In the cellar it was particularly thick because of the depth of the water that had been allowed to stand stagnant for days. Our next task was loading the mud into buckets and carrying it out. Everything in the cellar had to be taken out, washed and cleaned, including dozens of jars containing canned fruits from the preceding summer.

Had we been at home that morning, Father felt we could have kept the water from going into the cellar at all by building small emergency dams, about six inches in height, around the cellar window openings. This seemed fatherly hindsight at best but later, in 1915, the town was flooded again, not quite as seriously as in 1903, although for a few hours the water did reach the same level. I was home on leave from West Point at the time and with my two youngest brothers we made certain, by building such dams, that not a drop of water got into the cellar.

When the 1903 flood had subsided, the town was a wreck. Yet crops that year were of record size. I remember Father talking about the ancient Egyptians and how they profited by the overflow of the Nile. He remarked that if farmers could have one flood early each year, it would be a fine thing even though they would lose some of their first plantings. For my part, floods were a bad idea all around.

From time to time we heard about the wandering Uncle Abraham. His first venture into the ministry joined him and Aunt Anna, his wife, with a Brethren preacher, D. H. Brechbill. They traveled in a cumbersome covered wagon to the Cherokee Outlet country in Oklahoma Territory, an area opened to settlement only a few years before. Until approaching winter drove them home, they conducted what Aunt Anna described as a "highway and hedge call."

Back in Abilene, Uncle Abe designed a better vehicle for the next trip. This was seven feet wide, fourteen feet long, and six and one-half feet high to the canvas roof. It held a table and chairs, a stove, four cots, and a sliding curtain that divided it into sleeping compartments. This contrivance Uncle Abraham christened a "gospel wagon" and after a dedicatory ceremony, they set out again with two companions.

Even as a preacher of the Gospel, my uncle had a streak of the carnival barker in him. When he reached Herington, Kansas, ten days or so after leaving Abilene, the small town was crowded with July Fourth celebrants. One man in the street, with a large megaphone, was directing the crowds toward an assembly at the edge of town where bands would play and speeches would be made. Uncle Abraham, confronted with this worldly competition, whipped his team and gospel wagon into the line of march. At the next intersection, he turned down a side street, brandishing his whip as he stood upright, and shouting at the top of his voice: "This way to heaven!"

The lustiness of his tone, the vigor of his gestures, the novelty of his vehicle had the desired effect. The crowd followed Uncle Abraham to the other edge of town where, assembling them around his wagon, he delivered what was described as a soul-rousing sermon.

In an even smaller town, hard pressed to gather a group together, he planted himself on the sidewalk, lying on his back. He elevated his feet against a wall, and resting his head in one hand, began to read his Bible. In no time at all, naturally, a crowd gathered and when he considered the group of reasonable size, he sprang to his feet. He had his congregation and the congregation got his sermon.

The following year, after a third highway and hedge season, my uncle and aunt returned to Pennsylvania. For a short time, they lived at an orphanage conducted by the River Brethren. They, childless, fell in love with the children. And there they got the idea that out in the newly-settling Oklahoma Territory, they should open up a similar home for orphans.

With no qualms about where money would come from or where orphans would be found, they filed a homestead claim on a quarter section of land outside the present Thomas—then only a stopping place on a wagon trail eighteen miles from the nearest railroad. In a sod-covered dugout home, they planned their enterprise.

With his own funds and mainly with his own hands, Uncle Abraham built a frame house. When the building was ready, he and Aunt Anna traveled to Guthrie, the territorial capital, were granted a charter, and incorporated the Jabbok Faith Missionary Home and Orphanage on August 26, 1901. The children came to fill the house, they were fed and clothed and taught. Uncle Abe farmed the 160 acres, well enough to feed the children with something left over for cash sale. Aunt Anna wrote endlessly to friends and relatives for cast-off clothing and she also reported regularly to the River Brethren through the columns of the *Evangelical Visitor,* everything that was going on. And in 1906, the church formally took it over.

Among the River Brethren, Uncle Abraham came to be known

as Mr. Jabbok. Today, on the site of the orphanage he and his wife started, Jabbok Academy, a thriving school, is a monument to the faith of two people who dared to dream and to do something about it.

Although two of my uncles, Abraham and another named Ira, were preachers, other men I knew were hardly candidates for the pulpit. Law-abiding though they were, they had their roots in that fascinating period of Abilene history when Wild Bill Hickok, the town marshal, made it famous—or less infamous.

Across the street from our house lived a man named Dudley, who claimed he had served for a time as a young deputy under Wild Bill. His tales of the man's prowess with a revolver were entrancing. Other men well acquainted with revolvers and their use were the town marshal, Henny Engle, and the Wells Fargo agent, a Mr. Gish.

Sometimes they went out to Mud Creek and would let me accompany them as they held a shooting contest. Occasionally, I was permitted to shoot several rounds. Each man carried his revolver differently. Gish wore his in a shoulder holster under his left arm. Henny Engle used a conventional holster on his right side. Mr. Dudley slipped his revolver inside his belt, the barrel pointing toward his left foot and the grip handy to his right hand. I would watch intently as they would draw and shoot. While none of them had the skill I've seen in shooting exhibitions, they were all above average in marksmanship and at least two had personal experience in gunfights.

My hero was a man named Bob Davis. He had long been a traveler, a fisherman, hunter, and guide. He was also a bachelor, a philosopher, and, to me, a great teacher. Bob, about six feet tall, a little stooped, quiet and gentle, was in his fifties when I knew him, roughly from age eight to sixteen. He never seemed to be annoyed when I went along on expeditions to the Smoky Hill River. The river, as I have said, had no really good fish, but using nets, illegally, Bob caught channel cat and sold them to the markets for something like ten cents a pound, dressed. In fall and winter, he trapped muskrat which abounded, and mink, which were scarce. For partially cured muskrat hides, he got eleven cents. For mink, $1.50.

Bob had an old double-barreled shotgun. At the time it seemed perfectly natural for him to bring down two ducks, from high overhead, with two shots. Years later, when I began to try the same sport myself, I realized what a remarkable shot Bob Davis was.

He taught me how to use a flat boat, with one paddle—to keep the paddle on one side and feather. I learned how to set and anchor a net, with the opening downstream. He was full of questions, his favorite method of teaching. "In the woods, it's raining. How do you find north?" (The moss on the trees tends to be on the northern side. This won't always work but if you look at enough moss and enough trees, it's apt to give you direction.) "Bub, how do you catch a muskrat?" (You go and look for his slides, then put your trap on a short chain so he'll drown.) "Do you use bait?" (No) "Meat?" (No) "How do you catch a mink?" (You look for a secluded place and put out a skinned muskrat with a stake through the body, near the trap, etc. etc.)

We spent weekends together on the river, with my mother's blessing. One thing he taught me, without sanction, was the rudiments of poker. Bob was an illiterate and he had difficulty writing his own name. He started it with straight lines around which he laboriously drew the necessary curves to spell out *BOB DAVIS*. But he knew poker percentages. He would deal me five cards and ask me whether I had a pair.

"Yes, nines."

"All right," he would say, "how many nines are there out of the forty-seven cards that you have not yet seen?" Of course the answer was two.

"Well, then, the chance of your drawing a nine as you take each card is two out of forty-seven—since you are drawing three cards you have six chances out of forty-seven cards of catching a third nine."

He dinned percentages into my head night after night around a campfire, using for the lessons a greasy pack of nicked cards that must have been a dozen years old. We played for matches and whenever my box of matches was exhausted, I'd have to roll in my blankets and go to sleep. Since I was fascinated by the game, I really studied hard to keep it going. Often, he would pick up part of the pack and snap it across my fingers to underscore the classic lesson that in a two-handed game one does not draw to a four-card straight or a four-card flush against the man who has openers.

So thoroughly did Bob drill me on percentages that I continued to play poker until I was thirty-eight or forty and I was never able to play the game carelessly or wide open. I adhered strictly to percentages. Since most tyros and many vets know nothing about probabilities, it was not remarkable that I should be a regular winner. When I found officers around me losing more than they could afford, I stopped playing.

I never have lost my zest for food cooked over a campfire—particularly for fish caught in a cold, clear stream and broiled within an hour or two on hot coals. In later years, when I have presided over a fish fry, the utensils have been less rudimentary than on my trips with Bob Davis. The wealth of instruments and gadgets I came to enjoy would have made my eyes pop as a boy. Even then, I must have hankered for the country-club touch in outdoor living.

While we were in high school, a group of us decided to camp on Lyons Creek, about twenty miles south of town, and so far as I know the only clear-water stream in that part of Kansas. Fine trees and beautiful campsites made the whole prospect attractive—if we could get together the right kind of money. We planned to be gone two weeks and each boy was supposed to find five dollars to put into the pot to take care of food and incidental expenses. There were about a dozen of us and we hired a fine old Negro man as our cook.

After this first venture, which we had been compelled to cut short, we modified our ambitions. The cost of the livery rig that had taken us down to Lyons Creek, plus the cost of food and the five dollars a week for the cook broke us. We still wanted to make the outing an annual affair and next time we would do the cooking ourselves.

We decided that each day two boys should do the cooking. Ames Rogers, a banker's son, and I paired off together.

I had already acquired some rudiments of the art at the time when Milton fell ill with scarlet fever. The doctor quarantined certain rooms in the house and because it was impossible for my father to stop working, he and the rest of the boys lived downstairs while Mother and a neighbor woman remained with Milton the entire time. It was a prolonged illness. Arthur and Ed had part-time jobs of their own and so the kitchen chores fell to me.

Mother would call instructions from the sickroom and I would carry them out. It was a new experience and I felt very important indeed. Although we didn't use the word then, cooking gave me a creative feeling. I don't think the family lived too well during those weeks but I learned something about the preparation of simple dishes for the table. My principal contribution was a hearty vegetable soup, always a family favorite. Under Mother's directions broadcast from upstairs, I got together soup meat and big joints and vegetables, well seasoned, which produced a really passable dish. By starting out each meal with a bowl of vegetable soup, it was no disaster if the main courses that I prepared did not come off too well.

On coming back from the first camping trip to Lyons Creek, I asked Mother for more help, and she taught me to bake and boil potatoes, handle steaks—which in those days were pan grilled—and even to produce a satisfactory peach, apple, or cherry pie.

When the next summer came around, it was soon discovered that Ames and I were better prepared than any other pair to do the cooking. The whole gang wanted us to cook every day. We weren't particularly adverse to the idea but naturally we demanded our price for the deal. The other boys had to do the cleaning up, getting the wood, building the fire. And we demanded on top that we also get first helpings in generous portions of any scarce commodity.

Even with the savings accomplished by do-it-yourself cooking, we began to run short of money again in the last two or three days. Most of our supplies came from a little store nearby. With only enough money to pay for our return trip to Abilene, the rations became meager. Although it was summertime, I took an old shotgun and went out to see if we could come by a few rabbits and squirrels. The hunting expedition was not notably successful but I did get two or three squirrels—very little indeed to feed a sizable group of hungry boys. With a few potatoes and beans, I tried to build a good stew. When we saw that we were going to be short, Ames and I began to talk as we cooked, a little louder than usual. Among other things, we said that we hoped that the crow we had just shot would make an edible stew.

Quickly, the word got around to the boys who hadn't been close enough to hear. They drifted over to the kettle in the fire, looked in, turned around, and said that they weren't really hungry. Several said they'd be content with some scraps of bread and a little butter. Of course Ames and I ate heartily and near the end asked, "What's wrong with you people? Don't you like squirrel stew?"

The last of the group, sitting off to themselves, had been looking at us with barely disguised distaste. Now they looked at us with menace, jumped up, and began a rush.

Ames and I did not stand upon dignity. We took off as fast as we could, well knowing that they would stop to get a share of whatever was left.

Despite threat of dismemberment, this experience did give me a continuing interest in cooking. I learned that even good food could be quickly ruined by bad preparation. When I became an officer in the Army, and had the usual chore of inspecting the enlisted men's mess, I found that here again it was not enough to bring good supplies into the kitchen. If we were to have a happy company, decent preparation was essential. I volunteered for Cooks and Bakers School on the post where I was first stationed. There I hoped to learn more about cooking for large groups of men.

I didn't learn enough at the Fort Sam Houston School to qualify as a cook. But I did learn about the problems of trying to bring four-star cuisine out of recipes which use hundreds of pounds of ingredients and gallons of water. I knew enough so that I could discover what was wrong with the food that men in my command were getting. I have made things miserable on occasion for young captains or lieutenants, responsible for messes, who limited their inspection to questioning whether pots and pans were shined brightly enough. Some had no idea whatsoever about a balanced meal and others cared not at all whether food not only tasted properly but looked appealing. I insisted that officers learn enough about their business, including the kitchen, to oversee it intelligently.

My interest in cooking has always seemed to be of interest to the press. I haven't the slightest idea how many miles of film have been wasted in photographing me as I broiled fish or steaks over a fire. I did not merit such attention as a chef—but I have noticed that my friends in the press not only reported on my productions, they devoured them with gusto.

While I was at Columbia, a home-style recipe for chicken soup* got as much attention and space in the press as any statement I made as University President. Much of the interest in that recipe may have been due to my suggestion that nasturtium stems be added to the soup. This was not only a novel idea but apparently an exotic ingredient and a considerable number of letters which came in after publication of the recipe reported that the writers could not buy nasturtiums in their neighborhood grocery stores. Would I suggest a place where they might be bought?

* See Note 2.

CHAPTER VII

Footnotes for Biographers

THE LAD was exactly my age but somewhat smaller and although I cannot recall the cause of the quarrel, we were squaring off and hitting at each other as hard as we could. There was no semblance of science. Our only hope was for one to outlast the other.

Gradually, I gained an advantage and was pounding my antagonist with satisfying rhythm. Suddenly, an avalanche struck me in the back. My opponent's older brother had come racing through the ring of yelling spectators and, hitting me right at the shoulders, bore me to the ground. There, he began slamming me all over the place.

Although he was somewhat stronger and larger, I did manage to get up, realizing now that I had two rather than one to try holding my own against. The outlook was not cheerful but I was stubborn enough to keep up the contest.

It happened that Edgar, just coming back from Northside School where he was in the eighth grade, saw what was happening. He pushed his way into the crowd of boys and, walking into the center, interposed himself between the bigger brother and me. I shall never forget his immortal words. "Now," he said, "you and I will settle this while Dwight finishes the job on this brother of yours."

The bigger boy looked at Ed, turned around, and pushed off. The younger boy left too.

Ed and I walked home for our lunch. I cannot recall any time, even in World War II, when unexpected reinforcements were more gladly received.

The fight I just described is remembered only by the participants. The one in which I was unfortunately engaged a year or so later has been described in such exaggerated terms by biographers that, although scarcely earth-shaking, possibly the record should be set straight.

Through the first six grades, I attended Lincoln School, directly across from our Fourth Street home. The darkness of the classrooms on a winter day and the monotonous hum of recitations, offset only occasionally by the excitement of a spelling bee or the suppression of a disorderly boy, are my sole surviving memories. I was either a lackluster student or involved in a lackluster program.

The time came for me to enter Garfield on the north side to complete seventh and eighth grades. Traditionally, there was hostility between boys from the north and south sides of town. Whenever any south-side boy was ready to go to Garfield, he was a stranger entering a rather closely knit group and he had best be prepared to take care of himself.

If no natural, personal rivalry sprang up between individuals, the crowd picked out two who would provide sport. By student consensus, pressure grew for a fight between a boy named Wesley Merrifield and myself. Why fight? There was no good reason. Actually I rather liked Wes and, as far as I knew, he had nothing against me. He was short and stocky. I was long and thin and rangy.

Other fellows, some of them older and all of them warriors who loved to watch a battle from side-line safety, kept running back and forth between us, trying to get us involved in an after-school engagement. This went on for days. Finally one evening, by the time we had walked down the street about three or four blocks, the two of us were practically forced together. Neither of us had the courage to say "I won't fight."

We began to slug away at each other awkwardly, doing little discernible damage. The only thing that made the fight notable was its length. We weren't skillful but we were stubborn and persistent so we kept pounding away, with occasional pauses for breath, for well over an hour. By that time, complete exhaustion overtook us and by mutual consent we stopped for a moment. Wes said, "I can't lick you." I said the same thing. And that was that.

When I got home, I quickly sneaked into the bedroom to take a look and found that I had a discolored eye. This signal, of course, was instantly noted by my parents when I came to the dinner table. Because they were both opposed to indiscriminate brawling, the fat was in the fire. I got off with a strong reprimand but I had to stay out of school for two or three days.

Some biographers have tried to paint Wes as a bully, bigger than myself, and the one who had forced the fight. Instead it was just the case of two boys not being able to withstand mob pressure. The fight had no unpleasant aftermath and later years when I saw Wes Merrifield, we were both amused in recalling the brawl.

Those of us from the south, in Abilene's Civil War, were less numerous than the northern tier but we liked to think of ourselves as being tougher. We numbered in our membership all the farm boys who lived south of town. But encounters between the two groups rarely reached the stage of real damage. Oh, occasionally there would be brick-throwing or threatening. But this was rather lackadaisical. Now and then snowballs with cinders or small rocks packed in the center were employed and resulted in a well-blackened eye. By the time I entered high school in 1905, the rivalry had flown out of favor and I cannot recall any further difficulty of any kind. One reason might have been that the south side boasted more than our share of pretty girls—Gladys Harding, Ruby Norman, the four Curry sisters, and Winnie Williams.

The move from Lincoln to Garfield School produced no transformation in my attitude toward academic subjects. In grammar school, spelling was probably my favorite subject either because the contest aroused my competitive instincts or because I had learned that a single letter could make a vast difference in the meaning of a word. In time I became almost a martinet about orthography, inclined to condemn as beyond redemption a man who confused principle with principal and the like. Arithmetic came next because of the finality with which an answer was either right or wrong.

Penmanship, the one ability which was thought to be the chief index to the educational progress of a child, was largely self-taught. The pupil, using a copy book in which each page was headed by a motto in handsome Spencerian script, filled its pages with laborious imitations. Neither then nor since has my handwriting resembled Spencerian or the English language. Although I began, in my late fifties, to paint in oils, fascinated with colors, my handwriting remains angular and slurred at best. My hand was made less for the use of the pen than of the ax—or possibly the pistol.

The town school superintendent visited classrooms regularly. He seemed to be as much concerned with discipline as with academic proficiency. Several times my deportment was reported to him, and not as a model.

Although in later years he described me in a newspaper interview as "a typically lively schoolboy with a very engaging nature and a boyish grin," I cannot recall now any sign on his part that he harbored such feelings.

When I entered high school, the educational facilities were meager. We were installed in the old city hall which also included the town fire station. During my freshman year, a new high school was built and it was a most magnificent structure. The faculty was enlarged.

Even at that, a course of study such as we were offered would mean that a community of Abilene's size today would be held up to obloquy for its criminal backwardness. A freshman took four subjects: elementary Latin, English, algebra, physical geography. No electives were permitted except that German could be substituted for Latin.

The most dramatic difference between high schools of today and those of my time is probably not in the curriculum but in the life expectancy of the students. Then, except for the common cold and chilblains, any illness might easily be fatal. It was taken for granted that a Fourth of July celebration would produce injuries and suffering ranging from powder burns to lockjaw. Quarantines were imposed for the more common ailments of diphtheria, scarlet fever, and the like. Treatment consisted of a few simple medications and a nourishing diet while the victim and the family waited cure or death. Diagnosis was hardly exact. "Blood poisoning" was a favorite phrase to cover a multitude of mishaps.

Racing down a wooden platform one evening with some of my friends, I slipped and fell to one knee. The damage seemed slight except for ruining a brand-new pair of trousers that I had bought and of which I was exceedingly proud. There was no bleeding; instead just a raw, red spot on my knee. The next morning there were no ill effects and I went to school.

On the evening of the second day, I did not feel well and I lay down on the sofa in what Mother always called the "front room." I dropped off, it seems, into delirium. My parents were alarmed and called for the doctor. There ensued a hectic time in our life, lasting for a couple of weeks. My mother was the day nurse and a friend of hers the night nurse and they stayed constantly at my bedside. The doctor came two or three times a day and only occasionally was I conscious—usually when he used his scalpel to explore the wound. On one of his visits, I heard him mention the word "amputation."

At that time, my ambitions were directed toward excellence in sports, particularly baseball and football. I could not imagine an existence in which I was not playing one or both. When I heard

Doctor Conklin talking about amputation, I became alarmed, and even furious.

When Ed got home, I called him and made him promise to make sure that under no circumstances would they amputate my leg. "I'd rather be dead than crippled, and not be able to play ball." The doctors—for by that time Dr. Conklin had called in a consultant from Topeka—were frustrated by my attitude. But my parents understood. While they were against such contact sports as football, they agreed to accept my decision. After drastic measures, which included the painting of a belt of carbolic acid around my body, the progress of the disease was stopped. I was ill for so long and so seriously that I remained out of school the rest of the spring and had to repeat that year.

This episode has often been told in biographies or magazine articles. One story said that my parents remained in prayer, day and night, for two weeks. This is ridiculous. My parents were devout Christians and there is no doubt that they prayed for my recovery, but they did it in their morning and evening prayers. They did not believe in "faith healing."

Except for my extracurricular reading of history, no school subjects set me afire until we took up the study of geometry. I was more excited by the summer and after-hours jobs I began to get.

I spent the month of September picking apples, at one point, and on Saturdays after the harvest, gathered apples from the ground and carried them to a cider mill. I was too small to grind the apples, but I did earn twenty-five cents a day.

The next July I got a wheat-harvesting job. The binders were horse-drawn and the wheat, once bound into bundles, was picked up by the men and shocked. These men were the highest paid in the whole harvesting operation. I, the lowest paid, rode the lead horse. There were four horses on the binders, three pulling abreast while the lead horse helped guide the binder to cut a full swath. For two years I earned fifty cents a day. The harvest season was short and I was still too small to take part in the later threshing of the grain for market. After the two years, my employer told me he could not use me because I was getting too big. He said he needed a lighter boy on the lead horse. (I suspect he probably feared that because I was getting older, I'd soon demand more than fifty cents a day.)

A few days later I learned of a temporary job. A family moving from Abilene to Hutchinson had a little livestock to take along. Because the animals were to ride in a boxcar with the household effects, railway regulations required that someone ride with them. This looked like adventure to me and I badgered the man for the job. He said I was too small and turned me down flatly.

That evening I complained at length to my folks. In one week I had been told that I was too big for one job and too little for another.

This may have been my first lesson that human relations are governed by neither fixed rules nor logic. One side in a difference of opinion may be blind to what the other side considers obvious decency and common sense. For years I had been taught that it takes two to start a quarrel. Now, I saw that in any organized effort there may be as many disagreements about policy and practice as there are participants.

Abilene citizens and educators took little interest in school athletics. The authorities left the matter to student initiative. We had to do our own financing. Each participant provided his own baseball shoes and gloves but uniforms, balls, bats, and transportation required outside support. To meet such needs we organized the Abilene High School Athletic Association.

We tried to enlist every boy, and most girls. Dues were twenty-five cents per month. While many students were often in arrears, they were not suspended. We carried them in the hope that once in a while they would provide a quarter for our always ailing treasury.

One year, a close contest developed in the election of officers, though for the life of me, I cannot remember why. The officers had little power. They did have a voice in preparing schedules. Certainly the treasury could not confer any influence upon its custodians. But when the election was over, our star pitcher and our fleet-footed left fielder found themselves among the defeated. They left the Association and refused to play. In addition we lost other members, causing our revenues to decline further. This deplorable result was accentuated because gate receipts fell off with our poor showing on the field.

The rest of us made the best we could of the season but we had a miserable record. Fortunately, the following year a left-handed pitcher appeared who was a real find. "Six" McDonald and I became fast friends. The revolt was forgotten. The AHSAA regained its strength.

In my senior year I was elected president of the association. Afterward, I felt I had helped assure its enduring future by a simple device—writing a constitution. As I reported in the high-school yearbook,

. . . We improved the condition of the Association itself by drawing up the constitution, which makes the organization a permanent one, and each year it will be simply a question of electing new officers.

My optimism, natural and perhaps even commendable in a youngster, was more wishful thinking than realistic. Many times since I have come to realize that a fervent speech, or a painstakingly written document, may be worth no more than the good will and patient co-operation of those who say they subscribe to it. The multiplication of documents, resolutions, exhortations, and declamatory documents seems to be the major growth business of the age. I fear that we too often lay more stress on words than on the stark necessity of deeds to back them up.

I recognize that we are seldom excited to either a renewal of conviction or its visible and tangible expression unless inspired by finely wrought words and ringing appeals. People are so inclined to put up with what they know, however inadequate or ineffective, that they must be shocked or excited somehow.

Abilene had accepted makeshift high-school quarters for years until the new building went up. Few people could see any "practical" results in continuing education. It was a male-run society and schools were preponderantly feminine. At Abilene High, girls outnumbered boys more than two to one; in my graduating class by twenty-five to nine. This was, I suppose, inevitable when a job of some sort awaited every boy of twelve or so who wanted work.

But the new building invited pride—and it attracted better teachers, teachers whose professional training was commensurate with the size and cost of the new facility. None of us could complain in our final high-school years about the competence or enthusiasm of our teachers.

We did manage to find fault with the subjects, though. I despised algebra. I could see no profit in substituting complex expressions for routine terms and the job of simplifying long, difficult equations bored me. While I made passing grades, I by no means distinguished myself.

The introduction of plane geometry was an intellectual adventure, one that entranced me. After a few months, my teachers conducted an unusual experiment. The principal and my mathematics teacher called me to the office and told me that they were going to take away my textbook. Thereafter, I was to work out the geometric problems without the benefit of the book. In other words, the propositions, as well as the auxiliary problems, would be, for me, originals. This was a fascinating challenge and particularly delightful because it meant that no advance study was required. They said that for the remaining months, unless the experiment was terminated by them, I would automatically receive an A-plus grade.

Strangely enough, I got along fairly well even when a new proposition meant a big departure from past methods. But not always. While others were confronting a new problem one morning, my mind was far away on what was called a wool-gathering expedition.

The project before them was a construction problem in drawing a figure that was exactly the square root of 2. One by one, the teacher called on students to draw this line and none could do it. He turned to me and said, confidently, "Well, Dwight, you do it."

I simply had no idea of how to start.

After a long and embarrassing silence, the teacher said, "Draw a right angle with each side the length of one unit, then you have the square root of 2." I was red-faced and felt that I had let the teacher down.

This simple application in reverse, so to speak, of the Pythagorean proposition that in a right triangle the square of the hypotenuse equals the sum of the squares of the other two sides, should have been obvious to me and to any of the others who knew the proposition. Apparently we were all misled by the phrasing of the problem into thinking we were confronted by an entirely new and to us unknown mathematical principle, instead of one of the most ancient and fundamental theorems. Some of life's newest problems, turned around, are revealed as old ones, which have backed onto the scene.

The end of high school plunged us into a world of commencement activities that were novel to me, especially socially. Commencement week itself was the high point of our lives. Because we antedated by a good many years the time when a high school is really an appendage to the auditorium and the field house, our commencement was in the Seelye Theatre, the largest gathering place in Abilene. There, on Sunday evening May 23, 1909, baccalaureate was held. On Monday evening there were to be class day exercises; on Wednesday evening the senior play; and on Friday evening, the grand event, commencement itself.

Our baccalaureate speaker was a picturesque figure, Dr. F. S. Blayney, minister of the Presbyterian Church, a man whose spectacular, snow-white beard, covering much of his waistcoat, added a patriarchal note to his every word and gesture. As to the words themselves, well . . . the local newspaper said: "The sermon was full of the best thoughts and was listened to with marked attention."

The senior class play was a local version of *The Merchant of Venice*. This was not quite a cultural landmark. Shakespeare might have laughed at its slapstick. Shylock, for example, was a wealthy gambler deeply interested in high-school athletics and particularly football games from which he derived much of his income. Although other names in the cast were recognizably Shakespearean, a few characters never conceived by the dramatist were also included for good measure: a professor who was an X-ray photographer—X-ray was then the latest thing in science—a policewoman, and Miss Abbie S. Threedice.

Edgar played the Duke of Venice, and I was Launcelot Gobbo, servant to Shylock. The newspaper reviews of the play were glowing. Edgar, according to the town's paper, "invested his character with dignity and art." For once in our school careers, however, I got more of the spotlight than Ed. That night, my hair was long and all over my face, powdered red, while black gum had taken two of my front teeth out. It was a part written for a blunderer and seemed to have been made to order. The review should have brought talent scouts:

Dwight Eisenhower as Gobbo won plenty of applause and deserved it. He was the best amateur humorous character seen on the Abilene stage in this generation and gave an impression that many professionals fail to reach.

I have in later years been reviewed along similar lines, but never because I intended to be so.

The commencement speaker, Henry J. Allen, editor of the Wichita *Beacon*, who would become governor and United States Senator, said:

"I would sooner begin life over again with one arm cut off than attempt to struggle without a college education."

For Edgar, whose plans to enter the University of Michigan in September were far advanced, this statement was an endorsement. For me, determined to go to college but with only a sketchy notion of how this might be done, such an emphatic pronouncement was iron in the spine of purpose.

The following summer was busy. Edgar's plans for enrollment at Michigan meant that both of us had to work to gather as much money as was possible to get him started. I changed from one job to another, depending upon the prospects for an extra dime an hour or an extra dollar a day. Because I did jump about, certain biographers have suggested that I was going through a period of indecision and had no idea what I wanted to do. The exact opposite was the truth. Ed and I had it all doped out. He was going to drop out later if necessary, to get me started. His choice of Michigan looked good to me and I was ready to join him two years later.

CHAPTER VIII

Toward Annapolis

ED AND I had just one idea that summer: to get our hands on every cent we could possibly earn.

He started working at once for the Belle Springs Creamery Company. My best chance seemed to be on a farm owned by a Mr. Bryan. We worked from dawn to dusk, the owner, his son, and I.

During the summer I learned of a small company which was making steel grain bins. These were sheet steel, galvanized, cut into lengths and cold riveted together. The manager offered more than I was making on the farm so I took him up on it, worked there for months, and became a sort of straw boss. When the time came for Ed to go to the University, I knew that I could earn more money at the creamery than at the little factory. I said my good-byes and started off over there as an iceman.

The ice was frozen in cakes of three hundred pounds each. Three or four of these had to be hauled up each hour on a windlass run by hand. The can containing the newly frozen ice was then put into a contraption with its open top sloping downward, and water was run on the can until the cake slid through an opening, a sort of doorway formed by sacks, into an adjoining room. I had to go in there with a pair of tongs to stand the cake on its end.

The rest of the hour I spent helping load the wagons for delivery of the ice around town or the boxcars which would carry it off. Though far from intriguing, the job did develop muscles. From iceman I was promoted to fireman. This exalted position was a tougher but better paying job.

In the furnace room there were three large fire-tube boilers. We used slack (almost powdered) coal and clinkers formed periodically. With a slice bar, twelve feet or so in length, I would push the burning coal to one side, loosen the clinkers from the grates, then haul them out with a hoelike tool while another man turned a stream of water on the clinker. In this small inferno, life lost its charm but the job led to another promotion.

I became, for my last year in Abilene, the second engineer in the creamery's ice plant. The work week was eighty-four hours, from six P.M. until six A.M., and my agreement called for fifty-two weeks a year. (Three or four times a year I was successful in getting a helper to take my place briefly.) But the salary was impressive—$90 per month.

Through my early teens I had formed a friendship with Everett Hazlett, son of one of the town's physicians. He was a big fellow, too, but he had been raised in a quiet atmosphere and occasionally a few people, smaller than he, would try to bulldoze him. I felt protective, a sort of obligation to him, and I took it upon myself to tell a few of the so-and-so's to lay off.

Our deep friendship endured to the day of his death in 1958; our correspondence over those forty-odd years would fill a thick volume. I drew on it for *The White House Years* because Swede Hazlett was one of the people to whom I "opened up."

While I was in high school, he attended a private military school, in Wisconsin, I believe. There he acquired an interest in the service academies, particularly the Naval Academy at Annapolis. After his Wisconsin schooling, Swede applied for an appointment to that institution and took the entrance examination. He failed the mathematical section of the test and, coming back to Abilene, told me that he had a reappointment and would again take the examination. He wanted me to make the same effort.

It was not difficult to persuade me that this was a good move—first, because of my long interest in military history, and second, because I realized that my own college education would not be achieved without considerable delay while I tried to accumulate money. With Ed already in college and receiving some help from Father and with Earl and Milton coming on in the future, I could see that if I could made it, I would take a burden off my family.

Swede Hazlett and I wasted no time. We immediately began to study together. He wrote to the Navy Department for copies of past examinations which were, incidentally, almost identical to those for entrance to West Point.

I was working in the creamery as night engineer, and my afternoons were, for three or four hours, my own. Swede was in charge of a small gas lighting store that had been acquired by his father. While he had to keep the place open, there were few customers and, undisturbed, we did our studying in his place of business. Day after day, during that summer, we asked each other questions and then graded the answers by comparing them with those given in the naval documents. With the close of summer my friend went to what he called a "cram" school to make sure that in his next try for Annapolis he would be successful. I went back to take a review course in selected subjects at my old high school where my teachers were anxious to help. I had to make certain that I made no bad grades at all—and I had been out of school for two years.

My congressman had no additional vacancy in either military academy. I wrote to Senator Joseph Bristow requesting appointment as a cadet or a midshipman and asked various influential men in town to write letters to him in support of my application.*

One thing was stressed in each of the letters. Because of my father's reputation and his insistence on paying cash for all he bought, each writer had something to say about the unimpeachable honesty of David Eisenhower. I never ceased feeling grateful to my father and to the people who recognized the virtue of simple honesty in all his dealings.

There were two steps. First was a request to take an examination to determine which candidates would be eligible for appointment and to take the entrance examination. The second was the exam for Annapolis itself.

Senator Bristow authorized me to participate in a competitive examination for appointment. His instructions contained a provision that the examination would apply to both academies if the applicant so chose. Even before the results of the examinations were published, I learned that I would be barred from going to Annapolis. The entrance regulations for that academy specified an age from sixteen to twenty, but Swede and I had earlier assumed that the

---

* Among others, I sought the help of Mr. Harger, who published one of the town's newspapers and of Mr. Heath, postmaster. Mr. Rogers, a banker, was eager to help, while Mr. J. B. Case volunteered to do his best. Mr. Case, incidentally, was the father of Charlie Case, now in his eighties and still my warm friend. The elder Mr. Case, a first cousin of Mrs. George Custer, was filled with tales and stories of the old west of the 1870s, and was a mine of information on the early days of Kansas. Another man helpful to me was a jeweler named Ward. I suppose there must have been some score or more letters sent to the Senator endorsing my application.

maximum applied until the twenty-first birthday had been reached. After taking the first examination, I learned that because I would be almost twenty-one by the time the next class enlisted, I was ineligible for entrance to the Naval Academy.

This was a blow. Swede and I had hoped to enter in the same class of the same academy. Because he had been given a naval appointment, my preference was for Annapolis. Another reason was that in the examinations I had come out as number one for the Annapolis appointment but as number two for West Point. I could expect a West Point appointment as an alternate only.

The man who ranked above me in the West Point examinations failed to meet the physical requirements. I got the appointment from Senator Bristow in the spring of 1911.

This was a good day in my life. The only person truly disappointed was Mother. She believed in the philosophy of turn the other cheek. She was the most honest and sincere pacifist I ever knew, yet at the same time she was courageous, sturdy, self-reliant. It was difficult for her to consider approving the decision of one of her boys to embark upon military life even though she had a measure of admiration for West Point because one of her instructors at Lane University, a favorite of hers, had been a West Point cadet.

When the letter of appointment came, I told Mother she shouldn't worry because I hadn't yet passed the final examination. Most boys went for a full year to schools for special training to prepare for service academy exams and so the chances were that I would fail. This did not appease her in the slightest for the simple reason that she could hardly hope one of her boys would fail a tough examination. Because she and my father always insisted that each boy should be the master of his own fate, she kept her own counsel.

From the minute the appointment arrived, I redoubled my study efforts. In the spring, I took the examination at Jefferson Barracks, Missouri, just outside St. Louis. The farm boy was completely unprepared for the sights of the river metropolis. One night, while quartered there for the examinations, I left the Barracks with another applicant and we wandered around the city.

We walked the streets for a time. Thinking we'd see more of the city, we took a streetcar and, riding it to the end of the line, found ourselves at a car barn in East St. Louis, on the eastern side of the Mississippi River. Now we had a problem.

No more streetcars were running. We saw no sign of any other kind of transportation and we were lost. A heavy fog lay over the city and we could not orient ourselves by the stars. We did think that by following the tracks backward we would soon reach the river. This ruse failed when we came to a point where the line branched and we had no idea which one to take.

Fortunately, in a nearby building, we saw a dim light. There we hoped to find a friendly soul who would set us on the right road to the city. We knocked on the door and soon heard someone in the room moving toward us.

The door, which was massive, began to open slowly and the first thing we saw was the muzzle of a revolver.

A voice said. "Who are you?"

We stammered that we just wanted help in getting back across the river. The man, who proved to be a bartender, apparently decided we were harmless young fellows, and he let us in, lowered the revolver, and gave us explicit instructions.

We were within a block of the bridge. We crossed it at double-time, hoping to catch the final car for the Barracks which we had been told left the St. Louis side of the river at 1:00 A.M. We made it but we had not yet solved the problem of avoiding discovery upon reaching the Barracks; and because we had violated instructions to be in bed by taps, we were afraid that we would be barred from completing the examination.

At the main gate, a guard would have taken our names, of course. We decided to avoid it. Instead we went down along the wall through the darkness, under the trees, to find a spot where we would be undetected as we scaled the wall. I have often thought that we were fortunate. The nation was at peace and there was no thought of subversion, sabotage, and so on. Security was lax and we got over the wall undiscovered and sneaked into the building. So far as I know, no one ever learned of our silly escapade.

We got into our beds and lay there breathing heavily. Then my friend said, "You know, when I looked down the barrel of that big pistol, I could see a whole funeral procession."

After returning to Abilene, time had to pass before I would hear from West Point. The waiting was almost unbearable. I had passed my physical examination, but the mental tests were something else again. Again and again, I went back over all the questions we had been asked. There was no longer any question of relative standing.

Having won the competitive examination for the appointment, all that was now necessary was to make passing grades.

And then I was informed that I had passed. I was directed to report to the United States Military Academy on June 14, 1911. At a later date, I learned that I had passed the exam somewhat above the middle of all those admitted. Since a number of those had undergone special training, I did not feel badly about my showing.

A minimum financial deposit was required from the new cadet, to cover the cost of his initial clothing issue, I suppose. I had been able to save the necessary amount and had enough to pay my transportation costs. By the time I reached West Point, I would have a total of about five dollars cash in my pocket. It was with such material wealth that I started a military career which, except for the interval of eight presidential years, still continues. It has been rewarding, in many more ways than monetary.

Between the notification of acceptance and my departure from home, each day was given over to preparing for a new kind of life. I had to say good-bye to relatives and friends and dispose of many possessions to which I attached incalculable value. One was a favorite shotgun, acquired some years earlier from Ed. It was a 16-gauge Winchester repeater, model of 1897. Another precious item was my dog, a smooth-haired wire terrier named Flip. She was an intelligent animal, obedient, sensitive, affectionate, and she had been my outdoor companion for years. After I left, she adopted Earl.

Milton and Earl, both growing boys, were proud of my new status. Each began to talk seriously about going to the Academy himself. As tactfully as I could, I had to make Earl understand that because of the loss of his left eye, there was no hope of a military career for him. (Some years later, when the First World War started, he tried to enlist. He memorized every item on the test cards used in the eye examinations and for a few days it appeared as though he would make it. But it was not long before he was found out and was discharged.)

But when I went off, no one thought of war. I can hardly imagine any time when we were so free from talk of war or seemed so far from it. Even that could not change things appreciably for my mother. But, she said, "It is your choice." She saw me off, and then went back home to her room. Milton told me later that for the first time in his life he heard Mother cry.

Book Two

THE PEACETIME ARMY

CHAPTER IX

Fort Sam Houston, Texas, 1916

BEFORE GRADUATING from West Point, each cadet was to express his personal preference for duty station. I put down the Philippines, the only one in my class who did, I think.

It seemed to be logical that I would draw this assignment. For many years, the Philippines tour of duty had been of the lowest priority as far as preferences were concerned. Because of this history, when the time came for purchasing uniforms, I went to the tailors and asked only for tropicals—khaki for field service and white for dress. I bought none of the other types of uniforms—olive drabs for garrison wear and the various types of blues for dress. These were expensive and I figured a number of years would pass before I needed them.

Toward the purchase of his first outfits as a commissioned officer, each cadet made forced savings during his entire four years. Regulations called for the Treasurer of West Point to take out of each pay $14 or $15 per month. Since my tropical purchases were far below average in cost, I was given upon graduation a considerable sum of money—at least in my eyes. This promised a fine vacation.

The President himself was required to sign every commission and when I graduated, Mr. Wilson was somewhat preoccupied with the Mexican troubles and with a war that had been going on in Europe since August 1914. I received no orders for assignment immediately.

Returning to my home, I set out to have a good time, and did. It was not long before the several hundred dollars I had received from my equipment fund surplus was completely exhausted. My father was an understanding man and now that I was a grown fellow of twenty-five years, instead of his giving me an allowance, I made an arrangement to borrow sums from him to be repaid after my commission. This indebtedness didn't disturb me because I was sure I could soon pay it off. Then, with my equipment fund spent, and in debt to my father, I received orders to go to Texas.

Assignment to a continental station meant that all the uniforms necessary had to be in an officer's possession. I was really up against it. In Leavenworth, Kansas, there was a uniformer named Springe, one of the best in the United States—and also one of the most expensive. There was nothing to do but go down to see Mr. Springe. I told him my problem and told him I would have to buy on credit. This was agreeable to him and he made all my necessary O.D. and blue uniforms, including full dress coat (a big frock coat used only on the most ceremonial occasions) and evening or social full dress.

The reason why the assignment to the Philippines didn't come through was understandable. It had to do with part of President Wilson's concerns. Since 1911, our relations with our neighbor to the south had steadily worsened and more and more of the Regular Army was stationed along the common border, all the way from California to Brownsville in Texas. This service was disagreeable. Usually, it separated a man from his family. Living conditions were rough. Anything was better to most officers than the border, so the requests for service in foreign stations, even the Philippines, outnumbered those put in for domestic assignment.

Of course, as the youngest second lieutenants in the Army, many of the members of the West Point Class of 1915 went to the least desirable places.

When I finally reached my regiment, with headquarters in San Antonio, Texas, I was properly uniformed but also badly in debt. First, I received my delayed three months' pay and this gave me a substantial payment on my debt to Mr. Springe. (At that time, a second lieutenant's pay was $141.67 per month.)

Many of the other second lieutenants in the regiment were in approximately the same situation as I, for one reason or another. Because I was not intrigued by the social life of the post, and because I began receiving small checks from participants in poker games of cadet days who had been temporarily impoverished, gradually I started to pay off some of my debts.

One Sunday afternoon in October, as Officer of the Day, I walked out of the Bachelor Officers Quarters to make an inspection of guard posts. On the walk across the street was a small group of people, one of whom was Lulu Harris, the wife of Major Hunter Harris and a lady popular with all the second lieutenants of the post.

"Ike," she called, "won't you come over here? I have some people I'd like you to meet."

"Sorry, Mrs. Harris," I called back, "I'm on guard and have to start an inspection trip."

She then turned to one young girl, as I discovered later, and said, "Humph! The woman-hater of the post."

Naturally, this caught the attention of the girl, who said something to Mrs. Harris that caused her to call once more. "We didn't ask you to come over to *stay*. Just come over here and meet these friends of mine."

I hadn't any objection and so, in guard uniform, which was olive drab with campaign hat and blouse and sidearms, walked stiffly across the street to say a polite greeting to the little family gathered around Mrs. Harris. Their name was Doud. They were from Denver and they spent the winter months each year in San Antonio. Out for a ride in a large car, they had stopped to pay a brief call on their friend, Lulu Harris. The one who attracted my eye instantly was a vivacious and attractive girl, smaller than average, saucy in the look about her face and in her whole attitude. If she had been intrigued by my reputation as a woman-hater, I was intrigued by her appearance. I said that I had to make the rounds of all the guard posts and asked whether she would like to go along.

To my astonishment, she turned to her mother, said a few words, and went off with me. Eventually I found out that one of the things that she was least fond of—to put it mildly—was walking. But apparently the little colloquy that had taken place, especially Lulu Harris' remark, caused her to take a second look at the Second Lieutenant who seemed rather brash or indifferent. Possibly she went along just to take me down a peg. In any event, that was the entrance into my life of Mamie Geneva Doud.

While it soon became almost routine for me to call on her, except on the nights when I was on duty, I had more time than money to spend on courtship. With debts to pay off, and a young woman to impress, I became, if possible, even more parsimonious.

When we went to dinner, it was usually to a Mexican restaurant called "The Original" on the San Antonio River in the middle of the city. The menu was unchanging: chili, tamales, enchiladas. There we could have dinner for two for about $1.00 or $1.25 including tip. The Orpheum, a vaudeville house, was more than popular—it was the Palace of San Antonio. Once a week, everybody had to go to the Orpheum. These two places, The Original and the Orpheum, in-expensive as they were, made up the largest item in my weekly budget. When I was not out with Mamie, I lived the life of a hermit. Except for my board bill, $30 a month, and my laundry, $5.00, it was difficult to get me to indulge in any kind of spending. During the late fall, however, I had one very fortunate evening in which there was more income than outgo. Two of my former class-mates had come to San Antonio to take physical examinations for transfer to the Aviation Section of the Signal Corps, as our air force was then called. They were heroes; anyone who succeeded in getting into Aviation was automatically assured of a 50 per cent rise in pay. To money-conscious shavetails, this was tremendous. The two young men, celebrating their forthcoming entry into what they said was the "elite" of the whole service, had organized a little gambling game, shooting craps. The game had been under way in the Infantry Club for an hour or so when I walked in.

They greeted me joyfully, saying, "Come on, get in here. We're getting everyone's money because we want to give a big party to cele-brate our start in flying."

"I'm sorry," I said. "You fellows don't want me; I've got two sil-ver dollars in my pocket and that's all. You can't use me in that game."

They jeered, good-naturedly, and one said, "Come on and put it in. Every little bit helps."

By dinnertime, I had run my two dollars up to a hundred.

Earlier, when I had not been wiped out in the first few minutes, I had warned my fellow players that I had a date and would have to leave at seven. When the time came and I made noises about keeping my date with Mamie, they protested. I couldn't go away and leave them losers, they said. The two new flyers, now flying low, insisted I had to keep on playing.

"Well, I'll tell you what we will do. Both of you seem to be losers in about the same amount," I said. "I'll take my two dollars, put them back in my pocket, and I'll divide my winnings into two equal piles. Each of you can take one roll. You can either lose or win and it's O.K. with me."

Lucky or not, they just couldn't see themselves taking a shot at fifty dollars each on one turn of the dice. So they politely refused and the game was over. I went to my room, took the two dollars out, put the other money in a drawer, and the following morning sent a draft to Leavenworth. That completed my payments to Mr. Springe for uniforms. Now I was out of debt to everyone except my father.

The colonel of our regiment, the 19th U. S. Infantry, was Colonel Millard Waltz. He was a veteran of the Spanish-American War, a short, heavy-set, swarthy, and heavily mustachioed man, and, as might be expected, all second lieutenants stayed as far away from headquarters and the Colonel as possible. My first encounter with him, other than the strict formality of reporting upon arrival, left me . . . well, a little up in the air.

Second lieutenants were a clannish group. Except when we had the money for an evening on the town, we often roamed the post in a rather aimless search for excitement. There were one or two, somewhat more serious than most of us, who spent part of their time going to concerts and museums, and, to our dismay, to lectures. Mostly, we wandered.

A small group of us happened to be standing one evening near the post flagpole, a tall, stately affair with strong supporting cables to hold it straight against the winds of the region. These cables reached from the ground to a point fifty or sixty feet up the pole.

I mentioned that I had once or twice climbed, overhand, similar though somewhat smaller cables just for the fun of it and said that I could easily climb one of these. One of my companions spoke up skeptically. I repeated my assertion that I could climb one of them, using hands only. The skeptic, a man I didn't know well, said that it was tommyrot to talk about overhanding my way to the top.

Although I was the junior second lieutenant of the regiment, I ignored his seniority, grew angry, and retorted, "What would you like to bet?" He had a little bit more money than most of us and he produced five dollars. It happened that I had one lone five-dollar bill in my wallet, so I put it into the hands of one of the other lieutenants, as stake holder.

Next we agreed on the conditions of the contest. I was to climb the slanting cable to the top but without touching it with my feet or legs. A time limit was set. This was satisfactory and I stripped off my regulation blouse and started up. I had no difficulty—at West Point one of my favorite exercises had been rope climbing—and was chuckling cockily about a windfall that would pay for an evening out with my girl when from somewhere below I heard a bellow.

"Who is that up on that cable?"

With a shock, I realized who was talking—our commanding officer, Colonel Waltz.

"Who are you up there?" he demanded.

"Mr. Eisenhower, Sir."

"Come down here," he said.

This was disaster. I tried to save my bet, remembering that Colonel Waltz was said to gamble on any sporting event.

"Sir," I called down, "Mr. Adler and I have a bet. He put down five dollars that I cannot overhand my way to the top of this cable. I am almost there—so could I please go on up and touch the pole and then come back down right away?"

"DO AS I SAY AND DO IT RIGHT NOW. GET DOWN HERE!"

Sheepishly, I let myself down along the cable and as quickly as my feet touched the ground came to a stiff salute. First he ordered me to don my jacket, and then he offered a few suggestions for improvement. I was, it seems, foolhardy, undignified, untrustworthy, undependable, and ignorant. He wanted no more of this on his post. Once he had finished taking me over the coals, he stalked off, saying, "There'll be no more of that on the part of anyone."

No sooner was Colonel Waltz out of earshot than Adler spoke up to claim he had won the five dollars.

"Won it?"

"Yes," he said, and he asked the stake holder, Wade Haislip, to turn the money over. I objected flatly and vigorously. The bet was, at the least, a draw because it had been nullified by the intervention of the C.O. None of us could have anticipated such an outcome and therefore the bet was null and void. Moreover, I said, everyone could see that I was easily making the ascent and morally I had actually won.

The argument got hot and heavy, growing in intensity, until I suggested that we finish the discussion with fists. One of the others said we could go down behind the barracks where no one would bother us. Adler refused, saying that we'd all get into real trouble. At the same time the majority declared the bet to be a draw and the money returned to each side. Adler (no relation to the Corporal Adler of West Point mentioned earlier) kept grousing; he still believed I owed him the five dollars. But now I had my temper under control.

Actually, I was happy that the matter had not gone too far. My knee was still troubling me and I was fearful that Adler, a big, strong fellow, could have helped me fix it so that I would have been nursing a knee again for a week or more.

As the winter wore on, I became more and more enamored of the girl I had met in October. I spent every evening possible with her. Occasionally, we'd go downtown in a jitney—an automobile of the cheapest make which ran, from dawn to midnight, over fixed routes somewhat in the manner of a streetcar. The fare was five cents; this gave the vehicle its name. We would go downtown in a jitney, pay a jitney, have a Mexican dinner at the old Original, see a movie, and get home neither out of breath nor out of pocket to any extent.

Engrossed in ourselves and our conversation after coming home, we would find now and then that the nightly transportation had stopped running. The distance from the Doud residence to my quarters on the post was two miles and it was unwise to overstay the Cinderella hour. San Antonio nights, however, made an evening stroll more of a pleasure than a chore, and to a young man in love, it was something of a pleasure—even though, or perhaps because, the girl I left behind could not help feeling sorry for me.

As the winter wore on, Mamie and I decided to become engaged. I gave her my class ring on Valentine's Day, 1916. Her father was then in Iowa, where he conducted his business, and would not be back until later in the winter or early spring. He reached there early in March and I took courage in my hands and heart in my mouth to ask him for the hand of his daughter. She was nineteen. He said this was far earlier than he had expected to see his daughter married, but he had no particular objection to me and would approve, provided we would wait a reasonable time. We tentatively agreed to plan on the wedding for the following November, when Mamie would be twenty.

Months earlier I had applied for transfer to the Aviation Section. I had more or less forgotten this because we could not expect an early answer. Almost as soon as Mr. Doud had given his tentative approval of our engagement, I had the answer. The application had been approved and I was to report to the post hospital at Fort Sam Houston to take a physical examination. That night I went to the Douds' house walking on air. I liked the idea of flight training and of course the 50 per cent more pay held out great and glittering promise to a man on his way to marriage. To the assembled family I told my story. There was some chilliness in the atmosphere; indeed, the news of my good fortune was greeted with a large chunk of silence.

The silence was broken by Mr. Doud himself, who said that they had been ready to take me into their family but if I were so irresponsible as to want to go into the flying business just when I was thinking of being married, he and Mrs. Doud would have to withdraw their consent.

He thought flying was a dangerous experiment. I saw it as a new military venture which some people thought was going to have real value, as well as providing excitement. That night I left in a glum frame of mind. For the next couple of days, I pondered the matter in misery.

As anxious as I was to try it, the Aviation Section was just another form of military service. Now, with a more serious attitude toward life, perhaps I should take a broader look at my future in the military. Possibly I had been too prone to lead a carefree, debt-ridden life. Now I would set my sights on becoming the finest Army officer I could, regardless of the branch in which I might serve.

After looking at the matter seriously, but not grimly, I phoned the Douds and made a date to see the family once more. When I arrived, I announced that I was ready to give up aviation. It turned out that my decision was an immense relief to the family because Mamie had been raising quite a fuss. She understood the way I felt about getting into flying.

Although everything was smoothed over, it had brought me face to face with myself and caused me to make a decision that I have never recanted nor regretted. The decision was to perform every duty given me in the Army to the best of my ability and to do the best I could to make a creditable record, no matter what the nature of the duty.

Soon, my fiancée went back with her family to Denver. As a symbol of my new seriousness and sacrifice, I stopped smoking ready-made cigarettes, which were then about $1.00 a carton, and went back to rolling my own.

☆　☆　☆　☆　☆

At about the same time, the troubles with Mexico became more intense and the National Guard was mobilized on the border area. Although most Guard regiments were poorly equipped and untrained, they had some semblance of organization.

I left the post to live in a camp where I became an Inspector Instructor of a Guard regiment. My duties were to help straighten out administrative snarls and to supervise training. I enjoyed the work. My assignment was to the 7th Illinois Infantry under command of Colonel Daniel Moriarity. Fittingly, practically the entire regiment was Chicago Irish. The reports of the Officer of the Day were filled with fights and all sorts of disputes. A night without serious disturbance was the exception.

Colonel Moriarity was a fine old fellow who didn't like to bother much with the details of training and administration. Although he was jealous of his subordinates, he was happy to have me, as an instructor, take over in effect the running of his regiment. I wrote all his orders, prepared reports and other official papers for his signature, and became the power behind the Irishman's throne.

As I look back on it, it was one of the valuable years of preparation in my early career. Although I didn't have the primary responsibility of training, disciplining, and equipping such a large command, the arrangement made by the Colonel gave me the feeling of personal authority. I began to devote more hours of study and reading to my profession, although I did not neglect my courting, now carried on by correspondence.*

Relations between the United States and Mexico had deteriorated throughout 1915 and early 1916. In 1915 President Wilson had recognized General Carranza as the head of the "Constitutionalist" government of Mexico. Pancho Villa, chief of the Mexican opposition, who until then had been fairly co-operative, became belligerent. In the fall of that year, President Wilson permitted the Carranzistas to move troops by rail across American territory to reinforce their garrison at Agua Prieta, across from Douglas, Arizona. The combined force sallied out of the town, until then invested by Villa, drove his troops away in disorder, and so disheartened them that in a short time he could number only fifteen hundred men or so against an earlier strength of ten thousand. Villa swore vengeance against the United States and all Americans.

* During that period I came to realize that it was not quite enough to keep my nose above water financially. If we got married, it would be necessary to accumulate at least a small stake for the protection of my wife. To that end, I took out small insurance policies. One was in the Army Mutual Aid Association which provided $3000 of insurance at low cost; another small policy was with a commercial firm. These two policies represented the only estate I could possibly leave a widow in the event anything happened to me.

In January 1916, nineteen American citizens removed from a train in Chihuahua were shot to death. Although Villa disclaimed responsibility for this specific crime, he did march his irregulars toward Columbus, New Mexico, intending to stage a raid across the international boundary. Colonel Henry J. Slocum, commanding the 13th Cavalry at Columbus, could not cross the border to reconnoiter. Mexicans, persuaded by him to report on Villa's movements, came back with word that the irregulars had split and were moving in various directions. The surprise attack began before dawn on March 9.

The American cavalrymen reacted instantly and, by the light of the burning hotel, set on fire by Villa's men, they mowed down the attacking forces. More than two hundred of Villa's irregulars were killed while the American losses were comparatively slight—seven soldiers and eight civilians killed. Moreover, the infuriated troops attacked the Villa rear guard twice in the retreat and finally flanked the main body, pouring a heavy fire into it. Retreat turned into rout.

This set off a reaction in the United States and although Wilson seemed to be a most patient President he now decided that the time had come to punish the organized forces and irregular units that were causing us so much trouble. As a consequence, the so-called "Punitive Expedition" was put together and given the mission of capturing Villa and totally dispersing his men. It was put under the command of General Pershing.

Because of factual news and grapevine rumors, letters from my fiancée as the spring wore on began to show more and more alarm about the possibility of my going into Mexico. That seemed to Mamie like going around the world. I told her that my application for service with the Punitive Expedition had gotten me nowhere but she was nervous nevertheless about the United States getting into one war or another, the more so because relations with Germany, which was then at war in Europe, were steadily getting worse.

Throughout the winter of 1915–16 there had been a rising clamor for the United States to act more vigorously against both German submarine warfare, in which many of our ships had been sunk, and against Mexico, whose depredations across the border seemed to us unconscionable. Many people became impatient with President Wilson. He was well aware that America was not militarily capable of joining immediately in any major war abroad and so he continued to apply reasonable arguments in an attempt to get the Kaiser and his subordinates to stop the inhuman submarine campaign.

All the trouble, of course, was reflected in the daily newspapers and in our correspondence. Finally, we reached the conclusion that we should advance the date of our wedding. We decided that we would do so after Mamie had contacted her parents, then in the East, and if I could get a short leave from the Army, which was then serving on almost a wartime footing.

I asked for twenty days. Although War Department instructions denied leaves or furloughs for any purposes except an emergency, it seemed to me that imminent marriage was just that. This didn't impress the Colonel. He did send my letter on to the department commander, General Funston.

To my surprise, I was ordered to report to Department Headquarters to see the General. Frankly, I didn't know how to get to the General's office except by asking questions. I marched over to his headquarters, dressed in my best uniform, shoes polished and everything spic and span. I didn't want any carelessness or sloppiness on my part to create a bad impression on the brass.

It was just as well that I had shined up because the brass was prepared to create a bad impression on me. First, I waited in the adjutant's office. Adjutants are inclined to be both liberal and negative in the dispensation of advice—and he said that he thought it was a poor time for second lieutenants to be getting married.

After that poor start, I went to the chief of staff's office. He didn't say much, at least nothing to depress me further, but he remarked that the General was busy. While I waited, I thought back to my one other meeting with the General.

The preceding fall, one of the local military academies in San Antonio had proposed that I coach their football team. They were prepared to pay $150 for the season. This was munificence itself but with my new sense of responsibility, I refused, saying I was an Army officer, and therefore had no time for football. Although this must have sounded stuffy, the head of the school, a man named Peabody and a friend of General Funston's, apparently told the General what had been said.

General Funston walked into the Officers Club one day when several second lieutenants were having a beer. He looked us over and said, "Is Mr. Eisenhower in the room?" I stood up and said,

"Sir?" I couldn't imagine what he had on his mind. He called me to the bar and said, "Have a drink."

I couldn't say that I was already having one so I took another. "Mr. Peabody tells me that he would like you to coach his team at the academy."

"Yes, Sir."

"It would please me and it would be good for the Army if you would accept this offer."

"Yes, Sir," I said.

He indicated that the conversation was over. I saluted and went back to my friends. The idea was, I suppose, that helping to coach the kids would encourage them in their military training and give them a favorable impression of the Army.

Now the chief of staff said I could see the General.

"I understand you want to get married," the General said immediately.

I confirmed that impression.

Then he looked up at me for the first time. "Oh yes, Mr. Eisenhower. I remember you very well." Then he wanted to know what the rush was about the marriage. I had to tell him a little bit about the circumstances and the change of plan. He smiled and said, "All right, you may have ten days," adding, "I am not sure that this is exactly what the War Department has in mind but I'll take the responsibility."

I had to get to Denver. I had no wedding ring and it was Sunday. Also, as usual, I had no money. I looked up a friend who worked for the Lockwood National Bank of San Antonio, told him my story, gave him an estimate of my needs, and exposed my cash resources, which were somewhere on the order of $250.

He laughed and said that this would be satisfactory to the bank and any overdrafts that I might write during the period would be honored. In those days the credit rating of an Army officer was of the highest order.

Next I went, still on Sunday, to find another friend who was the manager of Hertzberg's, a jewelry store. I told him I needed a wedding ring—which Mamie and I had tentatively selected earlier—and I had to keep enough cash to pay railway fare, to say nothing of my wife's when we started back from Denver. He opened the store, gave me the ring on credit, valued at something like $70. So with a new ring, new debts, ten days, and high hopes, I started on my journey.

The train ran into a flood in northern Texas and I lost one day of the precious ten. This did nothing for peace of mind—the trip from San Antonio to Denver took about fifty-six hours and we wanted to return by way of Kansas to visit my family.

We were married by a Presbyterian minister from Britain, named Dr. Williamson, who had been occupying temporarily the pulpit in the Central Presbyterian Church. Our honeymoon was a weekend at a nearby mountain resort, Eldorado Springs. We went back to Mamie's home for one or two days, then took the Union Pacific to Abilene, reaching there at about four in the morning. My father met us at the station and we went home. We could stay only a matter of hours.

My mother was determined that we would have at least one fine meal in her house and so instead of the normal breakfast, our meal that morning was a monumental fried chicken dinner. For two hungry young people, it was an early but welcome banquet.

Earl and Milton were excited about meeting my bride and pleased that they were almost her age. They were friends instantly.

After a full eight hours, we took the train again. For part of the time, we traveled the old Missouri-Kansas and Texas Railway, called the Katy Railroad, on which my father had gone to work in 1887.

We reached San Antonio to be greeted by young Army friends, laden with all sorts of packages. Because the advancement of our marriage date was a sudden decision, formal announcements had not been sent. But the post grapevine had given our wedding complete coverage. In our old bachelor quarters of two rooms and a bath, there were all sorts of packages, most of them containing the latest electrical appliances. There was a chafing dish, a coffee percolator, a toaster, a broiler, and a tiny stove. They seemed to me at first glance more decorative than functional but as we soon discovered, we'd have use for them.

The officers' mess was located across the street. It was convenient. Once inside, the only thing enjoyable about it was the company. Mamie, young, full of life, and attractive, was the pet of the post. She was showered with attention from officers and ladies of all ages, and thoroughly enjoyed the experience of company eating except for one detail—the food.

Although the viands brought in the back door to the kitchen were undoubtedly of good quality, by the time they had been transformed at the hands of the alleged cooks, they lacked flavor, glamour, probably even nutrients. Tapioca pudding and mashed potatoes, often cold, seemed to be indistinguishable as well as permanent items on the menu.

Of course, once in a while we could take a jitney downtown to dine at one of our old haunts but even on the salary of a first lieutenant—I had been advanced one grade in rank on our wedding day—we could not indulge too often in such luxury. More unhappy each day with the officers' mess, we began supplementing our diet by using our wedding presents to make coffee, candy, and other minor dishes. Mamie was so pleased with the results that she surprised me one day by buying a small icebox so that we could test our ability to subsist entirely on our own efforts. If my cooking experience had been spotty, and was now some years in the past, Mamie knew even less about cooking than I. But our table fare began to include pot roast, steaks, and chicken—all of which were plentiful and cheap—and the meals became so presentable that now and then we could invite in a couple of friends.

Soon after we were married, I was made Provost Marshal of the post. We had a certain amount of trouble keeping order for a while, with untrained soldiers and time on their hands, and conflict between the Regular Army and the National Guard. I went out on a patrol with two men one evening, one walking behind me and one across the street. We were checking on bars and other establishments of dim repute. Suddenly there was a shot in the street, almost beside my ear. I heard it thud, saw the flame but did not hear the whine. We looked around and there was a second shot. By then my corporal, a huge fellow, had located the shooter and he dragged him out of an alley, not being unduly gentle about it.

"Hey, watch it," the man said harshly. "I'm an officer." And he was, a lieutenant.

"I don't care what you are," said the corporal. "You shot at my lieutenant."

We turned him in and a National Guard court fined him five dollars. Penalties were stiffer later but there were times when I was frightened for Mamie. One of the few women in an Army camp, there were many occasions when she had to be alone. I gave her a .45 pistol and showed her, carefully, how to use it if such ever became necessary. She took it all seriously.

One morning, as a check, I said, "Mamie, let's see you get your pistol out—as if there were somebody trying to break in through the front door."

She went to look for it. We had rented a piano and she had the pistol hidden behind the piano, inside a bedding roll, under other possessions, and in general so far buried that she couldn't have gotten it out in a week, much less in a hurry. I decided to keep on concentrating on trying to make the camp safer.

In early fall 1916, I was approached to coach the football team of another preparatory school. Peacock Military Academy, where I had coached the year before, had acquired a graduate of the University of Texas who had been a fine football player. The school now after me was St. Louis College. This was a Catholic school where the student body was somewhat larger than at Peacock. They made me an attractive offer.

After meeting the faculty and student body, I went to work. Their football team's coaching had been only that which was given by one or two of the Fathers. The team had not won a game for five years. At least I started with a record that shouldn't be hard to beat.

We tied our first game, then ran along for four or five straight wins, and reached the finals of city competition. There, with a combination of bad luck and nerves, we lost a close one. But the season was cause for a celebration. The Fathers had Mamie and me out to a victory dinner and thus started a friendship which has continued over the years. The college now has a different name, after consolidation with St. Mary's of San Antonio, but as late as 1962 I went out to see the faculty and the student body and we had a good time replaying the old games.

By early spring 1917, the dangers and irritations along our southern border had been reduced and conditions between the United States and Germany had worsened. The War Department recalled many of the National Guard regiments and Camp Wilson, home of the 12th Provisional Division to which I had been attached, was now abandoned. I returned to Company F of the 19th Infantry.

The Germans had announced that they were going to resume unrestricted submarine warfare. President Wilson warned, in a stern speech, that if they did so, they would bring the United States into the fighting. He spoke in February, sometime later the sinkings began again, and by early April President Wilson went before the Congress and asked for a declaration of war.

As usual, our country was sadly—close to totally—unprepared. While we had mobilized a few more regular regiments in 1916, the strength of the Regular Army was awfully small. Intensive efforts had to start at once to bring our strength up to a position where it could participate in a conflict that had been raging in Europe for more than two years.

One of the methods for expanding the Army was to draw cadres of officers and men from each regular regiment to form either one or two more regiments around them with recruits. The 19th Infantry was directed to form the 57th and I was chosen to go with the new group. When Mamie and I got this news we were crushed. We had regimental spirit—in those days the man stayed with a regiment as long as possible. She had many warm friends in the 19th.

Nevertheless, the new assignment was of such importance and required such exertion that we had no time to moan over disappointments. Our outlook had to be forward. The cadre to which I was assigned had only five or six officers including the colonel, and so all of us had to fill several posts until more officers could be obtained. My job was to be regimental supply officer. And my orders were enough to dismay a young man who had less than two years of commissioned service.

The Colonel, D. J. Baker, told me that within two or three days three thousand recruits would reach the now vacant Camp Wilson, just out of Fort Sam Houston. They would be coming with only their clothing and barracks bags. I was to be responsible for giving them supper that evening and providing them thereafter with shelter, food, supplies, and anything else that men needed to subsist and train. For the next five days, I was on the move almost around the clock.

Fortunately, I had one experienced non-commissioned officer with me, named Alexander. He had been in the supply business a long time. We borrowed trucks here and there, we found enough tent shelter to cover the arriving men from the weather, and we somehow appropriated enough food to give them at least a meager sort of meal both the first evening and the next morning.

With men on hand now to work, even though they had no training, things began to move faster and more help arrived with a contingent of newly commissioned officers who had just graduated from a short course at Leavenworth.

Shortly it was decided that we would not stay in our present position but would move twenty miles out of San Antonio to a place called Leon Springs, along Fredericksburg Road, a well-known highway. Leon Springs boasted no advantage except a large area, with room for training movements, and the fact that it was already in the possession of the Federal government. There was not a building or shelter on it of any kind. It did boast one well, from which we could draw fresh water.

From the beginning, the great mobilization of 1917 meant that the competition for supplies was keen among the new regiments. I made friends with every officer from every supply service. I haunted the quartermaster, ordnance, engineer, and medical services, was constantly pleading the case of our new Infantry regiment, now approaching full strength. We were at full strength in numbers, at least, but the men were denied almost everything needed with which to prepare for war. The days were filled for all of us and we were working so hard that the Colonel determined that Sunday should definitely be a day of rest. Except for services by chaplains under the trees outdoors, we were free to do as we pleased.

This was a limited privilege because there was no transportation of any kind to go down into San Antonio. Mamie was determined not to let this situation defeat her. Although she had never driven a vehicle powered by a gasoline engine, and our own little car was uncertain in performance, she was determined to learn enough about it to come to the camp and spend some Sundays with us there. Her first venture was lively.

The only thing she could remember about the car was how to start it. She did recall how to get it into forward gear and so she began a twenty-mile trip after telephoning me in advance. To avoid traffic, she started out early in the morning. She wanted the whole road to herself and I must say she needed it.

She had asked me to meet her at the gate because while she knew where to turn off Fredericksburg Road, she knew nothing at all about the camp. I walked the mile or so to the entrance and waited. I was finally rewarded by seeing Mamie coming down the hill.

As she approached I could hear her calling. She got closer and closer and when I made out her words, she was saying, "Ike! Get on, get on quickly—I don't know how to stop this thing!" I started toward her and she said, "Jump on!"

Cars in those days had broad running boards and it was no trick to hop aboard, get the door open, and take over from her. She leaned back with a sigh of relief and when we had drawn to a stop, she told me about her expedition.

First she had learned that she not only did not know how to stop, she was not at all sure that if she ever did stop that she'd remember the right way to get it going again. When she reached a railroad crossing where she was supposed to stop and look, there was no hope . . . she had to go straight across, fortunately without incident. She had learned a lot in this early form of on-the-job training. The real accomplishment was that she got there at all.

The day was pleasant; a few of the other officers had succeeded in getting some of their families to the camp. I spent part of the day in giving Mamie driving lessons. She seemed to have difficulty. Nevertheless, she became passably proficient. Sad as I was to see her go, I induced her to make an early start back and got a promise that she would telephone me as soon as she arrived. Two hours later I got the welcome news that she was safely at home. From then on I tried, whenever Mamie wanted to visit the camp, to arrange for a more experienced driver to go along. It was difficult to judge who was in more danger—the men on their way to war, or the women on their way to the men.

We remained short of critical supplies. I kept hammering away and the War Department frantically accumulated everything that was already manufactured and sent it along. Training was intense and the Texas summer made it anything but easy. But the supply department seemed to be the focus of all trouble. The companies and battalions wanted more—more of everything. We couldn't get the supplies, by and large, so we were resented by our own people and repelled by the supply services.

I assembled the junior supply officers of the regiment—those who worked with companies and battalions—for a lecture on supply in the field. Needless to say, I had been poring over the textbooks, because there was no one in the regiment, except our one noncommissioned officer, who knew the subject. It was a cloudy day and the officers and enlisted men to whom I was speaking gathered around just outside my tent, under a large tree. A drizzling rain started but we put on raincoats and kept on. While I was talking, the weather became more threatening. Then there was a terrific bolt of lightning, and all that I was conscious of was a sort of ball of fire in front of my eyes.

The next thing I knew I was lying on my back in the mud and an enlisted man was pushing down on my ribs, trying to bring me back from unconsciousness. I did not feel any particular harm except when they picked me up and I shook myself, I had a splitting headache. For the moment, the lecture was off and I went back to my tent. The adjutant, Captain Walton Walker, was a friend of mine. Feeling a little woozy, I walked over to his tent. He was in a state of upset himself. Walton had been telephoning when the big shock came—it hit the telephone line—the phone flew out of his hand and across the room and he had an arm that was rapidly turning black and blue.

Colonel Baker often remarked that he was the only regimental commander in the Army whose entire staff had been struck by lightning and lived to tell about it.

During the summer months of 1917, our regiment rapidly rounded into form. The training program was intensive and in most respects enlightened. Because Walker, the adjutant, and I were so close to Colonel Baker, he gradually heaped more and more jobs upon us. For example, the Colonel was something of a dyspeptic and fussy about his meals. He complained constantly about the quality of the food and after having tried the mess officer's job on several other people, he gave me the position. This of course was in addition to my other duties of trying to supply a regiment of 3500 men with mules, transportation, weapons, shelter, and all manner of hardware.

But supplying the Colonel was its own war. The meal at which Colonel Baker was always present and about which he voiced his sharpest criticism was breakfast. I had heard him talk often of his liking for game. This gave me an idea.

Both Walton Walker and I liked to shoot. We took off each morning at about 4:00 A.M., got on our horses, and went to one of several fields in which we found doves in plentiful supply. We would shoot a few, bring them back, dress them, and by the time the Colonel was ready for breakfast at about 8:00, he'd have a fine meal out of our morning shoot.

Our horses were well trained and we could shoot from their backs, while an orderly came along with a bag to pick up the birds. We learned to bring in at least a half a dozen because the Colonel liked the birds so much that he would frequently say, "Any of these for lunch?" With the best cook we had, we experimented and wasted a good many birds in trying to find something that we thought would amuse the Colonel. We tried broiling them with little pieces of bacon on their breast; we made stews out of them, adding a few mild vegetables—potatoes, carrots, and the like; finally we hit on making dove pies. By giving the Colonel a regulation breakfast of bacon and eggs about once a week, and on another day locating some lamb chops and dressing them up fancily, we seemed to keep him satisfied. The other officers got little attention because we were preoccupied with keeping the Colonel in a good mood. This was good for everybody; we all enjoyed life more when he was.

Getting ready for a shooting expedition one morning, Walker found that his horse was lame. He took a new one from the picket line. It didn't occur to us to test the new horse for behavior under fire and the first time that Walker had a chance at a dove, he let go with his shotgun, an automatic. In those days, a magazine carried five cartridges. As Walker fired his first shot, the horse came up off the ground about four feet and Walker, throwing the gun up with one hand and grabbing for the reins with his left, had little control over his reflexes. When the horse's feet hit the ground with a jar, another shot was fired almost automatically, while Walker was trying desperately to keep his seat and control of the horse. With each succeeding shot, the horse went higher.

By the time the second shot was thrown in the air, the orderly and I were both off our horses and were trying to stay close to them on the side opposite to the source of danger. Four straight times the horse hit the ground, the gun went off, and Walker, miraculously, kept his seat. Each of us was perspiring freely by the time the gun was empty and was more than glad to get out of the mess with a whole skin.

Everybody in the regiment became interested in equipment. All of us implicitly believed that once we were fully supplied and equipped, we'd be sent overseas. This was every man's ambition.

Each Saturday morning, I reported to the officers during breakfast on the state of supply and what we were still missing. Finally we got to a time when the only things we needed were entrenching shovels and carriers to put them on the pack of foot soldiers. They were on urgent requisition. Then a huge box of them arrived at the supply tent.

We were elated at our success. The Colonel, the adjutant, the battalion commanders, and my assistant came to see this last vital item of supply unpacked and distributed. The box, on the order of five feet by four by four, was bound up with strap iron and securely nailed. We got it opened up and looked in at our prize. Then our faces fell in dismay. They were shovel carriers, all right, but they were the old style and not the new ones with which the Army was then to be mass-equipped.

Immediately, we nailed the box back up, put on the strap iron, and shipped it back to the ordnance department. This was not the end of the story. Its sequel gave me a sharp lesson in bureaucratic red tape.

Army regulations prescribed that whenever anything was missing or wrong with a shipment, the receiving officer was required to remove every item from the box, count it, check it, and give a full report on the deficiencies. We, of course, had taken nothing from the box; one look showed us that the equipment was not right and we sent it back.

Months later, when I was on other duty, I got a bill from the ordnance department for $22.04. That was the price, according to them, of nineteen items missing from the box of supplies we had opened. I wrote a letter, explained the circumstances, and enclosed affidavits from several of the officers and men who had been with me. I thought the explanation and evidence were valid.

I still had to send Ordnance my check for $22.04.

When the canceled check came back, Mamie, who was secretary of the family, pasted it in the back of the checkbook as a receipt and perhaps as an object lesson. Many months later, I got another bill for $22.04, with a letter saying that I owed this amount for the loss of items from the box. A model of restraint, I made a copy of the canceled check, sent it back, and heard no more.

If this was my first encounter with bureaucratic blundering, it was far from the last before World War I was over. More humiliating than costly, in a way, I felt that in that nebulous region called the War Department, I had been found wanting.

Anyhow, the regiment was in good shape. We were sure that we were one of the best outfits in the whole Army and were confident that we were destined for overseas duty. Instead, I got a special order detaching me from the 57th Infantry and assigning me to the training camp at Fort Oglethorpe, Georgia, to be an instructor of candidates for commission. This was distressing. I wanted to stay with a regiment that would see action soon. And I thought that my wish could be easily taken care of; another officer, one year senior to me, was anxious to go into the instruction business. So I asked the Colonel, who was kind enough to say he wanted to keep me, to telegraph the department commander to ask whether orders could be changed to send Captain —— instead of Eisenhower (I was now a captain). The request was promptly answered: disapproved.

Though I didn't know it then, the 57th Infantry, completely trained, fully manned, and equipped (except for the latest model shovels), was not to be sent to war. Instead, it was assigned to garrison duty in and around Houston and never saw any action overseas. For me this was a hard lesson that if the mills of the gods grind slowly and exceedingly small, the mills of the War Department seemed to grind to no purpose whatsoever.

My parting with Mamie was particularly difficult. She couldn't go along because I was going to field duty. Also, she was expecting our first child.

At Oglethorpe, I reported to Colonel Henry Slocum, son of a Civil War general, and went to work training candidates in an intense program for commissions as second lieutenants. The training was tough—designed as much for weeding out the weak and inept as to instruct.

We went to the field and lived in trenches, constructed dugouts, and prepared for warfare on the Western Front. I came out of those trenches on the twenty-sixth of September and found a telegram dated the twenty-fourth, saying that my son had been born. His name was Doud Dwight.

The work was fatiguing but I enjoyed it. Luckily, over the months I had been following the progress of the war and read everything that I could find about minor tactics of infantry. This was paying off. We could put into practice what I had been reading as theory.

With that camp closed, new orders came in to proceed to Fort Leavenworth to instruct provisional second lieutenants, who had passed their examinations but as yet had no training. Enough time was allotted so that I could go by way of San Antonio to see my new son and spend a day or two with my wife.

When I reached there, I reported in at the post and learned that a machine-gun battalion was being organized for overseas duty. It was to be commanded by a friend, Captain Gilbert Allen of the old

19th (he was now a lieutenant colonel), who heartily endorsed my instant application. We sent it forward with great expectations. Again, a curt reply, adding only that I was considered to be a young officer with special qualities as an instructor. Disappointed, I trekked off to Leavenworth.

I had been on duty there for a few days when an order arrived to report to Colonel Miller, the post commandant. He read me a letter from the Adjutant General which noted that I had several times applied for duty with troops headed overseas. The War Department did not approve of young officers applying for special duty; they were to obey orders and, in effect, let the War Department run the war. I suspect that someone in Washington who had seen my requests put me down as one of those who, in later years, would be classified as an eager beaver. Whatever the case, the message was loud and clear. A man at a desk a thousand miles away knew better than I what my military capabilities and talents were; and he did not want to be bothered by any further exercises of initiative on my part.

This made me furious and when the Colonel proceeded to add several reprimands of his own, I reverted to the old, red-necked cadet. I was asking nothing, after all, except to go to battle.

"Sir," I said, "this offense—if it is an offense—was committed before I came under your jurisdiction. If there is punishment to be given out, I think that it should be given by the War Department and not added to by yourself, with all due respect."

Strangely enough, I heard him say, "Well, I think you're right. And I respect you for standing up to your convictions." The Colonel sent me out in a friendly mood toward him, although my views of the War Department continued to be beyond easy conversion to parlor language.

I was made assistant instructor for Company Q, a large group of the provisional lieutenants. In addition, I was to supervise all the physical training of the entire regiment, to be responsible for bayonet drills, calisthenics, and exercises. The winter was severe and we had lots of snow—but if conditions were frequently unpleasant, and at times bitter, my duties were one way of keeping warm.

CHAPTER X

Camp Meade, Camp Colt:
Training for the Invisible War

SINCE coming to Gettysburg to make it our home after leaving the Presidency, I sometimes receive letters from young people, men and women in their thirties as well as high-school and college students, in which an underlying theme recurs. This theme is expressed by the question, in one form or another, "What can *I* do?"

What is happening, of course, is that they are, in part, in the grip of youth's eternal conviction that most of what they are studying, and much of what they are working on, is pointless or irrelevant or futile. Added to this is the probability that in an age where atoms appear to threaten life and automation seems to threaten vocation, they feel that they may be losing their identity and any control over their destiny. Either implicitly or explicitly, the letter writers tend to blame forces beyond their control.

Those who write really want more inspiration than explanation, but at least they are questioning and that is healthy in itself. Their letters cannot be answered by one of my old proverbs or succinct statements of rosy optimism.

I could say, if we were talking together, "My friend, I know just how you feel. Everyone, including ancients like myself, feels the same as you do at times. The only thing to do is keep questioning but keep plugging." I never make that reply. It would be fast rejected as the pat answer of a man who, already in the evening of life, does not appreciate what happens when day to day work seems sterile or purposeless.

On the other hand, it is easier to point out that if they were to examine the correspondence of any of their heroes out of history, they might find that he had revealed his feelings in pessimistic moments in the same sort of letters. I've done no special research but George Washington's letter, written in the autumn of 1758, months before the fall of Fort Duquesne and the collapse of the

French empire in the Ohio Valley, would be an example. As he camped at Fort Cumberland, a hundred miles or so from the enemy, he was doing absolutely nothing, in his judgment, toward victory. He put his feelings this way (capitalization, punctuation, and spelling are General Washington's):

We are still Incamp'd here, very sickly; and quite dispirited at the prospect before Us. That appearance of Glory once in view, that hope, that laudable Ambition of serving Our Country, and meriting its applause, is now no more! . . .

Not very pleased with himself, and grumbling about powers beyond his control, he added:

Tis dwindled into ease; Sloth, and fatal inactivity, and in a Word, All is lost, if the ways of Men in power, like the ways of Providence are not Inscrutable; and, why [are] they not? for we who view the Action's of great Men at so vast a distance can only form conjectures agreable to the small extant of our knowledge and ignorant of the comprehensive Schemes intended . . .

Washington got his gripes off his chest, much in the mood of those who write me, by putting them down on paper. Then he went back to work.

To me, his method makes good sense. Early letters of mine displayed a dazzling ignorance of coming events. Whenever I had convinced myself that my superiors, through bureaucratic oversights and insistence on tradition, had doomed me to run-of-the-mill assignments, I found no better cure than to blow off steam in private and then settle down to the job at hand.

Unfortunately, the cure is never total—we all suffer from feelings of futility, at times—and I cannot propose it to my correspondents as a panacea. It troubles me that I cannot express myself more eloquently and helpfully, for I appreciate their gloom when the road traveled seems to have a dead-end. The early months of 1918 were such a period.

By this time I knew enough about officer training and organizing new units—or thought I did—that the prospect was one of falling into dull routine. I tried to recognize that in preparing young officers to lead troops, we were making a constructive contribution. This kind of thinking was small comfort, at times, for a man who had finally decided to make the Army his career.

For one thing, all the West Point traditions that nourished élan and esprit centered on battlefield performance. The leadership of the men who had gone before us, faced with headlong attack, stubbornly defending and then causing their troops to follow them was in our minds the hallmark of the true soldier. My mastery of military paper work, even of rudimentary training methods, hardly seemed a shining achievement for one who had spent seven years preparing himself to lead fighting men.

Some of my class were already in France. Others were ready to depart. I seemed embedded in the monotony and unsought safety of the Zone of the Interior. I could see myself, years later, silent at class reunions while others reminisced of battle. For a man who likes to talk as much as I, that would have been intolerable punishment. It looked to me as if anyone who was denied the opportunity to fight might as well get out of the Army at the end of the war.

My elation, then, can well be imagined when I received orders in late winter to report to Camp Meade, Maryland, to join the 65th Engineers. This, I was told, was the parent group which was organizing tank corp troops for *overseas* duty.

That word put new spirit into me. I rushed back to San Antonio to see Mamie and our youngster, then took off for Camp Meade.

Our first job was to complete the organizing and equipping of the 301st Tank Battalion, Heavy. These men were to man the big tanks, a rarity on World War I battlefields where even the small "whippets" were not common.

Morale was high. As soldiers promised a new weapon always will, we convinced ourselves that we would have it in our power to clinch victory. We were *different*. We and the Air Section were taking only volunteers. In those tanks (not yet arrived), juggernauts of combat, titanic in bulk even though snails in speed, there was an irresistible force that would end the war. The men dreamed of overwhelming assault on enemy lines, rolling effortlessly over wire entanglements and trenches, demolishing gun nests with their fire, and terrorizing the foe into quick and abject surrender.

All of us were itching to move. We quickly completed basic training but having no tanks we were not yet ready for the battlefield. We were sure that within weeks we'd be in France to dissolve the stagnation of trench warfare with the latest in ultimate weapons. For once, the soldiers' expectations were realized.

In mid-March, I was told that the 301st would soon be taking a ship at New York. I was to go along in *command!*

As a regular officer, I had to preserve the sedate demeanor of one for whom the summons to battle is no novelty. But my exuberance, I'm sure, was shown in every word and gesture to the battalion. I went to New York to see exactly what would be required. I wanted no hitch in embarkation and shipment. Too much depended on our walking up that gangplank for me to take a chance on a slip anywhere. The port authorities may have thought me a worrywart about trifles, but I worked my head off.

Within two days I was back at Meade. The plan had been changed. My chief said he was impressed by my "organizational ability." I was directed to take the remnants of the troops who would not be going overseas, and proceed to an old, abandoned campsite in Gettysburg, Pennsylvania, of all places.

Because the camp in Gettysburg had to be established quickly, while I still had to complete all the details of shipping the 301st to New York, I took a small detachment to the new campsite, named Colt. My mood was black. I decided to leave them in the charge of a good man named Garner, a captain who had been commissioned a year earlier from the non-commissioned ranks. I knew little about him but he seemed quite capable.

We ran up the United States flag on a pole that had been left there. As I was ready to get into an automobile to start the long drive back to Baltimore, I saw Captain Garner watching the flag flapping at the top. I paused and he said, without looking at me, "Captain, the last time I was on this ground was many years ago. At that time I was standing before a general court-martial which sentenced me to six months in the guardhouse, and then suspended the sentence.

"Now," he said, "I'm a captain in that same Army, and I'm standing here as temporary commander of the camp in which I was disgraced." As I looked up, this old, hard-bitten, gray-headed former non-com had tears streaming down his face.

All I could manage to say was, "Look, Garner, I know you'll do a splendid job. Good luck." And I sat back in the car and started off. To this day, whenever we stand to salute the flag, that memory is with me.

The War Department abandoned the title of the 65th Engineers and set up, in its place, an organization called the Tank Corps, putting it under direction of Colonel I. C. Welborn, an Infantry man who had won the Medal of Honor during the Boxer Rebellion. He was an active officer, in many ways brilliant. His office was located in Washington and I had to report to him twice a week for instructions. Otherwise, I was very much on my own at Camp Colt.

The Tank Corps was new. There were no precedents except in basic training and I was the only regular officer in the command. Now I really began to learn about responsibility.

One bright spot was that tents were easily available. We began to erect them, and although we had no materials with which to build tent frames and floors, we managed to make the men comfortable enough. Five or six men went into each tent, rather than the eight for which they had been designed. We established a personnel and records section. Within a short time the command was functioning, making its reports, and getting along.

My personal orders were specific, indeed rigid. I was required to take in volunteers, equip, organize, and instruct them and have them ready for overseas shipment when called upon. The orders warned that no excuses for deficiencies in their records or equipment would be accepted and that my camp was not only a point of mobilization but of embarkation. This meant that troops sent from Gettysburg would go directly to a port without any intermediate stops.

Most of our work was improvisation. At first hand, every day, I had practical lessons in the Republic's lack of preparedness for war —including its unreadiness to care well for men who answered its call.

In early April, a storm came upon us and it was so sudden and so furious that we were snowbound for days. The tents were not heated. As the snow fell and I suspected what we were in for, I got through the snowdrifts into the town. These days, despite stop lights and speed limits, I ride from our old campsite to the town square in two minutes. That morning, it took two hours. At the first hardware store, I bought every stove that would fit into a tent. By the time I reached the last shop, I had cleaned the town out. For the time being, at least, the Tank Corps had a local monopoly on one kind of equipment.

We still didn't have enough stoves to go around. I had the men build stone cairns from piles of rock and shale built up when they had cleared the area. These permitted modest fires inside the rest of the tents, although they required a patrol of men all night to keep the fires going and make sure that no tent burned down.

Had the men been at home in civilian life, many would have taken one look out the front or back window at the mountains of snow and gone back to bed. If they had gone to work, some would have sniffles and others pneumonia. Nothing of the sort happened at Camp Colt. And certainly the air should have been thick with complaints that Army negligence had exposed volunteers to premature death. Not so. They seemed to take the storm as a splendid way to demonstrate their robust health. To me, the spirit of the men proved the best disease preventive.

When the storm ended, we were ready to tackle anything in the way of work. I expected that most of the men would be on their way to the port within a month, to be replaced by a shipment of fresh volunteers. My job then would become just a repetition. At that time the camp was at a strength of about five hundred men. Once again, I had not counted on the powers that be.

The British and American governments, because of a crisis in troop strength along the Western Front, made the "Abbeville Agreement." The British were to provide all sea transport across the Atlantic; the United States would, temporarily, move to ports of embarkation nothing but infantry troops and machine-gun battalions. This meant that for an unpredictable period, we could not move tank troops overseas.

Our numbers at Colt began to grow rapidly. I could foresee that before summer several thousand men might be in camp. Once they were competent in basic drill, they would have little to do. With time hanging heavy on recruits' hands, we could be sure of one thing: morale would deteriorate quickly.

I began to look around for ways to instruct the men in skills that would be valuable in combat and prevent the dry rot of tedious idleness. We had no information from France on what types of training best suited soldiers for survival and success in that form of warfare; not until World War II did the War Department set up a smooth system of communication between the combat zones and the training camps. Our chief source of information in 1918 came from newspapers and we had to use our imaginations. Fortunately for me, I had three excellent civilian officers who had both common sense and flair. At the outset, we had not much to work with. Soon ideas came.

In earlier wars, crushing defeats had often been the product of lost or misunderstood messages. We realized that anyone who could learn telegraphy and master Morse code would be useful in the Tank Corps. A first-rate telegrapher might prove himself worth more than a company of riflemen.

Enthusiasm was contagious and in short order we had a telegraphic school in operation. We established a motor school, with secondhand motors of all kinds, and several men who were competent to instruct.

I went to the Tank Corps headquarters in Washington to ask for small-caliber cannons. Only a few Navy guns, of the swivel type (we called them "three pounders"), were available. We drilled with these anyhow, even though we lacked ammunition and sufficient backstops. A number of machine guns came in and we trained gunners until they could take them apart blindfolded and put them together again. Then someone had the notion of mounting the machine guns on truck trailers or on flatbed trucks, and so we were able to train the men to fire from mobile platforms at both moving and still targets. The only satisfactory place for firing was Big Round Top, a terrain feature that has a prominent place in the history of the Battle of Gettysburg. Its base made a perfect backstop. Soon, soldiers were shooting from moving trucks at all kinds of targets there and the firing might have been heavier than during the great battle fifty-five years earlier.

All this we took on without orders from Washington but with the approval of my chief, Colonel Welborn. It was just as well—the camp continued to expand and toward the end of July, we had ten thousand men and six hundred officers.

By mid-summer we were operating efficiently because repeatedly we found in the mass of officers and men certain outstanding individuals who took to soldiering and leadership with zest.*

* A man named Whittington, for example, who was placed in charge of all supply and logistics of the camp, was a real find. He never had to be told anything twice. Another, Floyd Parks, whom I found among the second lieutenants, showed such promise I gave him a company to command and succeeded in getting him promoted to first lieutenant. Shortly thereafter we were authorized to train as provisional battalion units but we were not allowed any "official" formation larger than that of the company. Parks made such progress with his company that even though he was not yet—I think—twenty-two years old, I put him in command of a battalion. After the war was over, he stayed in the Regular Army and rose to the rank of lieutenant general before he retired.

As was inevitable, however, in receiving men of many backgrounds and from recruiting stations of varying standards, some had serious physical defects or mental blocks. The awkward, hay-foot, straw-foot soldier to whom keeping in step meant concentration and co-ordination beyond his capacity did not bother me. After all, in my first days at West Point, close order drill was a trial for a corn-fed youth who had been accustomed all his life to American independence in stride and pace.

But as the war wore on, trainees who were really unfit became more numerous. Because this was happening in camps all over the United States, the War Department started "Development Battalions." Rather than reject or discharge a man as soon as he displayed any deficiencies, he was transferred to one of these battalions. If he showed no improvement there under special instruction, he would be discharged.

Because over the years I have more than once complained of War Department rigidity and inflexibility, I should stress here that the Development Battalion was an exercise of the imagination at the highest levels of the Army, arising as much from concern for the individual's own well-being as for his military use.*

There are a good many dissenters, I'm sure, but the American Army, in my experience, has a substantial respect for the latent potential in every man. Although it had become an axiom in some European armies that every private carried a field marshal's baton in his knapsack, the man himself had to fight and claw to any distinction on his own. In our Army, it was thought that every private had at least a second lieutenant's gold bars somewhere in him and he was helped and encouraged to earn them.

Beyond military considerations, the Army, firmly committed to the doctrine that in a Republic the backbone of wartime force is the citizen soldier, had to demonstrate that most civilians could become effective fighters as well as responsible, thinking men who understood the purposes of combat.

At Camp Colt, because our enlisted personnel were volunteers showing an exemplary zeal, our troops were a few cuts above average. College and high-school graduates were not unknown, although the man with about eight years of school was normal. Illiterate men were few; in fact, I encountered none. But with a

* See Note 3.

mushrooming command, we obviously needed an agency like the Development Battalion. This was authorized and Colonel Welborn remarked to me that this would be the only Development Battalion in the country where the camp was run by an officer below the grade of brigadier general. I was below that grade, all right, but I had one officer who did the camp more good than a star on my uniform.

Weeks earlier, a classmate of mine named Randolph had reported in. He had a genius for training. The men liked him and so it was sensible to give him command of the new battalion. Two or three hundred men were transferred to it. Those who were physically defective were discharged; there was nothing we could do for them. But for those who were slow or inept or, as the expression became later, oddballs, Randolph and his assistants did a great deal.

I am inclined by nature to be optimistic about the capacity of a person to rise higher than he or she has thought possible once interest and ambition are aroused. If I were not, the experience of watching Randolph with the Development Battalion would have made me so. Today, they might be tagged retarded people. What Randolph accomplished has always convinced me of the Salvation Army's theory that a man may be down but he is never out. The majority were transferred within a few months back to regular organizations. Indeed, out of the battalion, twenty-one men were sent to officers school and eighteen finally became second lieutenants. Others became high-ranking non-commissioned officers and technicians.

Even as we saw the redemption, so to speak, of hundreds of men who had been thought incompetent, the supervising of thousands of other young men of intelligence and loaded with animal energy had to be a twenty-four-hour-a-day occupation.

Gettysburg, when we set up camp there, was a borough of about three thousand people. The big events since the battle of July 1863 and President Lincoln's eloquence, had been GAR encampments and football games at Gettysburg College.

Most residents welcomed the soldiers, if for no other reason than patriotism. A few saw in them a source of quick and easy profit, catering to all their appetites. In any community, this minority can cause endless trouble, sometimes seriously affecting, by a sort of contagion that runs through the ranks, an entire command. From the beginning, we were eager to establish good relations with our civilian neighbors and protect the community and the troops against the offensive few.

Good morale within an outfit is usually reflected by good conduct away from it. In the first few weeks a recruit is too dog-tired to want to do anything except rest his feet and escape observation by corporals and sergeants. When he develops some soldierly ability, he also develops pride—*if* his officers are not ignoring him or abusing the privileges of rank. This sort of officer can be a menace to any command.

A quick brush with politics involved a congressman and a trouble-making officer. The officer had been caught cheating at cards by some of his colleagues. They brought the packs of cards to me and after listening to their story, I sent for the man.

When he came in, I had laid out the packs of cards on the front of the desk. He stood at attention, in a manner of speaking, and I said:

"Do you see these cards?"

"Yes."

"Are they yours? Do you recognize them?"

He flushed and said, No he couldn't.

"Well, I can show you exactly where you have marked them. Would you like me to do it?"

He stammered, refused to touch the cards, and said, "No."

To end it, I asked, "Would you rather resign at once for the good of the service or would you like to be tried by court-martial?"

"I'll submit my resignation this afternoon," he said.

For me that was too long a wait. "Right outside this room is a man who takes shorthand. I suggest that you write out your resignation, bring it back to me, and I'll send it forward to the War Department today."

Two or three days later, the congressman from his district came in, accompanied by the officer's father. The congressman introduced the latter as one of his most important constituents and suggested that I withdraw the son's resignation and transfer him to another camp. I declined politely, saying I could have nothing to do with such a move; this would be passing the problem on to another commander, and the man would repeat the same offense. After the congressman argued and blustered a bit, he said that he would accept my judgment and asked whether I could get taken out of the resignation the words, "for the good of the service." Not as far as I was concerned, I said; the man had been guilty of cheating and he had to take this request to the War Department. Here the congressman got angry and said he thought I was acting arbitrarily for a Major.

"I'm acting as an Army officer protecting my command."

I heard no more from him but I did learn later that he had succeeded in getting the young officer back into the service.

This was not the end of my encounters with congressmen of the day. The War Department had been issued orders by the government that every commanding officer of a camp could, at his discretion, close all saloons or other places where liquor was dispensed within a distance of five miles of his camp. My provost forces were well acquainted with all such places in the Gettysburg area and they thought it better to allow them to stay open and to keep an eye on them, rather than close them down and cause a surge in bootlegging, a business they couldn't control. Each man licensed to dispense liquor was given instructions that he could not sell intoxicants to a man in uniform and if he did, we would close his place. Things seemed to be working out until I got a report that a man who owned a sizable hotel with a bar had been surreptitiously serving liquor to men in uniform.

Because he ran a hotel as well as a bar, I was not exactly sure of my authority. So I simply put a provost guard around the hotel and allowed no soldier to enter it. Naturally, with this restriction enforced, visitors who had come to see their brothers and husbands and sons and sweethearts would not go into the hotel either. The hotel owner came to see me, made a promise, and I gave him another chance.

He didn't keep his promise and the guard was returned to the hotel sidewalk. I sent word that he had had his warning; I had allowed him to conduct business under his oath to carry out the orders of the War Department and my instructions; and I wouldn't again withdraw the guard.

For our next meeting, he came equipped with his congressman and the congressman's secretary. I listened to his story and said that I still stayed with my position. After debate, the congressman said, "Well, we have means—we can go to the War Department. If you're going to be so stubborn, I'll have to take up the question of replacing you."

I said, "You do just exactly that."

He looked a little startled.

"Nothing would please me better than to be taken out of this job. I want to go overseas. If they take me out of here, maybe I can get there."

The dialogue ended on this note and he left with his secretary and his constituent. Within minutes, the secretary came back and said, "Look, Major, don't pay any attention to all this. The congressman had to do this because the hotel man is a very important supporter of his but we don't want to start a quarrel."

"That's all right with me," I said. "Let it go."

It became obvious, after a time, that the man had gone to the War Department because I got a letter from the Assistant to the Secretary of War. He wrote that the Secretary wanted to commend me for diligence in looking after the welfare and well-being of my soldiers.

There was nothing for the owner of the hotel to do but to come back, apologize, and renew his promise of good behavior. He asked me whether he could operate as the other hotels were doing. I told him that he didn't deserve a second chance but I couldn't be sure that he had not reformed.

"Let me warn you of this," I said in effect, "I shall probably put some of my provost guards in civilian clothes and they'll be haunting your place. If they ever see you sell or give a drink to a man in uniform, I'll put you out of business." We had no more trouble.*

In spite of the Abbeville Agreement, we began to get special

* Of another hotel in town—the Gettysburg—I have very pleasant memories. There I stayed as a cadet when my class came down from West Point in 1915 for our pregraduation visit. There I had my first meals when I arrived to assume command of Camp Colt.

It was then managed by the elder Henry Scharf who was scrupulous in observing all regulations that applied to soldiers. However, during the flu epidemic because he thought a stout eggnog a sovereign cure for almost any human ailment, he engaged himself in mixing many gallons of that beverage which he contributed to the hospitalized troops.

Almost forty-five years later, on December 14, 1964, his son Henry M. Scharf and the latter's wife had Mamie and me to dinner with them in the hotel grill. When we had finished eating and reminiscing, Mr. Scharf turned the key in the lock, closing the doors on an historic Gettysburg establishment. We were its last diners.

requests for soldiers with certain skills. A request from the American Expeditionary Force came to the War Department for sixty-four telegraphers. This request gave some of us around headquarters a bit of sardonic amusement. We had been told that the Tank Corps in Europe had no need of the specialized training we had set up.

The orders told us that a ship would be leaving Philadelphia within thirty-six hours. The troops were to be on that ship with all their records and personal gear in perfect shape. We immediately selected sixty-four qualified men, had to check up on their vaccinations, inoculations, give them complete physical and equipment inspections, and process the complex paper work. All this was time-consuming. But we figured we could do it if we could get the equipment to Philadelphia hours in advance of the sailing.

Checking schedules, we found that the next freight train would not make our deadline. We didn't have enough truck transportation to send supplies to the port. So I told a trainmaster in Harrisburg to attach a baggage car to the next through passenger train. It worked. We had a wakeful weekend. For thirty-six hours, several of us had not a wink of sleep. Finally, we could congratulate ourselves when a call came through that the ship had sailed and that nobody was turned back because of any deficiencies.

Again, the bonus was a yard of red tape. A letter arrived from the Quartermaster General which said that I should read the Army regulations, specifying the paragraphs, and that I was to show cause why I personally should not pay the difference between the *express* charges for shipping the gear from Gettysburg to Philadelphia and the charges for ordinary freight.

This time I was prepared to protect my pocketbook against another raid.

Immediately, I got copies of my initial orders for the establishment of Camp Colt which said that no excuses for deficiencies would be accepted. I also attached the orders specifying that I was to get the men and their supplies to Philadelphia in time.

The documents had their effect. At least, I have not yet paid.

During the summer we saw our first tanks. Although we were part of the Tank Corps, we knew about tanks only from hearsay and newspapers. With the cheerful cynicism of soldiers, we had not expected to see one until we reached Europe. Even at that, we couldn't be sure whether we would be operating them or facing them. However, someone in the war zone apparently thought that there might be virtue in letting the Tank Corps recruits and trainees get a preliminary look at the machine that one day we were to operate.

Three small tanks were sent to us. It was an exciting time. They were French-manufactured Renaults, each weighed about seven tons, and each, in combat, carried either a machine gun or a small one-pounder cannon, mounted in a revolving turret. Each *was* to carry, I should say; the tanks arrived without weapons. Again, we improvised.

At about the same time, two British officers appeared as advisers. Thus began my connection with allies, a word that was to become vitally important to me as the years rolled on. The British officers helped us to understand the uses of these new, armored weapons. In their conversations, I heard about a British political figure named Winston Churchill. According to the two officers, this Churchill had had a hand in producing the first tanks. They admired him extravagantly. And I must say that from their descriptions, he sounded like a good chap.

When I had been first sent to command Camp Colt, I must have shown or expressed my disappointment. I was told that this would be a temporary arrangement. After I had the training operation organized, Colonel Welborn would consider my assignment overseas. Now that the camp was operating smoothly, the Colonel had a change of heart. In his new mood, he said that he could not possibly recommend my transfer to Europe until the end of mild weather.

A major shift was inevitable then for when we moved into midwinter, our temporary camp, unsuitable for the severities of climate, would have to be abandoned. Before this happened, Welborn promised he would take up the matter of my going overseas. Once again, my hopes had been temporarily frustrated.

Colonel Welborn accompanied the refusal with a recommendation for my promotion to lieutenant colonel. This came through on my twenty-eighth birthday, the fourteenth of October, 1918. (Months after the war was over, I lost this rank because of the contraction of the Army. I was not to regain it again until 1936, while serving in the Philippines.)

The Colonel said he would put me in command of the November shipment of troops. After hearing this in late summer, I began to assemble the troops I wanted to take over. Understandably, I gave them particular attention because I wanted to make certain that they were without any faults that I could eliminate.

Once the basic provisions of the Abbeville Agreement had been fulfilled, we began to make monthly shipments of Tank Corps troops to Europe. Each time, we had information about the ships sailing so the work of final polishing did not require the sleepless nights of the emergency calls received earlier. We were proud of the fact, and remained so until the end of the encampment, that not a single man of ours was turned back from port because of any defect in his instructions, records, or physical condition.

Frequently, men from other camps, on reaching the embarkation depots, had gone absent without leave, or had imbibed too freely while roaming the fleshpots of the eastern cities. Warned, we took measures to see that our men arrived at exactly the right moment, were put aboard ship, and all records turned over without giving them any special opportunities for peccadilloes. Some of them were unhappy that they had been denied a last, wild fling. Happy or not, they may very well have been saved from a protracted tour of hard labor, a blot on their records, or if they had managed to get aboard ship in time, from the violent seasickness that can follow a spree on the town.

If the embarkations went well, the fortunes of those of us who stayed behind were unpleasant. Our next problem was nationwide, almost worldwide.

The only group of inductees (or drafted men) that we received came sometime in September from another camp. They reached Colt late one evening. Many of the men were feeling headachy but the doctors discovered that just before they boarded a train for Gettysburg, they had received typhoid fever shots. Because people normally experience some reaction to these shots, the sick men were sent by the doctors to our "replacement company" for the night. They would quickly throw off their aches and pains.

The next morning, alarming reports started to reach me. Some of the new men, I was told, were registering high fevers and were obviously very ill. The camp surgeon immediately took countermeasures. Before noon, "Spanish flu" was recognized. Because the men had not been confined to quarters and some of them were obviously carriers, the whole camp had to be considered as exposed.

There was spare space available because of the numbers of men who had been shipped overseas. We started a program of isolation.

We put up every kind of tent with makeshift bedding and any man with the slightest symptom was isolated from the others—if only by putting canvas partitions between beds. No more than four men were allowed in any tent; three wherever we had room. Each who had been directly exposed to the disease was, wherever possible, put into a tent by himself.

By the second day, some of the men had died. The week was a nightmare and the toll was heavy. The little town had no facilities to take care of the dead—which were to number 175. There were no coffins. We had no place to put the bodies except in a storage tent until they could gradually be taken care of more suitably. The doctors not only treated every soldier with symptoms but they moved also to assist the civilian population.

Churches were taken over for hospital use as the numbers of sick mounted rapidly. The whole camp was on edge. No one knew who was going to be stricken and death came suddenly. Near my office, I saw a man unloading a truck. I had seen him several times before and was struck by his fine appearance. This time I remarked on his healthy condition. The following evening, the doctor came in and said: "That man you thought looked so well yesterday morning is dead this evening."

The doctors were giving every kind of inoculation they could conceive of to see that no other infectious or contagious diseases sprang up to complicate the situation. Regulations called for every man who had not received all his smallpox, typhoid, and other inoculations, to get them as soon as possible. The hospital was about a hundred yards from my office. As I was looking out the window, watching a long line of men inching their way to one of the hospital tents for typhoid inoculations, I heard a shout. All the men in the line scattered like quail. They went over much of the ground on which Pickett's charge had taken place years earlier—and it took some time to collect them again.

I went to the hospital to see what had happened. There I learned that the line of men, like the rest of the camp, had been tense. In addition, they were reluctant to take inoculations, as usual. Everything was set for an explosion. As the men filed past the morgue tent, the spark appeared.

One man, who had been very sick and had apparently stopped breathing, had been carried out of the hospital by orderlies and put inside the morgue tent. Hours afterward, as the line of soldiers filed by, he came to. Completely bewildered by his surroundings, and alarmed when he saw that he was surrounded by naked bodies, he called out in a weak and weird voice, "Get me out of here." This started the stampede. No one stopped to reason. One man did report to the doctors and they in turn rushed to the tent and found the man alive. He was taken back into the hospital for care. He recovered and was a healthy soldier when he left our camp. The nerves of some of the other men may never have been the same.

During this period, I had my family with me. In April, not long after we established the camp, Mamie had arrived with our new baby, "Icky," and after several unfortunate trials, we found suitable quarters in Gettysburg. While I could not be at home all night, whenever possible I would go there in the evening. My duties required getting up early in the morning but it was fun to have the chance to see my son growing up and spend the evenings with my wife. Now, of course, I was desperately worried. Even my wife or my youngster could contract the terrible disease. A doctor from Oklahoma, a Lieutenant Colonel Scott out of the National Guard, had ideas of his own. In addition to isolation, he used a number of strong sprays on patients. He told me he would like to experiment with my family, and my headquarters staff which, including enlisted men, must have numbered forty or more. I told him to go ahead.

Each morning he would use two sprays on the throat and nostrils of each of us. One of them was intensely pungent and strong. On application, I felt as if the top of my head was going off. The other was, I think, a sort of soothing syrup to follow the first. The twice daily spray was anything but a tonic. Nevertheless, he insisted upon continuing this treatment on every member of my family and headquarters—though possibly he spared the baby. We were fortunate—or he was smart. Not a single person in my headquarters command or my family contracted the flu. Lieutenant Colonel Scott is another of those men to whom I will always feel obligated.

The losses were heavy but because of the strict measures taken by the camp surgeon the flu experience in other and bigger camps was far less satisfactory than ours. One week after our first death, the last one occurred and the epidemic was under control. As soon as this record came to the attention of the War Department, I was ordered to send thirty of the doctors from Camp Colt to show exactly what measures had been taken. This could have been a blow but since the detail was temporary, we were glad to be helpful. The remaining doctors were busier than ever taking care of the convalescent and the normal sick-call list.

When the epidemic was over, the War Department decided to transfer the remnants of my camp to get us out of Pennsylvania before the onset of winter. A place near Raleigh, North Carolina, was selected. This meant little to me. The move would not be made until after the November shipment of troops to Europe was complete—and I would be in Europe and no longer responsible.

Colonel Welborn called me in to say that if I would agree to give up my plans for overseas service, he was prepared to recommend me for full colonel. I declined. "I'm ready to take a reduction in rank to the average of my class—to major that is—if the lieutenant colonelcy which I have now stands in the way of my going overseas," I said. The November group was in good shape, with enough supernumeraries to take care of anybody who was called away by emergency or fell out by sickness or other causes. Nothing within our control would prevent meeting the target date for departure in early November. Fate, with the usual bad manners, intervened; I had made no provision for imminent German defeat.

In the first days of November, talk began about the weakening of German resistance. There was reason to hope for an early end to the war. Soon, the "false armistice" was noised around the country—and on the eleventh of November, 1918, the Armistice was agreed to and carried out. Even before that, the War Department had announced the cessation of shipments to Europe.

For Mamie and me, as a family, only qualified pleasure attended the rumors of an armistice for we had received word that her younger sister was dead. This was a terrible blow for both of us. The two girls had been close and I had deeply loved "Buster." She was a favorite of the entire family and among all who knew her. Mamie left for Denver and the funeral, taking Icky with her. I could not leave Camp Colt for the seven or eight days necessary.

Our parting, amidst all the rumors about the end of hostilities, and in the sadness of personal loss, was difficult, the most trying we had encountered in our less than three years of married life. For Mamie, only the most compelling call of heart could have strengthened her for the trip.

At Colt, on the other hand, I had little time for reflection. Nothing at West Point or in the forty months since graduation had prepared me for helping to collapse an Army from millions to a peacetime core. The new problem kept us even busier than we had been in the middle of summer.

No human enterprise goes flat so instantly as an Army training camp when war ends. Everything that sustains morale—peril to the country, imminent combat, zeal for victory, a sense of importance— disappears. The only thing that counts for a citizen soldier is his date of discharge. For the officers, the troops' preoccupation with this one objective made maintaining discipline and morale a major task.

To organize a make-work program (what in World War II was called eyewash), would have been self-defeating. To continue intensive training would have been ridiculous. A new aspect of leadership was demanded of every commissioned and non-commissioned officer —the ability to explain, reasonably and persuasively, all the necessary measures that would have to be taken before we could fold up the camp and the war.

The tempo of training slowed. To compensate, the tempo of policing areas increased. The War Department said that officers and men whose continuance in the service would impose hardships were to be returned home as expeditiously as possible. General demobilization, we were told, would be deferred until the necessary regulations could be formulated.

Foreseeably, a trickle of applications for immediate discharge from every unit in the Army began flowing into our camp headquarters. The trickle became a small niagara. Winter was coming on fast. Neither our tents nor the few temporary buildings provided the proper shelter against cold. Fortunately, the War Department reached a fast decision on the situation.

As quickly as possible, we were to clear the site we had occupied for nine months, complete our records, then move to Camp Dix where we would await final orders. The process was laborious. Although split-second timing was not then an inescapable component of military movements, endless hours of planning were required so that we would not find ourselves still camped at Colt, with our kitchen stoves on some railroad siding, and with the other fundamental impedimenta of all military organizations highballing toward New Jersey. We got through it and arrived at Camp Dix in early December. There the pace stepped up. Soldiers would be returning from France shortly, flooding the demobilization center, and room had to be ready for them.

Yet we had to be meticulous. Every soldier had to have a thorough physical. His financial records had to be checked to make sure that he had gotten all to which he was entitled in his final payments, including the $60 bonus the government gave him on discharge, and his transportation back home arranged.

We reached Dix with between five and six thousand people. Although almost every man wanted to shed his uniform on the spot, we persuaded some to stay on, at least temporarily. We were trying to make an effort to retain at least a nucleus of a Tank Corps. This was accomplished.

After the discharge of most of the men, we were left with between two and three hundred, the remnants of my command, plus the three Renault tanks of which we had been so proud. We were ordered to Fort Benning, Georgia.

The memory of that trip stays with me after more than forty-five years, etched deeply because of its discomfort. Troop train travel, even in peacetime, is far from luxurious. Nothing in those days was so pinch-penny as Army movement by rail. The War Department always made its rail moves by "land grant railways," on which governmental rates were far less than on other systems. The transportation officers had to select circuitous routes to take advantage of those rates. As we left Dix in mid-winter 1918–19, the route meandered tortuously through the eastern United States.

To prolong the endless trip, our train apparently had the lowest possible priority. Everything else seemed to have the right of way. Passenger expresses, accommodation and milk trains, slow freight and work crews, low-flying birds—each moved past as we sat on sidings, miserable, wondering which we hated most, the waiting or the whistle and jerk that would announce the beginning of our trip to the next siding.

Maintenance of the passenger cars had been one of the low or no priority jobs during the war, evidently. There were no lights, no heat, no hot water. The kitchen was a baggage car in which we had a couple of camp stoves and field rations enough to last the command for several days. We did get hot, although not very appetizing meals, now and then. I spoke to the railway officials and was always given the same excuse: "What do you expect when the government takes over the railways?"

During one of our lengthy stops, we purchased candles and gave one to each two soldiers so that they could have a little light during the evening. There were no candlesticks, of course, so each had to be set up by dripping wax on window sills. Everyone was tempted to huddle around them for warmth as well as light. Full clothing and blankets were necessary through day and night.

The trip lasted for almost four days, each a year long.

CHAPTER XI

Through Darkest America
with Truck and Tank

I HAD missed the boat in the war we had been told would end all wars. A soldier's place was where the fighting went on. I hadn't yet fully learned the basic lesson of the military—that the proper place for a soldier is where he is ordered by his superiors.

Our transfer to Fort Benning was only an interim until the War Department found a permanent post for the remains of the infant Tank Corps. Mamie was now free of worry about what might happen to me overseas; she and I were impatient for a reunion. But asking her to make a transcontinental trip from Denver with a little baby would be foolish. This sacrifice might be nullified within a week or so by an Army order transferring us to Texas, to California—or, with unintentional irony, to Colorado. It meant a brief spell of loneliness; brief, that is, meaning interminable.

As for my professional career, the prospects were none too bright. I was older than my classmates, was still bothered on occasion by a bad knee, and saw myself in the years ahead putting on weight in a meaningless chair-bound assignment, shuffling papers and filling out forms. If not depressed, I was mad, disappointed, and resented the fact that the war had passed me by.

At times I was tempted, at least faintly, to try my luck as a civilian again. An Indiana businessman who had been a junior officer at Camp Colt offered me a position at considerably more pay than a lieutenant colonel and certainly more than a captain, the grade I would hold as soon as the inevitable demotions came. Staying in the Army meant years of trying to stretch dollars and merge dimes. No one can be a more fearful worrywart than a young man trying to read his future in a bleak moment.

There was, after all, a brighter side. For an officer graduated from West Point less than two years before the United States entered the war, I had been singularly fortunate in the scope of my first three and a half years of duty. How to take a cross-section of Americans and convert them into first-rate fighting troops and officers had been learned by experience, not by textbook. Not to overstate the fact, I had a feeling for the military potential, in human terms, of the United States. My education had not been neglected.

At Benning I had far too much time on my hands. The Army fixed that. By early March, 1919, we were on the move again, this time to Camp Meade, Maryland. For me, this was full circle, Meade to Meade within one year. Unfortunately, even there we were on a mark time basis. The future of the Tank Corps was uncertain. Many experienced soldiers thought tanks clumsy and slow, mechanically unreliable, expensive, and tactically useless. On several counts they were right. On the last they were wrong.

To correct the deficiencies of the tank, which was still a primitive vehicle, would require its constant use in field exercises plus co-operation between military men and manufacturers. In those days, such co-operation was seldom thought of once the pressure of war was off. The use of the tank was, for the time being, turned over to the theoreticians. What was turned over to us at Meade, for the time being, were more soldiers to demobilize.

Mamie, our son, and I still had to be separated. Meade was a cantonment unsuitable for families. The few permanent houses on the post were occupied by senior or permanently assigned officers. To move my family to Baltimore or Washington, the nearest cities, would have made life difficult . . . transportation was meager and slow.

Tank officers were housed in Bachelor Officers Quarters. Because the cities were distant and the local recreation facilities were dismaying, there was every chance of going to seed. Several of us started a night school which met twice weekly for junior officers who hoped to enter the Regular Army once demobilization was completed. For those whose academic schooling had been cut off, we organized classes in mathematics, history, and English. For others we had a class in minor tactics.

On free evenings bridge and poker games sprouted up but they never amounted to much. Our demobilization duties soon became so pressing that most of us were putting in long hours and sleep consumed the rest of the time. Then, as spring wore on, a change of pace occurred again—the familiar change which millions of veterans came to describe in a more recent war as "hurry up and wait."

We might have filled the time at the card table or the bar. But there were chances to reach out, to search for duty that was more than perfunctory.

Major Sereno Brett and I heard about a truck convoy that was to cross the country from coast to coast and we were immediately excited. To those who have known only concrete and macadam highways of gentle grades and engineered curves, such a trip might seem humdrum. In those days, we were not sure it could be accomplished at all. Nothing of the sort had ever been attempted.

If only for my grandchildren, who have given up the word "airplane" in favor of "jet," and who have seen pictures of men wandering outside capsules traveling faster than 17,000 miles per hour, I should enlarge a little on American travel at a time when sixty miles an hour was breakneck. But I'll put that history lesson in the back of the book.*

I wanted to go along partly for a lark and partly to learn.

The trip would dramatize the need for better main highways. The use of Army vehicles of almost all types would offer an opportunity for comparative tests. And many Americans would be able to see samples of equipment used in the war just concluded; even a small Renault tank was to be carried along.

The War Department thought that it would be a good idea to send along a number of observers from several branches of the Army. So did we. Instructions came to Camp Meade that two Tank officers were to go. I promptly reported that I would be glad to make the trip, if my superiors approved, and the other man I'd select would be my friend, Sereno Brett. We got our orders and joined the truck train the next day.

An elaborate ceremony had marked the start of the transcontinental expedition. Just south of the White House grounds, the "Zero Milestone," which still survives nine Presidential administrations, was dedicated in the presence of the Secretary of War, Newton Baker; the Chief of Staff, General Peyton March; a handful of general officers; several Senators and Representatives. Each had some-

* See Note 4.

thing to say about the role of these road pioneers; not all of them were brief. My luck was running; we missed the ceremony.

The convoy was then directed to proceed overland to San Francisco without delay, via the Lincoln Highway. Delays, sadly, were to be the order of the day. The convoy had been literally thrown together and there was little discernible control. All drivers had claimed lengthy experience in driving trucks; some of them, it turned out, had never handled anything more advanced than a Model T. Most colored the air with expressions in starting and stopping that indicated a longer association with teams of horses than with internal combustion engines. It took a week or ten days to achieve any kind of march discipline. Roads varied from average to non-existent. Even in the earliest days of the trip where the roads were usually paved, sometimes with concrete, we were well supplied with trouble. First Lieutenant E. R. Jackson, the ordnance observer, was a meticulous recorder of all accidents, mishaps, and small disasters. I'll draw on his records for sampling of the first few days.

The convoy left camp at 8:30 in the morning, dedicated the Zero Milestone at 10:00, and left Washington at 11:15. At 2:50 P.M. the Trailmobile Kitchen broke its coupling. A fan belt broke on a White Observation Car. And a Class B had to be towed into camp at the Frederick Fair Grounds with a broken magneto. The weather was fair and warm, the roads excellent. The convoy had traveled forty-six miles in seven and a quarter hours.

Next, Lieutenant Jackson reported:

July 8.—Departed Frederick, 7 A.M. Fan adjustment let go on Class B ✗414674, 8:30 A.M. Unsafe covered wooden bridge, one mile south of Emmitsburg reached at 9 A.M. Two hours delay due to unsafe and covered bridges, too low for shop trucks, necessitating detours and fording. Engineers rendered valuable work in bridge inspection. Class B ✗414668 stopped to take up brakes at Gettysburg, 2:05 P.M., where we also had lunch.

Militor pulled Class B Machine Shop ✗414319 (10 tons) out of mud on bad detour near Emmitsburg, after two Macks in tandem had failed. Towed in another Class B with disabled magneto, 12 miles over rough detour. Militor made Piney Mountain on 3rd speed, with tow. . . . Mack trucks had difficulty making this grade on low gear. Packards also were lazy on hills. Mack Machine Shop ✗5 damaged top on low bridge between Emmitsburg and Chambersburg, Pa. . . .

There were no accidents to personnel. The weather was fair and warm, the roads excellent, with the exception of the two detours because of the unsafe bridge and the repairs to the highway. The second day the convoy had made sixty-two miles in ten and a half hours.

The third day, July 9, the Lieutenant's journal became repetitious. The convoy moved out at 6:30 in the morning, one vehicle bent its steering wheel drag link by going into a ditch at 7:45, another was held up by a broken accelerator spring, and a third by a sticky exhaust valve which caused the truck to lose compression. Oh, yes, it also had ignition trouble at the same time. It was then ten in the morning.

There was lunch at noon, apparently uneventful, and that afternoon

Class B delayed by bad valve tappet. Ignition trouble on Packard. Class B lost starting crank pin & had to be pushed or towed to start motor. Another Class B had valve and magneto trouble. Considerable magneto trouble on various types of trucks. Encountered heavy grades & altitudes exceeding 2200′ . . .

Other than these, there were no "losses or damages," wrote Lieutenant Jackson. A confirmed optimist, he said that the day's fifty-seven miles had been "excellent driving for untrained personnel." There was an enthusiastic reception in Bedford, Pennsylvania, with two thousand people on hand, a band concert, and street dancing. There were also speeches by a general, two colonels, and Dr. S. M. Johnson of the National Highways Association.

Despite the Lieutenant's good cheer, we had, in three days if my addition is correct, spent twenty-nine hours on the road and moved 165 miles. This was an average hourly speed of about five and two-thirds miles an hour—not quite so good as even the slowest troop train. Before we were through, however, there were times when the pace of our first three days would seem headlong and the four speeches at Bedford only a slight taste of the hot air ahead.

In some places, the heavy trucks broke through the surface of the road and we had to tow them out one by one, with the caterpillar tractor. Some days when we had counted on sixty or seventy or a hundred miles, we would do three or four. Maintenance crews were constantly on the job to keep the vehicles running. They did good work, as I recall. We lost only two vehicles by accidents and one was beyond their help—it rolled down a mountain. The weather continued fair and warm, reported the Lieutenant conscientiously in his meticulous catalogue of disasters.

One by-product of this trip, whose usefulness was entirely unpredictable in 1919, was the nodding acquaintance that I acquired with the face and character of many towns and cities across the east-west axis of the country. We were always, of course, routed through the main streets of each community. Our snail's pace enabled me to observe anything different or unusual. At every overnight stop where there was a town, we were welcomed by a committee and if only to demonstrate that I was not solely an Army propagandist, I tried to learn as much as I could about local interests. Much that I learned was quickly forgotten. But enough stayed with me so that decades later, it had its uses.

Approaching Fort Wayne, Indiana, for example, in the early fall of 1952, the campaign train on which I was traveling was boarded by a group of local citizens. They wanted to tell me the principal concerns of their neighbors about the approaching election. Some of them seemed a little flustered during the introductions and, to put them at ease, I began to ask about certain local enterprises and industries. Several of the younger men and women told me that they had never heard of the firms that I mentioned. Undoubtedly they were sure that I had gotten Fort Wayne mixed up with Kokomo or Keokuk in the manner of politicians. Fortunately for me, an older man who had moved to the edge of the group spoke up, saying that several of the companies—one manufactured pumps, I think— were early Fort Wayne enterprises and had either closed up or moved away during the depression or merged. This seemed to have a relaxing effect on the younger people in the group, they helped put me at my ease, and we had an animated conversation about the growth of cities like Fort Wayne.*

* Later, I learned that after leaving Fort Wayne, the group began to discuss my background knowledge, even if outdated, about their home town. Several expressed surprise that no one who had ever lived there could know so much about the community. Most of them agreed that I had a surprising knowledge, for a professional soldier, of civilian enterprises and the country's cities. One dissenter explained it: "Look, this is the way it works. The General insists on being briefed by his staff. Before he gets to a place where he is going to talk, his researchers tell him everything about it. Before he got on the train, he probably listened to a half-hour report on everything about Fort Wayne since the arrival of the French. If the length of the Maumee River had come up, he would probably have given us the exact figures. Military men are very thorough that way. They have to be."

Mamie and all the Douds met the truck train at South Platte in Nebraska and went along with us for the next three or four days, as far, I think, as Laramie, Wyoming. This was a fine interlude and I decided that it would be nice, being in the West already, to apply for a leave with my family at the end of the tour—if indeed we ever reached the end. We were kept busy taking care of breakdowns and trying to improve our march discipline. But it wasn't all work and it wasn't all discipline. Once we got into a reasonably dependable pattern, so to speak, for machines and men alike, there were effervescent spirits to take advantage of every lull—particularly after we had crossed the Missouri and were in more sparsely populated areas. A few of the stories I have used in later years whenever I could gather about me an audience willing to listen. Whatever most of them may have thought, my son John has always been my most appreciative listener. He has heard them so often that he knows them by heart and often retells them himself. For all I know, they may be passed on from generation to generation of Eisenhowers as family heirlooms.

Some of the commissioned officers were reserves and some were regulars. For most, camping out and taking care of oneself in the field was a matter of course. But as it developed, the train also included a number of young officers from the big cities of the East, who were innocent of knowledge of the West, their only impressions of that section of our country having been gained from highly colored books and stories, usually printed on pulp paper. Before long these men were identified and their inexperience offered a chance for escape from boredom.

Major Brett was a combat veteran from World War I. Sereno was of swarthy complexion, short, strong, and muscular. He had piercing brown eyes, the sort that seemed to look right through the person to whom he was talking. A few of us began to spread the word that Major Brett was a trifle touched, as a result of "shell shock," and was, perhaps, a bit of a crackpot. To confirm this talk, especially in the minds of the youngest officers, he took to setting up his own camp apart from the convoy itself. On pleasant evenings when there was no danger of a shower, he would pick up his bedroll and move out hundreds of yards from the rest of us. While getting into his sleeping bag, he began to utter weird and strident cries—and then, of course, he went to sleep. In the morning when he woke, he'd give one or more of these whoops just on general principles.

These mildly erratic habits began to worry the young men and they asked whether something could be done for him. We didn't want them to be too frightened, so we told them that it was I, and only I, who could control Sereno when he had one of his "fits." These, as time went on, became more frequent, naturally. All that was necessary to quiet him was for me to be present, to lead him off and talk to him for a time. For the next day or so, he would act as normal as anyone else.

It was some time before Sereno's fits became really promising. In the meantime, there were other theatrical possibilities. Early one morning, several of us, riding in a reconnaissance car across the plains of Nebraska, saw a jack rabbit loping along the road. At less than a hundred yards away, he paused. One of us had a .22 caliber rifle and, after stopping the car, shot the rabbit. Sereno had an idea. We carried the rabbit with us until we were a mile or so from our scheduled campsite. There, going off the road for a hundred yards or so, we found a bush against which we propped the now stiffened body of the jack rabbit. From a distance, it looked fairly natural.

That evening, we persuaded two of our eastern friends to drive out with us to do a little shooting. We took only .45 caliber pistols. As we drove along, Sereno suddenly said, "Stop! Stop! Look over there—see that rabbit!" At that distance, and in dimming light, one could see him only in imagination. We described him so carefully that the easterners admitted they could make out his outline. Sereno said that I was one of the finest pistol shots he had ever known. "Ike, why don't you take a crack at him?"

I carefully aimed the pistol in the general direction of the North Pole and fired. Sereno exclaimed, "You've got him! You've got him! He fell."

Never having seen the rabbit in the first place, the easterners agreed with Brett that it was surely a fine shot and they marveled at such skill.

I sat with them while Sereno raced out to pick up the big jack. Held by his ears, the rabbit must have been almost two feet long. Sereno brought the rabbit toward us but when he came within thirty or forty yards and was sure that we had all seen it, he threw it aside and said, "Well, let's turn back."

The two easterners protested. The rabbit would make a nice addition to our rations. We had to explain to them, patiently, that jack rabbits were absolutely no good—they were tough, stringy, tasteless (which they actually are). The easterners continued to act as though we were quite wasteful, but we didn't go back. No matter how un-appetizing the ordinary jack rabbit, we didn't dare let them see one which had been shot twelve hours earlier.

There were other modest hoaxes. At a spot in Wyoming, Sereno, on a clear night, climbed a bluff 150 feet or so above the camp, sat on this lofty height, and moaned and howled coyote-like. It wasn't too good an imitation for one who knew the real thing, I must say. Then he slept. Rising in the dim light of dawn, he threw his bedroll over the cliff and it came rolling into camp. We woke up, the easterners wondering whether he would follow. Instead, he came racing down a steep but perfectly passable path, kicking gravel, screaming, yelling, throwing things, and heading directly for the tent of one of the Easterners. The man, who had been looking out of the flaps of his tent, took off, shouting to me, "Stop him! Stop him!"

Well, I had my chore and dutifully performed it.

At times I was suspicious that these eastern types were doing a bit of acting themselves. They might have been leading us on. Still, there were many miles to go and our little troupe polished its per-formances.

Perhaps our finest hour was in western Wyoming. We had camped within a mile of a little settlement that boasted a combination restaurant and soft-drink parlor, a post office, a telegraph station, two general stores, and a half dozen houses. Going over there for a visit, we decided that one of the easterners back in camp, a man who was more gullible than he should have been about conditions be-yond the Hudson River, should be given a taste of the authentic West.

Sereno made friends with several of the local people who were in the restaurant. After he talked to them, we took a table and waited for the arrival of the easterner and a few of the other boys.

While we sat enjoying our dinner, the natives began to talk and argue heatedly and loudly about the possibility of Indian trouble. It appeared that an outbreak was imminent. They were terribly dis-appointed, we overheard, that the motor convoy had come into their region without arms. They had been informed that we carried nothing but a few pistols, with a .22 caliber sporting rifle here and there. Then they addressed us directly.

"We've been hoping you'd get here," one man said, "but I'm not sure it's going to help. We thought the Army might frighten the Indians away." He said they'd been troublesome lately and the community had hoped to have relief from their depredations for a while. But he added that the Indians were shrewd and that by now they knew that the visiting soldiers had no arms.

As they went on, Sereno and several of us expressed our anxiety. Before we left for camp, we proclaimed our intention of mounting a guard. We borrowed an old shotgun from one of the townspeople and loaded it with shells (from which we had removed the shot, so that in no event could anyone get hurt). Then we arranged for sentinels.

Courageously, Sereno and I and a few others took the early duty. We allotted the dreary small hours of the night to the officer for whom this episode was staged. Sereno, during his tour, just before midnight, let out an occasional shriek, not Sereno-like but more in the manner of carnival Indians. This added to the tension. As Sereno came in off post, we took concealed positions to watch our man.

The recruit took his duties seriously, marching at attention around the camp as if on parade. Brett and several others spread out and from a distance would let out an occasional short yelp. Finally, just as we hoped, the sentry let go with both barrels—to arouse the camp, he explained later.

After he explained, at length, we all went back to bed, pleased with ourselves.

There had been no Indian trouble since 1890, of course, but another kind of threat loomed instantly. It happened that one of the duties of our victim was writing up daily progress reports to be telegraphed back to the War Department. We learned that he had drafted a telegram in which, among other things, he described the local Indian trouble and reported dissatisfaction among the local population because we had come in with no means of defending the community in the event of attack.

Faster than any vehicle in the convoy, we shot off in all directions to find the man who was carrying that message to the telegraph office. We found him, took the story to the commanding officer, and pointed out that if such news reached the Adjutant General, he was unlikely to understand our brand of humor. The commanding officer went along with the gag, crossed out the Indian part of the telegram, and sent the rest of it off, not informing the man who had drafted it in the first place. Thereby, a number of us were saved lengthy explanations in original and three or more carbons.

At camp in the Nevada desert, we decided to play bridge. Nearby was an old wooden skeleton of a structure, covered entirely with screening. Because it was fly and bug proof, we hung a number of lanterns about the place, set up empty boxes and boards for two tables, and we began to play. My young eastern friend was on hand as a kibitzer. Before long, turning over my place to the easterner, I excused myself and went to find Sereno, who did not play bridge. He was, as usual, quite imaginative and after a short planning meeting, I went back to the bridge game and sat down while my stand-in finished out a rubber.

Suddenly, through the screen door came Sereno, screaming, "Help, he's killing me! He's killing me!" His neck and shirt front was awash in blood. Another young officer chased him into the enclosure, waving a knife also smeared with ketchup. Without pause and running blindly, Sereno rushed right through our flimsy bridge table, with cards, players, chairs flying and Sereno running on in circles. Finally, he dashed out the door again, his assailant stumbling after him.

The man for whom this had been arranged nearly fainted. He was white, and his hands were shaking. He did have the strength to cry out to me, "Colonel, you let him get out of your sight!" Now I had to rush out and join in the clamor and confusion. When I caught up with the other two, we had to devise a finish. We found a few bandages, did slapdash first aid and bound them around Sereno's neck and shoulder. The work was not artistic -but with one arm in a sling he did look like a wounded, in fact, a punished man. He wore the bandages for four or five days until one of the doctors solemnly pronounced him well enough to move his arm; no tendons had been cut and the jugular vein had not been touched.

From the beginning, we had expected that the fellow we had been riding in our horseplay would realize what was up. We had always intended to tell him long before we reached San Francisco. Instead we found that he had taken the whole thing seriously. Any attempt to explain it would humiliate him. This wasn't the idea and so the half dozen of us involved pledged that we would never, as long as any of us was in active service, tell the facts to our friend—who incidentally we all liked very much. I am sure that in the almost half-century since, he has had no inkling that what he and one or two others went through on that journey was as part of an audience for a troupe of traveling clowns.

We reached San Francisco at long last, although even in California, where the highways were the best we had encountered, we averaged less than ten miles an hour. Lieutenant Jackson continued to make his reports faithfully. On September 5, the next to last day, he wrote:

Departed Stockton, 6:15 A.M. . . . Drove over best section of entire Lincoln Highway. 2 Rikers & Packard broke fan belts. Class B trucks had broken spark plug porcelain, broken fan belts & brakes required adjustment. Indian motorcycle broke control wire.

But that was the last of our troubles except for final speeches. Now clothing was issued for a parade into San Francisco. We were met east of Oakland by city officials and the fire department, were escorted through flag-festooned streets, with whistles blowing around the Bay. There were elaborate electrical and fireworks displays, a dinner at the Hotel Oakland, a dance at the municipal auditorium. The next day we crossed San Francisco Bay on two ferries, paraded through the city, received our medals, and listened.

In Sacramento, the governor, William D. Stephens, had compared us to the "Immortal Forty-Niners." He reminded everyone of the hardship, privation, discouragement, and even death incurred to reach this new land. "Their blood is the blood of the western country," he said, "strong—virile—self-reliant. . . . So, in this journey of yours across the plains . . ." etc. On the last day, the speeches ran on and on, in a similar vein.

The weather was fair and warm.

The trip had been difficult, tiring, and fun. I think that every officer on the convoy had recommended in his report that efforts should be made to get our people interested in producing better roads. A third of a century later, after seeing the autobahns of modern Germany and knowing the asset those highways were to the Germans, I decided, as President, to put an emphasis on this kind of road building. When we finally secured the necessary congressional approval, we started the 41,000 miles of super highways that are already proving their worth. This was one of the things that I felt deeply about, and I made a personal and absolute decision to see that the nation would benefit by it. The old convoy had started me thinking about good, two-lane highways, but Germany had made me see the wisdom of broader ribbons across the land.

The request for leave was granted and I had four weeks with Mamie, our son, and her family. The Douds were ready for their annual trip to San Antonio to spend the winter. Because there was as yet no place for Mamie and Icky to live in or near Camp Meade, she would go along until we could make arrangements to be together again. I joined them for the early part of the trip, making mine almost literally a busman's holiday.

We had no sooner left Denver than we encountered rain. Never ceasing rains. As we got into Oklahoma, all the roads were mud and we bogged down. There were moments when I thought neither the automobile, the bus, nor the truck had any future whatever. Finally we got as far as Lawton, near Fort Sill, the artillery post. From there we could go no further. We stayed a full week, living in the hotel.

That was the week of the World Series when Cincinnati of the National League met Chicago of the American League. As in my boyhood, news about the series came by telegram. These were posted in the windows of drug stores and newspaper plants. Mr. Doud and I watched every bulletin, wondering why the great Chicago White Sox could not get going. Each of us considered himself a baseball expert. We spent hours debating what was wrong with Chicago and we not only plotted up every mistake of the Sox manager and coaches, we knew exactly how Cincinnati could be trimmed. We little dreamed that we were second-guessing an event that was to stand in athletics as an all-time low for disloyalty and sellout of integrity.

Out of the "Black Sox" scandal, I learned a lesson and began to form a caution that, at least subconsciously, stayed with me. It must be remembered that in the fall of 1919, the war over and the country back to business as usual, the World Series was a national preoccupation. Millions waited for each telegraph bulletin, scrutinized it word by word. Newspaper reporting was factual. The stories after each game, narrating the play, were strictly objective. But stark facts and objective reports could not give the whole story.

In the passage of years, whether because of the Black Sox scandal or not, I grew increasingly cautious about making judgments based solely on reports. Behind every human action, the truth may be hidden. But the truth may also lie behind some other action or arrangement, far off in time and place. Unless circumstances and responsibility demanded an instant judgment I learned to reserve mine until the last proper moment. This was not always popular.

During the White House years I found support from a distinguished American poet who had had more years than most of us to appraise life and had used them well and wisely. At a time when I was being criticized by many people who thought I was moving too slowly about matters close to their hearts, Robert Frost visited my office one day. He gave me a book of his poetry. On the flyleaf, at the end of the inscription, he wrote:

"The strong are saying nothing until they see."

It was a compliment that I appreciated and needed. His poetic craftsmanship had enabled him to express in eight words a truth many of us take years to learn, if we learn at all. I like his maxim perhaps best of all.

CHAPTER XII

Colonel George Patton

WHEN I returned to Camp Meade in the autumn, many changes had taken place. Senior officers of the Tank Corps who had seen action in France were back. Among these men the one who interested me most, and whom I learned to like best, was a fellow named Patton. Colonel George S. Patton was tall, straight, and soldierly looking. His most noticeable characteristic was a high, squeaking voice, quite out of keeping with his bearing. He had two passions, the military service and polo. Side issues for George Patton were pleasure riding—he had a fine stable of good horses—and pistol shooting. From the beginning he and I got along famously. I did not play polo (neither my background nor my knee was much help) but I was devoted to riding and shooting. Both of us were students of current military doctrine. Part of our passion was a belief in tanks—a belief derided at the time by others.

Before I left on the transcontinental trip, we had started at Meade tactical and technical schools on this new weapon. After my return, those of us who had not been abroad during the war badgered George and the others who had taken part in battle into giving us detailed accounts of plans and operations. We began to evolve what we thought to be a new and better tank doctrine.

In their World War I mission, tanks—as we understood it from battle orders and memoranda—were to precede and accompany attacking infantry. The prescribed distance between the deployed line of tanks and the leading infantry wave was about fifty yards. The immediate battle task of the tank was to destroy machine-gun nests, whose interlocking bands of fire made it impossible for infantry alone to move effectively. The enemy of the tank was field artillery (and later, the anti-tank gun, of course).

Because the tank was looked upon as a front-line infantry weapon in attack, those who followed the accepted doctrine were not interested in developing any machine that moved at higher speeds than infantry could walk—some three miles an hour. They did want the heaviest defensive armor practicable, armor that would be invulnerable against anything but large-caliber guns.

George and I and a group of young officers thought this was wrong. Tanks could have a more valuable and more spectacular role. We believed that they should be speedy, that they should attack by surprise and in mass. By making good use of the terrain in advance, they could break into the enemy's defensive positions, cause confusion, and by taking the enemy front line in reverse, make possible not only an advance by infantry, but envelopments of, or actual breakthroughs in, whole defensive positions.

Through a year or more of work, we expanded our theories and refined the tactical ideas. We described in some detail the characteristics of the tank we believed best for the American Army. We wanted speed, reliability, and firepower. We wanted armor that would be proof against machine guns and light field guns, but not so heavy as to damage mobility.

We were constantly experimenting. A man named Christy was designing a model that we thought had many advantages over those of the war vintage. Experimenting with what we had, we tore one tank to pieces, item by item, until there was no nut or bolt that had not been removed from the mechanism, including the engine. Now if a clock that has been disassembled can frighten the amateur, a tank, even a small one, is infinitely worse. I had doubts that we would ever restore the vehicle to running order.

We started the reassembly during our afternoon hours and so carefully had we done the work, that no pieces were left over and the machine operated when we were finished.

The Camp Meade reservation was broken up here and there by woods and deep ravines. We decided that by using the terrain to keep tanks under cover until we approached an imaginary enemy line, we could get surprise on our side. As in all forms of combat, even practice exercises, we were convinced that surprise attack would be far more successful than one without it.

The small tanks—the Renaults—bogged down much more easily than the big, clumsy Mark VIIIs of American manufacture. The engine in the Mark VIII was the Liberty, originally designed for airplanes and adapted for tank use. Often unreliable, the Liberty was powerful. We devised a system of using Mark VIIIs to tow the smaller Renaults through depressions and up slopes where they, on their own power, could not make the grade. On the side of each Mark VIII was an inch-thick steel cable, eighteen or twenty feet long. We used these as tow ropes to pull one, two, or three Renaults in tandem. This worked pretty well, increasing the small tanks' range.

With our commands out in the field one day, we were working out an attack problem, and testing our scheme through a deep ravine that was muddy at the bottom. Everything began fairly well. We got the first big tank across the obstacle. We had hitched three light tanks to it; we wanted to see how many big tanks we would need to get a platoon of small ones across such a ravine. Two of the Renaults became mired down and the big tank had to give out maximum power.

Patton and I were standing on the upslope as the big tank came through, crawling painfully to the top of the ravine. The noise was almost deafening; none of the tanks in those days was noted for silent operation. But in the midst of the racket we heard a ripping sound and we looked around just in time to see one of the cables part. As it broke, the front half whirled around like a striking black snake and the flying end, at machine-gun bullet speed, snapped past our faces, cutting off brush and saplings as if the ground had been shaved with a sharp razor.

We were too startled at the moment to realize what had happened but then we looked at each other. I'm sure I was just as pale as George.

That evening after dinner, he said: "Ike, were you as scared as I was?"

"I was afraid to bring the subject up," I said. We were certainly not more than five or six inches from sudden death.

Immediately instructions were published to our units that the utmost care was to be taken in the use of cables, that whenever extra strain was put on them, all personnel should be kept out of the way and tank personnel should be inside with all hatches closed.

We had no opportunity to use the small cannon with which the big tanks were armed but we were anxious to discover the best kind of machine gun to be obtained, and to test at length their accuracy, range, reliability, and, above all, their endurance. One day we took a .30 caliber Browning water-cooled machine gun into the field. We set it up where we could put the targets in front of a backstop and shoot to our hearts' content. At the time we had a lot of old ammunition. Because it showed evidence of deterioration, the War Department allowed us to use almost unlimited amounts.

Sustained firing does not improve a rifled weapon's accuracy of fire. As a machine gun heats up and the barrel expands, the rifling begins to be ineffective and the bullets fly in a pattern called "keyholing"—that is, instead of rotating around their long axis, they fly helter-skelter through the air. Our target that day was too far away for us to tell when keyholing began. Every few minutes or so, when we thought the gun might no longer be accurate, we walked down to take a look at the targets. In the first bursts we fired, we saw no change in pattern; about the third trial we decided to take an extra-long belt and fire it until it was near the end.

While George operated the gun, I used a pair of strong field glasses. As most soldiers know, if an observer concentrates intently on the trajectory of bullets he can often see how they are behaving in the air. After George had fired a long burst, the bullets were beginning to act strangely. I told him we ought to have another look at the target. We started forward, one on either side of the gun. Naturally, we converged to continue our conversation as we walked down. When we neared each other, the machine gun suddenly fired.

We both jumped back, looked at the gun, and then at each other in consternation. As we did so, there was another discharge from the weapon. "George," I shouted, "that gun's so hot it's just going to keep on shooting!" We raced off to one side, then ran back, and George twisted the belt so that no other rounds could feed into the piece. After that we looked up sheepishly. We had acted like a couple of recruits.

After the breaking cable and the self-firing gun, we decided that we had about used up our luck. As it turned out, we were to need luck but of another kind entirely—and George Patton, who was to become the finest leader in military pursuit that the United States Army has known, had little enough.

All our experimenting and training took time. If some of the conservatives in the War Department had known exactly what we were up to, they might have condemned it as a waste of time for soldiers who might better be employed in close-order drill and road marches. Eventually, these seniors had their inning. Until then, the small group around George and me knew we were pioneering with a weapon that could change completely the strategy and tactics of land warfare. In one respect, these circumstances were better than battle itself. Trial and error and the testing of alternatives is experiment and research—but in action, you are offered few second chances.

Every mistake we made, every correction, every scrap of information about the exploitation of terrain, was added to World War I's lessons. These were the beginnings of a comprehensive tank doctrine that in George Patton's case would make him a legend. Naturally, as enthusiasts, we tried to win converts. This wasn't easy but George and I had the enthusiasm of zealots.

As the months went by, we analyzed tactical problems used at Leavenworth in Command and General Staff School courses. After comparing our solutions with those approved by the Leavenworth faculty, we would add to the forces involved a complement of our dream tanks and solve it again. The troops supported by tanks always "won," in our revised solution.

Both of us began articles for the military journals; he for the Cavalry, I for the Infantry. Then I was called before the Chief of Infantry.

I was told that my ideas were not only wrong but dangerous and that henceforth I would keep them to myself. Particularly, I was not to publish anything incompatible with solid infantry doctrine. If I did, I would be hauled before a court-martial.

George, I think, was given the same message. This was a blow. One effect was to bring George and me even closer. We spent a great deal of time together, riding through our respective commands during the day, and talking, studying, and blowing off steam at night. With George's temper and my own capacity for something more than mild irritation, there was surely more steam around the Officers Quarters than at the post laundry.

Word arrived that the rifle matches at Camp Perry were to be resumed, now that the war was over, and the Tank Corps would be allowed to send a team. As a new organization, we were placed in the lowest classification. This was fine with us. We had a number of first-rate marksmen at Meade and we'd make a splendid showing in the C class. We set up rigid training, with incessant practice, eliminated cigarettes and drinking, limited the amount of coffee a man could have during the day. For competitive purposes, we established two teams. George did not like this form of rifle sport and he was non-shooting captain of one team while I captained the other. We debated every hole in the targets, shouting out claims of which shot had touched the black, etc.

Of course there was a spot of wagering. Whenever soldiers are asked to forecast anything, the one sure development is off-track betting. But the bets were small, with the losers paying off in Coca-Colas, for the most part. Morale was elaborately high. Then we got an order from the War Department that there would be no Tank Corps team. The Corps was to be only a branch of the Infantry.

Ultimately, we learned not to regret the long practice sessions. There was no trip to Camp Perry but it had been good training for many soldiers and from our enlisted group certain fine non-commissioned officers emerged. These men became excellent instructors.

George was an impatient as well as a self-confident man. When the defense legislation of 1920 was passed, the Tank Corps as such was abolished and was made part of Infantry. George applied for transfer back to Cavalry. This arm would, he hoped, display more imagination and receptiveness to ideas. I, a little less abrupt, began to hope for another assignment. In a new atmosphere, I might be more persuasive than in months past and might influence my superiors to take a look at the further possibilities of the tank.

Before George and I were separated, my little family had been reunited. First Mamie had come alone from Texas and had taken a room in a home in Laurel, a small town a few miles from Meade. She stayed a month but because I could see her only a few evenings and because we both so missed our little son, Icky, and worried about him while he was separated from us, she went back to San Antonio until we could all be together.

A few months later, permission was granted for post commanders to assign wartime barracks as quarters for officers and their families. All expenses of remodeling, renovating, and furnishing such barracks were to be borne by the officer himself. I was allotted such a set and George Patton a neighboring one. (At the time he was commanding officer of a light brigade, equipped with the old Renaults, and I had the heavy brigade, with the Mark VIII.) In the early summer of 1920, Mamie came back to help me transform an ancient set of barracks into a home.

The building was two stories high. Partitions had to be torn out, others built. One of the old common bathrooms, which had a concrete floor, was made over into a kitchen. Smaller rooms were thrown together to make a dining room. Upstairs, we created three fairly decent bedrooms. Much of the work was done with the help of soldiers who volunteered and whom I paid a nominal hourly sum. We had men who were skillful in revising plumbing and rerouting it. The existing pipes were good for sanitizing thirty or more men, but were not much good for washing three people, one at a time. We scrubbed and waxed floors and brushed buckets of paint onto beaverboard nailed over the rough lumber partitions.

A rented home can be distinguished from an owned home, I've always been told, because the lawn is late in being mowed, the garden in being weeded, the front porch in being painted. Renters, they say, are usually poor custodians of property. If these observers are right, an Army post should be a rather dreary demonstration of minimal care. All the inhabitants know is that their tenancy won't last long. Post commanders may issue orders that lawns be cut regularly and fresh paint applied. But no orders can make enthusiastic gardeners out of soldiers. Nevertheless, at most Army posts, the families are careful homemakers.

There's little likelihood that they will enjoy the shade of the trees they plant or that they will ever see the finest hours of shrubs and perennials that require years to reach maturity. But they are avid readers of seed catalogues and tireless sowers of vegetables and annual flowers. For years, I read through many a winter's evening with the Burpee's catalogue in my lap. Toward the end of my active military career, the care I gave my vegetables at Fort Myer and my vigilance in guarding the garden against the raids of squirrels and crows, even to standing guard over it on occasion with a rifle, earned a certain amount of comment from my neighbors. Perhaps, they said, this is one of the reasons we won World War II. Others thought that agriculture did not seem to be a part of my duties as Chief of Staff.

I suppose that neither West Point nor almost five years of Army duty had eradicated the feeling that spring meant gardening or that in every season of the year there are outdoor chores to be done. I had put in too many years coaxing corn and tomatoes and green grass up out of the Kansas soil ever to give it up. In the barren surroundings of Camp Meade, we had a challenge to test any gardener's enthusiasm and endurance.

Camp Meade was sand. There was scarcely a blade of grass to be found in the entire encampment. With a few men who knew something about landscaping, we got busy. They plowed up our front yard and sowed it with a sturdy grass. They even built a low picket fence around it, which they painted white. At the end, we were proud of the place which, counting labor and everything, had cost us about $700 or $800, not counting the labor Mamie and I had invested in the old barracks.

Perhaps it was the struggle to make it livable that made the place so attractive to us. Altogether, it was about two and a half months before we felt able to send for Icky, who was living with Mamie's aunt in Boone, Iowa. (For her trouble and his keep, we had paid her $100, somewhat under the going rates, I'm sure, but all we could afford out of our salary.) When Icky arrived, we settled down.

Along with the normal evening study that George and I continued, we also managed to find time twice a week for a poker game. Two members of my staff and I were regulars there. We normally were rather insistent that we play only with bachelors or others who could afford to lose. But there were a number of men going through the camp for discharge who had money to burn and who practically forced themselves into the games. This was true also of a few who were assigned to the regular command.

One man who appeared every night was a uniquely unskilled player. His style made me think of that old maxim of Hafiz, "If he being young and unskillful/plays for shekels of silver and gold/ take his money my son praising Allah/the fool was made to be sold." This was the philosophy which was part of my poker playing until I was shocked into a completely different attitude. The young man came to me one morning and asked whether I would take government bonds to pay for his losses of the night before.

I listened to his story. "Okay," I said, "I'd be happy to."

Then it turned out that these were "Baby Bonds," patiently saved by his wife during the years he had been away to war. Their face value was $50. I accepted them at that. But I was depressed; in fact, I felt like a dog. After thinking it over, I went to my other friends in the game and told them the story. We tried to remember exactly how much the man had lost. The total was considerable.

Without any argument, we agreed to find some way to let him get his money back.

We didn't want to hurt his pride by making him a charity case, so we decided to allow him to win. In our belated compassion, we agreed that he ought to win back not only the Baby Bonds but something extra. This was not achieved easily. One of the hardest things known to man is to make a fellow win in poker who plays as if bent on losing every nickel. Our system was to guess when the man we were trying to help had a good hand. Then we'd step in to drive everybody out. After we had driven them out with betting, which wasn't easy to do without driving the principal out, we'd let him win the hand.

It was trouble. For example, at one point the captain, my adjutant, found himself with a good hand. If he were called, he would have won easily. Since he had already drawn, it would have looked silly for him to throw in his hand. The only way to disqualify himself was to have too many cards. While the others were picking up their hands, he dropped his cards on one that was lying in front of him, and then said: "I'm sorry. I called for two cards and wanted only one. Now I have six cards. My hand is dead." That was just one stratagem. But it took until nearly midnight to get the job done. Finally the game broke up.

The three of us then divided our losses and I told the others that I would go to Colonel Patton, the man's commanding officer, and suggest that he give an order that no one in his brigade be allowed to play cards for money. This would be easy because George was no enthusiast about card playing. We were happy. The man had gotten back his bonds and almost the exact amount we thought he had lost.

The next day he dropped in and said, "You know what's happened? Old Patton has just stopped card playing for everybody in his brigade. Isn't that just my luck—just as I was started on a real winning streak?"

I had the presence of mind to say, "Well, you know that Patton's a tough man. If you disobey any order of his, it will be a mistake. Don't get into any card games. You can't get into ours because I can't allow it—and don't get into any others."

I decided that I had to quit playing poker. It was not because I didn't enjoy the excitement of the game—I really love to play. But it had become clear that it was no game to play in the Army. Most of us lived on our salaries. Most losers were bound to be spending not only their own money but their families'. If we had stayed with our original intention of playing only with bachelors, perhaps this could have been all right. But now I felt that it was a bad idea—and from then on I did not play with anybody in the Army.

Social life among the married couples was rather thin in the post-war months at Meade. Occasionally, a visitor would come up from Washington and his host would stretch himself to arrange a reception and dinner. One of the incalculable benefits I got from my friendship with George Patton was an invitation to meet a man who, as it turned out, was to have a tremendous influence on my life.

Brigadier General Fox Conner had been the operations officer at General Headquarters for General Pershing in France. When the Conners accepted an invitation from the Pattons to Sunday dinner, Mamie and I were included among the guests.

After dinner, in early afternoon, the General said to George that he would like to see the schools we had devised. He also wanted to hear our ideas about tanks. This was meat and drink to George and me.

General Conner went down to the shops with us, found a chair to sit in, and then began to ask questions. Apparently, George had told him about our friendship and some of our ideas about tanks, so the General directed most of his questions at me. Some could be answered briefly, while others required long explanations.

By the time he had finished, it was almost dark and he was ready to go home. He said little except that it was interesting, he thanked us, and that was that.

A few months later, General Conner sent word to me that he was going to Panama to command an infantry brigade. Would I like to go along with him as executive officer? This was a wonderful chance because, with our dream of a separate tank force shattered, I knew it would be an opportunity to have a tour of service with such a man. General Conner's reputation was splendid: he was one of the Army "brains."

I told my own commanding general about the opportunity. He countered that he had few experienced field officers and could not spare me.

As usual, at the prospect of a change, I had gotten my hopes up high. It was time, I felt, to do something other than what I was doing. I was too much out of sympathy with the War Department ideas of the day concerning tanks and I argued the point until General Rockenbach said he would send my application on to the War Department even though he knew it would be disapproved. He was true to his word. He sent it on and it was turned down.

CHAPTER XIII

The Tragic Road to Panama

IF MEADE was at times frustrating, it was also a school where I gained additional experience in handling men and in studying weapons.

At the beginning of my time there, I took on the football coaching job under instructions from General Rockenbach. We set up a training table, using the advice of the best trainers and dietitians I could find. Then I started to work. Although I did not believe in using officers on football teams, it was customary in the Army at that time. I did agree to have one officer on the team. If he proved capable as a player, he'd be able to exercise quick and effective leadership during the game. If rank has its privileges, it also carries weight in a football huddle. I found a man named Kelley, inexperienced in football, but who was young, enthusiastic, and who had been a sprinter in college. He had a good throwing arm and I used him at quarterback. Our teams did well through 1919, 1920, 1921.

Barracks or not, Mamie, Icky, and I had settled down to a fuller family life than we'd ever known. Icky, naturally, was in his element, and he thoroughly enjoyed his role as the center of attention. For a little boy just getting interested in the outside world, few places could have been more exciting than Meade. Deafening noises of the tanks enthralled him. A football scrimmage was pure delight. And a parade with martial music set him aglow. I was inclined to display Icky and his talents at the slightest excuse, or without one, for that matter. In his company, I'm sure I strutted a bit and Mamie was thoroughly happy that, once again, her two men were with her.

By now, I was entirely out of debt. Perhaps we were in a position to enjoy an amenity or two. Possibly we could afford a maid who would help Mamie in a makeshift house that required constant attention. We hired a girl in the neighborhood who was ready to work and who seemed both pleasant and efficient. When she accepted the job, a chain of circumstances began, linking us to a tragedy from which we never recovered.

We learned later that just before we met her the girl had suffered an attack of scarlet fever. Although her cure was quick and she showed no evidence of illness, the doctors finally concluded that she had brought the disease to the camp—and that our young son had contracted it from her.

We did everything possible to save him. The camp doctor brought in specialists from the nearby Johns Hopkins Medical School in Baltimore. During his illness, the doctor did not allow me into his room. But there was a porch on which I was allowed to sit and I could look into the room and wave to him. Occasionally, they would let me come to the door just to speak to Icky. I haunted the halls of the hospital. Hour after hour, Mamie and I could only hope and pray. In those days, before modern medicine eliminated scarlet fever as a childhood scourge, hope and prayer were the only possibilities for parents. At the turn of the year, we lost our firstborn son.

I do not know how others have felt when facing the same situation, but I have never known such a blow. Within a week he was gone. I didn't know what to do. I blamed myself because I had often taken his presence for granted, even though I was proud of him and of all the evidence that he was developing as a fine, normal boy.

Icky was completely devoted to soldiers. My own command had gotten together not long after his arrival and bought him a tank uniform, including overcoat, overseas cap, and all the rest. Every time they were out on a tank drill, one of them would come and ask Mamie's permission to take him along. They would put him in a tank; he was just one of the boys. With his death a pall fell over the camp, at least our part of it. When we started the long trip to Denver, to bury him with the others in Mamie's family, the entire command turned out in respect to little Icky. We were completely crushed. For Mamie, the loss was heartbreaking, and her grief in turn would have broken the hardest heart.

This was the greatest disappointment and disaster in my life, the one I have never been able to forget completely. Today when I think of it, even now as I write of it, the keenness of our loss comes back to me as fresh and as terrible as it was in that long dark day soon after Christmas, 1920. My wife and I have arranged that when it comes our time to be buried, to be laid away in our final resting place, we shall have him with us.

In the months that followed, no matter what activities and preoccupations there were, we could never forget the death of the boy. Sometime after my application for transfer to the Canal Zone had been disapproved, orders came out of the blue for me to proceed to that station.

What had happened? Fox Conner, a warm friend of General Pershing, now the Chief of Staff, had informed the Chief that he wanted me as his staff officer. The red tape was torn to pieces, orders were issued, and I was to arrive at the new station by January of 1922.

The arrival of the furniture packers from the Quartermaster Depot marked the beginning of our departure from Camp Meade. These men can, out of long experience, descend upon a household and leave it in a few hours a total void. Because our goods were to travel by sea and possibly be stored within a warehouse in the tropics, the Quartermaster men did an especially careful job.

Despite their expertise, Army movers have certain qualities in common with others. Delicate objects like china and porcelain are tossed by the man at the table or cabinet shelf to another man stationed beside a barrel. He drops the article in, drops on a covering wad of straw, catches the next piece, and repeats the process until the container is full. A third man, armed with a hammer and nails, attaches the cover and rolls barrel and contents like so much scrap iron down the steps and onto the waiting truck. On the other hand, articles that can stand almost any amount of abuse such as pillows and bedding and ironwork are carefully packed into cases made of the heaviest timber available, beautifully and meticulously lined with excelsior and paper padding.

General Rockenbach was very kind. He gave a party in our honor and presented Mamie with a handsome silver vase inscribed *To the Mascot of the Tank Corps Football Team*. He made his car and chauffeur available to us during the last hectic days after our own little car, a Model T Ford, had been sent up to New York for shipment on the transport to Panama.

Incidentally, when the car had been placed aboard, the ship's captain suddenly got orders to go to the mid-Atlantic to aid a storm-tossed transport just returning from Europe with several hundred bodies of our soldiers who had been slain during World War I. (The name of our ship was the *San Miguel;* as I recall the transport bringing back the bodies was the *Buford.*) The storm was severe but fortunately both ships reached port safely. The Eisenhower Model T had not done as well.

It hadn't been properly lashed down and during the storm it broke loose and raced around the deck to the eternal detriment of its finish and shape. The bumps and salt spray had made of it a rather sorry, although still mobile, vehicle.

In the meantime, we had gone to New York for embarkation and had to wait for the ship to return. With meager resources, we had several extra days to spend in that city. We suddenly developed an appetite for low-cost meals and museums where no entrance fee was charged. Finally, the great day arrived and we started on our first foreign tour of military service.

The accommodations were miserable. The Army Transport Corps evidently based their model loading pattern on advice given by sardine canners. To add flavor to this intimate use of space, we ran into a heavy storm along about Cape Hatteras. I was in charge of the enlisted detachment. Soldiers usually make poor sailors and my men were determined to prove the rule. We were busy day and night trying to make life easier for men who were convinced that neither they nor the ship would survive the voyage.

We rode the storm for several days before reaching Puerto Rico, our first stop, and along the way few passengers were healthy enough to come to the dining room for meals. Mamie and I found that we were fairly good sailors. In fact, in all the years in which we have used ships of various types, I think neither of us ever missed a meal because of the well-named and uncomfortable *mal de mer*.

From Puerto Rico we sailed directly to Panama and were met there by General Conner's aide. He helped us with arrangements for getting to Camp Gaillard with our gear, including the automobile. (The special distributor and carburetor I had installed at Camp Meade had been stolen.) When we got to the point on the Canal nearest to our station, we left the train to make our way to Gaillard.

The first necessity was to walk hundreds of yards in the tropical heat across the Canal on one of the lock gates.

For Mamie that walk was the worst possible avenue of entry to a foreign station. Crossing it, she probably thought that nothing in the United States was ever like this. An authentic American, and like many native Iowans, she considered the whole world a wonderful place especially when she was living neatly between New York and San Francisco. She thoroughly believed in the broadening influences of foreign travel—if she knew she could get back home soon.

Panama was not the best introduction to life beyond our borders. The houses at our new station were old, flimsy survivals of Canal construction days. To keep vermin out was difficult. They were infested with bats; and Mamie hated bats with a passion. Frequent thundershowers penetrated roofs and walls and windows and made living there too damp for comfort—except for those black, winged unwelcome visitors who seemed to thrive in the Turkish bath our house became after every storm.

Although Mamie did a little horseback riding, she never has and never will consider outdoor sports a worthwhile way to spend her time. During our Canal Zone tour, there was little to find in the way of entertainment, except a dance on Friday night and a club bridge party on Wednesdays.

The only easy way to get back and forth across the isthmus was by rail. Indeed, it was rumored that the railway company, owned by the government, of course, would not allow any trans-isthmian roads to be built because their use would reduce revenues from necessary travel back and forth. This gave us material of an evening for gripe sessions about bureaucrats and their ways.

We could, by advance arrangement, get an automobile across the isthmus by driving on top of the Canal gates. But this caused the lockmen a great deal of trouble and our contact with the outside world, consequently, was not close.

Although our families occasionally went shopping in the city, in the main we lived out of the commissaries and post exchange at Gaillard. Monotony was relieved for most of us by the unstable nature of the land. We lived on the edge of the Culebra Cut, where we were constantly bothered by mud slides that went into the Canal, blocking it to traffic. Gigantic dredges would tackle the task of moving the slide back into the hinterland for a few days, weeks, or months before the next mammoth movement. We didn't consider the slides a hazard; they were a foil to the daily routine.

It wasn't until I visited Panama after World War II, when I flew back and forth across the area, that I saw to my horror that the entire post where we had once lived had slid into the Canal and had to be laboriously dredged out of the main channel.

Except for such dubious entertainments, *my* tour of duty was one of the most interesting and constructive of my life. The main reason was the presence of one man, General Fox Conner.

The commander of our brigade was a practical officer, down to earth, equally at home in the company of the most important people in the region and with any of the men in any regiment. General Conner was a tall, easygoing Mississippian, he never put on airs of any kind, and he was as open and honest as any man I have known. One change in my attitude he accomplished quickly—with profound and endless results.

In asking me a casual question, General Conner discovered that I had little or no interest left in military history. My aversion was a result of its treatment at West Point as an out-and-out memory course. In the case of the Battle of Gettysburg, for instance, each student was instructed to memorize the names of every brigadier in the opposing armies and to know exactly where his unit was stationed at every hour during the three days of the battle. Little attempt was made to explain the meaning of the battle, why it came about, what the commanders hoped to accomplish, and the real reason why Lee invaded the North the second time. If this was military history, I wanted no part of it.

General Conner made no comment. I found myself invited to his quarters in the evening and I saw that he had an extraordinary library, especially in military affairs. We talked for a time and he went through the library and picked out two or three historical novels. "You might be interested in these," he said quietly. I remember that one of them was *The Long Roll* by Mary Johnston, and another *The Exploits of Brigadier Gerard* in the Napoleonic Wars. A third was *The Crisis* by the American Winston Churchill.

They were stirring stories and I liked them. When I returned the books, the General asked me what I thought. As we talked about them, he said, "Wouldn't you like to know something of what the armies were actually doing during the period of the novels you've just read?"

Well, that seemed logical enough and I expressed an interest. He took down a few books on the military history of those periods.

The upshot was that I found myself becoming fascinated with the subject. But fascination wasn't enough. After I read the first of these books, General Conner questioned me closely about the decisions made—why they were made and under what conditions. "What do you think would have been the outcome if this decision had been just the opposite?" "What were the alternatives?" And so I read Grant's and Sheridan's memoirs, and a good deal of John Codman Ropes on the Civil War. I read Clausewitz's *On War* three times and a volume that was the Comte de Paris' Army of the Potomac narrative. The General did not urge me to read the Comte de Paris in its entirety but only certain chapters that bore upon campaigns we were discussing. He had me read Fremantle's account of the Battle of Gettysburg, as well as that of Haskell. The best outline or summarized history of the Civil War, he thought, was *Steele's Campaigns*. As I began to absorb the material of these books, I became even more interested in our Civil War and we spent many hours in analyzing its campaigns.

The best chance for such conversations was when we were out on reconnaissance. In the tropics, the terrain, or rather the usable features of the terrain, change rapidly. A trail made one year through the jungle can be completely overgrown by the time the dry season makes travel over it possible once more; or a landslide may wipe out all traces of it. Because we were constantly laying out routes and charting them on maps for the rapid movement of troops and their supply trains (which were mostly pack animals), so that we might be able to meet with considerable force any enemy landing on our sector of the Canal, we spent a good deal of time during the dry season in this kind of work.

Usually, we were on horse eight hours a day, most of it at a walk. We would make camp before dark. Close to the equator, the sun sets early and during the long hours before bedtime, between 6:30 and 10:00, we sat around a small campfire and talked about the Civil War or Napoleon's operations.

Our talks went further afield. General Conner was a natural leader and something of a philosopher, both as a student and as a storehouse of axiomatic advice. He was the man who first remarked to me, "Always take your job seriously, never yourself." He was the man who taught me that splendid line from the

French, "All generalities are false, including this one." The range and curiosity of his mind was not limited to military affairs. (It's a pleasure to give credit here for two quotations that I used later in life on hundreds, if not thousands, of occasions.) He often quoted Shakespeare at length and he could relate his works to wars under discussion.

"Now when Shakespeare wrote his plays," General Conner might say, "he frequently portrayed soldiers, and not entirely fictional ones—historical figures such as Prince Hal and Richard. In describing these soldiers, their actions, and giving them speech, Shakespeare undoubtedly was describing soldiers he *knew* at first hand, identifying them, making them part of his own characters. Even when he was writing of Julius Caesar, the dramatist must have endowed him with an education, characteristics, mannerisms that Shakespeare knew in some of the leaders of his own time."

With this kind of lead into a discussion, sometimes hardly more than a rambling bull session, we would broaden it into a general conversation about the long history of man, his ideas, and works. Excited by these talks and thoughts, I read in the works of authors strange to me: Plato, and Tacitus of the Roman nation, and in historical and philosophical writers among the moderns, including Nietzsche. No matter what time of day or evening I would walk across to General Conner's house to ask for another book from his library, he seemed delighted that I was there. And when he got the book of my choice, he would usually volunteer a second. As I read each one, I tried to digest its main themes and important points —I could be sure that sooner or later the General would be asking me about them.

Our conversations continued throughout the three years I served with him in the isolated post of Camp Gaillard. It is clear now that life with General Conner was a sort of graduate school in military affairs and the humanities, leavened by the comments and discourses of a man who was experienced in his knowledge of men and their conduct. I can never adequately express my gratitude to this one gentleman, for it took years before I fully realized the value of what he had led me through. And then General Conner was gone. But in a lifetime of association with great and good men, he is the one more or less invisible figure to whom I owe an incalculable debt.

☆ ☆ ☆ ☆ ☆

If the education of one young officer was under way, I found myself contributing to the education of a horse. Now I'm not an old cavalry man who believes that a horse is human. (In fact cavalry men of my day were convinced that most horses were better than most humans; only in moments of complete frustration, when everyone else is out of step except myself, do I ever agree with this sentiment.) On the other hand, in teaching skills, in developing self-confidence, the same sort of patience and kindness is needed with horses as with people. But I was not moved to tackle this project to prove a theory. I got into equine education because I had to have transport.

Horses and mules were the standard transportation at Camp Gaillard. There was one road leading to the Canal gate and an antiquated ferry there, eight miles away. Shortly after I arrived, I went to the corral to select a mount from twenty or more horses. All were mature, although not superannuated. They had been well picked over by officers who had arrived on the station before me. None of those remaining was trained, because the enlisted men at the corral, all from Puerto Rico, as it happened, had not been trained.

One of the soldiers who was on duty that day struck me as being both intelligent and at home with animals. His name was Lopez and I asked him to go with me as I walked among the horses to make a selection. His quick replies to all my questions about the health, strength, and temperament of each horse so impressed me that even before choosing one, I asked whether he would like to be my orderly. The broad smile that accompanied his "Sí, Señor Captain"—the grade I then held—made us friends at once.

I picked a big, coal-black gelding a bit over sixteen hands. He was splendid in the conformation of hindquarters, barrel, and legs. But forward of the withers he was pure mule with a short, thick neck and a large head. He looked stubborn. But this didn't bother me; from early boyhood I had had horses to care for, ride, and train and I decided that he was the best of the lot for use in the jungles surrounding us.

Lopez beamed. He said that my selection was very fine and he asked whether, in his new position, he could select his own mount from among those allotted to enlisted men. I said yes and from that moment on the four of us, Lopez and I and the two horses, became a closely knit unit.

After selecting Blackie, I found that my suspicions that he might be stiff and unwieldy were unfounded. Although at first he knew only two gaits, the walk and the extended gallop, he soon learned the slow and full trot and the canter. In a few weeks he was responding satisfactorily to the simpler aids. In the records, his age was given as fourteen years but his progress seemed almost miraculous. I was so pleased that I began to work earnestly. He learned normal movements and others more showy. He learned to two-track, turn on the forehand or haunches, either at the halt or on the move, to change leads at the canter, although this last he found difficult.

I began to teach him other movements—tricks, they could be called—that I'd never attempted to teach any animal. He learned to put one foreleg in front of his head when I was ready to dismount and to use his other leg to kneel. After that I taught him to follow me at a distance of about ten paces when I was on foot and stop as quickly as I did. I taught him to obey the word "Halt!" no matter when or how given and whether I was mounted or on foot. He not only stopped promptly but he would remain immovable until I called either "March" or "Come."

The commands were no trick; they were necessary because along the jungle trails were stretches littered with heavy boulders that could not be negotiated except by leaping one to another. On these stretches we would have to dismount and walk. By training Blackie to follow me at a distance of ten yards, I could hop and jump through the boulders without the danger that a horse would jump on my heels. As the General, his aide, our two orderlies, and I prepared to jump from one rock to the next, I would take the last position in the column and put Blackie at the head of the animal column following us. The other horses would not jump onto his spot until he had vacated it.

Blackie's complete obedience to command saved his life. One day we reached a deep ravine, filled with mud and muck, and obviously impassable. With my orderly and another man, I began to work upstream, riding Blackie to higher ground, hoping to find a place where we could cross.

We reached a spot that looked suitable. I started slowly into the ravine and found to my horror that it was exceedingly deep and nothing but soft, muddy slush. As quickly as I felt Blackie go down,

I threw my feet out of the stirrups and stepping up quickly on his haunches, leaped backward to the bank we had just left.

One of the orderlies there grabbed my hand. But the horse, badly frightened, began thrashing around and sinking deeper and deeper. It looked as if he would disappear in minutes. Because he was partly on his side, his position may have prevented him from sinking faster.

Realizing what was happening, I shouted, "Blackie, halt!" At first this didn't get through. After I had shouted the command again and then again, he suddenly stopped and did not move. Had he been a thoroughbred, he would have fought the mud until he was smothered; there would have been nothing we could do. Now he lay there quietly and we tried to figure ways to get him to firm ground.

Each orderly had a stout piece of rope on his pommel. We got one of these around Blackie's neck and the other around the top of his saddle, wedging the rope in by long sticks under both cantle and pommel. After tightening the ropes, we realized it was impossible to pull the horse backward. So, leaving the other orderly with Blackie, I took his mount and Lopez and we pushed our way rapidly on up until we got to a place where the ravine petered out. Crossing there, we rushed swiftly back to Blackie.

Now we had the ends of the ropes thrown over to us and we began to pull. I had the rope round his neck and had to be careful not to choke the horse. Nevertheless, I realized that he was still sinking, although slowly, and if we couldn't do something soon he would be gone. So now I said, "Come, Blackie," constantly repeating the command and he began again to move.

Throwing his feet out, he got himself nearly erect, and then, in the fashion of a horse trying to swim, he leaned forward into the muck as our two horses began to pull. We took it slowly but within a half hour we got Blackie onto sound ground.

A proud animal, he looked sheepish when he turned his head to look himself over. His saddle blankets, saddle, all his accouterments, to say nothing of the horse himself, were completely covered with black mud. Fortunately there was a beach only a mile away where Lopez and I gave him a thorough washing.

Blackie was not only proud, he was sensitive to applause. I taught him to go up a set of steps on a hillside, fifteen feet in height, and after turning around on a stone at the top, to make his way down.

At first descent was difficult; a horse doesn't like to go down a steep path because he can't see his feet and is unsure of his footing. However, once he had mastered the trick, Blackie became the talk of the post, and I frequently had to take him to the steps to show him off for the General's visitors. Whenever he learned a stunt, he did it thereafter almost at his own volition and, having completed it, would snap his ears forward and walk more like a conquering hero than an ordinary GI horse that had been bought for $150.

General Conner got word that a horse show was to be held in Balboa. He told me to enter Blackie. Knowing that my horse would have to compete against thoroughbreds and purebred Arabs, I protested. I didn't want to shame the horse in that kind of competition.

"Well . . ." the General said—he always spoke in a drawl—"I'm not sure he'll do well in the equitation but I'm going to arrange for him to do that step trick of his." So the General had a set of wooden steps made, and had them hauled out to the place of exhibition.

When we reached Balboa, we found that the equitation show was going to take place before any other events. Every horse that was going into a special event had to be entered in the earlier equitation.

Although my horse was well trained and nicely mannered, his conformation was simply not up to that of the six or eight others in the show. However, it had to be done and he did beautifully in all the exercises, except for his old stubbornness about changing leads. When he came to the jumping, he did better than any other. But the grading list that we had been handed by the judges called for a 45 per cent value for conformation, while manners, training, disposition, grooming, and tack were worth 55 per cent.

We were among the first to finish the equitation event. I sent Blackie to the stable and went into the grandstand to wait with Mamie until the stair-climbing act was scheduled. We were sitting there when the judges finally began to announce the winners. The blue, red, and white ribbons were awarded and I silently approved every one of them. The chosen animals had done well indeed. Next, the judges said something that I didn't hear but I saw little Lopez jumping up and shouting to me in excited pidgin English—or pidgin Spanish: "Come—*venga!*—come!"

He rushed off for the stables which were a few yards back of the grandstand. I was not sure what was going on but I went down promptly, Lopez came back at a fast trot, jumped off the horse, and said, "You won a ribbon, you won a ribbon!" My face a mask of concealed astonishment, I got up on my horse and went to get the last ribbon in the show, the yellow.

Afterward, the head judge said to me in an aside, "You stole that ribbon. Your horse was just a ham. As he went around there, his head perking forward, his trot and big black shining coat caught the eyes of the judges. I couldn't make them understand that you were just riding a plowhorse and had no business getting a ribbon." I laughed at him—he was a full colonel so I laughed courteously. But I said that I thought Blackie was a better horse than any of the others in the show and that it was a pity he didn't get the blue.

We did the step climbing and the ham showed up strongly in Blackie when he heard the crowd. I made him go to one knee in pretense of bowing. Then his ears went forward and he really looked like a champion—up the steps, around, and down again.

The General and I were riding one morning over a section of the post I had never seen before. Ahead was a great wall that the General told me was a housing for the water line through which our water supply came. The wall was perhaps three and a half feet wide and stretched out to our right across a valley. On the other side of the valley, the structure joined the road on which we were then riding, going straight ahead like the chord of an arc. I said to the General, "I think I'll take Blackie over the short cut and see how he likes it."

For a few moments, everything went well. In the middle of this long stretch, which must have been three hundred yards long, Blackie looked down. On each side he could see that he was standing, without visible support, about fifty feet above the ground. He halted. For the first time in my life I saw the flesh of a horse shaking all over. From the poll of his head to his feet, he began to shiver and I realized that he was panicky. I started to soothe him with my voice and decided to dismount.

There was no way to walk around his front quarters so I had to slide off carefully underneath him. Crawling forward, I got hold of one of his legs and slipped past him until I could stand. I took his reins, dropped them over my arm, and started walking, trying to give him confidence. Without hesitation, he walked behind me. At the far end of the wall, I told the General what had happened.

I was sure that Blackie had regained his confidence. I said to the General that when we returned, I would ride him back the same way.

This we did and Blackie walked the wall, ears forward, knowing that he was doing something special.

Whenever we came along that road, my horse, without command or movement on my part, would stop until the General and the orderlies had gone on, then he would turn onto the wall and march across proudly and happily to wait for the others. As long as I was in Panama, the horse did the same thing, showy as a peacock.

When we left Panama Blackie was seventeen years old. I planned to buy him from the government, to let him live out his days in a pasture. But the station to which I was assigned was one where it was impossible to take a horse. I found an old friend who had just come to the post and who was a good horseman. With the permission of the General and of the succeeding commanding officer, the horse was allowed to go to Captain Adrian Bryan, who kept him as long as he stayed in Panama. After that, I lost track of Blackie. He had lived to a rather venerable age for a horse and I can only hope that he had kind treatment to the end of his days.

In my experience with Blackie—and earlier with allegedly incompetent recruits at Camp Colt—is rooted my enduring conviction that far too often we write off a backward child as hopeless, a clumsy animal as worthless, a worn-out field as beyond restoration. This we do largely out of our own lack of willingness to take the time and spend the effort to prove ourselves wrong: to prove that a difficult boy can become a fine man, that an animal can respond to training, that the field can regain its fertility.

Long after Camp Colt and Panama, when I observed the young soldiers arriving in Europe, thousands of whom in appearance and attitude were evidently victims of heedless homes and a heedless society and were now expected to assault and destroy the Nazi elite, I determined that some day I would seek an opportunity to help correct this neglect, often forgetful of the precious value of every individual. Eventually, out of this determination, was born a project at Columbia University which I'll describe later.

In those Columbia years, when Mamie and I drove down to Gettysburg to look at a farm to buy, one of the attractions about the place we examined was the evidence of run-down soil. This was a chance, I thought, to prove that careful husbandry could restore land to its original fertility. The challenge outweighed certain obvious faults. Although we haven't achieved the greatest success—the soil to start with, two centuries ago, was probably thin and after a few plowings was spotted with gravel and stone patches—there are enough lush fields to assure me that I shall leave the place better than I found it.

The tutoring by Fox Conner and the rewards of working with Blackie were important to me in Panama, but the heart of my life was my family. Consequently, the most important event during my Camp Gaillard assignment was the news that we were to have another child.

Knowing that the baby was to be born during the month of August, Mamie took a steamer, in the early summer, to New Orleans. Then she went to Denver with the understanding that I would follow when the birth of the child was imminent. I reached there in time and on August 3 we had another boy, one who in appearance so resembled the one we had lost that, for my part, I was seldom able to see any difference between them when comparing their pictures at similar ages.

Mamie stayed in Denver until the baby, John, was a few months old and then returned to Panama. The most absorbing interest in our lives was his growth into a walking, talking, running-the-whole-household young fellow. John did much to fill the gap that we felt so poignantly and so deeply every day of our lives since the death of our first son. While his arrival did not, of course, eliminate the grief that we still felt—then and now—he was precious in his own right and he did much to take our minds off the tragedy. Living in the present with a healthy, bouncing baby boy can take parents' minds off almost anything.

Mamie had brought along a nurse to help. Kathryn Herrick was one of the most handsome and cheerful persons I ever knew. She was, I suppose, about the same age as Mamie, but instead of being tiny— Mamie weighed about one hundred pounds—Kathryn was a large girl. When she carried the baby around under her arm, it looked as if she were carrying a corsage. John adored her and before he could talk, he was trying to sing songs with her. Certainly by the time he was a year old, he was far ahead of any other youngster I had seen of that age. The companionship between the two was a beautiful thing to see. Kathryn stayed with us until John was about four years old, at which time we were sent to quarters that were so small there was no room for an extra person in the house. For years we have kept in touch and even now, occasionally, get a word from her.

One of the most profound beliefs of General Conner was that the world could not long avoid another major war. He did not seek war and he thought that if the United States had been part of the League of Nations, it might have been possible to avoid one. But under conditions as they were he was quite certain that the Treaty of Versailles carried within it the seeds of another, larger conflagration. He urged me to be ready for it.

Among the suggestions he made for my professional readiness, he told me that I should try one day for an assignment under a Colonel Marshall. He often said, "In the new war we will have to fight beside allies and George Marshall knows more about the techniques of arranging allied commands than any man I know. He is nothing short of a genius." In spite of my anxiety to take advantage of General Conner's advice, there was never an opportunity to serve under George Marshall prior to World War II. Indeed, before that time I had met him only twice, and then momentarily. One of the first things I noticed was that he was a man who had many of the characteristics of Fox Conner.

Panama was a peaceful but for me an eventful and, pardon the pun, pregnant tour of duty. I've always regarded General Conner and that period as considerable influences in my life. Had he been at the proper age for a high command in either World War I or World War II (in the first, he was a young brigadier) he would have been one of the outstanding leaders in either conflict. The joy of life with Mamie and John would have made a station far worse than Panama a happy place for me. Nevertheless, the first hint via the military grapevine that I would be transferred was welcome news. I could dream about the orders until they arrived. Then I came back to earth with a thump.

Back into the rut I had started to dig for myself a decade earlier. I was ordered back to Meade—to help coach a football team.

CHAPTER XIV

The Generals: Pershing and MacArthur

THE WAR DEPARTMENT moves in mysterious ways its blunders to perform—this sentiment expresses my mood in the fall of 1924. Why, three months ahead of schedule, I was moved thousands of miles from Panama to the Chesapeake Bay to join three other officers in a football coaching assignment is still a cosmic top-secret wonder to me. Then or now, one guess would be as good as another.

The whole thing may have started in a heavy think session of staff officers as an attempt to (what is now called) "improve the image" of the Army. On the other hand, it may all have come about because some bright young junior officer, relaxing with his seniors after a golf game, remarked for lack of anything more constructive to say, "Wouldn't it be dandy to get an Army team together that could play an undefeated, untied season and smear the Marines?"

Such a casual question, if dimly comprehended by a senior officer who nods his head in silent acquiescence as the easiest way of being good company, can result in an amazing amount of activity. A younger man, loaded with energy, interprets the nod as official approval to start things moving. In no time at all, a Big Project is under way. The initiator simply announces that the General wants it. The same thing, I am sure, happens in other human organizations. But I suspect that it happened most easily in the Army of forty years ago when hot lines of communication were unknown and a hint that the old man wanted something done was a peremptory summons to action.

Whatever the origin of the business about football at Camp Meade, someone made a decision; mimeograph machines began clicking out travel orders; officers and their families began packing.

Though working with soldiers was always fun, by 1924 I was getting exceedingly weary of the football coaching interludes that in the wisdom of the War Department were continually being inserted into my career. For one thing, evident to me personally, I was hardly a first-rate coach; I brought to the field only the system I had learned at West Point, slightly improved by a few innovations made over the years. These were field expedients, so to speak, that took advantage of one man's prowess or capitalized on a reported weakness in an upcoming opponent. I was largely an ad hoc coach, cutting the suit to fit the cloth. In only one tactic was I a confirmed practitioner; whenever I could find a good passer, I always tried to open up the game.

Before football recruiting became big business, opposing teams were often on a par in brawn and muscle. Ground plays, depending for success on brute strength, produced a seesaw struggle around the center of the field, as exhausting to the fans in its monotony as to the players in its bruises. When one team took to the air, however, an accurate passer and a receiver with sure hands and fast legs could turn a stalemate into a rout, even though the other nine players were muscle-bound behemoths confronting eleven of their counterparts.

That lesson I had learned once and for all when Knute Rockne and Gus Dorais of Notre Dame had stunned the country's football fans—and me, sitting on the bench—by their two-man defeat of West Point in 1913. My efforts to apply the lesson of that afternoon to Army football were usually thwarted by the lack of a really fine quarterback who could throw the ball accurately and for distance, a player who ever since the forward pass became legal had been absolutely necessary to a winning team. To develop such a player, once a lad of promise was found, took more time than the Army would permit when I was still an off-and-on coach. Senior officers expected instant delivery from the victim assigned to produce a winning team. That went double for the coaches at Meade in 1924. The War Department itself had issued the directive. What more could we want?

That much done, the War Department was no help. Although an Army team of championship caliber was wanted, we got no assistance in helping us recruit talent. Possibly they thought that, given enough good coaches, players could be made out of any material.

It is true that we, who were not by nature humble, would have been the first to concede that they had assembled a splendid array of coaches. The head man was a classmate of mine, Vernon Prichard, who had been quarterback at West Point when I played on the team in 1912. A man named Bridaster was his line coach; the ends were tutored by another old friend, Ralph Sasse, who had made a splendid record in the tank forces overseas during the First World War; and I was the backfield coach. We were the War Department's total contribution to a successful season. Recruiting was our responsibility. We could draft any soldier we wanted, regardless of his assignment—so long as we recruited within the gates of Camp Meade.

If we had been given the right to search out the best talent in the continental Army, the season record would have delighted even the crustiest War Department officer. Their insistence that we had to do the job with the material immediately at hand may have been good character training for coaches, but the results on the scoreboard won no plaudits from press or spectators for our brand of soldier football. The players tried hard. We seldom won. Against any small college we might show up fairly well for a quarter or so. In the Western Maryland game, a drop kick did put us in the lead. Thereafter, Western Maryland solved our plays and made three touchdowns while we were helpless to increase our three points. In the climax game against the Marines, who we were sure had scoured the entire corps for players, we lost by 20–0 or something of that sort. For all of us, the season had been far from inspirational.

On the other hand, for me there was a possibility of personal profit. If, in my semi-professional failure, the War Department never again showed any interest in me as a football coach, the season was a huge triumph. That was not to be. Even 1924's dismal record did not weaken the adhesive on the label I wore. It still said *Football Coach.*

At least the football duties were temporary. My permanent orders were cut before the end of the season. They ordered me back to command a battalion of tanks—the same old tanks I had commanded several years earlier. The orders were to take effect after a sixty-day leave, already approved.

It was high time I was getting to one of the established Army schools, I thought, and after the orders appeared, I went to see the Chief of Infantry. I asked whether the orders could be changed, and whether I could be sent to school. I should have known better; he refused even to listen to my arguments, and said I would have to go to Benning to command the light tank battalion.

A strange telegram arrived. It was from Fox Conner, serving as Deputy Chief of Staff to General Hines. General Conner knew of my disappointment in not getting detailed to the Infantry School at Fort Benning. The telegram was cryptic in the extreme.

NO MATTER WHAT ORDERS YOU RECEIVE FROM THE WAR DEPARTMENT, MAKE NO PROTEST ACCEPT THEM WITHOUT QUESTION SIGNED CONNER

What could be in the wind? The only reason I could accept the advice was my complete faith in General Conner.

For several days I was in a quandary until orders arrived. Normally, they would have been so difficult to accept that it was well I had advance warning. The orders detailed me to recruiting duty in the state of Colorado!

They relieved me from duty with the Infantry. To be assigned to the recruiting service, in those days, unless it was to meet an immediate and temporary personal requirement of an officer, was felt by most of us to be a rebuke a little less devastating than a reprimand.

To further confuse me, I had a note from a captain I knew, John Thompson, who had seen a telegram come through the office of the Commanding General of the 8th Corps area at Fort Sam Houston:

My dear Ike:

Just happened to see the above telegram on the board file this morning and though [sic] that you might be interested in seeing its contents, especially the part I have underlined in red. Congratulations on having such a fine rep. Best regards and best wishes for a happy New Year. If you come down this way look me up. Oiseau King and Gessler are also stationed around here.

The telegram itself, sent to the Commanding General at San Antonio, whose jurisdiction extended over Colorado, and with four words underscored by Captain Thompson, read:

DESIRED DETAIL MAJOR DWIGHT D. EISENHOWER, INF'Y AN EXCEPTIONALLY EFFICIENT OFFICER NOW ON LEAVE IN DENVER COLO ON RECRUITING DUTY THAT CITY ABOUT NINE MONTHS PERIOD YOUR RECOMMENDATION DESIRED SIGNED DAVIS

After my gloomy interview with the Chief of Infantry, I had reached the somber conclusion that he and I did not see eye to eye on my place in the military sphere. If I were inclined to overestimate my own abilities, certainly nothing could persuade me that he rated me above average. The new assignment—until I saw the telegram—confirmed me in this opinion. Now I saw myself described in writing as "an exceptionally efficient officer." This stumped me until I learned that the Chief of Infantry had been circumvented, not converted, to enthusiasm.

A letter arrived from General Conner. He said that because Benning was under the exclusive jurisdiction of the Chief of Infantry, it was impossible for an infantry officer to go there except with the Chief's approval. Instead, General Conner had arranged for my transfer from the Infantry on a temporary basis to the Adjutant General's office—which was in charge of recruiting. I had never thought of so drastic a measure. Had anyone else suggested to me that I desert an arm for a service, I would have been outraged. Now it had been done without consultation. But with my solid belief in Fox Conner I kept my temper.

Under his novel arrangement, a final order came to me which said that I had been selected by the Adjutant General as one of his quota of officers to go to the Command and General Staff School at Fort Leavenworth. I was to arrive there in August 1925.

I was ready to fly—and needed no airplane!

☆   ☆   ☆   ☆   ☆

To the cynic, all this may seem proof of "It's not *what* you know, it's *who* you know." There is just enough truth in that phrase to assure its survival so long as humans must save face or nurse an ego. Certainly, had I been denied the good fortune of knowing Fox Conner, the course of my career might have been radically different. Because I *did* know him, I did go to Leavenworth. And I must confess that the school there, a watershed in my life, might not have been half so professionally profitable to me had I gone there years later on the schedule the Chief of Infantry thought suitable.

But on this business of who you know, a one-minute lecture to any young person who may read these words:

Always try to associate yourself closely with and learn as much as you can from those who know more than you, who do better than you, who see more clearly than you. Don't be afraid to reach upward. Apart from the rewards of friendship, the association might pay off at some unforeseen time—that is only an accidental by-product. The important thing is that the learning will make you a better person.

That bit of pontificating done, I must admit that once my first exultation was over, I began to take a second look. The order assigned me to Command and General Staff School before I had any chance to get the usual preparatory infantry instruction at Fort Benning or elsewhere. This was like being sent to college without a secondary school education, in a sense. It could put me in an awkward position with classmates at Leavenworth, a highly competitive school. Graduation there was thought to be a passport to better assignments in the Army and graduation high in the class was said to mark a man for future advancement. An aide in the office of the Chief of Infantry gave me his felicitations: "You will probably fail," he said. His letter said that going to Leavenworth under these conditions would make me useless thereafter as an infantry officer. Up against the graduates of advanced schools, I might end up with another tour of football.

I wrote Fox Conner asking him what preparatory work I could undertake before arriving at Leavenworth. In his reply, he said:

You may not know it, but because of your three years' work in Panama, you are far better trained and ready for Leavenworth than anybody I know.

You will recall that during your entire service [with me] I required that you write a field order for the operation of the post every day for the years you were there. You became so well acquainted with the technics and routine of preparing plans and orders for operations that included their logistics, that they will be second nature to you. You will feel no sense of inferiority . . .

This was encouraging but I thought it would be a good idea for me to learn what I could. Again, I got copies of the Leavenworth problems and spent considerable time during the winter months solving them and checking my answers against the approved solutions as given in separate envelopes. It was by no means a chore. I loved to do that kind of work. Today, problems of all sorts are submitted to me by folks ranging from schoolchildren who want a suitable name for a newly arrived pet to senior citizens who would like a one-paragraph solution for juvenile delinquency or global overpopulation. But practical problems have always been my equivalent of crossword puzzles.

The spring of 1925 passed quickly and Mamie and I began to pack. At Leavenworth, I found the school itself to be exhilarating. There were no examinations as such, no tests of memory. There was a period of instruction covering medical, ordnance, quartermaster, signal services, as well as the operations of the fighting arms. Then we began to get problems—instructed under what is now called the "case" method.

A pamphlet outlined a suppositious force, located in a particular spot, with indications of the enemy's strength and the mission of the Blue Force, which the student always commanded. The first step was to decide what actions should be taken. Second, after your decision was turned in, the correct decision was given to the student and he was then asked to give the proper plans and dispositions to support it. Fox Conner had been correct. We had done this kind of "war gaming" in Panama.

As time went on, it was easy to identify those people who were studying too long and too hard at night and coming to the daytime sessions and the problem room without fresh minds and an optimistic outlook. I established a routine that limited my night study to two hours and a half; from seven to nine-thirty. Mamie was charged with the duty of seeing that I got to bed by that time. This went on five nights a week. There were no classes on Saturday and on Friday nights and Saturday nights we unwound completely at parties at the Officers Club or in friends' quarters. Sunday nights we began studying for the next day's lessons.

On the theory that study groups were better than individual work, most members of the class joined together in small committees, ranging from four to eight. I was invited to join one of these. After thinking it over, I declined. If I wanted to work two hours and a half, I didn't want to get involved with too much conversation, argument, and discussion. But there was a lot to be said for two men working together. Even the staking out of a problem by one man could be a long and difficult process. Plotting tactical situations on a map, for example, took time. One man read out the instructions from the memorandum furnished, while the other marked up the map, usually pinned to a wall. This legitimate teamwork saved precious hours.

Happily, in the class was a friend from 19th Infantry days, Leonard T. Gerow, a graduate of Virginia Military Institute. Two or three years senior to me in grade, we were approximately the same age.

His feelings about committees were the same as mine so we decided to study together.

Because my room on the third floor of our quarters was a little more commodious than his, we made my house the regular meeting place. This spot was off limits to all post and family personnel. We converted it into what I considered a model command post. The walls were covered with maps. The worktable was large and the bookshelves close at hand with every reference work we used. Above all, no sound, household or military, reached us there. We learned far more in quiet concentration than in the lecture room.

Of course, when we went into the afternoon problem sessions, everybody was on his own. That the method adopted by Gerow and myself was useful is proved, I guess, by the fact that we both graduated with high marks, separated from each other by something like two-tenths of one per cent.

In the mid-1920s, the Leavenworth course was for one year only. Mamie and I had to prepare for our next move. Sometime in late May, orders arrived from the Chief of Infantry—I had been retransferred—to go to Fort Benning to take command of a battalion. This was satisfactory. At the same time, two other possibilities appeared.

The first was a request at the War Department for a man to act as a Regular Army military instructor for an ROTC unit at a northwestern university, with the additional opportunity of . . . yes, coaching the football team, for an additional sum of $3500 a year.

The second was offered by General Edward King, the commandant of the school. He said he was putting my name on the list of instructors for the next year at Leavenworth. He asked if I had any objection.

I said, "No, Sir. No objection whatsoever." But I did tell him about the set of orders that I had already received and about the offer from the university. I told him that if given any choice, I would decline the latter.

While the additional income was attractive, I was tired of being taken off straight military duty to help coach football. "I don't think it's possible for a man to meet the requirements of two rather exacting jobs," I said. "If I have to coach football all the time, I might as well resign and try to concentrate on the sport."

A few days later, General King telephoned and said that the War Department was anxious that I proceed to Benning. Again, that was that. About mid-August, we set out in a new automobile for Georgia. Now Georgia, off and on, has been a favorite of mine in the fall and spring months when the air is balmy and the weather refreshing. Summer was something else again. But the quarters assigned to us were the nicest we had yet enjoyed and as soon as the temperature went down, we were glad to be there.

But if Georgia temperatures declined, mine didn't. A week after I reached Benning, I was told that I would have to coach the soldier football team. With an enormous effort of will, I said quietly that I just turned down $3500 a year additional to do the same thing. I asked the executive officer of the post if I could decline the responsibilities of head coach. I would take charge of the backfield and the offensive tactics but I didn't want to carry the administration or training or lining up of other coaches.

This was agreed, and I began working under another Texan, Captain Barry. Once again, the material at hand was willing but raw and the season was not one to divert attention from Notre Dame, Wisconsin, West Point, and the others. Fortunately, I didn't have to face another. In mid-December the War Department ordered me to report to Washington, D.C. for duty in the office of General Pershing.

☆   ☆   ☆   ☆   ☆

Whatever the wishes of the War Department to have me stationed at Benning, General Pershing, the famed "Black Jack" and leader of our AEF in World War I, outranked anyone else in the Infantry or in the Department who had designs on me. The new agency he headed, the Battle Monuments Commission, was not only building and beautifying the cemeteries where our war dead were gathered abroad but it was also preparing a battlefield guide, a sort of Baedeker to the actions of Americans in the war. The guidebook writing was assigned to me.

I had been in the job hardly long enough to do any damage when word was sent that I had been selected as a student for the War College.

The College was in Washington at the post now known as Fort McNair. To graduate from the War College had long been the ambition of almost every officer and I was anxious to take the assignment. General Pershing's executive officer, Xenophon Price, thought I was passing up a shining future with the Battle Monuments Commission. "Every officer attached to the Commission is going to be known as a man of special merit," he said.

"For once the Department has given me a choice," I said, "and for once I'm going to say yes to something I'm anxious to do."

I was a student at the College until the following June. In the meantime, graduating students had become eligible for assignment to the War Department General Staff and once again a choice was offered me: Did I want the General Staff or to go back to Battle Monuments? When I learned that to complete the work of revising the guidebook written earlier I would have to go to France to study them at first hand, my choice was easy.

This was my first chance to get to know a European country. In June 1928, I saw Paris for the first time. The job now took on new interest. It involved travel, all the way from the Vosges in southeast France to the English Channel, following the lines of trench warfare that had stabilized almost rigidly between late 1914 and the weeks preceding the Armistice in 1918.

In this way, I came to see the small towns of France and to meet the sound and friendly people working in the fields and along the roads.

Whenever possible, I stopped along the road to join groups of road workers who were eating their noonday lunch. Their tools at their side, the shovels, the hoes, pickaxes laid down, they were invariably relaxed and hospitable. When my chauffeur (he was always my interpreter) and I would ask if we could join them, their custom was to offer something from their lunchboxes. I developed a habit of carrying a bottle of Evian and an extra bottle of *vin rouge,* something I did not drink myself, but which was always welcome. In the trunk of the car, we began to carry certain specialties I thought they might like. At times it was just a fruit like oranges or bananas, sometimes a can of artichokes. One time I had half a dozen cans of sardines and opened one as an hors d'oeuvre. They went down so swiftly and with such exclamations of delight that I opened up another. There were just five of us in all and I didn't particularly care for fish; the others finished off the six cans of sardines in about as many minutes.

Whenever I could find no group along the road, I would save my lunch, look for a little *auberge,* or inn, and eat there to mingle with the people of the countryside. They were unlike some of the city people, warm and jolly and courteous.

Mamie and I had found an apartment on the Quai d'Auteuil over-looking the Seine and Pont Mirabeau. The apartment became a sort of informal, junior-size American Express for Army friends who were visiting Paris. Even if we had not wanted to see the sights our-selves, Mamie and I were drawn into their trips. In time we both became small-scale authorities on what should not be missed and what should be avoided.

Mamie, to be sure, was a specialist in the shops that ranged from the flea market and sidewalk stands to the *grands magasins*. I tried to find spots that would be new to American visitors, different from anything they were accustomed to at home. I became a salesman or tipster for several places and not always to the satisfaction of those whom I counseled.

One place, for example, and I think it is still in business, was the Musée Grévin. A waxworks not quite as large as Madame Tussaud's in London, but far more gruesome in its exhibits, this museum of French historic characters was absorbing. Most of my friends had never seen anything of the sort before and usually they were im-pressed. Occasionally, one of them would turn a corner and brush too close to a figure, concealed there for the purpose, and he would make a polite apology. This place—I suppose I was still an unsophisti-cated Kansan at heart—stayed in my memory as a unique Paris at-traction. The reaction of those who followed my advice was mixed.

Twenty-five years later, after I had assumed Supreme Command of the NATO forces, I lunched in the Hotel Astoria with two mem-bers of the staff. They seemed tired and worn-out after the rush and pressure of getting headquarters ready for my arrival. I insisted that they take an afternoon off to do a little sightseeing. They insisted in turn that they had already seen everything worth looking at—and anyway, Paris was a dull town on a February afternoon.

Their last remark set me off and, completely wound up, I lectured on the wonders of the Musée Grévin. Either persuaded or wanting to escape my address, they agreed to go. After spending two hours or so wandering from one exhibit to another, they finally returned to the sidewalk outside. One of them asked disgustedly, "Do you *really* suppose this was the most exciting spot he could find when he was still in his thirties?"

In the middle of the tour of duty, Mamie and I took leave. We went to Belgium, through Liége, Aix-la-Chapelle, on to Bonn and then up the Rhine, through the Black Forest into Switzerland, and finally into southern France. We were back in Paris in three weeks. With my tour of duty ending in mid-July, I applied for a terminal leave of a month and Mamie and I took our young son to San Remo in Italy. It was a preliminary look at Europe, a view of countries I would one day see again.

In two tours with the American Battle Monuments Commission, I served under General Pershing for a year and a half, or a little more. I never got to know him well, which was not surprising, perhaps. He was rather reserved and even remote in manner. He kept odd hours. Often, the General would not come to the office until one o'clock or later but frequently he stayed there until midnight. This must have played havoc with the social schedules of his direct subordinates. Several of us who were under pressure to get the guidebook out had to work late at night anyway. We became accustomed to the General's hours. He had few visitors.

One man did come to see him frequently. His name was McLaughlin and he was the editor of the Army-Navy journal. Mr. McLaughlin told me that he was one of those who thought that General Pershing should be a presidential candidate in 1928. This was my first adult encounter with a political campaign, though I was far over on the sidelines and the "campaign" was minuscule, and I didn't exhibit much interest. The General scarcely exhibited more. He was emphatic, as he had been immediately after the war, that the White House was not his choice of residence. McLaughlin was hardly the overpowering sort who might change the Pershing mind. There was a little talk about this in the office but by and large, the "boomlet" never got off the ground.

In his writing habits, the General was cautious and slow. Several times he asked me to draft speeches and in no case was I successful in producing anything he wanted. In drafting occasional letters, I was slightly more successful. In going over my work, he always edited carefully and with a precise regard for the exact definition of words. If I had used the word "exhaustively" I would find it changed to "thoroughly"; if I should use "speedily" he would change it to "rapidly." There was only one occasion in which I did much writing for him and this turned out, as usual, to be a futile expenditure of off-duty time.

The General was in the midst of doing his memoirs and he used as the basis his wartime diary. Whether the diary had been kept by a staff assistant or whether he wrote it out in his own hand, I do not know. But the entire format of his two-volume work on World War I was to be in diary fashion. This destroyed the continuity of any major episode, of course. A battle could not have a beginning and a body and an end for the simple reason that it had to be told in the form of General Pershing's daily experiences, along with a score of other affairs coincident with it.

One day he called me in. "I'm unhappy about this description of Saint Mihiel in the first part of September 1918—and also about the Argonne," he said. The last was a battle which began on September 26 and was waged to the last day of the war, November 11. "Read the parts of the book that cover these two periods and let me know what you think."

In a couple of days, I told him that these, the Saint Mihiel battle, followed by the Argonne campaign, were surely the two great ventures of the American Army in World War I. While I thought that other maneuvers, such as the deployment of divisions here and there, one in Italy and several up in Belgium, could be covered well in diary form, the climactic stories in the whole two volumes were these battles. I suggested he abandon the diary form for two chapters and instead tell the story of each battle as seen from his position as the commander of the American Expeditionary Forces.

"There's no reason to ignore your diary in telling the story," I said. "You can intersperse comments which will show where you were, what you were doing, and what you were thinking. This kind of treatment would give authenticity to the story you are telling."

He listened and seemed to be enthused. Then he told me to take the two chapters and draft them as I thought they should be.

With considerable effort I produced two chapters and left them with the General. After reading them over, he said he was happy with them. In such matters, he explained, he always looked to one man to give him final advice. That man was Colonel George C. Marshall, whose name had been mentioned to me by General Conner. Within a few days, Colonel Marshall came to General Pershing's office and stayed with him all through one afternoon. When his conference with the General was done, he came out through my office. For the first time in my life, I met George Marshall. He did not sit down but remarked that he had read over my chapters. "I think they're interesting. Nevertheless, I've advised General Pershing to stick with his original idea. I think to break up the format right at the climax of the war would be a mistake."

I said that there was some virtue in continuity. "Although I still think," I said, "that each of the two battles ought to be treated as a single narrative with the proper annotations to give it authenticity."

He remarked, rather kindly, that my idea was a good one. Nevertheless, he thought that General Pershing would be happier if he stayed with the original scheme.

After General Pershing's books were published, a number of my friends—most of them in the Army and all of them interested in the story—remarked that it was difficult to get the entire account of the war clearly in mind. They objected to it as a chronological recitation, based so completely on dates and limited to the day-to-day movements of the General, that it was not as interesting as they had hoped. Given my own work, I am probably no man to pass judgments on memoir writing but I still have to agree.

General Pershing was not a colorful man and he had one deplorable habit: he was always late—up to an hour or more—for every engagement. When no one else was available, I acted as temporary aide and it was always difficult, indeed embarrassing, to try to explain to the host why we were so late. The General seemed to be oblivious to the passage of time and he made no excuses for the long hours of waiting he imposed on any prospective host.

In his later years, I visited General Pershing in his rooms at Walter Reed Hospital. He grew weaker and weaker and it became almost impossible to talk with him. But whenever he spoke from his hospital bed, it was always as a senior commander. I had the impression that he was standing stiffly erect, Sam Browne belt and all. He managed to convey how much he appreciated visits by younger officers. Before he had taken to his bed, this slim, straight figure was an imposing presence. To all the veterans of World War I he is the single hero and they remember him with respect and admiration, even if not affection. He had a reputation for being something of a martinet but at the same time he was knowledgeable and fair. I liked him and we all owed him respect and admiration for the way he had carried responsibility in that war.

As time goes on and his image recedes into the past, General Pershing's place in history will probably not be as prominent as it might have been had he been more outgoing in personality. Early in life he had been the victim of a dreadful tragedy. His wife and two or three young children had been burned to death, in an Army post in Wyoming, I believe. Only one son, Warren, was left. He is, I understand, a successful and respected man who heads up a Wall Street firm.

When General Pershing died in 1948 I was visiting friends in Vermont. I went to Washington to be present at his funeral. This called for a long march from the Capitol to the cemetery at Arlington and at first it was thought that many of the senior officers, who were themselves reaching a venerable age, should not make the entire march. For my part, I refused the offer of the officer in charge of the funeral to have automobiles stationed along the line of march to take some of us middle-aged men out to the cemetery. In the middle of the march, rain poured down for some time.

The moment the rain started, cars were rushed to the head of the column to pick us up. This struck me as out of order in the funeral for General Pershing, who had commanded many American soldiers in Europe. I declined to get into the car. Actually, I was wet anyhow and I would have been more miserable in the automobile than continuing to walk. But I was certainly not going to give an example of brass running from a rainstorm when all the marching men in the long column had to take things as they came. Not in the last walk for General Pershing of the AEF.

A few months after we returned from France in 1929, I was available for assignment. It was my hope to go back to troop duty. But there was a new and different role ahead. The Assistant Secretary of War's office beckoned.

In those days there were two assistants to the Secretary of War: one was Assistant Secretary of Air; the other, and senior, was the deputy of the Secretary of War himself. One of the senior man's principal duties was to study ways of mobilizing American industry in the event of another war. This study became my task.

Working under an immediate superior, General George Moseley, a brilliant officer who had been on General Pershing's staff in Europe, I now undertook work that was intriguing, and frustrating, but that gave me an early look at the military-industrial complex of whose pressures I would later warn. Except at that point, the pressures were exactly reversed.

Two of us, ordinarily Colonel Wilkes of the Engineers and I, visited industrial firms. We pointed out that during the war they had been making fuses, or ammunition, or truck bodies. We would ask if we could see the plans under which they had operated and

wanted to know whether they could suggest improvements for re-
tooling rapidly to produce matériel we might need in case of war. It
was difficult to get any interest shown at all. After all, they felt, there
was never going to be another big war.

The beginnings of an industrial college were established in the
War Department. This was a school where officers, usually from the
supply services, were trained in logistics, and especially in solving
problems of converting a peacetime manufacturing plant to wartime
schedules. Because of the industrialists' disbelief that they might ever
again be called on to arm and equip a mass army, the work was
largely theoretical. But here and there, some manufacturers were
found who were ready to co-operate.

One of the questions was the organization of the government and
the War Department itself for control of production. To find out
about the experience of the War Industries Board of World War I,
I went to its chief, Mr. Bernard Baruch. He was a man who was not
only co-operative; he was anxious that the American public, as well
as the armed services, understand the complexities of conversion to
war. He was ready to talk to me at any time.

Mr. Baruch believed that immediately upon the outbreak of war,
preferably in advance, if the emergency could be foreseen, prices,
wages, and costs of materials and services should be frozen. None of
these could be changed except on decision of a special agency. In
this way, he hoped to avoid the inflation that had accompanied every
one of our prior wars. At the same time he advocated measures for
eliminating black marketing. He convinced me of the soundness of
his basic views and I made them part of the plans that I was
charged with drawing up. It was a long, irksome job. Many people
in the War Department were flatly opposed to Mr. Baruch's ideas.

High officials believed that a war should be conducted through the
normal, peacetime agencies of government. They did not favor price
controls. They saw no reason for special organization. Those of us
who believed in Baruch's policies argued that competition between
departments of government would interfere with maximum industrial production. They would answer that co-operation between the
Army and Navy departments would be enough to take care of the
problem.

All our experience has shown that this was convenient reasoning
and foolishness. Even during a war against a common enemy, ar-

mies and navies of the same nation have often delighted in warring against each other for guns, men—and applause.

Our antagonists persisted. Whenever we accomplished an industrial mobilization it was done on our own and in a rather isolated atmosphere. Indeed, the Chief of Staff of the Army, General Summerall, forbade any General Staff officer to go into the office of the Assistant Secretary of War.

Finally, General Douglas MacArthur succeeded General Summerall, late in 1930. Soon, the Assistant Secretary had a chance to talk with the new Chief of Staff. He was receptive to the ideas we had been advocating. General MacArthur, the Assistant Secretary, General Moseley, and myself discussed the whole concept, past experience, and what we intended to do with the interested agencies.

At the moment, the government was organizing, with congressional approval, a commission to study how to take the profits out of war. Many people believed that wars were started by munitions makers or industrialists, who wanted the bonanzas that had sometimes been obtainable under loosely drawn contracts. Undoubtedly some industrialists made more money than they should have out of war but most of them, as soon as peace came, were delighted to stop war production and get on with their own business, where they saw better long-range profit.

The commission called in witnesses and finally asked the War Department to propose a plan. We had been anticipating this and I was selected to draft the plan, working with Colonel Wilkes. The Chief of Staff presented it on behalf of the entire War Department. The plan was far from being a masterpiece but it did make an impression.

One stumbling block had been a question of rank and snobbery. Promotions were involved. In certain quarters, it was implied that anyone going into a technical service, particularly supply and production, was not up to the standards of a combat officer. The work had been looked down on by the General Staff. But now, assured the friendly co-operation of the Chief of Staff—which of course meant all those serving under him—our work went ahead faster. The Industrial College, which had been started in a little section of one room in the old Munitions Building, was enlarged. Better students were sent by the Army and Navy. Attention was given to credits earned there by officers for their eventual promotion. So, the arrival of General MacArthur, the new Chief, gave new impetus to our work and was certainly a morale boost.

My day-to-day boss, General George Moseley, was dynamic. He was always delving into new ideas, and he was an inspiration to the rest of us. He was always quick with praise and was ready to take responsibility for any little error or criticism that came our way from outside. Years later, his outspoken reaction to public questions, often political, got him a bad press. Many who did not know the man himself may have thought him a reactionary or a militarist. The impression he created was a distortion, I am sure; he was a patriotic American unafraid to disagree with a consensus. I continued with him until the elections of 1932. As a result of that election, President Hoover was going out of office and all presidential appointees in the War Department would change.

General MacArthur, it developed, had need for a personal military assistant other than his aides, a man who could be an amanuensis to draft statements, reports, and letters for his signature. He asked me to take the job. I moved over to General MacArthur's office about the first of January 1933, and established a working relationship with him that was not to end until December 1939.

☆　☆　☆　☆　☆

Douglas MacArthur was a forceful—some thought an overpowering—individual, blessed with a fast and facile mind, interested in both the military and political side of our government. From the beginning, I found that he was well acquainted with most of the people in government in almost every department. Working with him brought an additional dimension to my experience. My duties were beginning to verge on the political, even to the edge of partisan politics.

Most of the senior officers I had known always drew a clean-cut line between the military and the political. Off duty, among themselves and close civilian friends, they might explosively denounce everything they thought was wrong in Washington and the world, and propose their own cure for its evils. On duty, nothing could induce them to cross the line they, and old Army tradition, had established. But if General MacArthur ever recognized the existence of that line, he usually chose to ignore it. At times, this could complicate life for himself and his staff.

My office was next to his; only a slatted door separated us. He called me to his office by raising his voice. When I had visitors in my office, I always made sure that the door was closed because I didn't want to disturb the General. At the time he was fifty-three. He was decisive, personable, and he had one habit that never ceased to startle me. In reminiscing or in telling stories of the current scene, he talked of himself in the third person. "So MacArthur went over to the Senator, and said, 'Senator . . .'" Although I had heard of this idiosyncrasy, the sensation was unusual. In time I got used to it and saw it not as objectionable, just odd.

On any subject he chose to discuss, his knowledge, always amazingly comprehensive, and largely accurate, poured out in a torrent of words. "Discuss" is hardly the correct word; discussion suggests dialogue and the General's conversations were usually monologues.

One of the General's old friends, who had a fifteen-minute interview with him, sat and listened to him and was able to insert only an occasional yes or no. The Colonel left the office and realized that under the MacArthur treatment he had forgotten to bring up the subject of his visit.

Later that day, encountering another officer whose appointment with MacArthur had immediately followed his, the officer said: "You certainly made a tremendous impression on General MacArthur."

The Colonel, bewildered as he recalled the one-sided nature of the talk, asked, "What in the world do you mean?"

The other officer replied: "Why, the General said when I went in that he had just had a tremendously interesting chat with you. He said that he always looks forward to your visits because you are a fascinating conversationalist from whom he learns a great deal!"

Unquestionably, the General's fluency and wealth of information came from his phenomenal memory, without parallel in my knowledge. Reading through a draft of a speech or a paper once, he could immediately repeat whole chunks of it verbatim.

In several respects, he was a rewarding man to work for. When he gave an assignment, he never asked any questions; he never cared what kind of hours were kept; his only requirement was that the work be done. The difficulty was that I soon found myself engaged in a variety of reports, statements, estimates, and the like that kept me so busy I was in the office until 7:30 or 7:45 every night. Because General MacArthur kept unusual hours, including luncheons or other absences from two to four hours and then stayed on in his office until 8:00, my hours became picturesque. But if the occasion came up for me to take a week's leave, all I had to do was tell him I was going away for a few days and he would make no objection.

Of course, the work did pile up while I was gone.

In July 1932, an event occurred which brought the General a measure of lasting unfavorable publicity. This was the "Bonus March." The marchers were veterans who wanted the bonus money promised them by the Congress. Almost a decade earlier, the Congress—buffeted on one side by veterans who wanted immediate bonuses and on the other by an administration opposed to them—attempted to please both by authorizing a liberal grant for World War I service, postponing payment until 1945, when most of the Senators and Representatives would have left Washington and the earth.

This action, a poor compromise, pleased no one, least of all the veterans. Their claims had been recognized—but they could not collect on them for more than twenty years. This arrangement required them to have one foot in the grave before they could enjoy the money. As times got hard, many veterans came to think that the deferred bonus was identical to a deposit in the bank. This oversimplification, without any legal base, became an intensely emotional idea at a time when millions of families were hard pressed to feed and clothe themselves or to meet the rent.

We were in the depths of a depression. Men were out of work. The government had to alleviate distress and minimize hardships. Despite the fact that this was a national calamity affecting almost all citizens, some veterans seemed to feel that they should be regarded as a special class entitled to special privileges. They marched to Washington to get the promised money.

All in all, I think there were eighteen or twenty thousand men. Some were encamped outside the town, across the Anacostia River; others had taken over abandoned buildings not far from the Capitol and were living in them, with blankets thrown on the floor. When existing buildings were occupied, others built miserable little shacks out of cast-off materials, tin cans and old lumber and the like—anything to shelter them from the rain and bad weather. Over outdoor fires, they cooked their scanty meals, sometimes a dozen veterans pooling all the foodstuffs they had to make a stew.

To a number of citizens, they were a nuisance whose picketing and placards disturbed the quiet of Washington. To others, they were the menace of Bolshevism attacking the government at its very

Capitol. In fact, most of them, after their arrival on Pennsylvania Avenue, however misled they may have been by a few agitators, were quiet and orderly. They insisted on enough discipline within their ranks to guard against lawlessness or collapse into mob anarchy. Nothing of the sort had ever been seen in Washington. And, except for "Coxey's Army" in my boyhood, there was little or no precedent for the march itself. Thirty years before demonstrations would become an accepted mode of protest, the bonus veterans were pioneering direct action against Federal legislative authority. Both sides in the dispute were neophytes in conducting or facing such protests.

Restraint and a reasonable amount of good humor marked the veterans' attitude. Restraint and a decent sympathy marked the government's. For many days, nothing happened.

The time did arrive when the government, because of building construction in the neighborhood, had to move the marchers from the immediate vicinity of the Capitol. The veterans refused to move. This brought on trouble with the police, who were outnumbered and trained only to deal with criminals, not with large groups organized under discipline learned in the Armed Forces. Then the President called our regular troops to clean out the area.

I cannot remember exactly how many soldiers were involved but my impression is that there were five or six hundred. As quickly as the order was announced to us, General MacArthur decided that he should go into active command in the field. By this time our relationship was fairly close, close enough that I felt free to object.

I told him that the matter could easily become a riot and I thought it highly inappropriate for the Chief of Staff of the Army to be involved in anything like a local or street-corner embroilment. (Of course this was no "street-corner" matter—but it still did not require the presence of the Chief of Staff in the streets.) General MacArthur disagreed, saying that it was a question of Federal authority in the District of Columbia, and because of his belief that there was "incipient revolution in the air" as he called it, he paid no attention to my dissent. He ordered me to get into uniform. (In that administration officers went to work in Washington in civilian clothes because a military appearance around the nation's capital was held to be undesirable.)

I reported back at the hour fixed by the Chief and then, with his aide and a couple of others, we went out. One of the officers was George Patton, then a major commanding a squadron of cavalry at Fort Myer. A few old-fashioned tanks were brought in but, so far as I can recall, they took no part whatever in the movements to evacuate the veterans.

The veterans made no more vigorous protest than a little cat-calling and jeering at the soldiers, who were only performing their duty as they edged the men away from the area under dispute. The veterans were guided or nudged in the general direction of the Anacostia River and the bridge over it. The movement proceeded slowly.

Instructions were received from the Secretary of War, who said he was speaking for the President, which forbade any troops to cross the bridge into the largest encampment of veterans, on open ground beyond the bridge.

These instructions were brought to the troops by Colonel Wright, Secretary of the General Staff, and then by General Moseley of the Assistant Secretary's office. In neither instance did General MacArthur hear these instructions. He said he was too busy and did not want either himself or his staff bothered by people coming down and pretending to bring orders.

In any event, we marched at the head of the column right on across the bridge, halting the troops on the other side. Shortly afterward, the whole encampment of shacks and huts just ahead began burning. I know that no troops started the fire; they were too far away. Some of the veterans themselves, to show their displeasure, must have started the blazes going in scattered spots throughout the camp.

The whole scene was pitiful. The veterans, whether or not they were mistaken in marching on Washington, were ragged, ill-fed, and felt themselves badly abused. To suddenly see the whole encampment going up in flames just added to the pity one had to feel for them. Later the troops were dismissed except for a small group that was left to watch for any attempted return of the veterans into the city itself. But the whole action, from beginning to end, did nothing to alleviate the lot of the veterans or to enhance the reputation of the government and the Army. When General MacArthur got into his automobile to go back to the War Department, I remarked that there would probably be newspaper reporters trying to see him. I suggested it would be the better part of wisdom, if not of valor, to avoid meeting them. The troop movement had not been a military idea really, but a political order and I thought that the political officials only should talk to the press. He disagreed and saw the newspapermen that night.

I think this meeting led to the prevailing impression that General MacArthur himself had undertaken and directed the move against the veterans and that he was acting as something more than the agent of civilian authorities. Popular impressions are difficult to eradicate and I have read in recent years at least one account that said that this was one of the darkest blots on the MacArthur reputation. This, I feel, is unfortunate.

Ordinarily, General MacArthur would have been relieved as Chief of Staff in the fall of 1934. However, reorganization in the War Department was going on and it is possible that the President had not yet chosen the man he wanted to appoint as the next Chief. General MacArthur's tour was extended by one year.

Toward the end of this period, a bill had been passed in the Congress bestowing commonwealth status on the Philippine Islands for ten years. The ten years would give the Philippine government, then headed by Manuel Quezon, an increasing degree of autonomy, as it went about preparing for an independent existence. This included the design and buildup of its security forces.

Most new countries, bent upon achieving complete self-rule, cannot understand what is in store for them in carrying the responsibilities as well as the pride of independence. But in the case of the Philippines there was a reasonable understanding of these responsibilities and the need for careful planning. The United States constantly expressed its intention to free the nation and also to support an effort to develop among the Filipinos the talents and skills necessary for self-rule. At times the pace may have been slow because the target date for independence was undecided and the preparatory period's length was anyone's guess. But the law of 1935 set up a fixed date and thereafter the race was on within the Philippine government to prepare for nationhood.

In all history, the American decision was at that time unique. So far as I can recall, never before had a great power, a war victor, deliberately proposed independence at a certain and fixed date for an occupied country except under the pressure of armed revolt. The congressional action on the future of the Philippine people had a unique effect on my own professional life. After two decades, the wheel of fortune had made a full turn. In 1915, forecasting my future, I was sure that the Philippines would be my first assignment.

Now, although no hint had ever been raised that I might go there—for one thing there were no Filipino football teams to coach—Manila was to be my next destination. In the happenstance of Army life I had become associated with General MacArthur and the General was a natural candidate for a special role in the Islands.

Of all American names, after William Howard Taft, MacArthur's carried weight to the point of veneration in the Philippines. His father, our last military governor there, was a symbol of American might in battle and American understanding around the conference table. The son, a general officer in our forces in the Islands before he became Chief of Staff, had won the confidence and admiration of Manuel Quezon, who was about to become the head of the Commonwealth government. In Quezon's judgment, no other man could generate in the Philippine people the esprit as well as the willingness for work and sacrifice needed in the development of defense forces that had to be created from scratch.

Quezon proposed that General MacArthur become Military Adviser to the emerging nation. MacArthur accepted the invitation enthusiastically.

During my last months in the office of the Chief of Staff, Major James Ord and I were engaged in devising a defense program which we hoped would be within the economic capabilities of the Philippine government. Although I was not ecstatic about the prospect of going to the Islands—I thought I deserved, after years of staff work, a chance to serve again with troops—General MacArthur was still Chief of Staff and was very insistent that I go along with him for a year or so.

He said that he and I had worked together for a long time and he didn't want to bring in somebody new. In addition to the implied compliment, this insistence revealed a human quality in the General who even then was thought to be a mysterious, romantic figure far above the frailty of dependence on others. Only a few months earlier he had dared to take on the President, opposing Roosevelt's request to the Congress for unlimited authority to control Army strength. At all times, he seemed so certain of his own professional superiority over his fellow officers and of a high place in American history that he developed in the American public a like appraisal of his merits. His was truly a case where self-confidence breeds self-success. Those about him knew that he was made neither entirely of gold, nor even of brass for that matter; he had his share of human clay, of oddities and affectations. At times he acted like any other member of the office staff, although I never recall him actually descending to such chores as running the mimeograph. Nevertheless, his emphatic insistence on my continuing with him was a distinction that I could not fully appreciate yet. In the decades that followed, I came to understand better that in making his request General Mac-Arthur made himself more like most of us. Whatever our position, whatever the power we exercise under the weight of responsibility, we need familiar faces about us as much as we need expert opinion or wise counsel. Although the faces at times may be reminders of past tests endured and passed rather than a guarantee of success in future trials, they are heartening. They show loyalty, visible evidence that one does not stand alone.

The faces around a man need not be ever-flowing sources of profound judgments or the source of cataracts of staff memoranda. In the White House years, the numerous excellent minds about me, and the wise counselors from the departments of government, sustained and sometimes inspired me. But the faces need not be topped by gray hair. The presence there of my grandchildren—the toys strewn across the path to the office, the children's extreme audibility when they cut loose with tongue and larynx—was a similar stimulus. John and Barbara's children somehow helped to remind me that the country would not go to the dogs nor the world collapse in ruins. Perhaps they suggested, too, that it must not. They, together with Mamie's mother, Mim, represented for me a personal link with the long past before I was born and with the long future of the Republic after I would go.

But when General MacArthur lowered the boom on me, so to speak, I could not comfort myself with such perspective. Duty with troops was my first desire. Psychologists might argue that my wish was simply a preference for the known over the unknown. I do not know. Whatever might have been going on inside me, I was in no position to argue with the Chief of Staff.

Nor did I succeed in getting from General MacArthur a fixed period for the assignment. One privilege he did permit, possibly realizing that a familiar face meant as much to me as to him. He said I could pick one associate from the Regular Army to go along with us. I contacted Major Ord, a classmate, and a man whom I wanted with us not only because of his quickness of mind and ability as a staff officer but because he was as much at home in Spanish—the principal language of the Philippines after Tagalog—as he was in English. Jimmy Ord was eager to go.

The defense plan he and I had worked up did not recognize that we already had a principal enemy: money, or its lack.

We had made assumptions about the availability of munitions and set a meager pay scale for the conscript army, favorable to a low budget. We came up with a program of 50 million pesos—that is $25 million—in an annual budget.

General MacArthur had been in communication with President Quezon and even before we had this outline plan completed, we were called before the General, who told us that the sums we had been contemplating were entirely beyond the financial capabilities of the Philippine government. We'd have to reduce our estimates, he said, by 50 per cent. So we started off anew, discarding the earlier plan.

We decided that during the early years, at least, the Philippines could get along with obsolete American Army equipment. We assumed that we could get it on loan and without cost. We reduced the pay of the Philippine conscript to little more than cigarette money, and cut down the contingent of officers to the point where this would be dangerously close to an army of recruits only. We thought that such a makeshift force would be rejected out of hand as worthless for defense.

Instead we were told that Quezon could produce a revenue of 16 million pesos a year for the project but no more. This made for a paper-thin plan. Once again, we reduced the numbers of divisions and the length of training. At first we'd insisted that one full year of training was necessary; now we wrote in a six-months tour, suggesting for longer service only certain types of specialists who would have to be taught maintenance and technical tasks necessary in any army worthy of the name.

By this time, Jimmy and I were muttering to ourselves that "They also serve who only draft and draft." We were fast learning that the is attached to any proposal in any nation, funds are made available, I've often read that once the label of defense or military security is attached to any proposal in any nation, funds are made available, that newly independent nations prize military establishments as the chief symbol of their freedom. This was not true of the emerging Philippine nation. So far as I know, Manila did not house a single pacifist. It did not house a single free spender, either. And the people there had not yet been persuaded that deficit spending fosters prosperity. All Jimmy Ord and I could do was to assemble our proposals for a skeleton force that some day might have flesh put on its bones. We turned it in with fingers crossed.

This done, we set about drafting a law to present to the Philippine legislature to have the force authorized. We could no longer think of a Navy of any size whatsoever and for the moment we abandoned the possibility of developing a small air force—capable of reconnaissance and possibly light bombing against any attempted landing.

Of course, during the intervening ten years before independence, we had to assume that American forces with land-based aviation and with U. S. Navy and Philippine Scouts would take care of defenses of the Islands. Indeed, that was still an American responsibility. With the limited funds available, however, no matter how ingenious our schemes might be, we knew that we could not hope for any respectable force earlier than the date of complete independence—that is, the year 1946.

CHAPTER XV

With MacArthur in the Philippines

WHETHER or not those of us in the small group that departed Washington for Manila thought that we were on a singular and striking mission—a great power was deliberately and voluntarily proposing to arm and train a dependent people—I don't recall. Even though our Chief, Douglas MacArthur, spoke and wrote in purple splendor, his subordinates were restrained in the language we used about the future. We played it down as just another job.

We knew we would be scraping for pennies and pesos. In the judgment of outsiders, of course, the presence of General MacArthur outweighed limitless amounts of money and men. Unhappily, at the very outset, he suffered two shocks.

The first struck while we were still en route to the West Coast. One moment Douglas MacArthur was Chief of Staff of the United States Army, whose arrival in Manila would be dramatic testimony that our country considered Philippine independence and defense so important that the head of our Army had been sent there to help; and the next moment, after he tore open a telegram from Washington and read it in silence, he learned that he was now only a former Chief of Staff, and was reduced from four-star to two-star rank.

Firmly fixed in the General's mind was the conviction that President Roosevelt had agreed to retain him in the top position until a month after his arrival in Manila. The prestige of those four stars in the eyes of the Filipinos would have been a certain help, he thought. He would be retiring as Chief of Staff to aid the new cause. Suddenly, out of the clear at an isolated railroad station hundreds of miles from Washington, to learn that a new COS had been appointed caused him to express himself freely. It was an explosive denunciation of politics, bad manners, bad judgment, broken promises, arrogance, unconstitutionality, insensitivity, and the way the world had gone to hell. Then he sent an eloquent telegram of congratulations to his successor.

In the long run, except for personal resentments, no harm may have been done to our mission. The second blow, falling months later, had a more deeply personal effect. It deprived the General of a lifelong source of inspiration and strength, his mother.

The widow of General Arthur MacArthur was among the most remarkable of Army wives and mothers. All her life she had been with the Army on the frontier and in the Pacific, as well as in Washington. She was imbued with assurance that her son was destined for greatness; she lived for him and his success. Despite his own immense talents, the General relied heavily on her when the going was tough; he shared with her as a partner the joys of achievement.

Shortly after we boarded the *President Harding*, she became ill. Not long after our arrival in Manila, she was dead. Her departure from his side, and from his counsels, affected the General's spirit for many months.

We settled temporarily in the Manila hotel. The Ords and their two children looked for a house in the city. Because Mamie had decided to stay in Washington so that our son, John, could complete the eighth grade in that city, I continued to live in the hotel.

From the outset, the work was difficult. We tried to figure new and better ways to provide a reasonable defense establishment once the Islands were on their own. This meant that the Islands would have to be dependent to some extent upon the United States government, upon its generosity and readiness to accept the security of the Philippines as a matter of vital interest to the United States. We worked full tilt to polish up drafts of the necessary law, getting advice from Philippine legislators. As soon as the law was passed, we started to build little training stations—nothing more than barracks and cleared spaces in various sections of the Islands. To minimize transportation costs we built more than ninety of these stations, with about two hundred conscripts in each place.

We soon saw that it was necessary to have a small "air force" even if for nothing else than to get to the training stations. The roadnet of the Philippines archipelago, comprising something over seven thousand islands, was still primitive except in Luzon. Light planes that could land and take off from short strips would make every training site accessible.

So, aiming at two birds with one stone, we bought a few primary

trainers of the type used at Randolph Field and borrowed two instructors from the Army Air Corps.

Though we worked doggedly through 1936 and 1937, ours was
a hopeless venture, in a sense. The Philippine government simply
could not afford to build real security from attack. We had to content ourselves with an attempt to produce a military adequate to
deal with domestic revolt and to provide at least a passive type of
defense around the perimeter of the Islands to slow up the advance
of any aggressor until some friendly nation, presumably the United
States, came to their aid.

We were encountering then an example of the costs of independence that others have met more recently when so many dependent
colonies find themselves on their own and a little bit intoxicated by
freedom. Too many Filipinos, even those high in government, were
concerned with the privileges of independence and too little with its
responsibilities and costs. Often President Quezon and I talked this
over. He had prepared a private office for me in his Malacañan
Palace because of the amount of work I had to do between his
office and ours as liaison agent. He understood but insisted that
national pride would demand that they have at least some kind of
military force.

Then there was an incident that chilled the warm relationship
that Jimmy Ord and I had with General MacArthur. The General
had an idea that the morale of the whole population would be en-
hanced if the people could see something of their emerging army
in the capital city, Manila. He suggested a large demonstration of
strength, bringing units from all over the Islands to a field near the
city, and camping them there for three or four days. The city's
population could visit them and it would all end with a big parade.

Jimmy and I estimated the cost. We told the General that it was
impossible to do the thing within our budget. Carrying out this
demonstration would take money that was desperately needed for
more important purposes. But following the General's orders, we
began to do the necessary staff work.

Among other details, we had to arrange with island shipping
firms to bring in the troops. It wasn't long until news of this reached
the Philippine government. President Quezon called me in from
the little office in Malacañan, said he had heard about the planned
troop movement, and asked me what it was all about.

I was astonished. We had assumed that the project had first been agreed on between the President and General MacArthur. When I discovered that this was not the case, I told Quezon that I thought we should discuss it no further until I could see General MacArthur. But Quezon was disturbed and said he was going to telephone the General. I said I would withdraw to my office and when he wanted me again, he could reach me there.

He didn't call and I returned to my other office in the Walled City within the hour. General MacArthur was exceedingly unhappy with his entire staff. By the time I saw him, he was visibly upset. He said he had never meant for us to proceed with preparations for the parade. He had only wanted us to investigate it quietly. Now the matter had come to the ears of the President who was horrified to think that we were ready for a costly national parade in the capital. Because General MacArthur denied he had given us an order—which was certainly news to us—there was nothing to do except stop the proceedings. This misunderstanding caused considerable resentment—and never again were we on the same warm and cordial terms.

In the beginning of 1936, we fixed up a field outside the city limits, selected a few students, and started a miniature air force. The students learned rapidly and I decided to take flying lessons, informally, from Captain Lewis and Lieutenant William Lee, the American instructors. Because I was learning to fly at the age of forty-six, my reflexes were slower than those of the younger men. Training me must have been a trial of patience for Lewis and Lee.[*]

Little more than thirty years had passed since Kitty Hawk. One had to react alertly to changes in sound or wind or temperature. The engines were good but the pilot who asked too much of one, in a steep climb, for example, learned that the roaring monster could retreat into silent surrender.

The seat of the pants was a surer guide to navigation than the few instruments and beacons we had. The pilot depended on his eyes, scanning terrain for landmarks, and on his ears to tell him that all was well under the cowling. There was a compass to help, when mineral deposits did not excite it into a dance. Other instruments were few and fairly primitive. Once the pilot left the ground, he was

---

[*] After a time Lewis left, was replaced by a Lieutenant Parker, who, in turn, was replaced by a Lieutenant Anderson—all of which suggests that I wore out lieutenants fairly fast.

on his own, lord of all he surveyed or its victim. He was alone as he never could be in cities or towns.

To attract attention for a landing or a message, we buzzed a building until its occupants ran out. They never knew whether we were just visiting or in trouble. To communicate was a simple matter: you wrapped a message around a stone and dropped it as close as possible to them. We did have maps. One slight problem was that tropical landscapes, viewed from several thousand feet up, bore slight resemblance to the best map. In my examination for a pilot's license, on July 19, 1939, I wrote:

To locate position on map get into clear area where ground is visible. Seek prominent landmarks such as railways, rivers, main roads, cities, which may be readily located on map. If possible, fly low over a railroad station or other structure on which name of locality may appear.

If these means do not immediately help, then fly compass course toward a general area of known fair weather, and again seek landmarks, etc.

In other words, just keep flying until you run out of gas or your luck changes. But it was fun and at the end of the tour, I had 350 hours in my flight log.

After World War II, I had ceased to fly altogether, except that once in a while, on a long trip, to relieve my boredom (and demolish the pilot's), I would move into the co-pilot's seat and take over the controls. But as the jet age arrived, I realized that I had come out of a horse-and-buggy background, recognized my limitations, and kept to a seat in the back.

Jimmy Ord was not only a congenial fellow, he was a top-flight officer. He helped to make light work of the heavy chore of building defenses out of little or nothing. He had to make a trip to Baguio one day. I was in the hospital for the moment and when he came in to say so long, he mentioned that he was taking one of the Filipino students as pilot. "No, you won't," I said. "Get one of the American flight instructors. They'll be glad to do it."

He laughed and said, "Our Filipino boys are doing really well. I'll use one of them. I won't be gone more than a few hours. See you late this afternoon."

As they neared the air strip in Baguio, up in the mountains of northern Luzon, Jimmy decided to drop a note near the house of his friends, the Fairchild family. He told the pilot to circle the place. In circling, the plane lost speed and crashed. The pilot and the plane were not badly damaged. But Jimmy, who was leaning out of the back seat, had his body whipped around so violently that his injuries were grave. He died within a few hours.

From then on, more of the planning work fell on my shoulders, but without my friend, all the zest was gone. We looked around for a replacement and a staff officer, Lieutenant Colonel Richard Sutherland, serving with the 15th Infantry in China, was assigned to us. As a companion and comrade, no one could fill the void left by Jimmy's death, but Sutherland was capable and I appreciated his help.

President Quezon seemed to ask for my advice more and more. He invited me to his office frequently. This was partly because of the office hours General MacArthur liked to keep. He never reached his desk until eleven. After a late lunch hour, he went home again. This made it difficult for Quezon to get in touch with the General when he wanted him. Because I was the senior active duty officer, my friendship with the President became closer.

Our conversations became broader and deeper. They were no longer confined to the defense problem. Taxes, education, honesty in government, and other subjects entered the discussions and he seemed to enjoy them. Certainly I did.

From time to time, I suffered attacks of bursitis but these were nothing at all compared to a strange intestinal ailment. The doctors called it a "partial stoppage." For a long time I was on a bland diet but I suffered no acute attacks and gradually drifted back to old habits. As a result, I suffered at least two more attacks after the first serious one in 1936. When, finally, twenty years later I had an attack requiring surgery, the doctors had a new name: ileitis.

In 1938, my family and I went back to the United States briefly. I wanted to ask the War Department for more help. At first they were unsympathetic. As long as the Philippines insisted on being independent, the War Department's attitude was that they could jolly well look out after their own defenses. To end the interminable frustrations at lower echelons, I went to the top. The Chief of Staff of the Army was General Malin Craig. I told him my story, adding that General MacArthur's view was that a friendly Philippines, with a government able to provide at least delaying action in the event of enemy invasion, was vital to U.S. interests. General Craig agreed and in short order the word seeped down to his staff. Doors that had been tightly closed began to open and we secured a number of concessions and much assistance.

It has to be remembered that the American Army itself was starved for appropriations. The Army was down to about 118,000, its total expenditures perhaps $300 million, including its Air Corps. There wasn't much the Army could do for the Philippines without cutting the ground out from under U.S. preparedness. The War Department did put us in touch with manufacturers who were ready to do business at the right price, and the Army provided obsolete but useful equipment—such as the World War I Enfield rifles. We couldn't do much about getting light training airplanes or infantry mortars.

After begging or borrowing everything I could from the Signal, Quartermaster, Ordnance, and Medical groups, I went to Wichita, bought several planes, then to the Winchester Arms Company in Connecticut. With what I had "liberated" and bought, I went back to Manila. (My family had joined me and John went to school in the mountains at Baguio.)

There was uneasiness about the possibility of war. The Nazis were in the saddle and riding hard in central Europe. Among other things, they were persecuting the Jews unmercifully and many of the Jewish faith were fleeing Germany, trying to find homes elsewhere in the world. In Manila, arguments started between those people who for some strange reason were supporters of Hitler, and the rest of us. It was difficult to keep the arguments, even in social gatherings at the Army-Navy Club, under control. The Philippines had undergone four hundred years of domination by Spain. The results were mixed. Almost without exception, though, the Spanish community was on Hitler's side, partly because they believed that Hitler supported the Franco government to which most of them gave their support. Hirohito got little attention. There was a considerable Jewish community in the city and I had good friends among them.

Out of the Jewish ordeal in Europe, an unusual offer was made to me. Through several friends, I was asked to take a job seeking in China, Southeast Asia, Indonesia, and every country where they might be acceptable, a haven for Jewish refugees from Nazi Germany. The pay would be $60,000 a year, with expenses. The first five years' salary would be placed in escrow to be delivered to me if I should be separated from the new job for any cause whatsoever.

The offer was, of course, appealing for several reasons. But this time, I had become so committed to my profession that I declined.

The arguments and tensions developed there caused apprehension about what might happen to the Philippines if war should break out. It was almost universally conceded that a European war would rapidly become global. General MacArthur did his best to allay fears. He wrote a long paper, describing why it would be to the disadvantage of Japan, for example, to attack the Philippines. He assumed that the Japanese leaders were rational and not only would be friendly to the Philippines but would try to make treaties with the new nation. Because he believed this, he went to some lengths to assure the Filipinos that they would never be attacked. At the same time, he speeded up the military training program.

I became certain that the conflict that General Conner had consistently predicted fifteen years earlier was likely to break out. We did our best to keep up with the news, with what came in by radio and cable, and what could be gathered by the intelligence office of the Regular Army forces in the Philippines. I saw the intelligence officer at least once a week.

One evening I went to visit a friend, Howard Smith, a colonel in the Public Health Service. Howard had an antiquated radio that, under favorable conditions, pulled in transoceanic messages. We listened to it with earphones, while Mamie and Mrs. Smith chatted. And so it came about, as we were listening closely, that we heard the British Prime Minister, Neville Chamberlain, in a stiffly formal but stricken voice, say:

This morning the British ambassador in Berlin handed the German government a final note stating that, unless we heard from them by 11 o'clock that they were prepared at once to withdraw their troops from Poland, a state of war would exist between us. I have to tell you now that no such undertaking has been received, and that consequently this country is at war with Germany.

You can imagine what a bitter blow it is to me that all my long struggle to win peace has failed. Yet I cannot believe that there was anything more or anything different that I could have done and that would have been more successful. . . .

Now may God bless you all. May He defend the right. It is the evil things that we shall be fighting against—brute force, bad faith, injustice, oppression, and persecution—and against them I am certain that the right will prevail.

General MacArthur had been retired from active service for the United States but he still headed the American Advisory Group developing the Philippine Army. I went to him. "General," I said, "in my opinion the United States cannot remain out of this war for long. I want to go home as soon as possible. I want to participate in the preparatory work that I'm sure is going to be intense."

MacArthur said that I was making a mistake. The work I was doing in the Philippines was far more important than any I could do as a mere lieutenant colonel in the American Army.

I reminded him that because the War Department had decided I was more useful as an instructor in the United States than as a fighting man in World War I, I had missed combat in that conflict. I was now determined to do everything I could to make sure I would not miss this crisis of our country.

Manuel Quezon was far more emphatic than General MacArthur in insisting that I remain. He handed me a blank contract for my services and said, "We'll tear up the old contract. I've already signed this one and it is filled in—except what you want as your emoluments for remaining. You will write that in."

"Mr. President," I said, "your offer is flattering. But no amount of money can make me change my mind. My entire life has been given to this one thing, my country and my profession. I want to be there if what I fear is going to come about actually happens."

He finally accepted my decision and before long we had a beautiful farewell luncheon in the Malacañan Palace, overlooking the river that flowed past.

Mamie, young John, and I departed for San Francisco by liner. We spent Christmas in Hawaii and were in San Francisco to celebrate New Year's. That city, I know, is surely one of the world's most stimulating places. Along with London and Paris and Rome, it is not to be missed by those who seek the unique and the exhilarating. Although I have spent more time in the English and French capitals, I have a special fondness for the city by the Golden Gate. On New Year's Eve, one side of Market Street was so crowded with enthusiastic celebrants that the nimble-footed might have walked on their heads; the cable cars were festooned with passengers who hid the vehicles from sight; the whole city that night, in all its extravagance of blaring horns and shouting people, was unforgettable. The noise and the glitter were the end of our peaceful decade of family life together. Ahead of John lay four years at West Point; for Mamie, premonitions about the future, and long and lonely months when both her son and her husband would be far off.

For me, the next six years would be thronged with challenges and chances, work and decisions, for which all my life I had been preparing. As we said farewell to 1939 and welcomed in a new year and a new decade, we thought grimly but optimistically of the nation's future. I hoped that a field command awaited me. When dawn broke over the Presidio of San Francisco, only the job just finished in Manila and the unknown job immediately ahead were in my mind.

Book Three

AT WAR

CHAPTER XVI

The States Again

THE ORDERS sending me to Fort Lewis, Washington, were changed by the Army commander in San Francisco. I was to remain on temporary duty at his headquarters for planning work.

Mamie and I had been anxious to incur the least possible interruption in John's schooling. Believing that we were going to be on duty in Tacoma, we had entered him in the senior high-school class. Fortunately, my brother Edgar lived in that city and he and John had long ago formed a natural attachment. Mamie and I sent John to Ed and then tried to catch up on what was going on in our country, the one to which we were so glad to return. The government had become convinced that the United States could no longer hope that our distance from Europe and Asia would serve as security. Although isolationism was still rampant in parts of the country, and its spokesmen, often men of integrity and indisputable patriotism, were insistent that we were in no danger, an increasing majority of our people saw that if we had to go to war unprepared, the penalty would be disaster.

Selective Service was enacted and assured manpower for an expanding Army. National Guard divisions were readied for active duty, military budgets were substantially increased. Using hindsight, we were not doing all that we should have. Still, in the circumstances of the time, at peace with the world, our government and people alike were showing a sharpened sense of responsibility.

The Army commander at San Francisco, General DeWitt, sent for me and explained the reason for the emergency change in orders. "These headquarters, Ike," he said, "have just received from the Chief of Staff a directive to concentrate for training exercises in California all the National Guard and Regular Army troops of the whole area." His army area comprised the entire West Coast and stretched northward into the interior, including the state of Minnesota. "One of our problems is to move all the troops, mostly by rail, into a training area in southern California for maneuvers."

The National Guard troops were authorized to be on active duty for a short time; three weeks, as I recall. The assignment was to get camps established, bring them all into the proper station, and start training as quickly as the first units arrived. The orders had been specific—all the training was to be done in one spot.

A quick study of the problem showed that someone in the War Department had not done his homework. To bring troops from Minneapolis, for example, to the single spot in southern California would take so many days that the last train bringing the last unit from Minneapolis would arrive just in time to turn around and start the trek back. General DeWitt had put me into a planning section under a Colonel who was a stickler for orders. I reported to this officer that the limited transportation facilities available by rail would not allow us to train all the troops in one spot. There was no solution, I suggested, except to establish at least two mobilization points and camps.

"I'm accustomed to obeying orders," the Colonel said stiffly, "and there will be no shift from the specifications given us." He instructed me not to take my conclusions to the Army commander.

This brought our planning activities to an impasse. At about that time, the Army was putting on a field exercise with an amphibious landing on a California beach south of San Francisco. The Colonel and I went down to observe the operation. While walking along the beach, we ran into General Marshall and General DeWitt who spoke to me briefly. General Marshall's only comment, a laconic reference to the luxuries we had in the Philippines, was "Have you learned to tie your own shoes again since coming back, Eisenhower?" As an old Philippine hand himself, he was mindful of the servants and services available there.

I grinned and said, "Yes, Sir, I am capable of that chore anyhow." This was the second time General Marshall and I had met.

General DeWitt then took me aside. "How're you getting along with the planning?" I told him about the difficulty in transportation but said we were carrying out the plans as ordered.

He said, in mixed surprise and annoyance, "If this is true, why haven't you been in to see me?"

"Because the Colonel felt we shouldn't bother you."

He said he would straighten it out.

A day or two later, when General DeWitt called the Colonel to his office to ask about the plans, the Colonel said, "Eisenhower has worked out all the schedules for shipping and camping and everything else. Everything is in order except for the fact that the troops from Minneapolis can't reach the concentration area in time to participate actively in the exercise." General DeWitt said quietly that the War Department orders were not intended to be impractical and asked him to draw up a plan for two concentrations. I completed the work in a few days.

Then I was free to go up to Fort Lewis.

The assignment to the 15th Infantry Regiment, restoring me to active duty with troops, was fine. In the main, the men were seasoned. Many had seen service in China before the Regiment's return to the States two years earlier. The rest were volunteers. The 15th and the other regiments of the 3rd Infantry Division were ready for maneuvers by mid-summer. Although my regiment was undermanned by 400 troops, understaffed in experienced officers, underequipped in trucks, machine guns, and mortars, we did a thorough job of combat training over some of the most difficult terrain in the country, the "cut-over" land of Washington State.

Stumps, slashings, fallen logs, tangled brush, pitfalls, hummocks, and hills made the land a stage setting for a play in Hades. Although I was regimental executive, I asked for and got command of a battalion. Through the day, like everyone else on maneuvers, I sweated and accumulated a grime of caked dust. At night, we froze. Never in any one stretch did I have more than two hours' sleep. At times, I was really fagged out. But all of us learned lessons that would pay off in combat. The experience fortified my conviction that I belonged with troops; with them I was always happy.

I made my desires for continued service with troops clear to every Army friend I met, particularly visitors from Washington who were involved in personnel administration.

Then, in the mail one early fall morning of 1940, I had reason for outright elation: a letter from George Patton seemed almost a guarantee that in case of war I would not be left at home. He wrote that he expected to get one of the new armored divisions to be organized soon. He intended to ask for me as a regimental commander under him.

Immediately, I got off a note to my good friend, Mark Clark, then assigned to General Headquarters, where he was in close touch with the Chief of Infantry. I asked him to try to make sure that I would be

let alone for a while, so that I would be available for the Armored
Force when the time came. By no means did I want the reputation
of an eager beaver—but having a temporary success as a fugitive
from the staff, I hoped to remain so.

For a few weeks, I continued to dream about an armored command under George Patton. But the roof fell in on me shortly after
the middle of November when the signal officer at Fort Lewis passed
to me a telegram from Leonard Gerow, my classmate and associate
at Leavenworth in the two-man command post we conducted in the
attic of my quarters there fifteen years earlier. Now a brigadier general and Chief of the War Plans Division in the War Department, he
wired:

I NEED YOU IN WAR PLANS DIVISION DO YOU SERIOUSLY OBJECT TO
BEING DETAILED ON THE WAR DEPT GENERAL STAFF AND ASSIGNED
HERE PLEASE REPLY IMMEDIATELY

Despite the compliment implicit in the word "need" in connection
with duty at the highest Army level, shock waves of consternation
hit me, faintly described in the opening sentence of the letter I wrote
him: "Your telegram, arriving this morning, sent me into a tailspin."

In the few hours between the arrival of Gerow's telegram and my
reply, I reviewed in my mind and tried to evaluate the ramifications
of this new development. There was the possibility that once again
—should we go to war—I'd be shut out of combat duty. An attack
of shingles, the first and last of my life, did not make things easier.
The doctors thought it serious enough to recommend hospitalization.
I managed to dodge, for I was less miserable when I had something
to occupy my mind. But straight thinking, in the midst of physical
pain and a disturbing query, was a little difficult.

I did not want to be considered as a slacker or a cry baby but I
honestly felt that after all my years of almost constant staff assignments, I really deserved troop duty. So I decided to tell Gerow the
whole story. I pointedly told him at the outset that after he had read
the letter, if he should decide that I belonged in the War Department,
all he had to do was issue the orders. I continued:

In the first place, I want to make it clear that I am, and have always
been, very serious in my belief that the individual's preferences and desires
should have little, if any weight in determining his assignment, when superior authority is making a decision in the matter. So all the rest of this
is because, by implication, you asked for it!

In the body of the letter, I tried to present, as factually as I could, my record and my wishes.

At the moment, I may very well have thought that letter one of the most important I had ever written. Unknown to me, the long train of gears in War Department processing were about to mesh.

In the letter, I had mentioned that General Thompson, commanding the 3rd Division stationed at Fort Lewis, planned to put my name before the War Department to fill another staff job—as his Chief of Staff. So far as I knew, no one in Washington was aware of his intentions. I was wrong. A few days after writing Gerow, I got a radiogram from him that ended my fears of a Washington desk job and my hopes of field command.

AFTER CAREFUL CONSIDERATION OF CONTENTS OF YOUR LETTER AND THE WISHES OF GENERAL THOMPSON AS INDICATED TO GI I HAVE WITHDRAWN MY REQUEST FOR YOUR DETAIL TO WAR PLANS DIVN WILL WRITE DETAILS LATER REGRET OUR SERVICE TOGETHER MUST BE POSTPONED

When I next wrote Gee Gerow, I said: ". . . in trying to explain to you a situation that has been tossed in my teeth more than once [my lack of extended troop duty in recent years], all I accomplished was to pass up something I *wanted* to do, in favor of something I thought I *ought* to do, and then . . . find myself not even doing the latter."

When I answered the first telegram, Mamie would not give me a hint of what she preferred. She did not want my decision to be affected by her personal wishes. But somehow I learned that what she desired more than anything else was an assignment to Washington.

My feelings about the whole mess were expressed in one short sentence: "Actually, Gee, the job of staying with a regiment is a damn near hopeless one." And that is exactly how I felt. Well, at least I could recommend others. The letter ended with:

P.S. Serving on the G.H.Q. staff is one of the finest officers in our Army, Lt. Col. Wayne [Mark] Clark. When you get a chance, get hold of him and have a half-hour's talk.

While we were at Fort Lewis, in 1940, Mamie and I had a conversation with our son when John had informed us he wanted to try

for a West Point appointment. I thought it wise, before his desire
became decision, to ask him to consider, objectively, the possible
advantages of a civilian educational institution.

I had known a few Army brats whose parents had virtually forced
them to try for a West Point appointment because of the strain a
college would put on the family budget. I did not want John to feel
that this was happening to him. My purpose was not so much to
discourage him as to suggest the diversity of opportunity. "While we
don't have any money to speak of, we can still finance a college education—even if it extends over eight or ten years." I contrasted the
relatively relaxed attitude of student bodies in colleges I had visited
with the highly disciplined cadet existence. I talked about what he
might expect in later years. If he could develop as a lawyer, doctor,
or businessman, he could probably go just as far as his character,
abilities, and honorable ambitions could carry him. In the Army, I
had said, things are ordered somewhat differently. No matter what an
officer's ability might be, his promotion was governed strictly, under
laws then current, by the rule of seniority until he reached the grade
of colonel. To make the point, I took myself as an example.

John knew that I had been in the Army since 1911 and a commissioned officer for twenty-five years. During all this time, the reports rendered by my commanders (after West Point) had always
been satisfactory and I had been informed officially that among field
officers I was classed in the top category. I had graduated from both
the War College and Leavenworth Staff and Command School,
standing at the head of my class at Leavenworth. But, I emphasized,
no peacetime record had any influence in pushing a man faster up
the ladder of promotion until, after slow seniority, he had reached
the grade of colonel. Then he became eligible for selection to a
brigadier generalcy, regardless of seniority, for the first time in his
career.

Personnel offices of the Army had shown me that my class would
not reach the grade of colonel until something like 1950, at which
time I—as one of the older men in my class—would be sixty years
of age. Because the War Department did not promote colonels to
general officer grade with a short time remaining before compulsory
retirement, the chances of my ever obtaining a star in the Army were
nil. (I had put in a caveat by saying, "Of course, in an emergency,
anything can happen—but we're talking about a career, John, not
miracles.")

John must have wondered why I stayed in the Army at all. To give him the less gloomy side of the picture, I said that my Army experience had been wonderfully interesting and it had brought me into contact with men of ability, honor, and a sense of high dedication to their country. I reminded John of the incident in the Philippines, when a group wanted me to leave the Army with an ironclad five-year contract at $60,000 a year. The offer had few temptations.

Happy in my work and ready to face, without resentment, the bleak promotional picture, I had long ago refused to bother my head about promotion. Whenever the subject came up among the three of us at home, I said the real satisfaction was for a man who did the best he could. My ambition in the Army was to make everybody I worked for regretful when I was ordered to other duty.

John listened seriously and promised to think it over. A few days later, my brother Ed dropped in to see me. Edgar's law business in Tacoma was thriving and he had been thinking about passing it on, at a future time, to a relative. He liked John and believed he had a logical and what he called a "legal" brain. He had offered John a proposition:

"If you'll go to any college of your own choosing for four years, and then through three years of law, I'll pay the entire expenses of your education. If you join my law firm, I'll pay you twice your military salary at any comparable stage of your career—until you're earning more. Then, you're on your own."

Ed said, rather ruefully: "You know, that young devil just looked me in the eye and said, 'Thanks, Uncle Ed; I appreciate your offer. But I've made up my mind.'"

John was around the house somewhere and I called him.

"Obviously, John, from what Uncle Ed says, you've made up your mind to try to enter West Point."

"Yes, that's right."

I asked him about his reasons. The substance of his answer was: "It's because of what you told me the other evening. When you talked about the satisfaction you had in an Army career, and the pride you had in being associated with men of character, my mind was made up right then." He added, "If I can say the same thing when I've finished my Army career, I'll care no more about promotions than you did."

☆   ☆   ☆   ☆   ☆

On the last day of November, with Pearl Harbor twelve months and
one week off, my active service with troops came to an end. Orders arriving that day detailed me to the General Staff Corps, assigned to
duty as Chief of Staff, 3rd Division, Fort Lewis, effective immediately. I was back on the staff—but at least with the designation
"General Staff with Troops." I had escaped Washington and, to that
extent, felt lucky.

Because of rapid Army expansion, Lewis was one of the busiest
spots in the country. Day and night it was clamoring with construction crews working and thousands of recruits moving in to replace
thousands of soldiers who had finished their basic training. My stint
lasted three months.

At the beginning of March 1941, I became Chief of Staff to the
IX Army Corps, commanded by General Kenyon Joyce. Although
my post was still Fort Lewis, my duties were considerably enlarged.
The Corps was made up of all posts, camps, and stations in the
northwestern part of the country. A few days after the transfer, I
was promoted to temporary colonel. I was too busy to meditate on
the fact that I had now reached the rank that for a good many peacetime years had stood as the certain terminus of my career.

Our army was getting ready for field maneuvers. In scope of operations and in magnitude of the forces involved, they would be the
largest in its history. I was catapulted to a spot in those activities
around the end of June 1941, when orders transferred me to headquarters, Third Army, in San Antonio. Arriving there on our twenty-
fifth wedding anniversary I took over as General Krueger's Deputy
Chief of Staff and in early August I became the assigned Chief of
Staff of the Third Army.

By now General Krueger's command, which stretched all the way
from New Mexico to Florida, had a mobilizable strength of 240,000
officers and men. During August and September, we concentrated
these forces in Louisiana and undertook maneuvers against the Second Army, commanded by General Ben Lear, whose troop strength
was around 180,000. Old Louisiana hands warned us that ahead lay
mud, malaria, and mosquitoes. Their description was accurate. But
they didn't add to such attractions the fact that we would also
meet head-on the problems of 400,000 men moving into rela-

tively unsettled country, where the roadnet was designed for a car or two at a time, not an army, and a climate which seemed calculated to produce exhaustion. But the work was gripping.

The lack of practical experience was particularly evident. World War I staff men of all echelons above a regiment had largely passed out of the service. The rest of us, under pressure, had to transform textbook doctrine into action. The nervous energy, technical competence, and drive required of all those present were tremendous. But those qualities alone were not enough; eternal patience was necessary, too. The commander also needed iron in his soul for one of his chief duties was to eliminate unfit officers, some of whom were good friends.

After each stage of the maneuvers, we tried to assemble the principal officers for a critique. In these morning chats we emphasized everything that went right; encouragement was essential to the morale of men tiring physically. At the same time, we had to uncover and highlight every mistake, every failure, every foulup that in war could be death to a unit or an army. With every one of these critiques the self-confidence of each participant seemed to grow.

The stamina of officers and men and their ability to take care of themselves in the field increased. Their ability to live through the ardors of a campaign in Louisiana's sticky heat sharpened their willingness to endure. Toward the end of the maneuvers, just as we were starting out on a final problem, the tail end of a hurricane swept the Third Army area. But the troops took it in stride.

During maneuvers, my tent turned into something of a cracker-barrel corner where everyone in our army seemed to come for a serious discussion, a laugh, or a gripe. These visitors prolonged my hours and considerably reduced sleeping time. But I never discouraged those who came to complain for I was often astonished to see how much better they worked after they had unloaded their woes; and, of course, the harder they worked the smoother things went for us at Army headquarters. In these sessions I was kept up-to-date with the latest in Army humor. This revolved largely about the simulations of reality in peacetime maneuvers. The granddaddy of all these stories, I think, was this one:

An umpire decided that a bridge had been destroyed by an enemy attack and flagged it accordingly. From then on, it was not to be used by men or vehicles. Shortly, a corporal brought his squad up to the bridge, looked at the flag, and hesitated for a moment; then resolutely marched his men across it. The umpire yelled at him:

"Hey, don't you see that that bridge is destroyed?"

The Corporal answered, "Of course I can see it's destroyed. Can't you see we're swimming?"

I heard that one so often that I passed it along in a letter to Gerow:

Stories such as the above float around and give us an occasional smile. . . . Handling an Army staff that has had very little chance to whip itself together has its tough points—in spite of which I am having a good time. But I would like a command of my own.

The maneuvers ended I got, instead of a command, the star of a brigadier general. My reaction was expressed in a short note to my friend:

Things are moving so rapidly these days that I get almost dizzy trying to keep up with the parade. One thing is certain—when they get clear down to my place on the list, they are passing out stars with considerable abandon.

Shortly afterward, I was given unsought publicity in a newspaper column whose author attributed credit to me that should have gone to General Krueger. I still have no idea why I became the target for his praise. But I was happy that, if the item had to appear at all, it came after the General had recommended me for promotion.

While in Louisiana we heard how narrowly we had escaped a legislative failure. In the Congress of the United States, the extension of Selective Service was passed by a single vote. I still shudder to think how close we came to returning trained men home, closing down the reception centers for new draftees, reassembling a fragmentized force into its Regular Army core—all within weeks of our entry into the most colossal war of all time. It was reported that for achieving this victory, however slim, one man was largely responsible, General George Marshall.

Of course, I still had no idea that our commitment to battle would be precipitated by the Japanese. In fact, when I asked in 1939 for reassignment from the Philippines to the United States, I did so in the confident belief that should war break out the initial battles would be in the Atlantic Theater. If we really got into war—and with each passing week I became more sure we could not stay out—

I felt sure the Nazis would provoke it. And that was where I wanted to be. Again, I was wrong, at least about where the United States would be drawn into the war.

Eating lunch on Sunday, December 7, my ambition was short-range. I wanted to capitalize on the Sunday afternoon lull and take a long nap. A few extra hours of sleep would enable me to tackle the next day's work with vigor. The nap did not last long. Orders that I was not to be awakened under any circumstances were ignored by my aide, who wisely decided that news of the attack on Pearl Harbor was adequate reason to interrupt my rest.

Five days later, I was suddenly summoned to Washington for "emergency duty." I had no intimation of how long I was to be there or what my duties were to be. The telephone message was, "The Chief [General Marshall] says for you to hop a plane and get up here right away."

Mamie and I quickly revised our plans. First casualty among them was a visit to our Plebe son at West Point during a two-week leave I had hoped to get around Christmas. She hurriedly packed a bag for me and I got into a plane. Forced down at Dallas, I took a train to Washington, where I reported to the Chief of Staff on December 14, 1941.

What might be called my official reminiscences of World War II have been recorded in *Crusade in Europe*. But during the war there were incidents that provided some break in tensions, some insight, or some amusement, that I did not report. If I now recall any episode that may have appeared in *Crusade,* I am by no means going back to scan every line of it to see whether I have been guilty of duplication. Here, it will be fun just to wander, with no worries about verbosity, coherence, repetitions, or literary criticism.

CHAPTER XVII

Incidents at War

MY CONCERN about the fate of the Philippines did not end after we had left Manila. In fact, I guessed that I had been ordered to the War Department in Washington for that reason. Through many hectic weeks following Pearl Harbor, I tried desperately to use my knowledge of the Islands and the people to come up with ideas for their relief under attack. In the tragic days of their isolation and collapsing defenses, I harked back to a final review of the situation as I had seen it in 1939.

Before I left, Jorge Vargas, secretary to President Quezon, had relayed a request from the President that I prepare an objective and comprehensive report of my *personal* observances about the Philippine Army and the Defense Plan for the Islands. Aboard ship, returning to the United States, I jotted down notes. When I submitted the report, it was with the provision that it be cleared with General MacArthur before Quezon saw it.

One had to assume that any armed attack against the Philippines would not be "an onslaught by the full naval, military, and economic might of a great empire." Such an expedition, I said in the report, would be limited in size, and would hope to overpower defenses through surprise. This assumption was not susceptible of proof, but with Japan then preoccupied with China, it seemed unlikely that if she came into the war on the Axis side, that she would concentrate all her imperial weight against the Philippines.

In that light, I continued,

There is one line, and one only, at which the defending forces will enjoy a tremendous advantage over any attack by land. That line is the beach. Successful penetration of a defended beach is the most difficult operation in warfare.

If any attacking force ever succeeds in lodging itself firmly in a vital area of the Islands, particularly on Luzon, 90 per cent of the prior ad-

vantage of the defender will disappear. Behind the protective lines established by such attacking force, more and more strength can be brought in,
by echelon until with superior armaments and with naval and other support, the whole will be strong enough to crush the defending army.

The enemy must be repulsed at the Beach.

Item by item, I went through what I considered the essential elements in further organization of forces, training, finances, personnel.
As always, I stressed morale.*

The Monday morning quarterback is obnoxious to me—and I
don't want to play that position. The Japanese did attack, using surprise rather than the full weight of their forces. The beach defenses
were broken and dispersed at an early stage in the action. Despite
heroic resistance by both Filipinos and Americans, the morale of the
people and the combat troops sagged far too fast. But much of the
blame for the overwhelming of the Philippines should be placed
squarely on us Americans at home.

For months before Pearl Harbor and Clark Field, we had been
trying to fool ourselves that war was far away. When the first Japanese bombs fell on the planes parked a few miles from Manila, our
ships at sea were carrying troops *away* from not *to* the city soon to
be the enemy's target. Though Congress had extended the draft, it
had required the discharge of all Selective Service men over twenty-
four. Days before the war began, these men left Manila for San
Francisco.

In Washington, through the cruel days and nights of that winter,
I had little idea of what had happened to my report. Not until two
decades later did I learn the full story.

In 1960, I met Jorge Vargas again for the first time in two
decades. He told me what had happened. Then he wrote it out:

June 16, 1960

Dear Mr. President:

The attached letter [Mr. Vargas refers here to a flattering note to Mrs.
Eisenhower and me] was prepared more than twenty years ago for airmail-
ing to you, but waiting to first revise it so as to give it a more personal
tone, I kept postponing its sending and was never able to get to doing
it because of the stress of events at the time. Moreover, I also wanted

* See Note 3.

to first clear your report with General MacArthur as suggested in your letter to me of December 20, 1939. This I was not able to do either.

Then the war you had so prophetically warned us about and had so painstakingly prepared us for suddenly came upon us with such terrific impact and bewildering swiftness that the only thing I could do was to try to hide your report and accompanying papers from the Japanese.

Fortunately I was able to store these particular documents which I considered of inestimable value to the history of the Philippines and specially of the Philippine Army, away from the enemy, together with a truckful of West Point uniforms and other personal effects of General Dick Sutherland. And now twenty years later I hope you will accept my apologies for my inefficiency and will receive these papers, even if only to serve as an imperishable reminder of your memorable sojourn in the Philippines.

In accordance with your expressed wishes, except for Ricarte who typed the final report, nobody else outside of President Quezon and myself have ever seen or read these papers.

Very sincerely yours,
Jorge B. Vargas

During the frantic, tumultuous months I spent in the War Department in the Planning Section and later as Chief of Operations, I was with General Marshall every day. I knew about his reputation, of course, but before long I had conceived for him unlimited admiration and respect for my own reasons. He inspired affection in me because I realized the burden he was uncomplainingly carrying. He never seemed to doubt that we could win, even when the Philippines had fallen. And there were surely strong reverses ahead. But George Marshall was rather a remote and austere person. He was one man who never, except on one unwary occasion, used my nickname. I had been known in the Army as Ike since the day I entered West Point. He constantly addressed me as "Eisenhower."

In his office one afternoon, a detail arose about the promotion of an officer. General Marshall stopped to give me a bit of his philosophy on the subject. "The men who are going to get the promotions in this war are the commanders in the field, not the staff officers who clutter up all of the administrative machinery in the War Department and in higher tactical headquarters. The field commanders carry the responsibility and I'm going to see to it that they're properly rewarded so far as promotion can provide a reward."

To illustrate his point, General Marshall cited a number of cases in World War I where outstanding leadership of combat troops seemed to him to have been ignored. His opinion was that the staff had been constantly favored and pushed ahead of field commanders. This time, he said, he would reverse the practice. Finally, possibly because he realized that I had been brought from the field into the War Department on his personal order, he turned back to me and said:

"Take your case. I know that you were recommended by one general for division command and by another for corps command. That's all very well. I'm glad they have that opinion of you, but you are going to stay right here and fill your position, and that's that!"

Then, to underscore the point, he said: "While this may seem a sacrifice to you, that's the way it must be."

The frustration I had felt in 1918 because of my failure to get overseas now returned briefly. By General Marshall's word, I was completely condemned to a desk job in Washington for the duration. Well, he had turned the general subject of promotion into something personal so I impulsively broke out: "General, I'm interested in what you say, but I want you to know that I don't give a damn about your promotion plans as far as I'm concerned. I came into this office from the field and I am trying to do my duty. I expect to do so as long as you want me here. If that locks me to a desk for the rest of the war, so be it!"

Momentarily, I was really resentful and I got up from my chair and started toward the door. It was a long march from where he was sitting. By the time I reached it, I was feeling sheepish about the outburst; it did nothing to help either of us, and certainly it didn't ease any of his job. Something impelled me to turn around just as I started out the door and, seeing his eyes on me intently, I had to grin a little bit at my own childishness. A tiny smile quirked the corner of his face. I left the office.

About three days later I was startled to find on my desk a copy of the General's recommendation to the President that I be promoted. I looked at it in bewilderment. He had just told me vehemently that staff officers were not going to get the promotions. As I read the memorandum of explanation, I was even more amazed. He had told the President that, as his operations officer, I was not really a staff officer in the accepted sense of the word. Under his

direction, he said, all dispositions of Army forces on a global scale—
and this included the Air Corps—were my responsibility. I was his
subordinate commander. This was the way it had to be, he said,
because his operations office had to be able to function without
constantly referring problems to him.

When this explanation was typed up, it had been routed through
normal channels and came to the officer in charge of War Department personnel. He, well knowing that it was incorrect to say that I
was a "commander," revised the text of the statement, assuming it
had been drawn up by a green subordinate. He was chagrined when
he was called in to the Chief's office and icily told that the statement
had been drafted by General Marshall himself.

A question arose in my mind that I have never been able to
answer satisfactorily. Had the years of indoctrinating myself on the
inconsequential value of promotion as a measure of an Army man's
worth influenced my reply to him? Certainly, in the years past,
knowing that I was locked in because of age and grade, I had
known a wonderful sense of freedom from awe when in the presence
of superior officers. But without my outburst I often wonder whether
General Marshall would have had any greater interest in me than he
would have in any other relatively competent staff officer. In any
case, I was now a major general.

General Marshall asked me for a directive for a Commanding
General for our forces in Europe. I drafted one. When he had
asked for a recommendation for a Commander, I proposed the Air
Force's General McNarney. Instead, General Marshall sent me to
London to command the European Theater of Operations. This
brought me up closer to the war—and the desk job in Washington
was behind.

War, as so many men have said, is the most stupid and tragic of
human ventures. It is stupid because so few problems are enduringly
solved; tragic because its cost in lives and spirit and treasure is
seldom matched in the fruits of victory. Still, I never intend to join
myself with those who damn all wars as vile crimes against humanity. World War II, not sought by the people of the United
States or its allies, was certainly not, on their part, either stupid or in
vain. Satisfaction, and memories precious beyond price, rewarded

those who survived and who, in loyalty to country and to ideals, answered the attacks.

The tragedy of it all was immense. From the Sunday morning when unarmed church parties of our men died under hundreds of Japanese bombs and shells to the final days when men, women, and children of Japan perished under two bombs at Hiroshima and Nagasaki, millions died. The loss of lives that might have been creatively lived scars the mind of the modern world.

In England, on the Fourth of July, 1942, we had little to celebrate. Our future was murky and foreboding. Two days before, Russia's Crimean fortress of Sevastopol had fallen to the Nazis after a 245-day siege. With their flanks free from threat, the enemy could plunge ahead across the Volga and into the Caucasus, to exploit the vast oil resources for further conquest. In Africa, though Rommel had been stopped in his eastward drive to engulf Egypt, the Nile delta was only a few hours from his advance Panzer units. Tobruk, symbol of British staunchness, had been lost once again with all its men and guns.

In the Pacific, the battle of Midway had already been fought—but we did not yet realize its destructive effect on the strategic plans of the Japanese. Their southward movement toward Australia would continue strong for another six weeks. We were sure that land battles would soon be fought in the Pacific Theater but we could not know that the Marines, staging for movement into the Solomons, would a month and a few days later halt one prong of the Japanese advance at Guadalcanal and, reinforced by the Army in October, destroy it; nor that less than a fortnight after the Guadalcanal landing a handful of American and Australian soldiers, by repulsing the Japanese at Milne Bay, would halt the enemy's southward tide.

What we did know was that a stroke, dramatic and decisive, had to be taken in Europe. President Roosevelt had approved the basic plan (ROUNDUP) for the invasion of Europe but he realized that it could not be carried out until late 1943 or early 1944. He and Prime Minister Churchill wanted to confront the enemy with a campaign when and where we chose. The President called for American ground action in the Atlantic Theater during the coming year. This was a tough one for we were not fully trained and we did not have much of the essential equipment.

A decision was made to invade French North Africa. Our forces were to clean out resistance from Morocco to Tunisia, and then

co-operate with Alexander, whose units were to advance from the
east, driving Rommel before them. Prime Minister Churchill brought
up the matter of command. He thought the TORCH expedition
should be as American in appearance as we could make it. This
was because of the difficulties between the British and French since
France surrendered in 1940. There had been the incident at the
French port of Oran, where the British had bombarded the harbor
and the ships in it. At Dakar, the *Richelieu,* pride of the French
fleet, had been crippled by British guns. There were clashes between
British and French in the Middle East.

Because we wanted our invasion of French Africa to be more a
peaceful occupation than an all-out attack, everyone present at the
London meeting of the Joint Chiefs of Staff agreed that it should be
under an American commander. Who was to be given the responsibility? I learned later that Admiral Ernest King, the American naval
officer at the conference table, who had a reputation for being a
tough, blunt man, remarked: "Well you've got him right here. Why
not put it under Eisenhower?"

This was agreed to and so the deed was done.

The Admiral's attitude had not always been one of unqualified
endorsement. Much earlier, in Washington, General Marshall had
sent me to see him on an important matter. In those days, Admiral
King was performing true to form. He scarcely looked up from his
desk. He said only one word in answer to the question I had proposed: "No."

Resenting his manner, but somewhat his junior, I still managed
to say that he was not giving my Chief's suggestion the proper
consideration. Stretching my luck, or my neck, I also added that
his attitude could not do much to assure co-operation between the
two services.

At that, King got up from his desk, and said, after a long moment,
"Sit down, Eisenhower."

The two of us moved to a settee in the office and after we had
talked for a few moments, he said, "Look, I sometimes wonder
whether in making decisions I depend too much on old naval customs, disciplines, prejudices—or whether I'm really thinking my
problems through. Now just state that question again."

I did and he said, "Why, I think we can do it, surely."

From that time on, I had a friend in the Navy.

Planning TORCH brought us face to face with the acute lack of not only trained troops and vital equipment but shipping, and, on the American side, experience. After a preliminary survey of the problem, I concluded that we should make the landing in French North Africa so overwhelming in strength and so secretly prepared and executed that hopefully no bloodshed would ensue.

TORCH hardly began as a flaming success. Throughout the war, I was always amazed that tens upon tens of thousands of tons of supply, from safety pins and aspirin to huge tanks and guns, usually reached their destination with dispatch. But through a crazy mixture of mistakes and oversights in the United States, the first matériel for the North African invasion arrived without one crate or box properly labeled. When this was discovered, panic was quite possible among the supply men. We were confronted with the necessity of going through every package, item by item, before we could have the faintest idea what was on hand and what was missing. Confronted by the awful headache of opening boxes, checking items, and recrating them, our supply people undoubtedly wished that war had never advanced beyond the bow and arrow. In time, they got the job done but their complaints must have been audible across the ocean.

Another example: for the drive on Algiers, all signal equipment for the *entire* task force had been put on one ship. When that vessel was shot up by an enemy ship, the task force was badly embarrassed. We learned to disperse specialized equipment.

More and more, I came to realize that brainpower is always in far shorter supply than manpower. The staff around me included intelligent officers who thought no problem beyond their ability to solve, no work load too heavy to endure. Such men became increasingly rare as our forces built up and the magnitude of our mission became more apparent. Late in August, I wrote my classmate, Vernon Prichard:

I have developed almost an obsession as to the certainty with which you can judge a division, or any other large unit, merely by knowing its commander intimately. Of course, we have had pounded into us all through our school courses that the exact level of a commander's personality and ability is always reflected in his unit—but I did not realize, until opportunity came for comparisons on a rather large scale, how infallibly the commander and unit are almost one and the same thing.

This letter was prompted by one received from Prichard that had been exactly two months to the day in traveling from Pine Camp in New York to my headquarters in England. It arrived at a time when, for my own peace of mind, I was impelled to get a few notions off my chest. I also wrote:

This is a long tough road we have to travel. The men that can do things are going to be sought out just as surely as the sun rises in the morning. Fake reputations, habits of glib and clever speech, and glittering surface performance are going to be discovered and kicked overboard. Solid, sound leadership, with inexhaustible nervous energy to spur on the efforts of lesser men, and ironclad determination to face discouragement, risk, and increasing work without flinching, will always characterize the man who has a sure-enough, bang-up fighting unit. Added to this he must have a darned strong tinge of imagination—I am continuously astounded by the utter lack of imaginative thinking among so many of our people that have reputations for being really good officers. Finally, the man has to be able to forget himself and personal fortunes. I've relieved two seniors here because they got to worrying about "injustice," "unfairness," "prestige" and—oh, what the hell! The purpose of putting down all these platitudes (which you must undoubtedly find rather tiresome) is my conviction that you have these things. Many of your qualities I have envied—even attempted to imitate.

In writing General Prichard, I was thinking aloud and talking to myself as well:

In the early days of a tremendous undertaking, such as this war, appointments and selection of individuals are based upon a number of unimportant factors—among which, as we all know, are: personal propinquity, wild guesses, school records, past acquaintanceship, and a number of others, of which few really search down into the depths of character and ability. But the stark realities of distress, privation, and discouragement will bring character and ability into their own.

All jobs are important, but your eventual one, whatever its nature, will bring big formations under your direct influence. So, if I may venture one suggestion, it would be this. While you are doing your stuff from day to day, constantly look and search among your subordinates for the ones that have these priceless qualities in greater or lesser degree. As the War Department moves you on up, you will find greater and greater need for people upon whom you can depend to take the load off your shoulders. The more you can develop and test these people now, the greater will be your confidence in them when you are compelled to thrust bigger and bigger jobs upon them.

Two months later, in the tunnels of Gibraltar, as we awaited the first news of our landing, the same sort of thoughts were in my head. The key to success was the quality of leadership we had provided our troops. The men were well armed and partially trained by now and as Americans they had both the initiative and the ingenuity that, fed by courage, could decide the course of battle—if their leaders, from platoon to division, were men who could inspire them to their best. The outcome was far from sure.

Even if the Mediterranean were not an Axis lake, as the enemy claimed, it was dangerous water. Our troop and cargo ships would be targets for all-out submarine and plane attack before we could provide sufficient air cover. The land on which we would campaign, although we expected to be among friendly people, for the most part, would be brutally hostile unless we occupied it swiftly and maintained intact our sea supply. We could not expect to live off the land; barren desert and mountains paralleled the coast with a narrow and fertile strip there that would provide wine and fruit—tempting but hardly a source of strength for fighting.

Our initial landings in North Africa were fairly successful. But soon after the initial landings on November 8, 1942, the French commanders in the region felt that honor required them to resist to the end. We, hoping to make the local French an ally again, tried in every possible way to persuade them to sign an armistice. The stumbling block was French insistence upon legal authority to sign; they would have to fight to the end unless authorized to quit by an official they considered to be a direct representative of Marshall Pétain. Enter Admiral Darlan—and the start of one of the most discussed episodes in the six-month campaign.

Admiral Darlan, a member of Pétain's cabinet, was taken as a political prisoner by our troops. Because he was one of the Vichy French and because it was believed that he collaborated with the Nazis out of enmity toward the British, I wanted nothing to do with him. But the local French military leaders, seeking a legal cover for ordering a cease fire, insisted that only Darlan could be recognized as the official empowered to authorize them to take such action. I was faced with my first "political" problem as a commander.

In the long run, we could defeat the local French forces. That would also defeat our hope of making the French in Africa our allies—and would hamper later operations in the base from which we would be attacking the Axis. Another certain result would be a delay in our hope of seizing Tunisia before it could be occupied by

Axis forces. On the other hand, if I should decide to deal with Darlan, we were assured of an immediate cease fire, no more casualties, and a chance at Tunisia.

To deal or not to deal, that was the question.

In my offices in the dank and dripping tunnels of Gibraltar, we discussed the military advantages versus the questionable effect on morale at home and in Great Britain. I talked at length with my political advisers but they couldn't help much. After going off alone for an hour or so, I returned to the conference room and announced the first major political decision I had ever felt called on to make:

"The military advantages of an immediate cease fire are so overwhelming that I'll go promptly to join Clark [Wayne Mark Clark, my American deputy] in Algiers and if the proposals of the French are as definite as I understand, I shall immediately recognize Darlan as the highest French authority in the region. He can act as the interim head of such civil government as exists, on condition that he carries out any orders I may issue."

I went on, "None of this should be under any misapprehensions as to what the consequences of this action may be. In both our nations, Darlan is a deep-dyed villain. When public opinion raises its outcry our two governments will be embarrassed. Because of this, we'll act so quickly that reports to our governments will be on the basis of action *taken*."

In a war such as the one we were engaged in, I told the assembled group, governments had to be concerned with public opinion and, as much as possible, must never be thought to be wrong in vital decisions. Our aim had to be to give them the benefit of a necessary decision in the field. But I had to add a warning. "If public opinion becomes too inflamed because we seem guilty of dealing with the enemy, the governments must be free to disavow us and indeed remove us from our posts.

"I'll do my best to convince our governments, by detailed explanation, that the decision was right. If they find it necessary later to take action against this headquarters, I'll make it clear that I alone am responsible."

The outcries came. Columnists and commentators made much of the "Darlan deal." Most of the time, I was too busy to worry about personal problems. But when the furor was at its height, I did reflect uneasily that sensational charges of incompetence as a political man, a role for which I had little training and little liking, could end my career. If I were through, I would feel sorry for myself, probably, and angry at the critics. Nor would I have excused them even though I knew that, confronted with a deadline and distant from the problem by a few thousand miles, they had to turn out within hours an interpretation of the Darlan episode, plus an assessment of blame. This situation of the analyst is what on occasion saddens me when I read a column or hear a commentary that in a few hundred words completely clears up, to the author's satisfaction, a most complex situation and then uncovers the culprit in one man or one group. The search for a scapegoat is the easiest of all hunting expeditions.

More important to me was the probable effect on my staff and the future of the allied campaign. If my head were removed, a replacement would be appointed immediately. But its fall, inescapably, would affect the position of every staff officer close to me. They constituted the cream of the American and British officers on the Atlantic side of the war. Guilt by association was not a development of the Second World War, but in an age of quickening communication, the dubious process is hastened.

Both President Roosevelt and Prime Minister Churchill saw the situation clearly and each effectively explained the circumstances to their countrymen. Their support, and the fact that we simply went ahead with the job at hand, meant that no heads would roll.

In the stories that began to circulate about me, I should have seen ample warning that the printed word is not always the whole truth. It didn't occur to me that I would spend part of my life after the war trying to sort out facts from fiction. At the time, the hoked-up details usually provoked from me no more than a grimace or, once in a while, a hearty guffaw.

A story appeared in *Yank*, the newspaper edited by and for our troops, shortly after the Darlan case was closed. This purported to describe activities at my headquarters in England as we prepared for the African landings:

The General, they say, was calm as a cucumber the whole time he worked in those cramped quarters. He liked doing his own packing and hung up his own clothes. And, as for giving his batmen and orderlies an easy time of it, there wasn't even much preparing involved in whipping up the General's favorite sandwich—raw beef with onions and plenty of pepper.

One London newspaper said that General Eisenhower—a Texan and former cowboy himself when he worked his way through the University of Texas—even managed to indulge in a little of his favorite reading (Wild West stories) while he was planning this vast campaign.

This story may have been the origin of all the succeeding reports that I never read anything but westerns. If so, I wonder that the other two bits of information were not as permanently incorporated into my public personality. They would have added considerable color to background stories and particularly to cartoons. Sketches of the President devouring raw meat sandwiches at his desk, either at Columbia or in Washington, or of Ike galloping on a cow pony around the White House lawn, would have provided a change of pace from golf clubs with which I was usually armed by cartoonists.

During the seven weeks that Darlan remained in power in North Africa, he never once broke his word to me or did anything that we thought was inimical to Allied interests. On Christmas Eve, while I was on the front lines, far from Algiers, Darlan was assassinated. His murder created another political crisis—the identity of the man to take his place.

Giraud, the French general who had accompanied the expedition into Africa, was initially believed to have such prestige that all the force there present, as well as the population, would follow his lead. He proved wholly incapable of influencing anyone.

The winter of 1942–43 was a time when we worked harder, I think, than we ever had before. My headquarters was at Algiers. The battle line lay hundreds of miles to the east. Because of my anxiety to keep in touch with the front, I made frequent trips, sometimes in a DC-3 but often, because of weather, by automobile, in a long, tedious trip that took thirty-six hours. I became run-down and life was not improved by a murderous case of flu. The way to deal with the flu, I thought, was to keep working.

In early January, we were told that heads of our governments were going to meet in Casablanca. We had to figure how to protect them and how to supply all their requirements. I received word that

I should attend the conference and we started out one morning in an old B-17. The plane was rated "battle fatigued." And it did look tired. The designation meant that the plane had been on bombing missions and had not had proper maintenance. We did not want to lose planes over enemy territory from mechanical failures; we did use them in a limited way within our own lines.

During the trip to Casablanca, we had to cross the Atlas Mountains, a formidable range in Morocco. While over the mountains, one engine started to give the pilots trouble and one stopped completely. Shortly thereafter, another began to sputter. The pilot called back, "All passengers put on their parachutes."

I asked my naval aide, Commander Harry Butcher, to help me get mine on and I would do the same for him. In the process, he pulled off one of the stars on my shoulder, leaned down to pick it up and put it back. He had difficulty. "What's the matter, Butch?" I said. "You've often pinned the stars on me. What's your trouble?"

"Yes, Sir," he said, "but never when I had to put you in a parachute!"

His hands were trembling so that I said, "Give me the star, Harry, I'll pin it on when I get time."

We stood, as ordered, by the nearest exit, ready to jump. Only one of the engines was working properly but by this time we had passed the crest of the range and the pilot put the plane down on a long glide to the coastline. Just as we approached the field at Casablanca, he got one more engine working briefly and with increased power made a fine landing.

As soon as we were on the ground, knowing that I had to be back at my headquarters next morning, I called the airfield commander to the plane and said, "Your first priority is to get this plane repaired so that we can go back." He had the work started at once.

An hour and a half later, while the conference with the combined Chiefs of Staff was in progress, an orderly came in and handed me a note. It was from the airfield commander:

It is impossible to repair your plane. It's being scrapped immediately and will never fly again.

When I saw that report, the realization of how lucky we had been to make the landing struck me full force. A good friend of mine,

General Ira Eaker, of the Air Force, said he would lend me his plane for the return trip.

At the end of the conference, General Marshall visited me in Algiers. He made two or three trips to the front. While in Algiers, he learned that I had been suffering for more than a week with flu; indeed, at the moment he arrived, I was carrying a high temperature, while the doctors also said my blood pressure was high.

The General said that he was worried about me. I said it was only because I had been exposed to bad weather at about the time of the Darlan assassination and I had a heavy cold.

"You're trying to do too much," General Marshall said. "You're making too many trips to the front. You ought to depend more on reports."

"Well, General, your headquarters are in Washington and yet you've come over here, and you've made several visits along the front to see for yourself."

He looked at me rather fiercely. "I don't come to the field very often," he said.

"Well," I said, "you can understand that because I'm closer to the thing here, and I have to give my interest over entirely to this one problem, I've got to do it with some frequency."

He did not withdraw his suggestion but he did not press it. Soon he remarked: "You ought to have a masseur. They're great for relaxing you before you go to bed." General Marshall added that General Pershing always had such a man traveling with him throughout World War I and had a good rubdown every evening.

I said frankly that I had never liked rubdowns even when I was playing football thirty years earlier. They made me more nervous than relaxed.

Finally, he came up with a suggestion that had some appeal. In substance, he said: "In this sprawling theater, with demands on your time and attention all the way from Casablanca to Tunisia, you just can't get to all the places you might like to visit. You ought to have a man to be your eyes and ears. Naturally, he'd have to be a man who has ability and someone you can trust. He should have a relatively high rank so that he could go into any headquarters and bring you back the information that you need. In other words, an extension of your own faculties. Ideally, you'd have far more confidence in his information than in daily situation reports from the front."

"That would be fine." We began to talk over the names of officers who might fit the description. When he casually mentioned the name Bradley, I said, "Go no farther." Back in Washington, he assigned General Omar Bradley to my headquarters.

This was more than agreeable to me. Bradley was not only a favorite classmate of mine at West Point, but a man whom I respected and admired throughout his military career. When he reached my headquarters, a close association began that has endured until this day—an association that was invaluable to me then and the memory of which is pleasurable now.

Of all the ground commanders I have known, even, and of those of whom I've read, I would put Omar Bradley in the highest classification. In every aspect of military command, from the planning of an operation to the cleanup after its success, Brad was outstanding. I have yet to meet his equal as an offensive leader and a defensive bulwark, as a wielder of every arm that can be practically employed against an enemy. In the aftermath of war, I'm surprised that he seems at times to be ignored or undervalued by those who write of the Mediterranean and European campaigns. Patton, for instance, was a master of fast and overwhelming pursuit. Headstrong by nature, and fearlessly aggressive, Patton was the more colorful figure of the two, compelling attention by his mannerisms as much as by his deeds. Bradley, however, was master of every military maneuver, lacking only in the capacity—possibly the willingness—to dramatize himself. This, I think, is to his credit.

Soon after Bradley began the kind of duty that General Marshall had visualized, I found that he had qualities so badly needed in command positions that it was not long before I assigned him to take over the II Corps. Later, of course, he became commander of the First Army and still later of the Twelfth Army group in Operation OVERLORD in 1944.

Because of our extended Tunisian position, we were in a tempting position for the enemy to try a counterattack. In February, such an attack was launched. But it did not come through the mountain pass which our intelligence officer predicted. And in the episode that followed, it was borne in upon me that a bit of personal caution might not be a bad idea.

By coincidence, just before the attack, I made a trip to the American II Corps, deployed on the southern part of the Tunisian line. Because of my illness and preoccupation with the Casablanca conference, I had not been to the front for three weeks and was getting uneasy.

When I arrived at the corps headquarters, the commander was absent on an inspection of his own. So I started out late that evening to make a reconnaissance. An aide-de-camp, an orderly, two drivers, and a II Corps staff officer went along. Finally we reached what was called the Faid Pass. Our intelligence officer had predicted an attack through the Fondouk Pass. Prediction or no, I talked about the defensive arrangements of the local command and was irritated to find out that although the unit had been there two days, it had not yet put out mine fields and prepared adequately for defense. Those officers with me minimized the importance I attached to organizing the position. They said they had been there only two days and their mine fields would not be started until the following day.

"Well, maybe you don't know it," I said, "but we've found in this war that once the Nazis have taken a position, they organize it for defense within *two hours*. This includes the scattering of many personnel mines along the front. We've learned to do the same thing. It's difficult for attacking troops to get through these deadly things. Get your mine fields out first thing in the morning."

About 3:00 A.M., we started back toward corps headquarters near Tebessa. There was only one road leading through the little village of Sbeitla and we had to use it to get back on the main highway. As we passed through the town, firing broke out. While I had no idea that there was any large force in the town, we had experienced a number of incidents in which Axis paratroopers would land behind the lines at a sensitive spot along our line of communications, to blow a culvert or bridge, and then make their way by foot into the German lines.

If there was going to be firing, we decided that we would organize as we pushed straight ahead. One man walked ahead as advance guard, two men came along right behind him as the main body, and I had a .45 pistol as the reserve. The two drivers brought along the Jeep and the Dodge in train. Our total armament was two carbines and three pistols. However, we got through the town without being fired on and we never did learn what the commotion was about.

Having escaped fire, the driver of my car fell asleep and ran us into a ditch. It took a half hour, using every sort of strength we had, to get it back on the road.

We arrived at headquarters without further mishap, reaching there shortly after daylight. I immediately sent for the corps commander and in plain language told him of my dissatisfaction with his defensive arrangements. I was in the midst of an urgent directive about the organization of our position when he told me that the Germans had already attacked through Faid Pass; in fact they had captured the entire garrison only two hours after I left it.

The events above initiated a battle that became known later as Kasserine Pass. We suffered a driving penetration into our thin line in the south and it was ten days before we finally regrouped and drove the Nazis back to where they had started. This was a painful lesson for green commanders and green troops. The units were far more efficient in combat from then on. Incidentally, my promotion to four-star rank came through just at the beginning of the battle. This grim coincidence was repeated later when I was advanced to five-star rank at the opening of the Battle of the Bulge. If this were a trend or a tradition, I came to feel it was fortunate that no higher rank could be conferred. There was no promotion worth such battles.

The complications of Allied command were intriguing. It's just as well; otherwise they might have been infuriating.

In the Casablanca conference, it had been decided that we were to plan, after the present campaign, to attack the island of Sicily. So, having forced the surrender of all the Axis military in Africa by mid-May, we were visited again by our political and military superiors.

The British were confident that a quick attack on the lower part of Italy would further our war aims materially. The Americans, agreeing that we should attempt anything that offered results, urged that we not forget that the next year—or certainly by the spring of '44—we were all committed to the OVERLORD campaign, the invasion of northwest Europe. It developed that General Brooke, Chief of Staff of the British Army, had never really liked the OVERLORD idea. At times during the two-day conference, he seemed to be reflecting the Prime Minister's thoughts.

He came to see me privately and argued that all Allied ground troops should stay in the Mediterranean, chipping away at the periphery of the Axis empire. But we should avoid any commitment of major ground forces. His idea was that we would be doing our part by building up our navies to kill off the Nazi submarines, while our bombers flew concentric attacks on the Axis and pounded Germany and Italy. The Russians coming in from the east, according to General Brooke, would carry on the ground battle. Of course this would have meant the complete abandonment of the OVERLORD plan. I believe that the British Chief of Staff was badly underestimating Allied strength and efficiency and overestimating Nazi power in Western Europe.

One question I asked: "How would you like to conduct a war according to the plan you've just outlined, and then find that all of Central and Western Europe has been overrun by the Russians? How do you think we could deal with the Soviets?"

General Brooke seemed to feel that this would be no problem. He thought that the Soviets would not try to maintain such an extended empire and would retire back into the limits of Russia once the war had been won.

I was reasonably confident that both President Roosevelt and General Marshall were determined to take no chances on such an outcome and I must say I agreed. In fact, this was implicit in the plan that I had outlined a year earlier, as head of the operations division. The Prime Minister did want us to carry on in the meantime a strong campaign against the Axis in the Mediterranean. I agreed with General Marshall that as quickly as we captured Sicily, we would do our utmost to exploit the victory until time came to concentrate strength for OVERLORD.

A small event that illustrates the difficulty of getting everybody agreed to launch a campaign is told in the story of Pantelleria. A tiny island in the Mediterranean, halfway between the northern tip of Tunisia and the island of Sicily, Pantelleria was heavily garrisoned by Italians. Popularly, it was said to be the "Gibraltar of the Central Mediterranean." The coastline was rocky, with no beaches, and the only approach was by sea through a narrow harbor perhaps three hundred yards wide. The interior was hilly, cut up into small plots by stone walls. Its capture would be a difficult feat of arms if the place were garrisoned by good, sturdy troops. It was almost out of the question to attack by airborne method; descending soldiers, blown up against the stone walls by prevailing winds, would be almost 100 per cent casualties. In the circumstances, some thought that the island was unassailable and that we would be foolish to try to take it.

There were other elements to consider, I thought. One was the fact that with the landing strip on the top of the island in possession of the enemy, our convoys going across from Africa to Sicily would be subject to strafing and dive-bomber attack. We would be denied the use of the field for both defense and offensive operations. My belief was that the officers and men of the Italian Army were sick of the war and wanted to get out of it. We knew that Mussolini had given orders that if any of the Italian garrisons surrendered, their families at home would pay the penalty. But with the theory that morale is the telling factor in war and suspecting that Italian morale was at a low ebb, I insisted on attempting the island's capture.

My immediate staff agreed. British ground commanders were doubtful. The attitude of Alexander and Montgomery was, "We must not risk a failure." Counsels were divided and unfortunately I didn't have an available American division that was amphibiously trained. I had to proceed cautiously to persuade my British associates that I was not going completely crazy.

We began an incessant bombardment of the island. To get a better picture, Admiral Andrew Cunningham, who was an ardent supporter of the plan, and I went up with a bombarding fleet from Tunisia to simulate an attack. As our dive bombers, fighter bombers, and high-level bombers turned their attention to the island, the ships, both destroyers and cruisers, bombarded the defenses full strength.

The reaction from the island was so feeble that I said, "Andrew, if you and I got into a small boat, we could capture the place ourselves."

When the attack was put on as scheduled, the men in the landing ships had not even completed getting into their landing craft when white flags began to appear all over the island.

Winston Churchill, by the way, was convinced that there were not more than three thousand Italians on the island. Our intelligence reports showed eleven thousand. On this difference of opinion, we had made a small wager. "If you'll give me an Italian sou for every soldier fewer than three thousand, I'll give you one for each man more than three thousand." At the surrender, we got almost exactly eleven thousand. Winston paid off the debt, remarking in a note that at this rate, he would buy all the Italians I could capture. I think the entire settlement came to about $1.60.

The Sicilian campaign lasted some thirty-eight days. Some two weeks later, the British crossed the narrow Strait of Messina and made an unopposed landing. Then the American Fifth Army assaulted at Salerno and made good its landing after a vicious, bloody battle. The fighting went on during the winter and again we were told to prepare to receive our political bosses. There would be a conference at Cairo, to be followed by one with Marshal Stalin at Teheran; the Marshal refused to go further west. Among other questions, the identity of the man who was to command the OVERLORD ("D-Day") invasion had to be settled.

The journey to Cairo provided a restful interlude. After a good meal, General Ralph Royce thanked General Marshall for a fine Thanksgiving dinner. "What's the matter?" someone asked me, seeing my surprised expression. "I'll be darned," I said "—is this Thanksgiving?"

General Marshall called me to his office and told me to take a couple of days off. I pleaded work, but he said, "Look, Eisenhower, everything is going well. Just let someone else run that war up there for a couple of days. If your subordinates can't do it for you, you haven't organized them properly."

I used the two days to go up the Nile to the Valley of the Kings and to go to Jerusalem. It was interesting and I saw just enough to create in me an ambition, still unfulfilled, to go back to the region some day. After the President left the meeting with the other leaders in Teheran I received a tattered piece of paper that, sealed in plastic, is one of my war souvenirs, you might say. At the bottom of the paper, General Marshall had written:

Cairo, Dec. 7 43

Dear Eisenhower. I thought you might like to have this as a memento. It was written very hurriedly by me as the final meeting broke up yesterday, the President signing it immediately.

G.C.M.

And at the top of the paper, these few words:

From the President to Marshal Stalin
The immediate appointment of General Eisenhower to command of Overlord operation has been decided upon

Roosevelt

After that note was passed, events moved rapidly for me. I wanted to make a final visit along the Italian front but because of time pressure, I had to confine the visit to the American sector. General Clark was doing well. Later, when he got to the Volturno River, he ran into real difficulties.

During the visit, we drove along the road on the south bank of the river. The opposite side was held by Germans. We were a little careless, I suppose, and a few shots were thrown in our direction but we speeded up and got out of the way.

This reminded Wayne Clark of a visit I had made to his headquarters just after the invasion started. He was in a tent pitched in the midst of a woods. There was heavy fighting to enlarge the bridgehead around Salerno and the atmosphere was taut. Wayne and I were sitting under the trees, making plans, when we heard a small shell coming. It exploded within the area. We were engrossed in our talk and paid little attention, although we did notice a few men diving into handy ditches bordering the road within the camp. It seemed to both of us a stray shell, and engrossed in our talk, we didn't bother to move.

A day or two afterward, we saw accounts written up that said that the two generals were so green they didn't realize that when shelling started, one took cover behind a tree or at least went flat on the ground. I wonder whether the writer would have been so sure about our greenness or nonchalance if he had seen us in the early days in Africa, ducking for the ditches every time we saw a plane in the air (with good reason—almost every plane then flying was an enemy).

After two visits with Mr. Churchill—one at Carthage, where he had a heavy cold and another at Marrakech, where he had pneumonia—I flew to Washington for two blessed weeks. There were conferences with the Chiefs of Staff, with the President, and a chance to see my family. Mamie and I had a secret meeting with John at West Point and I went to see my mother and brothers in Kansas.

The day before leaving, I went to see President Roosevelt. He was sick in bed with influenza. (At times, it must appear, the entire high command, civilian and military, shared the same illness. Perhaps this is not too far from the truth; perhaps fatigue and concern and responsibility were taking their toll.) We had a long conversation, much of it dealing with the final division of Germany. I argued for two things:

First, that we avoid dividing Germany into zones and arrange for the military government to be conducted under a coalition of the Allied forces—and the Russians.

Second, I felt that any division of the country would make administration difficult. On top of this, I told the President that I thought it would be far from certain that we could bring about the withdrawal of all Soviet troops, assuming their presence in the city, when the time came for civilian authorities to take over.

The President made light of my fears. He had no doubt whatsoever about the eventual restoration of a satisfactory German government under the aegis of the several occupying powers. What concerned him more than any relationships with the Soviets was his desire to have American troops occupy the northwestern rather than the southwestern sector of Germany. He had strong feelings about each region, felt that there was little in the southwest except "scenery and tourists," and knew that the northwest contained the Ruhr's productivity.

I pointed out that this would require some crossing of lines of communication between the British and ourselves but agreed that this was a relatively inconsequential matter. I did repeat that in my opinion, if we divided the country into definite occupational zones on a national basis, we'd have trouble. He finally said that this was one point he had already decided. This, of course, settled the matter.

I did add: "Then I hope the Western Allies will insist upon building a cantonment capital at the junction of the Russian, British, and American zones to avoid unnecessary trouble between ourselves and Russia." At this point, President Roosevelt became a little impatient, possibly, with my obvious distrust of the Soviets. He suggested that he would take care of it, that I should forget it, and let the political authorities make decisions of this kind. I subsided.

Even though confined to bed, he was zestful and, as he had since our second meeting, called me Ike. Mrs. Roosevelt came in briefly and we exchanged greetings. He asked me whether I liked the new title "Supreme Commander," and I acknowledged that it had the ring of importance, something like "Sultan." He wished me adios. It was our last meeting.

It is well for man to avoid superstitions, gossip, rumors, and, perhaps, possible portents. If I had taken what greeted me on arrival in

London on January 16, 1944 as a portent, I should have turned back. The fog in the streets was the heaviest it had ever been my misfortune to encounter if the expression is that the fog is so thick that you cannot see your hand in front of your face, this was worse. Our automobile lights could not penetrate the heavy, yellowish curtain more than a few inches. In front of the car, two or three men who were familiar with the area led the way. With their help, and traveling not over a half mile an hour, we finally reached the hotel.

The next day the fog had not lifted. My entire personal staff, already present in the city, tried to get me to the new office. It was quite an experience. After reaching the address, two men even got lost in the distance between curb, car, and front door. I was warned that near the door was an area-way into which anyone could easily fall. I called out that all of us would stand still until one man made it to the door. He did, opened it, and by a dim glow from the interior, we made our way inside 20 Grovesnor Square.

A genuinely auspicious sign was the presence of General Walter Bedell Smith, as my chief lieutenant, during the intensely busy period of preparation and planning for OVERLORD. General Bradley was to be commander of the American Army group when we had one established in France. There was a potentially delicate shift. I had communicated with General Patton and invited him to join us. But I told him that if he did so, the positions of him and Bradley would be reversed, with Bradley commanding a group of armies, and Patton a single one. He did not hesitate a second and I was happy to have him. After all, we had been friends for twenty-five years. There came a time when we needed all the friendship we could muster.

George Patton loved to shock people. Anything that popped into his mind came promptly out of his mouth, especially if it was bizarre. This may have seemed inadvertent but in my opinion he had, throughout his life, cultivated this habit. He loved to shake members of a social gathering by exploding a few rounds of outrageous profanity. If he created any effect, he would indulge in more of the same; if no one paid any attention, he would quiet down.

Not long after his arrival in England, he attended a meeting which he thought was private and off the record. Called upon for a comment, he made a statement to the effect that after the war was over, Britain and America would have to rule the world and other nations would have to conform. Georgie should have done three things: thought about what he wanted to say, watched his tongue, and checked the roster. There was a newspaper man present and the story made vivid headlines the next day. Again, George Patton was on the hot seat.

All kinds of protests arose and General Marshall cabled to say I would have to decide this one on my own and he would support my action, as usual.

I must say that it was tiresome at times to get George out of the noisy situations created by his own impulsiveness. But I always thought of him as a valuable Army man. While he did not like the heavy, dirty slugging necessary in breaking through heavily held defense lines, once a hole was made and he was turned loose with mobile forces, Patton had no peer.

I made up my mind to hang on to him. The offense he committed, though serious in the public mind, was just another product of George's thoughtlessness. I decided to let him suffer for a week or so to impress upon him that he could not continue to sound off this way and still be a worthwhile commander in a great Allied organization. I sent word that I would make a final decision in a few days and would let him know his fate.

George would sweat, I knew, because if there was one thing he wanted to do it was continue in the war. So, after an interval, I sent for him, told him that I had decided to keep him on, and said at the same time that he had to learn to keep his mouth shut on political matters.

Patton always lived at one extreme or another of the emotional spectrum. He was either at the top of his form, laughing and full of enthusiasm, or filled with remorse and despondency. When I gave him the verdict, tears streamed down his face and he tried to assure me of his gratitude. He gave me his promise that thereafter he would be a model of discretion and in a gesture of almost little-boy contriteness, he put his head on my shoulder as he said it.

This caused his helmet to fall off—a gleaming helmet I sometimes thought he wore while in bed. As it rolled across the room I had the rather odd feeling that I was in the middle of a ridiculous situation. Here was George Patton telling me how sorry he was he had caused me distress and anguish, and swearing by all our many years of friendship that he would never again offend, while his helmet bounced across the floor into a corner. I prayed that no one would come in and see the scene and that there were no news cameras at the window.

George could recover from emotion as quickly as he fell into it.

Without apology and without embarrassment, he walked over, picked up his helmet, adjusted it, saluted, and said: "Sir, could I now go back to my headquarters?"

"Yes," I said, shaking my head, "after you have lunch with me in about an hour."

CHAPTER XVIII

More War Stories

WE ALL think back to Sir Winston Churchill as a man who bespoke confidence. There can be no question but that his very presence in the British Isles, a presence of the spirit as much as of the mind, is responsible for the fact that those Isles survive today, so that their phenomenally distinguished history reaches into and includes the present. But Winston was a human being and there were moments when none of us could be sure of success.

Upon my return to London in January 1944 the Prime Minister and I resumed a habit of meeting at least twice a week. There was luncheon on Tuesday and dinner with the Chiefs of Staff and others on Friday. Occasionally, the dinner would be transformed into a weekend at Chequers, the country residence for the Prime Minister. At Chequers, other guests came for conferences, some rushing in for a few hours, others for the entire time. Fifteen months had wrought a tremendous change in the atmosphere of these meetings.

Even in the early fall of 1942, no one could have predicted how or when we would stop the Axis advance, the outcome of our counteroffenses in either theater of war, the survival of Russia as a fighting power, or our own capacity to wage offenses relentlessly on two fronts separated by half the earth's circumference. But now behind us was success in North Africa and Sicily. In Italy we had advanced almost to Rome, bringing down Mussolini's government. On the Pacific Front, the Japanese had been driven from Attu and Kiska, outposts on the Western Hemisphere they had occupied in 1942. MacArthur's troops were leapfrogging up the 1500-mile coast of New Guinea; islands in the southwestern Pacific had been liberated or their Japanese garrisons surrounded. Above all, clear to everyone, friend and foe alike, was the increasing might of the United States in men and weapons.

Nevertheless, in the meetings, tension and anxiety were inescapable. Across the Channel, scant minutes by air from our headquarters, was

Festung Europa. Behind the dunes and low cliffs the Nazis had through four years been fortifying beaches and ports. These were supported by mobile reserves who could be rushed to any point we might choose to assault, concentrating masses of armor and infantry against the relatively small numbers we could land by sea or from the air. Our lines of support, on the other hand, would be subject to fatal interruptions by stormy weather, by undersea attack, and, it was rumored, by assault from new projectiles whose range and speed would change the nature of war.

For the sort of attack before us we had no precedent in military history. Caesar and William the Conqueror had crossed the Channel to invade England successfully. But the England of that day was not guarded by an almost unbroken perimeter of guns and fighting men. Armies from Britain had been put ashore on the European coast— but they had always landed where friendly countries possessed a stretch of frontier or where the defenders were weak. OVERLORD was at once a singular military expedition and a fearsome risk.

It became quickly obvious that the Prime Minister was not oversold on its value, at least in the early spring of 1944. He felt that it would be far better for the Western Allies to wait for more significant signs of German collapse. Sometimes, in his contemplation of the possibilities before us, he spoke as if he were addressing a multitude. He would say, "When I think of the beaches of Normandy choked with the flower of American and British youth, and when, in my mind's eye, I see the tides running red with their blood, I have my doubts . . . I have my doubts."

There were doubts in many quarters. Some inevitably found their way into newspapers. During the spring, an expert opinion was offered by one writer who said that any attack on the northwestern coast of France would certainly create casualties on the order of 90 per cent. Because this prediction was highly publicized, Bradley and I decided that we must stress in all our meetings with American troops that such stories were nonsense. We were convinced that we were not going to have unusually heavy losses and we expressed our confidence that the Allies could successfully carry out the mission prescribed by the combined Chiefs of Staff and by our two governments. In this role, Bradley was superb.

While Winston might at times express his doubts in the close confines of an intimate meeting, he would never show pessimism or hesitancy in public, nor would he allow any expression of his to be distorted into the kind of article that had so disturbed Brad and me. Among ourselves, the Prime Minister would add, following his expression of doubt, "We are committed to this operation of war. And we must all, as loyal Allies, do our very best to make it a success." This I knew to be the true Churchill speaking and I always believed that his uncertainty about the wisdom of undertaking OVERLORD in the spring of 1944 was the result of the tragic experiences in World War I, when, in spite of tremendous British losses at Passchendaele, Vimy Ridge, and Ypres, their gains were often measured only in yards.

As for the American commanders, our confidence grew by leaps and bounds. We saw that our bombing operations were damaging German communications. We constantly cut into their supplies of fuel. We were destroying equipment and production capacity while, in the meantime, the Russians were making inroads on the Eastern Front. There was little opportunity for Hitler to reinforce the west even though he was aware that sooner or later we were going to attack. This confidence and optimism radiated. In private meetings, Winston said, more than once, "General, it is good for commanders to be optimistic, else they would never win a battle. I must say to you if by the time snow flies you have established your thirty-odd divisions, now in Britain, safely on the Normandy coast and have the port of Cherbourg firmly in your grasp, I will be the first to proclaim that this was a gigantic and wonderfully conducted military campaign."

Then he added: "If in addition you should have seized the port of Le Havre and have extended your holdings to include all the area including the Cotentin Peninsula and the mouth of the Seine, I will proclaim that this is one of the finest operations in modern war."

And finally, "If by Christmas you have succeeded in liberating our beloved Paris, if she can by that time regain her life of freedom and take her accustomed place as a center of Western European culture and beauty, then I will proclaim that this operation is the most grandly conceived and best conducted known to the history of warfare." To this, I invariably replied, "Mr. Prime Minister, we expect to be on the borders of Germany by Christmas, pounding away at her defenses. When that occurs, if Hitler has the slightest judgment or wisdom left, he will surrender unconditionally to avoid complete destruction of Germany."

Once I smiled. "Because of this conviction, I made a bet with

General Montgomery some months ago. The proposition was that we would end the war in Europe by the end of 1944. The bet was for five pounds and I have no reason to want to hedge that bet."

The Prime Minister's face curved upward into a splendid smile. "My dear General, I pray you are right." Ultimately, we held two substantial command and staff conferences to review planning and expectations for OVERLORD. At one of these there was assembled under a single roof as much civilian and military rank as may have ever been gathered for an operational briefing. Present were the King of England, his Prime Minister, several of the War Cabinet, all the British Chiefs of Staff, and all senior commanders of the proposed operation.

The meeting was notable for me not only because of the group itself but because of a statement by the Prime Minister. When the presentations were over, he said, "I am hardening toward this enterprise."

Winston repeated this two or three times and its meaning—certainly as far as the Americans present were concerned—was that while he had been long doubtful of the wisdom of OVERLORD, after hearing the explanations of the kind of resistance we expected to encounter, the help we would get from air and naval forces, and the special equipment we had for landing purposes, he had changed his mind and got caught up in the atmosphere of confidence and conviction. The smell of victory was in the air.

☆ ☆ ☆ ☆ ☆

There was a considerable difference in the methods used by the British government and those used by the Americans in communicating with and supporting a theater commander. The American Chiefs of Staff, with the approval of the President, gave the theater commander a mission, provided him with such supplies and troops as they deemed adequate, and let him alone to fail or succeed. If he failed, he was relieved and a new commander assigned. As long as he was succeeding, they largely let him make his own decisions.

The British government, on the other hand, kept in close touch with almost every tactical move in our theater of war. Often suggestions came to us for doing this or that and occasionally these seemed to indicate that London was focusing its attention on side issues.

If the suggestions were political in character, and if the other political leaders approved, they were promptly carried out. When they
dealt with tactics, I always answered courteously that I was ready
to discuss them with General Brooke or the Prime Minister himself
but it had to be remembered that I had the sole responsibility for
carrying out the directive of the combined Chiefs of Staff—the defeat
of Hitler.

In the reverse situation, the Prime Minister and his government
were sensitive, and properly, to anything they thought was a field
commander's intervention into a political situation. One time in the
Mediterranean, when we were trying to move air equipment (including steel plates for runways) from Tunisia to the area around
Bari, Italy, it became necessary for us to suspend bombing for a
few days. Trying to make a virtue out of necessity, we announced
that we were giving Italy a short respite, affording the Italian government a chance to quit the Axis and surrender. I had failed to tell
the British government in advance *why* I was doing this. Immediately, I had a copy of a telegram sent by the Prime Minister to
President Roosevelt which said there was no excuse for military
commanders meddling in things that were essentially political. Of
course, when I explained, everything was understood but the incident
did show how carefully the British government followed every single
detail of military operations.

Later, on the continent, after I had assigned the American Ninth
Army to Montgomery for the capture of the Ruhr in the spring
of 1945, I ordered it to return to Bradley's command for the major
drive we wanted to make through the center of Germany. I wanted
to link up as quickly as possible with the Russians coming from the
east and so divide Germany into two parts.

Instantly, there were complaints from the British government that
I was weakening Montgomery. This was hardly the case; I had
reinforced him materially during a critical stage of his operations
when a specific tactical problem had to be solved. With success
achieved, I continued with the other plans already laid out. This
hurt some feelings. But it was the kind of decision that the American
Chiefs of Staff thought belonged to the theater commander only
and never dreamed of bothering him about.

This sketchy analysis is no criticism of anyone and in particular
it implies no dissatisfaction with my British friends of World War II.
On the contrary, I liked them and always respected them. The story,

by and large, was one of extraordinary loyalty and teamwork between our governments and their fighting forces.

Here, my purpose is to show only that differences in tradition caused minor frictions on occasion, even in the most successful military coalition in history.

There were moments of grimness and sobriety that I can never forget. On the Fourth of July, 1942, I had my first intimate look at one of the consequences of our bombing raids on Germany. Needless to say, not all the consequences fell upon Germany.

The raids, from a small start, had come to be devastating. But our earliest American sortie was six planes accompanying a British formation in attack. The mission was well carried out and I went to visit the crews of the planes as they came in. While there, a Liberator, a big plane of American manufacture but owned by the British and flown by a Polish crew, limped in from another raid. As it approached the field, it wobbled drunkenly, or, to say the obvious, like a bird broken in flight. Clearly it was not going to reach the runway. It came in across field to earth and flattened out. Rescue squads and medical people were on the job. They reached the plane, opened it up, and got in at the crew. The sight was dreadful. Only two men were unwounded. While no one had been injured in the crash landing, the co-pilot had already been killed over the continent, the pilot was seriously injured, and two or three other men were dead. It seemed impossible that the plane had ever gotten back to base and indeed it was never flown again.

Although the days, and, as often as not, the nights, were crowded with conferences, with trips, and solitary thinking and pondering, there were occasional opportunities for visits to historic sites and the privileges of meeting personages who had been only names and photographs in newspapers.

Even before I was installed in London, the British were offering warm hospitality. In the spring of 1942 General Clark and others accompanied me on an inspection trip to Britain. We were given an opportunity to visit Windsor Castle one Sunday afternoon. The Constable, Lord Wigram, was our host. The party was made up of General Clark, Captain Sterling of the British Army, and myself. Lord Wigram told us that the Royal Family knew of our visit. In order to avoid any embarrassment to us, he said, they were remaining in their apartment during the afternoon hours so that he could take us freely around the castle and show us all the interesting places, including those which the Royal Family normally used for recreation on fair days.

Weeks later, I was fortunate enough to be presented to the King. When the King recalled that some time back, I had been to the castle, he laughed and said he had a story to tell me about that occasion.

It had slipped the King's mind that he had promised Lord Wigram that the Royal Family would remain inside during our visit. Because the day had been so beautiful and sunny, the entire family decided to take advantage of the weather and have tea in the garden. While they were sitting at the table, they glanced up the hill and saw, just over its crest, the bobbing heads of four men, one very tall—this would be General Wayne Mark Clark—and one who was Lord Wigram. The King instantly remembered his promise. Should Lord Wigram get a glimpse of the Royal Family in the garden, the tour would be immediately terminated and we might miss something the Constable wanted to show us. The King exclaimed to the others, "This is terrible, we must not be seen." The question was—What to do?

The first thing they did was to jump down quickly from their chairs to their hands and knees. This put them outside the line of vision of the party now moving upward on the hill. The courtyard in which they had been sunning themselves was surrounded by a stone wall and the King saw that by keeping low, close to the ground, all of them could remain concealed until they reached the wall and in its shelter could make their way toward their quarters.

So, the crowned heads of England, the Royal Family, held so high in the affections of all of us, crawled on hands and knees to the wall. Then, still more or less on all fours, they made their way to the castle door and disappeared inside.

When the King told me this story, he laughed uproariously and I couldn't help joining him. "Your Majesty," I said, "if all Americans could hear that story just as you've told it, I can assure you that never again will a man be elected mayor of Chicago by running against the King of England."

"What do you mean, General?" he said.

I gulped. "Well, years ago we had a man in Chicago, who in running for the mayoralty constantly attacked the King of England—saying what would happen to him if he ever showed up in Chicago."

I managed to point out that considering the amount of prejudice among some of our ethnic groups against the King of England and Englishmen in general, this was popular political claptrap for a local election. No intelligent person took it seriously.

More than two years afterward, in October 1944, the King decided to visit Americans in the field and we arranged an outdoor luncheon for him at one of the Army headquarters. In talking to the company, he started with, "I say, did you know that my father was a principal party in the election of a mayor of Chicago one time?"

This promptly gained the attention of everybody at the table and we listened to the story from its beginning. He told it well, not only in substance, but showing such an ability as raconteur that the whole group joined him in a lengthy peal of laughter. He seemed highly pleased with his success. The story was later retold me by his Queen, and then, still later, by the present Queen of England.

At the same outdoor luncheon, senior officers of both British and American armies were present. Seated directly across from the King was George Patton. During the conversation, the King asked General Patton if he had ever shot anyone with the pistols he was wearing.

George said promptly, "Oh yes." But he added, "Really, not these pistols. These are the ones I carry socially. I carry my fighting pistols when I'm out on campaign."

"How many men have you killed in war?" asked the King.

Without batting an eye, George said, "Seven, Sir."

This was too much for me. "How many did you say, General Patton?"

Instantly he replied, "Three, Sir."

"Well, George," I said, "I'll let you get away with that." George had often told me that during the Pershing expedition into Mexico in 1916, he and a small cavalry patrol ran into a handful of Villa's brigands and in the melee he shot one of the enemy. I think this was about the limit of his personal lethal accomplishments.

The King was popular with all the American forces, as were his Queen and his mother. He liked the simple life of a soldier and was perfectly at home with all of us. At the end of the war, he asked me to come to Buckingham Palace about tea time, mentioning that he wanted to see me privately for a few minutes in his office before we took tea with the Queen and the Princess.

The reason for the few moments before proved to be the presentation of one of the most prized decorations any man can receive in Britain, the Order of Merit. As I recall, only twelve men in the uniformed services and twelve civilians can hold the Order at any one time. The King, having handed me the box containing the decoration, passed to me also a sealed letter. He asked that I not read the letter until I'd left the Palace.

When I was free to open the letter, I found, to my amazement and pleasure, that he had written it in longhand. It was an expression of his gratitude and that of his people for my war services and was so beautifully stated that I have always held it as one of the most appreciated of all awards given me by any foreign government.

On the eve of my departure from Washington in 1942 to become American commander in the European Theater, General Marshall remarked, "Now, Eisenhower, when you go don't make the same mistake I did when I went over to get Mr. Churchill's agreement on the Roundup plan. I realized the British were short of many foods and I decided I'd take along a couple of cases of fresh fruit and vegetables. I gave instructions that I wanted the nicest and freshest I could get.

"When I got to Europe and started to divide the spoils among the British Chiefs of Staff, I found to my dismay that the two cases contained brussels sprouts, the one vegetable that's truly plentiful in the British Isles."

I thanked the General for his suggestion and told him I would be certain not to repeat his mistake. When I went over, I arranged to take several cases of oranges and grapefruit, which were exceedingly rare in that beleaguered island. I instructed an aide to watch them carefully. From the London Airport they were put on a truck to be unloaded at my hotel, The Claridge. A number of friends whom I had met during an earlier visit had come to call. I told them I hoped they would wait a few minutes because there was something I wanted to divide among them. They were delighted and waited patiently.

Finally, one of my orderlies said the cases had arrived and

asked if he could see me for a moment. I went out to a small room where he stood with a long face. Both cases were opened. In one there was a single fruit; the other was empty.

Ambassador John Winant was a popular figure in London. As a fellow American, he wanted to have a dinner for me, and invited a number of British and American associates, civilian and military. It was to be a stag affair and I did not see how I could refuse. Many military-governmental conferences were held as "dinner meetings," and though they could become relaxed, certain formalities were always observed—the toasts to the King and the President, for one.

Everything went well at the Ambassador's dinner, from my viewpoint, and when it was over I thanked him and went back to the hotel.

Winant, a gentle and soft-spoken man, telephoned me the following morning to ask whether he could stop in to see me a few minutes. I said, "By all means."

When he reached the office, he suggested that he would like to set me right about one important matter. I was appreciative. After all, it was wartime and anything anyone could do to help was welcomed.

He said, "General, I note that you are a heavy smoker."

"That's right."

"Well," he said, "of course at home our habit is to smoke at almost any place and on any occasion, unless we happen to be in church. But in this country, at every dinner of any consequence, it's a custom to avoid smoking until after the toast to the King has been drunk."

If this was a local tradition, I was grateful, so I said, "Thanks for your kindness in telling me about this. I'm sorry I didn't know about the custom and I assure you that I will not offend again."

And he said, "Thank you very much."

Then I added, "Last night was the end of my attendance at formal dinners in London."

This shocked Ambassador Winant and he begged me to reconsider. But I grinned and tried to assure the Ambassador that it was of no importance.

A few days later, my friend, Admiral Louis Mountbatten, invited me to a dinner. I said I couldn't come.

"Well, why not? A lot of your friends are going to be there and it is going to be largely a business affair but I wanted also to have a number of people who haven't met you, particularly some of the members of OPS [Operations]."

I started to speak and then he said, "You don't have to worry about smoking, General. You come along and I'll take care of everything." So I consented to go.

After the inevitable sherry, we sat down and found that the first course, a soup, had already been placed on the table. As quickly as it was consumed, the Admiral jumped to his feet and snapped: "Gentlemen, the King!" Still standing, he proposed: "The President of the United States." Then he sat down and immediately said to me loudly enough to be heard by more than a few, "Now, General, smoke all you want."

This was a silly performance on my part, I guess, but as I've often said, my smoking in those days was not just habit; it was a continuous performance. I did stick to one thing. After I learned that in London the service clubs allowed no smoking in their dining rooms and that a number of other clubs to which I was invited observed the same custom, I always found an excuse to get out of a dinner at such places.

The privilege of command allowed me to meet kings, queens, presidents, ambassadors—some in exile—and a rotund fellow named George Allen. We might never have met except for Mr. Allen's curious gift for prophecy.

A few days before I reached London, George Allen was sent by the President to the United Kingdom. He had been for a long time a member of the political group around Mr. Roosevelt and had been appointed, after serving as a Commissioner of the District of Columbia, to a position in the Red Cross. This required inspection trips during the war. After a visit to Ireland, he arrived in England and met a number of prominent people who knew of his connection with the President. So it came about one evening that he attended a dinner given in his honor by the American Ambassador to the Court of St. James.

The Americans present were hungry for news and gossip from their nation's capital. George, a constant storyteller, was not at all loath to give them the latest servings of both. As the evening ran on, the conversation turned to speculations about the future. Mr. Allen fielded most of these with competence until someone said:

"Who are the American generals likely to be prominent on this side of the water?"

Allen knew no generals of prominence. Indeed since World War I, in which he was a first lieutenant, he had no connection with the Army. He did know the name of one General—Daniel I. Sultan, who had been a fellow member of the District of Columbia Commission. He mused a bit about Sultan, stalling for time, and also thinking that Sultan, who was an engineer, might possibly be overlooked for combat command. Then he had a sudden inspiration.

Mr. Allen's wife, Mary, and Mamie, my wife, had been friends in Washington during the years when we had lived in that city prior to 1935. He remembered reading in the newspaper an account of the Louisiana maneuvers of late 1941 and of the operations of one Colonel Eisenhower, who had earned a little praise, and a promotion to brigadier general.

On the spur of the moment, and on the edge of desperation, he blurted out, "Watch Eisenhower."

Naturally, to demonstrate the scope of his knowledge, he had to enlarge on the personality and character of the man he had mentioned. It was of slight relevance that we had never met. The evening passed pleasantly and George returned to his hotel.

The following morning, one of the dinner guests called George on the telephone. He was awakened and sleepily wondered into the mouthpiece why anyone could possibly want him so early in the morning.

The reply was, "Why didn't you tell us? Why were you so coy?"

Allen muttered something unintelligible and quite possibly unprintable.

"Why didn't you tell us that Eisenhower was coming here in command?"

George, suddenly wide awake, and accustomed to thinking on his feet, now had to think on his back. "Well, the timing on these things is not only important, the moves of our senior officers are secret. I would have been badly criticized if I had let it out before the General got here."

George Allen lost no time in getting dressed because he could see only one way to retain his reputation as a man-in-the-know. It was clear that if someone called and talked to me about my friend, George Allen, Mr. Allen was going to lose stature within official London circles in a short time.

He knew that an old friend of his, Harry Butcher, a reserve commander in the Navy, had joined me recently, and he hoped that Butcher was in London. He telephoned and telephoned until he located Butcher and then told him the story. "Butch," he said, "I've just got to be seen with the General somewhere, otherwise people will call me the phony that I really am."

Butcher invited George to headquarters and said he would see what could be done. After keeping George on the hot seat for some time, Butcher came into my office, told me that he had a warm friend from Washington whose wife knew mine, and he thought perhaps I'd be pleased to send a message back by him. He added quietly that his friend was in a bit of difficulty and perhaps I could help out.

I agreed to see the friend and found a man of considerable avoirdupois, but with a sparkle in his eye. He told me the story. "General," he continued, "I'm putting myself at your mercy. If I could just be *seen* coming out of your office with you, or if a little item could be put in the paper that Mr. Allen had just called on the new commanding general, this would do the trick. But I would be grateful if you could do *anything* that would free me of the consequences of blabbing about things of which I know nothing."

Mr. Allen's obvious distress, and his anxiety to avoid fame as a teller of fairy tales, made me laugh. "I'll tell you what we will do. It's now about three hours until lunchtime at Claridge's, where I am living temporarily. While I don't like public dining rooms, this one time I'll have Butcher arrange a luncheon at the hotel, with you sitting on my right and a couple of American and British military friends at the table."

His gratitude was overwhelming. Allen promised to be my slave forever if I would just get him out of this predicament.

Butcher arranged the luncheon for seven or eight people and took care to reserve a table in the middle of the room and at the height of the lunch period. We all sat down together and had a wonderful time, although the reason for the luncheon was not divulged. For me, it was one of the few times I dined in public during the war, but for George, it was the saving of his reputation as a man privy to all the secrets of Washington. In the years since, George tells the story with embroideries and embellishments, and all the nuances of a born fabulist, and it never loses anything in the telling.

After such a beginning, we became friends. At times I thought he enjoyed my rank more than I did. He could speak of it in high-flown style. For example, now and then we would have a game of bridge. One evening we started out with only a single deck—for some reason it was difficult to keep two around my quarters—and in the first hand, George, who was one of my opponents, spoke up.

"Wait a minute, I have the joker. I have to have another card."

"Oh no you don't," I said. "That is the six of clubs. We lost the real six and you'll notice the markings in the corner."

George laid down his hand, leaned back in his chair, and said: "Now just a minute. If the Commander-in-Chief of all this armada, which is about to cross the Channel and lick Hitler, cannot afford one complete set of cards, then I have grave doubts that other and more necessary items of equipment with which we hope to win are adequate and ready."

"George," I said, "let me tell you this. We are not going to be playing games with the Nazis."

Late in the spring of 1944, I established an advanced GHQ near Portsmouth. Occasionally I would have to go back to London or to my base headquarters in Bushy Park. This involved an overnight stay which I spent at my increasingly familiar residence, Telegraph Cottage, just south of the City. Shortly after D-Day the fly bombs (V-1) began coming across from Europe with regularity and bomb shelters had been dug around the headquarters and housing areas. Orders about going to the shelters were strict. We couldn't afford, through negligence or carelessness, the loss of highly trained officers. Not far from my house was a dugout that would accommodate, with crowding, my household staff in the back, and people from neighboring houses in the front.

At noon one day we were having lunch and George was present. While at the table, we heard the signal that fly bombs were coming our way. If their course was determined to be toward our village, an "imminent alert" was sounded. Because the bombs flew at a rate of over three hundred miles an hour, no time could be lost. The alert sounded.

As we started, I warned George to keep up—but he, being generously fleshed and deliberate, straggled along yards in the rear. Seeing this, I said, "George, you'd better speed it up!" He still paid little attention. He was walking along with his eyes on the ground when Sergeant Moaney, who happened to look back, called out, "There it comes!"

George took one quick look and without pause shot past us as a sprinter would go by a pedestrian.

He rushed into the shelter, slammed the door behind him, and then, after a silence, realizing what he had done, shouted through the door, "Excuse me, General." He rushed down the steps. By the time we got the door open, the bomb had gone over.

(Most of us, whenever we saw one of the V-1s, would devoutly hope that the thing would continue on its way and not blow us to pieces. The second it had gone by, we would feel guilty that we wished ill luck on someone else, perhaps on people who did not have as good a shelter as we did. If we were caught distant from a shelter, we, like everyone, would lie down along a curb or in a ditch if one was handy.)

After the bomb had gone its way and we were back at the table, George began to talk. That was nothing unusual but I wondered how he would deal with any hint of embarrassment. First of all, he said, "General, I think you ought to practice your starts." The others at the table hurrahed him about saving himself at my and their expense and he continued: "Well, now, I decided as quickly as I closed the door what I would do in case the bomb exploded and all of you had become casualties. By no means could I let it be known, at once, that the Commander-in-Chief of the Allied forces now fighting on the Normandy beach was a casualty. So when I saw this secret telephone of yours in the shelter, I just planned to start issuing orders, just like you would. I would take full charge of things.

"In the meantime, I'd send for an orderly and send a secret message to the President to tell him that I had taken charge temporarily and ask him to name someone to take over from me. While I could easily handle things, I had such important business elsewhere that I could not be expected to carry on this job also."

As George went on, our happy faces were his reward and he has, in effect, never ceased telling the story.

George's stories were all accounts of actual happenings, and George, in almost every case, was the goat. A standard story of his is about a football game he played in in 1916. His side was beaten 222–0, all of which was accomplished in eight-minute quarters. He wonders what the score would have been if they had played fifteen-minute quarters. He claims that, according to one sports writer, the brightest player of the losing Cumberland College team was Allen himself, who circled right end with the loss of only five yards. At one point, he fumbled the ball and when it bounced toward his backfield partner, he called out, "Pick it up, Bill!" and Bill replied, in disgust, "Pick it up yourself—you dropped it."

For all the entertainment and companionship he provided, George Allen was one of those who at all times exemplified Fox Conner's admonition about taking one's job seriously, not oneself. George was chairman of the Prisoner of War Committee of the American Red Cross. In this role he had the chief responsibility, working through the International Red Cross and the Swiss, of establishing lines of access and communication to provide as much comfort—material and moral—to our men taken prisoner by the Nazis as could be given them behind enemy lines. That many of these unfortunate soldiers were able to survive the privations and rigors of the POW camps was due in part to the work done by George Allen and his organization.

If this gave him a role in history, George never thought of himself as a historic figure. If anything, he played down such associations. There is a marker he has had put on a boulder at the entrance to his farm on the Gettysburg battlefield, near my home. Thousands of other markers, commemorating valiant deeds, are in the immediate vicinity. The tablet on the Allen farm reads:

> N. O. N. Historical Society
> At this spot on February 29, 1776
> Absolutely Nothing Happened.

In the preparation of an immense military enterprise, the staggering multiplicity of decisions and details can tend to dwarf other things in life. But like all men in the services, I had personal concerns and worries, prides and fears, and a good thing too—they helped save us from degenerating into one-track machines. With the awesome potential of D-Day approaching, I found myself thinking as a father.

John's graduation from West Point was on June 6, the date of the invasion. General Marshall was characteristically thoughtful and he directed that John be sent to my headquarters, to spend a short leave before reporting to Fort Benning, Georgia, to complete infantry training.

John reached London on the *Queen Elizabeth* and for the next two or three weeks he and I had a grand time together. He was fascinated by the work at headquarters but he spent much time across the Channel visiting with people he knew in the field forces. As was to be expected, he soon began to argue that he shouldn't be sent back home. He said that he had gotten most of the training at West Point that they would give him at Benning and he felt that I should assign him to troops right here and now.

Things were not quite that simple. Such an action would lay John open to charges of favoritism. It wouldn't do him any good to be known as teacher's pet. So I told him that while I was sure that General Marshall would honor any request I made of him, I thought it was better for John to go along with the others of his class through the routine. He accepted my decision and we tried to crowd into his limited leave as much time together as was possible considering the demands of the war.*

After the landings on the morning of June 6, the battling stayed tough and constant but after weeks of fighting, Bradley started a heavy attack, captured Saint Lô, and about August broke through the left flank of the defending forces. For weeks the front was quite fluid and though the duties at headquarters were heavy, I managed to visit our forward units with some regularity.

General Haislip, one of my oldest friends, was commanding the XV Corps and I determined to visit him. As I reached his head-quarters about noon, he came out in a Jeep to meet me. His greeting was almost surly:

"General, I think you should turn around and go back right away."

"What's the trouble?" I asked.

"We've got Nazi artillery firing on our flank and we think there's a counterattack building up that just might overrun the area."

"Well, Ham," I said, "I'd like to see the development of their attack and I'm really confident you can handle it. Besides, I don't see you running."

---

* John went back to Benning and after his training was completed, joined the 71st Division. He came to Europe with the 71st and then General Bradley put him in a forward reconnaissance detachment called "Phantom." In the final days of combat, the work he did in Phantom carried him at one point far forward of our advancing troops—and I think that he found himself and his little detachment rather lonesome before we finally joined up again with them.

"Of course we'll handle it!" he said. "But in the meantime we could get some nasty artillery fire and you might get into it."

I reiterated, annoyingly, "After all, you might, too."

"This is my place!" he insisted. "But I don't want you here. Don't think I'm worrying about your possible demise. I just don't want it said that I allowed the Supreme Commander to get killed in my corps area. Now if you want to get killed, go into some other area."

I knew that in spite of his tone he was worried, but I was sure there would be no quick overrunning of the positions in spite of Ham's lamentations about the lack of reserves. So I said I was going to stay for lunch, at least. That lunch was a comedy, served in speeded-up, double quick-time, under Haislip's none too gentle prodding. He ordered soup for me without waiting for the others to sit down, and he had the main course on the table before I was through the first one. Just to plague him a little more I said, "Now look, Ham—you can bring this lunch in as fast as you want but I'm going to enjoy it. I had no breakfast and I ate last evening out of C rations and I'm not going to be hurried. You fighting guys serve good food."

He consented to my having thirty minutes for lunch. At thirty minutes plus one, he took me for a ride, saying that here was something interesting he wanted me to see.

After a couple of minutes, I remarked, "Okay, Ham, I'm just smart enough to know that this is the same road I came in on. What was it you wanted to show me?"

"I want to show you the shortest way out of this corps area!" he said. And that was that, for I found out that he was really worried.

When officers came back from nearer the front to my headquarters after the liberation of Paris—the Trianon Palace Hotel—I tried to see to it that they were treated with more hospitality than I was shown up forward. Bradley came to my winter headquarters at Versailles and I wanted to give him a fine luncheon. The day before I had received a prize, a bushel of oysters, still in their shells and packed in cool, wet moss. They had been brought over in one of our planes, tucked away in an odd corner by my friend Steve Early, who was the press secretary for President Roosevelt. I talked with my mess sergeant. "This noon, we'll have an oyster feast for General Bradley. Let's serve raw oysters, then oyster soup, and as an entree, fried oysters. Serve them with a salad and vegetables and give us something unusual for dessert. I want to do right by him."

I was smiling in anticipation as we sat down at the table; everybody loves oysters. When those beauties on the half shell came out, Brad looked up and said inoffensively, "I can't touch oysters."

I sent for the mess sergeant, and while we dawdled with our first course, I whispered frantically and impolitely, and he drummed up an edible meat—Spam, if I'm not mistaken—for the General.

I should have known better. Back in North Africa, I had had word from Secretary of State Cordell Hull, on a trip to Moscow, that he would spend an evening with us in Algiers. Along with his message came one from his staff with the information that the Secretary was on a strict diet. We were given a list of the things that Secretary Hull could not eat. The message was somewhat garbled but my A.D.C. was informed that among the forbidden foods was red meat.

We had just secured a large roast of beef and because the dinner group was to be eighteen people, the aide ordered it served, and at the same time arranged for an individual omelette for the Secretary. Things went off as planned and during the meat course my guests, almost without exception, praised the quality of beef. (It had come from a shipment sent me by another friend, Amon Carter, of Fort Worth.) When the waiters came back, everybody present—except the Secretary, of course—took a second helping. Mr. Hull was sitting on my right and, as the waiter started again for the kitchen, he spoke up in a plaintive voice, "Please, General, might I have a portion of that beautiful roast?"

I practically fainted with embarrassment. "Why, Mr. Secretary, we have a cable instructing us to serve you no meat under any circumstances. I'm terribly sorry."

"Well," he said, "the cable is wrong. I want some of that meat." Happily there was plenty left and I urged him to take all the time he wanted and he did. For the next meals I asked him what he desired and made sure he got it.

The war was not all oysters and beef and breakthroughs, as everyone knows. But, as noted, I have told the military story, as I saw it, elsewhere. From the start of OVERLORD, we knew that we would win—but we knew it not factually but with faith. When the Nazis' situation was hopeless, by any rational standard, they could still ex-

plode into fitful snatches of energy and deadliness. With the R
on the east, and the Western Allies driving in from the other sid
in the frenzied mind of Hitler and those hypnotized by him could
there have been the expectation of lightning strokes that would
liberate Germany from our tightening, encircling armies.

The Bulge was a dangerous episode but at Bastogne, the most
publicized (but possibly not the most critical) stand in our furious
defense, encircled thousands of paratroopers, hemmed in, held out
and wrecked the Nazis' time schedule. On a smaller scale, Bastogne
was repeated in scores of little places, hamlets and bridge crossings
and road bends, where handfuls of men might for hours hold up a
Nazi column. On December 22, 1944, our southern counterattack
was launched and in my order of the day I wrote:

The enemy is making his supreme effort. He is fighting savagely to take
back all that you have won and is using every treacherous trick to deceive
and kill. . . . In the face of your proven bravery and fortitude he will completely fail.

But we cannot be content with his mere repulse. By rushing out from his
fixed defenses the enemy may give us the chance to turn his greatest gamble
into his worst defeat. So I call upon every man of all the Allies to rise to
new heights of courage, of resolution, and of effort.

The enemy did fail. But to put it in those terms is to understate
grievously what happened. Our men responded gallantly. These were
the times when the grand strategy and the high hopes of high command became a soldiers' war, sheer courage, and the instinct for
survival.

More than the constant threat of imminent death, our men had
overcome all that the unbridled elements could inflict on them in
the way of snow and ice and sleet, clammy fog and freezing rain;
all the pain of arduous marches and sleepless watches. They had
given up their wives and children, or set aside their hope of wives
and children, overcome luxuries or poverty, fought down their own
inclinations to rest their tired bodies, to play it safe, to search out a
hiding place.

In the light of their record, I am skeptical about the critics of
young people these days—including myself—who bemoan their alleged desertion of traditional American standards. Many things now

going on naturally disturb me because they seem senseless or purposeless or graceless. In a nation whose numbers now approach two hundred million, tens of thousands will be found who skulk whenever danger looms, who seek safety for their own hides, or who are confused or questioning. In the days of the Bulge, not all soldiers were heroes. Seeking troops who could handle rifles or man guns along our extended lines, we offered men under certain court-martial sentences a pardon and a clean record if they would volunteer for the front. As I recall, all who had been sentenced to fifteen years or more of hard labor accepted the offer but very few of those with lighter sentences chose to abandon the stockade for the risk of combat. This refusal of duty by men wearing the American uniform was disheartening. But then, as now, I know that only a tiny minority create these doubts among their elders. Those who were in their seventies when I was in my teens probably felt the same way about some of my generation's doings and vagaries.

I believe that we can always rely, even as I had to in the Battle of the Bulge and the concurrent winter fighting from the North Sea to the Italian Alps, on the willingness and readiness of Americans, including young ones, to endure greatly in their country's cause.

☆ ☆ ☆ ☆ ☆

Moments from near the end. In mid-March 1945, we captured München-Gladbach, the largest German city that had fallen to the Allies up to that moment. I was up front with Van Gillem's corps. The troops had gotten into the city a couple of hours ahead of us but I was interested in watching their take-over. Suddenly there was the clamor of anti-aircraft fire. The target was an incredibly fast plane, a brilliant flash in the final fading moments of the Nazi Luftwaffe, the first jet I'd ever seen in flight. It looked more like a bright little silver fly in the sky than anything else and it seemed far out of range of our guns.

There was flak falling around us and because I never carried a helmet, the corps commander found one for me. But when it proved to be too small, he urged me to get under our Jeep. I said, "Look, Van, I don't have any false ideas about immunity to falling flak. I'm ready to take cover. But let me point out that across the road about three hundred yards, you can see a German woman and her children, all working the field and apparently planting the spring crops. She's not even looking up. Don't you think it would be a little silly to crowd under the Jeep?"

On May 7, 1945, a group of tired men met in my headquarters in Rheims. The moment was at hand. There had been long and tedious negotiations with German leaders who were backing and filling because of uncertainties as to who was really speaking for the deceased Hitler. When the signing finally took place, a little before three in the morning of May 7, I think no person in the entire headquarters gave much thought to starting a public celebration or participating in a private one. My group went to bed to sleep the clock around. And I waited up only long enough to get through on the phone to Omar Bradley.

"Brad, I've got good news. Get the word around." Then I issued the final and climactic order of the war in Europe. "Make sure that all firing stops at midnight of the eighth."

Book Four

AT PEACE

CHAPTER XIX

Stories Out of London, Berlin, Frankfurt

FROM Pearl Harbor Sunday until the German capitulation forty-one months later, I had been under all the pressures for which through my entire career I had been preparing myself. The size of the job, and the variety and uniqueness of the pressures, were unexpected, to say the least. No matter how jaunty my air at the conference table—some may have thought me cocksure—I wore a bit thin at times. Like so many other men and women who had been at war physically or emotionally, exhaustion rather than exultation was my first reaction to victory in Europe.

As I write, two decades later, my memory of the days immediately following the Rheims armistice ceremony is dimmer and fuzzier than it is of any other period of World War II. I had been liberated, too. In a deep sag of reaction, I luxuriated in the freedom from decisions about the life and death of human beings.

Most of us, when we are tired, are content with the good of the hour and are little given to planning for the months or even weeks ahead. It seemed perfectly obvious, anyhow, that nothing in my future could approach in magnitude what had engaged me during the recent past. After a short time, I did become excited by the idea of a purely sentimental venture, a nostalgic return to West Point. There is a traditional five-year reunion that every class observes (when possible). I thought I'd gather all my classmates who were stationed in Europe and go back.

Ours would be an unpublicized, even sneaky, expedition. That our travel time in a propeller plane, lumbering and poky by present standards, would consume three or four times as many hours as we would be at West Point, assuring for all of us a massive new case of fatigue and plane-weariness, troubled me not at all.

I called Colonel "Jodey" Haw and asked him to contact our class-mates with the invitation. Preparations went forward at full speed when a message from General Marshall knocked the whole scheme into a cocked hat. He cabled to say that because our troops could not return home for victory parades—the divisions that we could spare from occupation duties in Europe were to be sent to the Pacific —he thought we should bring representative groups from all units, including naval and air, to give the people at home who had worked hard and long a chance to cheer and blow off steam. I do not remember how many groups were to go but each was to be made up from all grades, from the youngest recruit to the Commanding General.

While preparations for the journey were under way, Prime Minister Churchill invited me to come from my Frankfurt headquarters to Britain on June 12. A ceremony was to be held in the ancient Guildhall where I was to be made a Freeman of the City of London. The honor at the Guildhall would require a speech and for a good many days in advance, I worked on a text. I knew what I wanted to say, but as usual, I wondered whether I could say it well.

So I got out the yellow pad and started to write with pencil in the evenings at my quarters in Bad Homburg. Weary at the end of each day from assaults on the papers that covered my desk, I got into bed each evening immediately after supper. There, propped against a pillow, I would go over the text of my speech until I fell asleep. Although I had spent many hours preparing drafts of reports and speeches for my seniors in the War Department, this was the first formal address of any length that I had to give on my own. I labored at it mightily, never satisfied with a single paragraph.

Each morning I would take the scribblings and corrections to the office and have the text retyped. Then I would bring it back home in the evening to correct and add to and cross it all up again with new hentracks—again for retyping. One evening, Frank Page, an old friend, came to dinner. During the course of the evening, he reminded me gently that the Guildhall ceremony was bound to be a solemn one and urged that I prepare carefully for it. "Frank," I said, "the speech is here somewhere. I always bring it back with me at night." After looking around, I had to say ruefully, "Well, this is the one night I forgot it. I didn't bring it along." Then I thought—and said, "Anyway, it starts like this . . ."

I began to quote from memory and to my astonishment was able to go through the entire talk without pause. At the end I exclaimed, "Frank, whether this is any good or not, it's done. As long as I can do this without notes, I'm ready."

Frank said the talk was adequate and, in fact, he urged me not to change it.

To fortify myself before I went to a ceremony that I knew would be held in strange surroundings, I wrote out on a small card the first words of each paragraph. My aides had to go to the Guildhall early and I decided to slip out the back door of the Dorchester Hotel. I was feeling confined, a little nervous, and thought that maybe I could have half an hour alone in the park.

As I crossed the street, a cab driver put his head out the window, called, "Ike, good old Ike," stopped, produced a piece of paper, which I signed. His passengers got out, and they asked me to autograph miscellaneous papers. As this went on, a crowd began to gather, and then, in moments, it seemed, hundreds had gathered.

It was flattering but it was also becoming difficult to extricate myself. As the crowd continued to grow, someone, looking over from the hotel, saw the trouble I was in, and called for a squad of police. They formed a flying wedge, got in to me, got me out again.

With my OVERLORD deputy, Air Chief Marshal Arthur Tedder, we proceeded to the boundary of the City and from there, in a horse-drawn carriage, were escorted through crowds to the historic hall.

The outside of the famous hall was not imposing but the interior certainly was. Before me was the sexton and the Lord Mayor of London, in uniform, and in wig. One carried a mace and Tedder whispered to me, "That mace is over six hundred years old." The hall was jammed.

I was given, as a symbol of the sword I was to receive, the Wellington Sword—a curved, oriental scimitar, encrusted with jewels. The actual sword, a Crusader type, was not yet ready but when it arrived, bearing the British Order of Merit insignia and other significant engravings, it became one of my prized possessions.*

As I spoke, the huge audience, made up of the officialdom of all Britain (except the Royal Family who cannot come down "into the City of London," so to speak), sat in absolute silence.

What I said, for anyone who wants to read the full text, is in the

---

* That sword, along with the Order of Grand Commander of the Bath and the Order of Merit are the few items that my son, John, chose out of the collection of things I offered him. He hopes to give them to his son, and so on and on, as long as there are Eisenhower boys in the family. Thereafter, I hope they will go to the Eisenhower Museum, in Abilene, Kansas, where the remainder of the collection is exhibited—but I hope this little collection will stay intact in my family for centuries to come.

back of the book.* But what I tried to express, in part, was that the honor was mingled with sadness—sadness that we had ever been faced with the tragic situation that compelled the appointment of an Allied Commander-in-Chief, and sadness which is known to any man who receives acclaim earned in the blood of his followers and the sacrifices of his friends.

The London papers greeted the talk warmly—and even, in an excess of friendly misjudgment, boxed it on the front page with the Gettysburg Address. After lunch at the Mansion House across the street, Winston Churchill and I stood on a balcony, greeting a crowd in the square below. Not an inch of road or pavement was to be seen, so dense was the gathering.

"Whether you know it or not, I've got just as much right to be down there yelling as you do," I said to the crowd.

"You see, I'm a citizen of London now, too."

☆   ☆   ☆   ☆   ☆

My headquarters was absorbed in the complexities of a new military move, one without precedent again—transporting more than a million victorious combat veterans to the Pacific Front. They were to engage the remaining member of the Axis while those combat veterans whose service had earned them early discharge would be returned home.

Here we were confronted by a human problem that among men of less discipline might well have ended in wild disorder. Inescapably, many of the men sent to the Pacific would feel that an injustice was being done them. Dissatisfaction, contagious in an Army fresh from battle with no enemy in its immediate front, could infect hundreds of thousands of men.

Our hands were somewhat tied by detailed directives from Washington as to how the turnaround was to be accomplished. Red tape festooned everything. One way to speed up our veterans' return from Europe occurred to me, possibly an echo of what I had seen in World War I.

Tens of thousands of our recovered prisoners of war, ready for embarkation to the United States and discharge, were crowded into a camp near Le Havre. Every day they saw Liberty and Victory ships

* See Note 5.

returning home empty, without cargo or passengers. They had to wait for the relatively few ships fitted up specifically for troop transport. Not realizing the impossibility of using cargo vessels because of the lack of sanitary facilities, etc., they were giving themselves and their officers a bad time when I arrived at the base.

No inspection had to be made to see that the men's complaints could easily expand into violent protest. Something had to be done. As I went about the base, in the back of my head I tried to come up with a device to speed the process. Refitting the cargo vessels would take months. The troop transports were making transatlantic crossings at top speed. As I gnawed at the problem the answer occurred—to double the passenger load on the transports, sleeping and feeding the men in shifts.

This simple solution would work only if the soldiers were willing to put up with considerable inconvenience and discomfort, especially if stormy weather was encountered. To many thousands of men gathered to greet our party, I asked a question over the P.A. system. "Do you want to go back home conveniently—or would you rather double up, be uncomfortable, and get home quickly?" I made it clear that this was no more than a brainstorm unsupported by a staff study. This proposal provoked a thunderous applause of approval.

The red tape was easier to cut in individual cases. My classmate, Dutch Aurand, was ordered to mainland China to take over a command there. He wanted with him his corps chaplain and close friend, Colonel Raymond Blakeney. At the last moment, he discovered that no chaplains could be transferred because Washington felt that they would be most needed in the European Theater during the turn-around period. General Aurand came storming into my office, denouncing bureaucrats and contributing to the general illumination in the room.

"Dutch," I said, "this thing is easy. I'll issue an order relieving Colonel Blakeney from his duties as chaplain without giving any reason or assigning him to any duty. Then he will be footloose and all you have to do is pick him up, appoint him your aide, and go off to China."

And so it was, by temporarily removing the collar of a man of God, we got him to a place where he could do his duty to both God and man.

Whatever the problems with our own red taping, I could cut those knots better than the knots of national prejudice. The French government had arranged a victory celebration to which I was invited. Naturally, all the principal members of my staff, British and American, went with me. At the end of the day, there was to be a dinner to which I assumed everyone had been invited. But about noon I learned that the British officers had not been. This made me furious. I sent word to the French officials that I was invited as commander of an Allied headquarters and I could not attend unless the principal officers of my staff were treated equally. I was assured that there was some mistake and that this would be corrected.

All seemed serene when we arrived at a cocktail reception before the dinner. The senior officers, both British and American, were present. When the reception was over, I was told that the dinner to follow would be a private affair, with only a few members of the French government and a few of my people to be present. I had to accept the explanation, particularly because one British officer had been included on the dinner list: my personal military assistant, Brigadier James Gault. But all of us felt that the British had been slighted.

On the trip to the United States, we visited Washington, New York, West Point, Kansas City, and Abilene. The ceremonies were a far cry from the simple, one-day, secret visit I had earlier and naïvely been planning.

I do not know the reactions of others, but I was amazed at the numbers of people who met us on the streets and the wild enthusiasm of their greeting. The trip to Washington was so overwhelming I thought everything to follow would be anti-climax. When we went to New York, however, the entire city seemed to be on hand. Hour upon hour, we traveled avenues jammed with people, with incalculable others hanging out the windows of towering office and apartment buildings.

In conferences at the Pentagon, we went over occupation policy in Europe, the movement of troops from our theater to the Pacific, and heard about planning for the invasion of Japan. This was to involve a new armada and assumed a defense of desperation. Whether or not the bloodbath of an entire people would have been the result, whether or not the operation was necessary, became within a few weeks a theoretical question. The explosion of the first atomic bomb at Alamogordo, and the bombs dropped on Japan in August, put an end to invasion plans and to the war itself.

In my home town, I got to see all the living members of my immediate family. This was a rich moment; we had been separated through trying years.

Going back home was a visit to memories. My father was no longer there. When he died in 1942, the house had lost one of its commanding presences. I remembered him as a modest, studious, and intelligent person. The two definite and serious financial reverses in his life had markedly affected him. In 1888, only three years after his marriage, he had found his business gone, his family growing, and he was without a job and in debt.

When drought and grasshoppers struck simultaneously, and southern Dickinson County, Kansas, a wholly agricultural community, was in distress, Father had such good relations with his suppliers that he and his partner were able to continue extending credit to their customers. Naturally, he and Mother were living on almost nothing but it had appeared that they would pull through. It was just at that moment that his partner decided to disappear, taking whatever small assets there were remaining, and leaving my dad holding the sack.

In after years, he could not be brought to talk about the experience. But, as I noted, he had started all over again, at the bottom, in the MK & T (Katy) shops at Denison, Texas, had come back to Kansas, had studied and become an engineer. Then, going over to a utility company where he started as an engineer, he rose to become Personnel Officer of the C. L. Brown Company, a group of central Kansas industries.

When the time came to retire, his pension and dividends made it possible for him and Mother to live comfortably. Then came 1929— and in time the company from which his income came went into bankruptcy.

He was never one for self-pity but he could never fully accept the idea that he might not be able to provide for Mother after he was gone or to leave each son a small portion of an estate representing a lifetime of work.

What he did not realize (though we tried to help him to understand) was that his integrity, his training, his discipline of his sons *had* resulted in dividends. We were all established in one career or another, and this was in no small measure accountable to his example and his reputation.

But he had always been sensitive about debt. He had not allowed Mother or any of the boys to buy anything not paid for at the moment of its receipt. Once, needing a new pair of trousers after I had ripped the ones I had on (which resulted in the infection and illness described earlier), I arranged with a storekeeper to let me have them until I could earn the money to pay him back. I asked the man to say nothing to my father. However, red tape went its way, even in Abilene, and some unmentionable clerk or secretary sent my father a bill for $4.50. He made no attempt to punish me but I could see that he was deeply distressed by my violation of one of his basic principles. Never again did I take a chance that any indebtedness of mine would come to his notice. But during my graduation leave, when I had no income of any kind and wanted to enjoy those months of free time, he had gladly and generously advanced me money.

His temper could blaze with frightening suddenness but when things were going along at a casual tempo, he was a good companion.

When the word came that he was gone, I was deputy to General Marshall for Operations of the U. S. Army. It was not possible to leave. But it was not possible for me to go ahead with business-as-usual. I closed the door of my office and sat thinking about the life we had all had together. On my desk was a clock-and-diary combination, and I made a few notes which still exist. They read, in part:

March 11, 1942

My father was buried today. I've shut off all business and visitors for thirty minutes—to have that much time, by myself, to think of him. He had a full life. He left six boys and . . . fortunately . . . Mother survives. He was not quite seventy-nine years old but for the past year he has been extremely old physically. Hardened arteries, kidney trouble, etc. He was a just man, well liked, a thinker. He was undemonstrative, quiet, modest, and of exemplary habits—he never used alcohol or tobacco. . . .

His finest monument is his reputation in Abilene and Dickinson Co. . . . His word has been his bond and accepted as such. . . . Because of it, all central Kansas helped me secure an appointment to West Point in

1911, and thirty years later, it did the same for my son John. I'm proud he was my father. My only regret is that it was always so difficult to let him know the great depth of my affection for him.

DAVID J. EISENHOWER 1863–1942

Later that evening, I made another note or two:

I have felt terribly. I should like so much to be with my mother these few days. But we're at war. And war is not soft—it has no time to indulge even the deepest and most sacred emotions. I loved my Dad. . . .

. . . Quitting work now—7:30 P.M. I haven't the heart to go on tonight.

The sight of my mother was one of the rewards of peace. Of course, she had paid the price of a lifetime of caring and working. As I first knew her, she was a tall woman, perhaps five feet six inches. She weighed about 135 pounds, with blue eyes and brown hair, untouched by gray. Now her hair was gray and, somehow, she was a little smaller.

My mother, as I have shown, was deeply religious. The Bible provided her favorite reading but she did not just repeat it by rote; she strove, always, to understand it. A woman as individualistic as she was not able to accept the dogma of any specific sect or denomination. Gradually, over the years, she had gravitated toward a local group known as The Bible Class. In this group, which had no church or minister, she was happy. Sunday meetings were always held in the afternoons at the homes of the members, including ours.

The usual program of worship included hymns, for which Mother played the piano, and prayers, with the rest of the time devoted to group discussion of a selected chapter of the Bible. The meeting was for serious study and for adults only. There was, eventually, a kind of loose association with similar groups throughout the country but, so far as I know, this was chiefly through subscription to a religious periodical, *The Watchtower*. After I left home for the Army, these groups were drawn closer together and finally adopted the name of Jehovah's Witnesses. A principal tenet in their beliefs was the rejection of force of any kind in human relations. They were true conscientious objectors to war. Though none of her sons could accept her convictions in this matter, she refused to try to push her beliefs on us just as she refused to modify her own.

Her happy disposition came from the depth of her faith. She rejected all concepts, common in those days, of eternal torment for the lost sinner. She believed in a God of mercy and of love, and while she believed the sinner would be "cut off" she was absolutely certain that those who were honest and faithful Christians would have a perpetual life of happiness.

To be sure, her life was one of almost ceaseless work. It had to be. She did everything imaginable to keep her boys well fed, sheltered, healthy, decently dressed, and in school. She cleaned, cooked, baked, mended, nursed, did the laundry and ironing, still had time to counsel with her sons and beyond that, to tend to her flowers, of which she was almost passionately fond. In the spring she would have us boys spade up the ground she chose for the planting of annuals, while they and perennials were carefully guarded and watered during the summer. In the spring geraniums would be set out in selected spots; in the fall they were potted and brought into the house for the winter. One room had a bay window opening to the west; it was bright throughout the winter, filled with the flowers she loved.

Many such persons of her kind of faith, selflessness, and boundless consideration of others have been called saintly. She was that—but above all she was a worker, an administrator, a teacher and guide, a truly wonderful woman. Possibly I can give a hint of her inner beauty by telling the story of her last moments.

When my father died in 1942 she was eighty years old. My brothers and I went to special pains to see that her remaining years should be as free of care as we could make them. We secured a competent and personable companion and provided the support to meet her modest needs. She wanted so little that each of us was constantly worried that she was denying herself. Instead we found that she was, true to the habits of fourscore years, saving money. Whenever any of us, visiting her as often as possible, would try to get a hint of any need or desire of hers that we might satisfy, she would invariably say with a smile, "Nothing more. Mrs. Robinson and I want nothing more."

One of her delights was to ride about the countryside in her old Dodge, driven by her companion. On a beautiful September day in 1946 she went out twice, coming home full of vivid memories of what she had seen. She went to sleep as usual and then, toward midnight, felt some abdominal discomfort. Waking her companion, who slept in the same room, she asked for a hot water bottle.

As Mrs. Robinson settled the bottle at her side, my mother looked up and said, "Please, get right back to bed. You might catch cold."

Her companion, going to her own bed, heard a faint rustle and a sigh and, turning back to glance at Mother, realized that she had died, quietly, with almost a smile on her face.

Ida Stover Eisenhower deserved such a peaceful start for the long journey.

Back in Frankfurt, the atmosphere was friendliness itself. There was a genuine welcome on the faces of the Germans who had been our enemies only moments before, it seemed. Whatever the postwar debates, it was easy to see that the population was relieved that the war was over and that Hitler was no more. American troops proved once again to be friendly ambassadors on the whole, free of ruthless vindictiveness or the looting of mercenaries.

In the little village between the town where I lived and the one where we had established headquarters, there was a school with students averaging eight or ten years of age. Rushing to the little picket fence that surrounded the school as my car, with its United States insignia, drove by, they would call "Heil, Heil Ice-en-hower. Heil Ice-en-hower!" Obviously, the little children didn't know anything about Eisenhower (despite its good Germanic origins), but it was just as obvious that they were reflecting sentiments that they heard at home. It was grimly ironic to realize that if they had said anything of the sort a short time earlier, their families would have been executed.

The headquarters in Frankfurt was in a magnificent building that belonged to the I. G. Farben Company. Scarcely damaged, it was one of the few intact symbols of Germany's pre-war industrial leadership on the continent. A story circulated that we had avoided bombing the building because we had already arranged to make our headquarters there. This was an indirect and silly compliment—presuming that our planners were so farsighted that we chose and saved headquarters offices, and that night bombing was without inaccuracies.

Next, I had my final brush with George Patton's impulsiveness. It was an example of a strong-minded man's tendency to oversimplify history. Whenever we met, George would say, "I hope you know, Ike, that I'm keeping my mouth shut. I'm a clam." Then, at a press conference, something was said about the Allies' policy of denying former Nazis a position of trust or responsibility in the German government. Patton, for reasons known only to himself, remarked that this was being overdone—and then had to add a few remarks which suggested that the Nazis were just another political party, like the Republicans and Democrats.

Perhaps other veterans said something of the sort on occasion. In part, such a remark might have had its root in the traditional American readiness to let bygones be bygones, or Patton might have admired the military efficiency of the Nazi party. But there is no point in speculating about motives. George Patton was aware that a principal purpose of our occupation mission was to cleanse the continent of Nazi control and influence. Now his words could have been misinterpreted by those who wanted an audible spokesman for a soft policy toward Nazi leaders.

This was senseless. I ordered George to my headquarters and said, "The war's over and I don't want to hurt you—but I can't let you be making such ridiculous statements. I'm going to give you a new job.

"You'll be the head of a study group that will codify, examine, and analyze the American war record in Europe and make conclusions on the major lessons of our campaigns." Patton was disappointed to leave his Third Army but he went to work on the new job, giving it the same kind of enthusiasm he gave to command and battle. From then on he had no occasion to meet the press and I had no occasion to criticize George for indiscretions.

For the governing of defeated Germany, the country was divided into four sectors, one each to be administrated by the Soviets, the French, the British, and ourselves. Periodically, the representatives of these countries, Marshal Zhukov, General Koenig, Marshal Montgomery, and myself, met in Berlin. In general, these meetings were friendly, but at times there was acrimonious debate between the Russians and any one of the western Allies about Russian interference with their forces in the city of Berlin or when they accused us of infractions of agreements.

Marshal Zhukov was rather standoffish with the other two representatives but between him and me there grew a relationship that permitted a frank exchange of views and a degree of mutual understanding. There was a sort of soldierly camaraderie that, under the circumstances, was useful. He and I talked at length about the war. He was particularly interested in the logistic arrangements that had enabled the Allies to make rapid advances across the whole of France. Indeed, he and Marshal Stalin later made this the subject of long conversation with me in Moscow.

I had to answer many detailed questions. They seemed surprised to learn that we had laid pipelines under the English Channel for bringing gas and oil to the continent and later put pipelines across France in order to reduce traffic on the roads. I described the "Red Ball" truck lines, with one-way truck roads and three shifts of drivers to keep every vehicle on the road constantly. I explained how we distributed supplies toward the front, with the reserves in such position that when a temporary shortage developed, it could promptly be filled. When our advances got too long and too rapid, and finally overran supply capabilities, we were forced to pause momentarily— and took advantage of those short lulls to regroup. To improve our situation, we captured and used Antwerp as a port and depot, adapted hundreds of transport planes as freight carriers, and brought many supplies in through the southern port of Marseilles. All this, to the Russians, who we must remember had not yet fully emerged from the age of horse-drawn artillery and supply, seemed amazing. Although they were able to make an atomic bomb within four years of the time we first exploded one and although they had in their scientific community a pool of theoretical genius and engineering talent, the ingenuities of mass production—except in artillery and ammunition—for the equipping of an army or for the convenience of a people were still a mystery.

They could not understand our democratic institutions, either. In Berlin one day, Marshal Zhukov came to me with a scowling face to speak in abrupt terms about what he called a personal insult. The Russians were receiving many of our news periodicals, including magazines. In one of the weeklies, a story about Zhukov was published which alleged, among other things, that he was shorter than his wife and that he had three children.

I tried to convince the Marshal that while this and other errors were regrettable, they were not official and were not meant to belittle him. He was unmollified. He said these were deliberate insults and he wanted to know what I was going to do to punish the responsible journalists.

My efforts to explain the workings of a free press were futile;

had the matter not been serious, my failure would have been funny. I explained that one of the reasons that I fought in the war—and, indeed, why my nation was fighting—was to defend the right of free speech and of a free press.

The Marshal would not admit that such a thing could exist. Again and again, he said, "If you were described like this by any publication in my country, I would see that it was eliminated immediately."

I pointed out that it was, first of all, not my inclination to silence all critical journals, and that we had libel laws, and a suit could be brought in court against a publication that printed falsehood and in so doing damaged the victim. But these were the limits of our legal reaction to this kind of story. The best I could get out of Zhukov was that he knew that I believed what I said but he was convinced that the United States government could control any publication and anything printed in it, if it really so desired.

Months later, when I attended ceremonies celebrating Red Army Day, I found Marshal Zhukov and his wife greeting people in a receiving line. His first words to me were: "Now—do you think my wife is taller than I am?" (She was not, of course. And he had two daughters.) I again confessed to the inaccuracies of our newsmagazine's story. This matter settled, he took his wife by the arm, abandoned the receiving line completely, led us to a comfortable corner, where with the aid of an interpreter we chatted amiably for a long time.

The Marshal had scant patience with political men.

Once, when I told him that I wanted to talk about a military matter and had not brought along my political adviser, I added that he could have his present if he liked. "No," he replied, "if you're not going to have yours, I'm going to throw mine out." He turned to Andrei Vishinsky, his adviser, and said, "Get out, I don't want you here."

Each conference held by the four of us at intervals was followed by a light supper—what I always thought should be not much more than a snack. Both the French and the Soviets, in their separate, proud styles, were inclined to transform the snack into a sumptuous banquet. It was a small war; each tried to outdo the other in the variety and attractiveness of the tables they spread, usually at 5:00 or 5:30 in the evening. Caviar, wine, vodka, fish, meats, the delicacies of each country, were displayed. I was more than annoyed because these feasts took place in a country which had for years been experiencing the privation of war—and which was not out of it yet. I urged that each of us, in his turn as host, produce sandwiches, coffee, and simple drinks. Everyone agreed in principle but in the long run, all of us were guilty of waste.

General Lucius Clay, my deputy in taking care of the day-by-day affairs of the military government, was forceful and thorough and tactful. After I was transferred to new duties in the United States, he became Commander-in-Chief of the American Zone. His masterful performance in that position has become history.

The Free World owes much to his firmness in handling the Berlin blockade and the airlift in 1948. I believe that had Clay's first advice been accepted at the time by his political superiors—to attempt by a resolute show of force to resupply Berlin by land—the clear rights of the United States would have been even more effectively demonstrated, and their respect for them underscored. In my opinion this would have had an advantageous effect on our relations with the Soviets. Clay's plan was too strong for the governments but he did get the administration's support in beginning resupply by air. From the above, you would assume that I am one of Clay's admirers —which I am.

☆   ☆   ☆   ☆   ☆

Back in the winter and spring of 1944, when all of us were straining to plan and prepare for the cross-Channel attack, most people talked of the war's duration in terms of two years. They believed that Germany, with its immense advantages of central position, and its overpowering victories of 1940–41, would put up such a defensive fight that it could not be overcome except in a long war of attrition. My own estimate was too optimistic by a matter of four months. But it was satisfying to all field commanders that almost exactly eleven months from the day we landed in Normandy, the surrender took place.

Then came the inevitable questions and arguments—Why was this done? Why was that done? Why didn't you do better? Why didn't you do it sooner? Why didn't you take such and such a place?

I do not mind saying that after the sudden release from the strain of responsibility, I was annoyed by carping criticism. Our actions were not above criticism, and a critique and analysis of such a segment of history is surely of value. But at times, as the post-mortems have gone on, it looked as if we had blundered throughout the campaign and had been defeated.

The Allied policy of demanding unconditional surrender, giving the Nazis no loopholes to treat for truce or terms, quickly came under attack. Many theorized that the war would have ended months or even a year earlier had we permitted the German people to hope that, by overthrowing Hitler, they could enter into negotiations. Those who thus theorized, then and now, fail to appreciate the rigidity of the Nazi structure, the iron discipline imposed on the German people, or the failure of previous attempts to bring Hitler down. Had the assassination plot against Hitler been successful in 1944, a series of palace revolutions might have so weakened the regime that the war could have ended in late fall or early winter. But this surmise is hinged on the death of Hitler.

So long as Hitler was alive, there could be no question about his control of the nation—and no alternative to unconditional surrender. His hold over a cultured and civilized people was eerily hypnotic. It was bolstered by the uncontestable evidence of immense success, from the obscurity of a Munich beer hall to the acquisition of a continental empire. Despite the loss of France and southern Italy, despite the retreat from Stalingrad even in the fall of 1944, Hitler still had control of Europe from the North Cape in Norway to the Aegean Islands. The Allies on both fronts were not yet on the German frontiers. Hitler's cause, to be sure, was hopeless. Through the last year of war, he may have been much of the time an outright madman. Nevertheless, those he ruled must have been convinced, until the final months, that eventually he would engineer another triumph for the armies of the Reich.

Of all the arguments and contentions, the one with the longest life at the moment is the question of why the Western Allies did not capture Berlin.

The question is heard repeatedly, now and then in a context that implies a conspiracy to promote Soviet control of Eastern Europe. No one has yet shown definitively why we should have captured Berlin. Indeed, considering the proximity of the Russian forces to that city as compared to our own when the final attacks from both West and East were launched, no one has yet produced any logical evidence of the feasibility of capturing it before they did. And if we had, we would not have gained much and we could have lost a great deal. The national zones of occupation in Germany had already been decided upon by our political chiefs. The orders I received from the combined Chiefs of Staff for conducting the war were: You will land in Europe and, proceeding to Germany, will destroy Hitler and all his forces.

That we did. To then jeopardize thousands of Allied soldiers' lives in an onslaught on the Berlin bunkers—if it had been militarily possible—would have been a sacrifice of men to gain a symbol.

On February 11, 1965, I wrote to Senator A. Willis Robertson of Virginia, who had asked for the bare facts as they then existed. In a concise rundown, I told the Senator:

(a) The mission of the Allied forces was not the capture of localities but the destruction of Hitler's armed might.

(b) No matter what German areas might be captured, each nation was required, under the political agreement, to retire within the lines prescribed—long before the end of the war—by Generalissimo Stalin, President Roosevelt, and Prime Minister Churchill.

(c) When our final operational plans had been drawn up, approved, and issued to Bradley, Montgomery, and Devers—in April 1945—the Western Allies had encircled the Ruhr but their main body was two hundred miles from Berlin. The Russian front was thirty miles from Berlin and its spearheads were already west of the Oder River. Under these circumstances, our plans made no mention of Berlin. Again, they were designed to accomplish the final destruction of Hitler's forces and at the least cost in Allied lives.

(d) My own headquarters had reported to our government in January that our advance in Germany would penetrate far deeper than the line which the political leaders had agreed upon as the eastern boundary for occupation by the Western Allies. Berlin was deep in the zone that was to be Russian. Our government decided that no change should be made in these boundaries.

(e) In the final stages of the war, American forces reached Leipzig and after the hostilities had ceased, we had to *retreat* 125 miles to get within the boundaries fixed by the Allied political leaders. During the Allied advance between the Rhine and the Elbe, which was so swift as to surprise all the Allied governments, Winston Churchill did suddenly suggest the possible political value of capturing Berlin. But the ground forces were accomplishing the prescribed objectives and to have changed these materially during such a movement would have been difficult, and, in my opinion, absolutely unnecessary and unwise. It is not correct to say, as some had suggested, that President Roosevelt *refused me permission* to take Berlin, but he was party to the earlier political decision that placed Berlin well beyond the Western Allies' sectors of occupation.

In early November, leaving for Washington, I expected to be away from duties in Frankfurt for only a few days. The main tasks ahead, as I understood them, would be appearances before congressional committees who wanted my testimony on unification of the armed services and on various proposals, particularly universal military training. My personal objectives were limited—to do some Christmas shopping that couldn't be finished in an overseas PX. Once again, my personal crystal ball was cracked: President Truman had plans for me.

CHAPTER XX

Lost in the Pentagon

THROUGH the many months of World War II in Europe, we had all heard about the wonders of the Pentagon. Every visitor arrived with at least one story about what happened to someone or other lost in that building's labyrinth of corridors. We came to know certain stories by heart and, after a dozen repetitions, even a polite laugh became extremely difficult. The one worn to shreds and tatters was told of an Army Air Corps captain who couldn't find his way and got so thoroughly lost that when he finally arrived at the office he was looking for, he discovered that he had been promoted to full colonel. I took all the stories with a large grain of salt. And then, in no time at all, I found myself at work there and the subject of another story.

I had been to lunch in the general officers' mess, located in the center of the building, just above the inner court and a considerable distance from my new office. Ordinarily, I went there with other officers and returned with them. Because they knew the way, I never paid much attention to the route we walked. This time, I ventured on the return trip alone.

Although I reached E ring safely, I discovered that this ring, the outermost corridor of the building, was an endless vista of doors, every one of them identical in appearance. I had not the slightest idea which was mine. Moreover, I didn't know the room number. I did recall that over the door was a signboard reading *Chief of Staff*.

So, hands in pockets and trying to look as if I were out for a carefree stroll around the building, I walked. I walked and walked, encountering neither landmarks nor people who looked familiar. One had to give the building his grudging admiration; it had apparently been designed to confuse any enemy who might infiltrate it. Finally, I gave up.

Immediately ahead was a group of girls, stenographers, I suppose, and I went up to one of them quietly and said, "Can you tell me where the office of the Chief of Staff is?"

She immediately said, "You just passed it about a hundred feet back, General Eisenhower."

By grapevine, the Army's astoundingly efficient bush telegraph, the word got around the Pentagon quickly. Then it got to the press offices downtown. When the story appeared in a good many newspapers the following day, the headlines may not have been so impressive as during the war, but they were just as bold and large. I'm afraid that any confidence in my ability, as new Chief of Staff, to manage the Army may have been considerably shaken.

No personal enthusiasm marked my promotion to Chief of Staff, the highest military post a professional soldier in the United States Army can reach. When President Truman broached the subject I told him that I'd much rather retire but he said he had special need of me at the moment. He promised that my tour could be brief if I chose, lasting only until he found a replacement (as head of the Veterans Bureau) for General Omar Bradley who would succeed me.

The job ahead was not pleasant. The demobilization of a wartime army is a dreary business. The taste of it I had during World War I at a far lower level did nothing to whet my appetite for the task now to be performed at the top. The high morale that characterizes the healthy unit in campaigns deteriorates as the time nears for its dispersal. The citizen-soldier and his family want him at home, today, at once! Yet demobilization has to be gradual.

Long before the end of the war, recalling the frenzy of World War I's much simpler demobilization, General Marshall had directed a commission of civilians and military men to prepare a charter for the orderly and speedy return home of our troops. Out of their studies came the "point system," a table of credits earned by each soldier for his time of service, time in combat, wounds and disabilities, his age and family obligations. Every officer and man could easily figure out his relative standing in priority for discharge. When it was first published, I think there was general agreement throughout the Army that the point system was a just and equitable arrangement. When I first saw it, before the Nazis' surrender, I felt that here again was a striking example of General Marshall's foresight and wisdom.

On returning from Europe, my professional concerns were maintaining the peace we had won, the continuing security of the United States, and demobilization. Washington seemed little bothered about the long-term future. Present pressures preoccupied most legislators and government officials. The most important was the widespread demand for a headlong return of troops from every theater of war. The past did get some attention, as I recall: there was an obsession among members of both houses of the Congress to find a scapegoat for Pearl Harbor and the early reverses we had suffered in the Pacific. But of the future, piled high with threats to our victory and to our continuing security, there seemed to be little thought.

This was frightening to one who had seen Europe devastated, especially in all its industrialized areas from the Polish border to the Atlantic. Although the will to survive was strong in those who had lived through battles and bombings, the means to live had been so thoroughly disrupted, in some places simply erased, that chaos was inevitable unless the Allied Armies in their occupied areas could provide for several years a temporary framework of administration and support. Without a framework, anarchy beyond precedent would engulf many of the liberated and conquered lands and when order was restored, the next masters of Europe could be either successors to the Nazis or they would be Communists.

In Washington, each month from V-J Day on, we exceeded the established quotas of soldiers to be returned to their families. By the end of 1945, the figure had reached five million, almost double the scheduled number. In part, this tremendous move was the result of a purely emotional surge in every echelon of command from the War Department down to the platoon—a determination to get every possible man home before Christmas. We were visited by committees of mothers, and an incalculable heat was put on Representatives and Senators. For a time, the Army let its heart run away with its head.

To every rational American, the immensity of the Army's mission and its direct contribution to world order, if carried out, must have seemed obvious. But words of caution and counsel by any military authority in early 1946 was overwritten in a mad rush to "get the boys home." Even as I recognized the deep-seated emotions and sympathized with them, I knew that any further yielding to insistent demands could produce the collapse of the demobilization system.

At the time I took over as Chief of Staff, there were in several camps mob protests that amounted almost to insurrections. These were intolerable in the American Army. I explained the situation to the nation and then issued orders, spelling out what disciplinary action would be taken by the commanding officer in camps where any disorders occurred in the future. This stopped the riots. It became possible, at least, to carry out the demobilization at an orderly pace.

Only six weeks or so after taking over as Chief of Staff, I had to go before the Congress. The Senators and Representatives, the principal targets of those who were demanding instant demobilization, were concerned by the evidence before them of what seemed to be a wave of national hysteria—and quite a few were concerned, too, for the possible disastrous effect on their own political futures. They were a difficult audience to face. After explaining comprehensively all the facts of demobilization, I made a personal pledge that in each case where unusual hardship or any injustice to an individual was claimed, members of my staff would investigate and report to me. Returning to the Pentagon, I directed that the first thing every morning I wanted a comprehensive digest of the pleas that had arrived the day before.

The correspondence section of my office was enlarged. Throughout the winter and spring, those working there, under the direction of Colonel Paul T. Carroll, a West Pointer of warm heart and clear vision, read through each letter and prepared summaries of the appeals for those that needed my personal attention. I read these every morning and on some days there were several hundred. The correspondence section's hours began at seven in the morning and ran far into the night, weekends not excepted.

Inevitably, complaints continued that we were not moving fast enough. Not everyone was prepared to accept our position that a globally dispersed Army, stationed on all continents and on islands from the Arctic to the edges of Antarctica, whose mobilization and transport had required years to effect, could not be returned home in a few months. The paper work alone, which would assure the veteran full credit for his service and back up any claims he might later make, was a task second only in magnitude to the initial mobilization of the Army. To assure myself that there would be no slowing down, I insisted on daily reports on the movement of troops through the discharge pipelines. Although we had no instruments called computers, we did use the most modern machines, as well as the most able statistical talent, in compiling these reports.

I must confess that the machines, perhaps feeling the pressure themselves, at times seemed confused by the data fed into them. Certainly the figures they turned out were confusing. More than one of my colleagues suggested that we junk them in favor of the abacus and slide rule. Eventually, so that we would know the exact number of men still in uniform, I ordered a hand count of every officer and man. It was to be made at reveille on July 1, 1946, I think. This old-fashioned census, laborious as it was, gave us our first accurate figures. We learned that our machines had been off by several hundred thousand men. Since then, I've always mistrusted, a little, even the most handsome, most intricate and guaranteed computer.

In the meantime, a representative from every military service was before the Congress begging for a peacetime establishment that could meet our nation's new worldwide requirements and obligations.

The Congress was tired of wartime spending and a number of its members showed every indication of wanting to go back to the old disarmed status in which the United States had always found itself when called upon to use its armed forces for self-protection. Military appropriations were cut down drastically across the board. Even when I went to Capitol Hill, with the President's approval, to ask for money with which to collect the Army's usable vehicles, scattered across the world, rusting away, so that we could concentrate them in places where they could be properly cared for, my recommendations were ignored.

It was idle for us—including General Carl Spaatz, Admiral Chester Nimitz, as well as General Alexander A. Vandergrift, the Commandant of the Marine Corps—to warn that the defeat of Japan and Germany did not mean that peace and light were going to be the order of the day for the coming years. We did not openly refer to the Soviets as a potential enemy in those days because our political leaders were trying to develop workable agreements with them. But there was no doubt what we meant when we kept warning.

Each of the Army budgets in which I had a hand was drastically cut down by the Executive and Legislative branches. The same thing happened to the other services. Indeed, the cutting continued long after I had left and gone on to a new post in New York City. Defense appropriations were insufficient to maintain the far-flung deployment of American troops that we believed necessary or to continue the necessary training, educational, and research work in the United States. It was this retrenchment and cutting away of appropriations that forced the Joint Chiefs of Staff to take nearly all elements of considerable military strength from Korea. In my opinion, that unnecessary conflict was thereby encouraged.

Among all the contemporary skills with which a soldier these days must concern himself, not the least important is public relations —a phrase almost unknown to the Army and a profession little practiced by it until World War II. That ignorance or negligence may be one reason why at the end of every war the Army was a budgetary stepchild. Chiefs of Staff might present and even argue their views that appropriations were inadequate—but they did it to their civilian superiors or to congressional committees. The general public, either as an interested audience or as a source of support, was largely ignored because of a long tradition, accepted by the Army, that soldiers should be seen but not heard.

George Marshall, who had a panoramic view of everything concerning and affecting the nation's defenses, remedied the lack by creating a bureau of public relations within the War Department. This was to explain the Army's mission, purposes, means, and needs. To the job, he assigned one of the wisest soldiers I have known, Alexander Surles. A major general, and a cavalry man who above all else wanted a combat command in armor, General Surles subordinated his own personal desires to the Army's good. Through the war years, he rendered the nation a service by his insistence that to the utmost limit possible within the requirements of military security, the American public be so well informed about the Army that there would be an authentic partnership between the civilians at home and the troops in uniform. Better than any man I had known until that time, he exemplified the fact that public relations could be a profession, one marked by candor, a respect for truth, and an inviolable integrity.

Cynics, I know, describe "PR" as a maternity gown designed to hide the true figure of fact. Undoubtedly, as abused by those who cover up or mislead, public relations can be stigmatized as mere propaganda or outright mendacity. Properly practiced, however, some form of it is necessary in a republic where the citizens must know the truth. After I had become Chief of Staff in the postwar period, and when Alexander Surles retired, I chose a man I had first met at Camp Colt almost thirty years before, Major General Floyd Parks, to succeed him. Parks was not experienced in communications but was so forthright, sometimes blunt, in his expression, so sure that truth could be effective in the forming of sound public opinion, so much more concerned with accuracy and substance than with timing and phraseology, that even though my choice of him may have shocked the experts, I never had reason to regret it. Nor did the Army and the War Department.

During the war, my relations with the press had always been frank and cordial. They were scrupulously careful—when they understood —not to compromise security. When secrecy had to be tightly observed, more than once I found that I could take correspondents into my confidence, telling them the full story of what was planned, and asking them to say or write nothing until the need for secrecy had ended. And the traffic in information was two-way: because they reflected far better than a military staff could the reactions of civilians at home and even of troops in combat, I learned much from them.

Timing, I did come to understand, is a critical ingredient in public relations. No matter what is said, the public may either ignore the news entirely or not hear or read it at all, if the story is released at a moment when more sensational or more exciting incidents pre-empt the headlines, or during a lull when relatively few people are reading or listening or watching. In conferences I attended then and later (in the White House), when an announcement of public policy or government action was under consideration, more attention sometimes seemed to be given to the exact hour of the news release than to its content.

In the Pentagon, I encountered with full force a phenomenon of American public life—the total lack of privacy permitted a senior officer of government, civilian or military. I had to live with the knowledge that every phone call I made or received was monitored from beginning to end, and possibly recorded in a stenographer's notebook; that no letter addressed to me, unless from my wife or a close relative or friend, would reach me until it had been read by at least one member of the staff; that every word I wrote, even the scraps I rejected and tossed into the wastebasket, would be scrupulously filed away for ultimate microfilming and scrutiny by students of history and its writers generations after I had left the earth. Life in the Pentagon, and later in the large white building that dominates Washington, had become a career in a glass bowl.

This sort of life may be difficult for men who are accustomed to sharing their thoughts with only a very few longtime associates—

businessmen, for example. Suddenly to find that their every spoken or written word, all their comings and goings, are the concern of people who are complete strangers, is disturbing. In fact I've heard it described as downright intolerable. I was less troubled than some people, perhaps, by the constant surveillance, possibly because the Army way of life, despite its multitudinous rules and regulations, is an open society. The actions of officers often provide the principal topics of conversation among all ranks and in all places from the Officers Club to the guardhouse.

As much as possible within the framework of organization, I have always sought to develop a family feeling with my staff. If I ever worried about the constant observation, I had the consolation that those intently watching me were friends. Now and then, they went to lengths in their meticulous guard over me that, had I known it at the time, would have struck me as carrying things a bit too far.

Almost twenty years after the fact, for instance, I learned that the ribbons I had worn on my jacket one day were a cause for alarm. Ordinarily, I wore only the Distinguished Service Medal. But when I was to visit a foreign embassy, I added the appropriate ribbon for the medal from that country's government. It turns out that on a certain visit, I had the wrong country—that is, the wrong ribbon. The Pentagon was shaken to its foundations. The following morning, this memo was published:

. . . hereafter when General Eisenhower's calendar indicates he is to call at a foreign embassy or to participate in any event in connection with a foreign dignitary, action will be instituted immediately to insure that he wears the proper ribbons. This will not be done at the last minute, but as soon as the event is put on the calendar.

In order to insure that there is no repetition of the ineffectual, perfunctory, lackadaisical performance of yesterday and that all concerned display necessary initiative without prodding or last minute apoplexy, the following measures will be taken:

1—When the engagement is made, Major Cannon will notify Major Schulz *immediately.*

2—Major Schulz will notify Sgt. Murray and is responsible that the ribbons worn by the General are proper and in order. *This will be done at once.*

3—Sgt. Murray will prepare the ribbons for General Eisenhower's blouse or jacket. *This will be done as rapidly as possible.*

4—Major Cannon will verify the propriety of ribbons.

5—Major Cannon will notify the undersigned when mission is accomplished.

6—Major Schulz will insure that Sgt. Moaney has ribbons and is informed as to when and where the General will require them.

7—If the General is required to be away on a trip and ribbons are necessary, either Sgt. Dry or Sgt. Murray will have required ribbons with them.*

All my life I have been an incorrigible reviser of written material. Whether I dictate a draft, or a draft has been prepared for my signature, I find that I have almost never said exactly what I wanted to say, in the way I hoped to say it. In the Pentagon, most drafts came back to me in either single- or double-spaced typewritten form. Each draft became a positive challenge for me to change its wording. My changes, inserted in pen or pencil between

* If this memorandum seems to border upon the ridiculous—and when I first saw it years later I thought just that—remember that in the matter of foreign decorations, none are so sensitive to inexactness as diplomats. Although I could hardly care less about the order in which a visitor wears his decorations, a decent respect for national feelings requires in an American officer a scrupulous observance of protocol. Had it not been for the vigilance of my staff, I might have hurt the feelings of foreigners whom I met at home or overseas.

All five men involved, I should insert here, survived the memorandum. Major Robert L. Schulz, now Brigadier General, U.S.A. (Ret.), has been with me for twenty-one years, is usually the first to see me of a morning in my office and the last to see me off at night. No crisis, even the small ones that upset most people, ever seems to unhinge him. He is the ingrained optimist who believes things will always work out; and he does everything he can to make them work out.

Major C. Craig Cannon, now Brigadier General in the Corps of Engineers, several times gave up his leave to help me at Columbia and was with me during the SHAPE period. Of all my aides, he was the most unflappable—so to speak—concealing under a perennially boyish manner a soldierly stiffness of lip and spine.

Sergeant Leonard Dry, who was with me from the North Africa campaign through the first year or so of Gettysburg retirement, was Mamie's favorite chauffeur at Columbia and in the White House. Since he left us to return to White House employment, he has had the same job with Mrs. Kennedy and Mrs. Johnson. He may well be unique in this association with three First Ladies.

Sergeant William Murray later became a warrant officer and, since his retirement from the Army, is now in hotel work in Washington where I see him now and then and enjoy a brief chat about old times.

Of Sergeant John Moaney, I have only this to say: He and I have been inseparable for almost a quarter of a century; in my daily life, he is just about the irreplaceable man.

the lines, were often indecipherable even to myself. My staff soon decided that all drafts would go to me *triple*-spaced with wide margins at top and bottom and on both sides. This increased the amount of white space on which I could demonstrate my profound disagreement with the submitted wording. Yet it seemed only to intensify my urge for revision. When one paper was returned to a staff member, with crossed-out lines and emendations all over the front and back of the sheet, winding around corners and tilted at many angles, he muttered in disgust, "What was the General using for a desk—a Lazy Susan?"

Revised or not, my writing had never threatened the standing of Twain or Hemingway. Nevertheless, many months before I left the Army, I was approached by representatives of various publishing houses, each with a different reason for wanting to publish my memoirs of the war. To all of these proposals I turned a deaf ear. For one thing, I was really tired; I wanted nothing so much as the opportunity to loaf a while and then try to find out what to do with the rest of my life. I had a notion that I might settle down in the vicinity of some small college, and to make a connection that would bring me in touch with young people. I had a suspicion that they could understand a little more about the world and its complexities than they were being taught.

Many of the publishing proposals were purely financial. While I was no one to scorn money and certainly wanted to live in fairly comfortable circumstances, money alone had no temptation. I continued to turn down all proposals. The head of a newspaper syndicate wanted me to do a number of articles. One of the popular magazines was interested in a book only because they wanted the privilege of serializing it. Each of these offers was for half a million dollars. Book publishers were more specific; other people approached me about movies, television rights, radio rights, and so on. All of this annoyed me, probably because I was also preoccupied with official duties. But finally two men, Douglas M. Black of Doubleday, and William Robinson, of the New York *Herald Tribune,* came to me with a different kind of argument. Roughly it went like this:

Historians, they said, are often inclined to use contemporary accounts as source material. Books about entire wars and whole campaigns written by authors who were not necessarily participants are frequently used as main sources, or, in fact, sole sources unless there are extant accounts by participants that differ in important facts and conclusions. They showed me, or reminded me of, a number of books which had been written hurriedly, so as not to "miss the market." Certain of these books on the African and European campaigns were riddled with inaccuracies. They contained conclusions that had slight basis in fact and were the hasty conceptions or misconceptions of authors who had a flair for writing rapidly and fluently. Mr. Black and Mr. Robinson, who were functioning as partners for the proposal, pointed out errors in these publications and said that since these were written during my lifetime and were not denied or corrected by me, the historians of the future might give them a high degree of credibility. "You owe it to yourself, to the country, and to history, to tell the personal story of your European campaigns on a factual basis, annotating the book as well as you can. It can serve as a better picture of what was done in your theater and by your headquarters than other, sometimes biased or prejudiced, reports."

This reasoning impressed me. After I thought it over for a time, they came back and I said, "I'm ready to undertake this task but on one condition only: it seems to me that every time the subject is brought up, people talk about all the various kinds of publishing rights and magazine rights and so on and I don't want to be bothered with such things. Now if you people can come up with a single package to cover the whole affair so that I don't have to argue with too many people, I will probably undertake something."

I added that I wouldn't attempt to start writing a document until after I had left the office of the Chief of Staff. "I don't believe that any man on active duty has the right or the time to undertake the writing of a book of this kind."

In another week or so they were back with the following suggestion. They said that the Internal Revenue Service had always considered that any book written by a non-professional writer and sold by him in its *entirety,* together with all rights of every kind, could be sold as a house and a lot can be sold. Thus, they said, by disposing of the entire group of rights along with the book itself, there would be no reason for others to bother me on the subject, and the whole process could be handled on a capital gains basis as far as taxes were concerned. I had never heard of such a thing and immediately asked the Treasury Department for an official ruling. Secretary of the Treasury Snyder wrote out a list of conditions that had to be observed, that the end product of a writing effort by a non-professional writer was to be considered a piece of property, to be sold not as income, but as a transfer of a capital asset. The Secretary, with his lawyers present, informed me that this had been common practice, was approved procedure by the Treasury and the Internal Revenue Service, and the only thing the author had to be careful about was to observe the conditions laid down.

The next time the publishers came to call, I told them that if the matter could be worked out on this basis, I was prepared to listen, after I had gotten the work done. But again I warned that I wouldn't do a single thing until I left the active service. I did say that I would use my terminal leave, which would take place in late winter, to undertake the job. I also said that there would be no sensationalism. I doubted that my writings would add circulation to newspapers or get a great many readers in book form and I recalled the competition for General Pershing's memoirs following World War I, which was livelier than the results. Mr. Black said, "All we want you to do is to tell your story, your way."

On February 8, 1948, I started on a writing program, at a speed that a soldier would call a blitz. Because the possibility of writing a memoir had pressed upon me for several years, I had given thought to the method I could use. There was a great deal of material immediately at hand. While I had never been able to keep up a diary consistently, I had years earlier formed a habit of dictating, at intervals of two to three months, long memoranda for my files, putting down the principal developments of the immediate past. My opinions and conclusions were included. All these from World War II were in my files.

In addition, I had carried on throughout the war an intermittent official correspondence with General Marshall, Prime Minister Churchill, Generals Bradley, Patton, and Montgomery, and the Operation Division of the American War Department. These, separately and chronologically filed, gave me, in sum, a handy and fairly complete record of events as I had seen them at the time of their occurrence.

I would use these records to jog and reinforce my memory. I assembled them carefully, arranging them so that they were immediately at hand whenever I felt the need of looking up any detail. World War II was not far in the past and my memory concerning details was fresh. It was my belief that in a personal memoir, only those things should be dealt with that were of such importance that I could not possibly have forgotten them. I did, however, need the dates and other details from the documents.

Initially, I intended to start the story with the decision I made in the Philippines to return to the United States. Then it began to look as if such an opening would demand a long account of that preparatory period. Instead, I decided on the device of describing first the circumstances of the surrender at Rheims in 1945 by Field Marshal Jodl. After that, I went back to review briefly the outbreak of the war and our entry into it on December 7, 1941.

From then on, I rapidly produced the first draft. In this case, I reversed the process that I had used in the past in making studies for the War Department. Because I did not intend to talk about things that were of less than top priority in my mind, I handed each chapter to my researcher as I wrote it. He then took it to the records to find documentation for every statement. Whenever it was not possible to find documents to establish the authenticity of any statement, I would then change the wording to separate those things that I recorded as absolute fact from those that could be found only in my memory.

After writing and checking the first draft, the necessary alterations were made and a new draft typed. In the next round I examined the text for duplications, omissions, bad arrangements, and other obvious errors. Then another clean draft was typed. Working this way, I kept three secretaries busy.

I do not recall the exact number of weeks that I put into the work, but I remember well that I worked approximately sixteen hours a day. Each day usually started with a short breakfast conference about the work immediately ahead and from then on I was dictating or correcting old drafts until something like 11:00 at night. At lunch I was frequently visited by two editors from the companies concerned, Kenneth R. McCormick, the Editor-in-Chief of Doubleday, and Joseph Barnes, head editor of the *Herald Tribune*'s foreign desk, who were very helpful.

Because I habitually arose at six, it was a tough grind for all of us, but in a way it was fun. The task was there to do. There were no delays for lack of material. My secretarial help was superb and at times my execrable handwriting provided the reason for a laugh.

After the initial drafts, the text went to experts who would come back with suggestions and frequently I adopted some of these. But whenever they seemed to change my meaning in the slightest degree, I rejected them. I was striving for logical presentation and continuity of story without any attempt to dramatize or reach for an elaborate and eloquent style of which I was not capable. I tried to write the text as plainly and straightforwardly as possible. Just before starting the work, I had reread Grant's memoirs, which I had always admired because of their simplicity and lack of pretension. I refused superlatives or purple adjectives and I would not indulge in the kind of personal criticism or disparagement of others that had badly marred many military accounts.

This striving for plain objectivity caused me uneasiness. I constantly argued that the lack of drama and the absence of criticism and argument would make the book banal and of little interest to the public. Whenever I voiced these feelings, I was immediately reassured by the editors, whose opinions I valued, who said that this war book would be better received if it were factual and personal without any trace of theatrics.

After the work of drafting and correcting, there was much else to do: selection of pictures, making of maps and sketches, approving a design for the jacket and other details, all of which took time. Commander Edward Steichen agreed to be picture editor for the volume. I asked him to search for photographs which would say, more vividly and powerfully than I ever could, what mud looked like; what the magnitude of the D-Day Operation was with its vast panoply of equipment spread out across the beaches; what our men looked like; and what the destruction of the enemy was. His photographic eye was that of a master of the art.

Even writing in such a breakneck style, the manuscript was finished on time, and in the fall of that year an ad hoc partnership of the *Herald Tribune* and Doubleday, in the persons of Mr. Robinson and Mr. Black, made an offer which I considered more than generous. Instead, I expressed again and again the fear that they would have a new and expensive white elephant on their hands. They smiled and said, to the contrary, that they were not sure they were treating me fairly. Both publishers and I later became warm friends.

So the deal was made, my writing was out of my hands, and I went to pay my taxes. Treasury Secretary Snyder said to me at a social function a little later, "Did you, as a young man in Kansas, ever dream that you would be writing your personal check in six figures?" The answer to that one was obvious.

The book sold unbelievably well. In the fall of 1966—eighteen years later—I asked Doubleday for a roundup of the story and I was assured that the book had been a profitable venture on their part. At least 1,170,000 copies of *Crusade in Europe* were sold in the United States and there were contracts for twenty-two foreign-language editions.

Even yet, orders come in every month for the book, which testifies not to its value as literature, but to the fact that people go on refighting the war.

My real acquaintanceship with James Forrestal began when, as Chief of Staff of the Army, I had met him during the war. After the Congress passed, in 1947, the first so-called "Unification Act" for the Defense Department I had many conferences with him, the first Secretary of the Defense Department. Shortly after I resigned the post of Chief of Staff of the Army to go to the University I became one of his close associates. At that time Admiral William Leahy, who was the President's personal Chief of Staff and who had been serving as an informal Chairman for the Joint Staff, was overtaken by bad health and was no longer able to act in that capacity. In these circumstances President Truman and Secretary Forrestal asked me to serve as a part-time and informal Chairman of the Joint Chiefs, although, at that time there was no legal authorization of such a post. I spent one or two days each week—sometimes more—in Washington to preside at the meetings of the Staff.

Forrestal was the first man in government who warned me during the war that in his opinion our government was being quite unwary in its dealings with the Soviets. He sent a number of informal messages to urge that I watch them carefully and not let the Soviets seize opportunities to take any unfair advantage of us. Since, from 1941 onward, I had, because of personal experience, become increasingly sure that the Soviets would not look upon the United States as anything other than a potential enemy, it was only natural that from the very beginning I had a high regard for Mr. Forrestal's opinion and for his foresight. In many ways he was an unusual person. I think it absolutely without question that he wanted only to do what was best for the United States and served in his very important post with as great a degree of selflessness as almost anyone I could name.

When he had been called to government service sometime early in the war, he was apparently a fairly wealthy man. I recall that when I was with him one day in 1948 he remarked that his service in Washington had used up practically all of his capital and that he would soon have to go back to private life again to restore the estate that he had hoped to pass on to his heirs.

During his youth in college his favorite sport was boxing, I was told. In carriage and general appearance, Mr. Forrestal was rather pugnacious. However, in carrying on the heavy responsibilities of the Secretary of Defense he seemed cautious and hesitant rather than pugnacious. He'd get into difficulties when tough decisions were placed before him and when his advisers—advisers in whom he had faith and trust—would engage in controversies among themselves. At times he would even come to a definite conclusion only to reopen the question or reverse himself some hours later. When this happened more than once I had my first inkling that he was a worrier; that he allowed problems to remain with him after they had presumably been solved and action started.

The most serious of those questions that I recall was one in which the Navy and the Air Force took opposite sides on the question of developing the big bomber known as the B-36. Hour after hour, I sat with him to listen to the opposing arguments and to the advice of our scientists. Finally, largely on the scientific counsel rather than upon military, the decision was made to go ahead with a B-36 program, though not, as I recall, in the magnitude proposed by the Air Force. The scientific advice was to the effect that if the United States was to have, during the next few years, any intercontinental bombing plane we had no recourse except to build a number of B-36s. This seemingly persuaded Jim Forrestal and, with my strong concurrence, he gave the go-ahead signal to the proponents.

This ended, I thought, all the repetitive studies and explanations and I was very happy to have it behind us. Within a matter of minutes after this decision was reached and I had returned to my office, Secretary Forrestal followed me, and said, "You know, Ike, I think we'll have to go into this B-36 matter a little bit more deeply."

I was shocked and for the first time realized that either the man was losing his memory or was becoming so confused that he could not concentrate.

Time went on, however, and though I watched for confirmation of my fears I came to the conclusion that it had been some temporary situation—probably brought on by intense study and sleeplessness (at times he mentioned insomnia). However, two of the Secretary's intimate civilian associates came to see me one day to say that they were certain that the Secretary ought to take a short leave. They said he was very tired and was showing every evidence of the beginning of a nervous breakdown. Something had to be done. I promised to do my best to get the Secretary to slow down.

This was far easier said than done but, finally, I felt it necessary to meet him head on about it. "Mr. Secretary," I said, "you showed a great deal of confidence in me by asking me to come back to act as your personal military adviser. Obviously, unless you can go away for a week or ten days without feeling the place will fall around your ears then you don't have that kind of confidence in me, and I might as well give up and go back to New York."

To this he reacted earnestly. "Oh, by no means," he said. "Stay here."

"Well," I asked, "will you start off this evening and go wherever you please, just letting us know where you are? We'll get in touch with you if anything happens that would require your presence." He faithfully promised to start at once.

When I came to the office early the following morning to find him in his office as if nothing had happened, I chided him about the point and it seemed as if he had completely forgotten the conversation. I now became convinced that there was something definitely wrong and talked again with his civilian assistants.

Ever since the election of 1948, Mr. Forrestal had become quite unhappy. It appeared that during the political campaign that year he had been anxious to establish in the public mind his conviction that the security establishment of the United States was not subject to partisan point-making or political strife. He thought that Defense, like the State Department, should be administered on behalf of the United States and without regard to party. For this reason, although a lifelong Democrat, he had declined to participate in any way in the actual campaign.

I heard him express this conviction many times and am certain that he was completely sincere. Shortly after the election was over he was informed that the Democratic National Committee was badly in debt as a result of the campaign and he did tell me that he sent them his check to help eliminate that deficit. He said that this was not any violation of principle because, while he was a good party member, the contest was over and it was perfectly proper for him to make such a donation. I agreed. However, according to Jim Forrestal, his attitude in the preceding fall had incurred the personal enmity of the politically-minded White House staff. He constantly referred to the staff as a group that was "out to get him." Whether or not these concerns intensified his nervousness, I cannot say, but I believe that its basic cause was overwork and the lack of co-operation, not only within the government at large but within certain sections of the Defense Department itself.

Time and again I urged him to require every subordinate to obey his orders absolutely or suffer the consequences of discharge and to make it clear that he was not impressed by any staff group, no matter how highly placed, that wanted only to challenge him and the work he was trying to do.

In the early months of 1949, it became obvious that the Secretary's physical and mental condition was deteriorating rapidly. When he would bring up the difficulties he was having and mention that if this sort of thing kept up he would have to resign, I never discouraged him. As much as I liked him, as much as I admired his good qualities, I came to believe that the best thing for Jim's sake and the Defense Department was for him to resign. Along about the first of March he made such a decision and submitted a letter of resignation to the President. He told me that his place was to be taken by Louis Johnson, a past commander of the American Legion, and an Assistant Secretary of War during Franklin Delano Roosevelt's administration.

Even before the date of transfer arrived, Mr. Johnson told me that he hoped I would continue the same kind of work I had been doing with the Chiefs of Staff. I agreed readily, not only because Mr. Johnson was a friend but because I was extremely anxious to see the Defense Department so organized that we could minimize the service rivalries that had plagued it.

Things went along fairly quietly for the next few days and then on March 21, I was struck with an attack of a most distressing kind (one that foreshadowed the ileitis attack of 1956). I was staying at the Statler Hotel in Washington and shortly after I got sick, I had a call from Mr. Forrestal who said he had to speak to me. "Ike," he said, "I simply can't turn over this job to Louie Johnson. He knows nothing about the problems involved and things will go to pot. I'll have to go to the President and withdraw my resignation immediately."

I replied with all my strength, urging him not to do anything so foolish. I said to even attempt it would lay him open to criticism and, worse, it would have no effect in any event because the ceremony had been set up for that day and it was impossible to stop it. He seemed to take this counsel and said he would go ahead with the ceremony.

Afterward, I was so ill that I lost touch with events. I read no papers and simply lay in bed. After a week or so, the doctors felt I was sufficiently recovered to go down to the warmer climate of Florida and try to shake off the aftereffects of these debilitating attacks. When I arrived, I soon felt like catching up with the news and found that Jim, whom I had not seen since March 21, was now in Florida himself, staying at a friend's house.

Soon I heard that he had to be returned to Washington to Bethesda Naval Hospital on an emergency basis and I assumed that he had had an accident. Later, the word was that his difficulty was mental and that he was in distressing shape. It was not long after that that we learned of his death, apparently caused by a leap from the top floor of the Bethesda Hospital to the pavement beneath. It was a sad end to the man with the fighter's face, the lonely responsibility of establishing a vitally important new Cabinet post, and a limitless devotion to his country.

Thinking back on whatever happened to my privacy, I have to think of what happened to my politics. Naturally, there were journalists who believed that I was a candidate for public office. All journalists know that political life can be rugged, yet each assumes, automatically, that every man who has the chance wants to get into political life and that anyone who denies such ambition is a liar. Among those people who pushed me toward office were those who were sincere, those who were not, those who were looking for stories, those who were looking for jobs. Among the ones to be respected were educators and writers.

One of the most earnest in the latter group was Douglas Southall Freeman. He had become convinced that our system of government was being endangered by one-party domination and that a President should be elected who was dedicated to constitutional government and to sustaining and maintaining the checks and balances. This great historian urged that I change my wholly negative attitude toward entering politics. He saw it as my simple duty to the nation.

Of course I valued his opinion. But I remained insistent in my belief that because a man had risen to high rank during war, and had been successful in a number of military campaigns, this alone was not important to the nation's peacetime progress. A number of people knew of my convictions about the need for balance among the several branches of government and the maintenance of the proper geographical distribution of political power. Those who held similar beliefs gave me little rest.

I had other personal ambitions. Mamie and I had always agreed that as soon as I got out of the service, we would go to that little college town, and probably buy a modest ranch. But it was not long after I entered the office of Chief of Staff that I found there were numerous offers to join either commercial or educational institutions of size.

The commercial offers I could decline out of hand. I did not believe it fitting for me, a man who had been honored by his government with military responsibilities, to profit financially for no reason other than that my name was widely known. Offers from the educational field were something else. I looked at those long and hard.

On the political side, pressures increased. Finally, I took a convenient opportunity to put my views before the public in an answer I sent to a newspaper publisher who wanted to enter my name in the New Hampshire presidential primary of March 1948. I worked over the draft of the letter carefully because I did not want to make it appear that I was arrogant or aloof or not complimented by such suggestions as had been made—but I did want to make it definite that I was not going to get involved in politics.

After four or five or six revisions of the letter, I decided to let it cool over the weekend. I did not take a copy home with me to Fort Myer. On Monday morning, as soon as I arrived at the desk, I called for it. For once I was satisfied. I did not think it should be mailed until I had shown it to Jim Forrestal. In his office, we went over it word by word. As I recall, he suggested a few minor changes that in no way affected either meaning or substance. One addition he suggested I was quick to accept. This was an insert recognizing the nobility of politics:

Politics is a profession; a serious, complicated, and, in its true sense, a noble one.

And then I added, in a model case of cracked crystal ball, "In any event, my decision to remove myself completely from the political scene is definite and positive."

CHAPTER XXI

New Student at an Old University

Wₕₑₙ a committee from the Board of Trustees of Columbia University asked me to consider becoming President of that great institution, I said (as I did later when other people had ideas about another Presidency) that they were talking to the wrong Eisenhower. My brother Milton was uniquely fitted for leadership because of his scholarly depth and his lifelong work in principal areas of American life—govermental, economic, and academic.

Without any disparagement to Milton, the committee, of which Thomas Watson, Sr. was chairman, countered that I had a broad, varied experience in dealing with human beings and human problems, a fundamental concern of the University; that I knew at first hand many areas of the earth and their peoples; that my interest in the training of young Americans and my wish to spend the rest of my life in such work offset my lack of formal preparation. They said that their invitation had the complete approval of Columbia's former President, Nicholas Murray Butler, and they were anxious to put my name before the Board for confirmation. I declined to accept because I felt the post should go to a man who was not only a good executive but was known as a scholar. The committee was not discouraged. For months its members applied pressures which would have been worthy of most super salesmen. I agreed, after a time, that if and when I left the military service, I would at least confer with the Board of Trustees before I made any move.

My preference, as I've said, inclined me toward a small school in a rural setting. In such a place, where friendly ties with students and faculty could be easily developed, I felt I might hope to share with them the lessons in hindsight from a reasonably full life. Possibly I visualized myself as a campus character whose lack of scholarly achievements would be offset by an ability to talk freely and fully about the world. Such a role I would have loved and it would have been easy. Columbia, on the other hand, was a formidable challenge.

Located in the world's greatest city, Columbia University was an international mecca for students and scholars. All sorts and conditions of men and women walked the campus. Its twenty-six or so acres, crowded with buildings, a self-contained and even self-centered community, were a microcosm of the intellectual world, as Abilene had been of small-town America.

Famed philosophers, scientists, historians were familiar figures on the sidewalks. "Names" in every field of human knowledge and research studded the University directory. The students, who in the undergraduate and graduate schools numbered around thirty thousand, were variety itself, in race, dress, speech. In all this diversity, a single concern—the search for knowledge and its dissemination— gave the Columbia community homogeneity. As everywhere, Columbia had its share of freeloaders, of students who were happy just to get by, of faculty and staff members who cherished the shelter of a rut to the windy and dangerous slopes leading up to peaks. But these were a small minority. Most were concerned with intellectual excellence.

My difficulty in reaching a decision was a natural fear that I could hardly hope to discharge the responsibilities in an enterprise so different from all my own experience and already so richly endowed with leadership in its deans and senior faculty. After all, I was approaching sixty years of age and although I still thought myself capable of adjustment to new scenes and new circumstances, Columbia would require a transformation in my way of life. The severity of the change might have been one element that tipped the scale against searching out a small college where life would have been, on the surface, at least, easier.

Above all, I saw in Columbia, because of its standing among American educational institutions and its influence on the educational process, opportunities as large and rewarding as the environment might be strange and difficult. If the faculty could stand me, I decided, I could stand the job.

Possibly I had worried too much about their reaction. Despite a surface excitement or curiosity or trepidation about the newcomer and what he might do to hallowed traditions, an old and great university takes a new president in stride with an aplomb and serenity that marks no other institution. As students come and go, so do presidents; but the university continues. Columbia, however, should have been an exception. For more than half a century, Nicholas Murray Butler had been its chief, as scholar and builder, as spokesman and showpiece.

The identification of the University with one man from the nineties of the nineteenth to the mid-years of the twentieth century could have spawned worries and fears when he departed the scene and a new face appeared in his place. After my selection as President was announced, there must have been rumblings and grumblings about the danger that a professional soldier might corrupt academic standards. But I soon learned that deep within the University structure, my arrival had caused little stir at all.

On Friday evening, for example, Low Library, where the University administrative offices were concentrated, closed its doors until Monday morning. Saturday, for me, was just another day in the week when I expected to put in at least a few hours at the desk. My peculiar attitude about schedules made no difference in the University's practice. For a while I did not realize this; on Saturday mornings I walked from our residence to the Library with a faculty or staff member who knew his way about campus, who knew the doorways, and who had the proper keys. One Saturday, without companion or guide, I attempted to penetrate the vastness of Low only to be confronted by a campus policeman who refused me entrance.

"I'd like to get into the President's office," I said.

"There won't be anybody there," he said.

When I added that my name was Eisenhower, his countenance and firm stand against my entrance changed not an iota. Nor did it when I assured him that I was President of the University. Whatever the outcome might have been of this confrontation between stalwart sentry and the new man, I have not the slightest idea. At that point, another policeman, who had apparently seen my picture in the paper, came along and vouched for me. The ivory towers of learning on Morningside Heights were guarded by other than venerable philosophers.

This was not the end of it. On another weekend during an austerity period when we had cut back on heating and lighting in all buildings not in use, I visited old East Hall late one evening. It housed the studios of the Fine Arts Department. I had heard about the work of one of the painters there and wanted to see it. During

NEW STUDENT AT AN OLD UNIVERSITY

the visit, a watchman, opening the first floor door of the building that should have been unoccupied as well as unheated and unlighted, shouted up the stairs. He wanted me to identify myself.

My name, shouted back as loudly as I could, probably seemed a Germanic garble. He wanted to know my business. When I called down the staircase that I was President of the University, a look of vigorous disbelief crossed his face and he was prepared to order my instant departure had not the artist, a well-known fellow, with his brilliant red beard, come out of his studio to urge my continued presence.

Later I learned that the watchman had reported to his senior that he had discovered in East Hall an elderly man who claimed to be the President of Columbia but did not look like it. The guard was undoubtedly accustomed to Nicholas Murray Butler, who looked the role to perfection. Butler, with his many-sided career, personified Columbia in the public eye. A scholar, as I have said, but no scholarly recluse, the world was a platform on which he played many roles. He had been all his adult life active in the Republican party and in 1912 was its candidate for the Vice-Presidency. His money-raising talents were enviable and some thought him a bit of a Machiavelli who seldom disclosed his hand as he moved and maneuvered to augment the prestige—and wealth—of Columbia. My own nomination might have been of his own doing, although the committee of trustees never hinted this to me. Whatever the case, he certainly supported the trustees' selection—and a good thing for me, too.

When Mamie and I first saw our future residence on Morningside Heights, I was a little disturbed by the mansion-like appearance of the place. Sixty Morningside Drive, in all its weight of marble and dark oak, was a grand and formal structure architecturally. It could be brightened, even warmed up, and Mamie immediately took on that task with Elizabeth Draper, the decorator. Even at that point, I saw that there was no room in which I could hope to flee grandeur. If there had been an attic I could have remodeled, I might have designed such a room. But there was no attic and the basement was beyond redemption. On the roof, which had once housed a water-tank as insurance against collapse of public supply, was a sort of "penthouse." From it, you could see all Harlem and on clear nights the lights of Long Island.

In this room, even as in the barn loft of my boyhood or my attic "command post" when I was a student at Leavenworth, I could find high above the street escape from the insistent demands of official life. Into the re-done water room, Mamie and I moved furniture utterly ineligible for a place in the gracious rooms below but dear from long association and worn by the years. A piano dominated one corner.

Access to the retreat was by a tiny elevator, unpredictable in operation, in which four passengers were a crowd. Up there, we were as cut off from the great city about us as we would have been on a remote island, and it was the one place where I could be myself.

An artist, Thomas E. Stephens, of New York, began a portrait of Mamie. I was an interested spectator. Having completed a sitting for the day, he asked Mamie to go with him through the house so that they could agree for a proper place for the portrait, when finished. Sitting alone after the two of them left, it occurred to me that I might as well make use of the paints remaining on his palette to try poking away on my own. The problem was to find anything on which to begin. It happened then that my old companion, Sergeant Moaney, came into the room and I had an idea. "Sergeant," I said, "in my room there is a little box about twelve inches on each side. Will you please knock out the sides, take any kind of white cloth you can find, and stretch it on the board by tacking the edges?" Within a matter of minutes, Moaney was back with a clean dustcloth and the bottom of the box. Together, we fastened the cloth to the board.

The only subject I could think of was right before me—Mamie's unfinished portrait. So I started out and kept going until the two explorers came back about forty-five minutes later. I displayed my version of Mamie, weird and wonderful to behold, and we all laughed heartily. Tom Stephens, for some reason, urged me to keep on trying. I did not even bother to argue; painting was beyond me. So when he said that he wanted my "painting" as a keepsake, I was glad to give it to him, this product of my first grand venture into "art."

A few days later a package arrived. Opening it, I found a present from Mr. Stephens: everything I could possibly need—except ability—to start painting. I looked upon the present as a wonderful gesture and a sheer waste of money. I had never had any instruction in painting; the only thing of possible help was a working knowledge of linear perspective, a subject we had studied at West Point.

I left the open package in my room. Each day I seemed to develop a little more curiosity about painting a picture. The result was that I took the plunge, to find that in spite of my complete lack of talent, the attempt to paint was absorbing. My most urgent need at the start was a generous-sized tarpaulin to cover the floor around the easel. The one thing I could do well from the beginning was to cover hands, clothes, brush handles, chair, and floor with more paint than ever reached the canvas. With the protection provided by the tarp, and with my painting clothes always stored in a dark recess of a closet, I succeeded in avoiding total domestic resistance to my new hobby.

The penthouse retreat at Columbia was an ideal studio. A professional might have objected to its lack of north exposure and a skylight. But privacy and quiet were more important to me than lighting. After eighteen years, I am still messy; my hands are better suited to an ax handle than a tiny brush. I attempt only simple compositions. My frustration is complete when I try for anything delicate. Even yet I refuse to refer to my productions as paintings. They are daubs, born of my love of color and in my pleasure in experimenting, nothing else. I destroy two out of each three I start. One of the real satisfactions is finding out how closely I come to depicting what I have in mind—and many times I want to see what I am going to do and never know what it will be.

In spite of this, I have frequently wished for more daylight hours to paint. Its only defect is that it provides no exercise. I've often thought what a wonderful thing it would be to install a compact painting outfit on a golf cart.

In the White House, in bad weather, painting was one way to survive away from the desk. In a little room off the elevator on the second floor, hardly more than a closet, the easel, paints, and canvases were easy to use. Often, going to lunch, I'd stop off for ten minutes to paint. In Gettysburg, I've tried many landscapes and still lifes but with magnificent audacity, I have tried more portraits than anything else. I've also burned more portraits than anything else.

The first member of the University family to greet Mamie and me at 60 Morningside when we arrived there in May 1948 was David Syrett. He was outfitted in cowboy togs with a toy pistol in a holster at his side. David, the son of a faculty member, was nine years old. Meeting us at the front door of our new home, he made a good

picture for the waiting photographers. Better still, the informality—
and the age of the University's unofficial greeter—set the right tone.
I think David was more interested in getting an autograph than anything else. Our picture made page one in eight New York newspapers the following day, I am told.

Fifteen years later, when I was in New York for the 1963 Alexander Hamilton dinner, David appeared again, we were photographed
together, and the six newspapers that had survived from the original
eight ran a "then and now" layout. At least one of them pointed out
that young Syrett had developed much more than I since our first
meeting; he was preparing for graduate work in history at the University of London.

The years between the two meetings had been for both of us, I
think, exciting, unexpected, and rewarding. Despite Columbia's
worldwide reputation as a prestigious center of learning, with its
unspoken suggestion that the University would be far removed from
the intimate, personal pursuits of daily life, David Syrett, on that
May day almost twenty years ago, crystallized for me the idea that
humanity would be present among the humanities and sciences. A
small boy had set himself one mission and wanted proof of its accomplishment. In his eager curiosity, forthright warmness, and initiative, he got it. My autograph was an urban counterpart to the jack-
rabbit a country boy might have exhibited after a chase in field or
forest.

I arrived at Columbia determined to enjoy a firsthand association
with the students and faculty. I insisted on a change in the location
of the President's office. Nicholas Murray Butler had worked on the
second floor of Low Library, reaching it by a private elevator from
the office of the University's secretary. This protected him against
intrusion by the crowds that often thronged the rotunda, usually
sightseers; it also made him inaccessible to visitors who had not
gone through the red tape of appointment-making. The office was
moved to the first floor. There, I hoped, both students and faculty
might have direct and easy access to their President and I would not
feel immured in a remote citadel.

Duties and responsibilities, whose scope I had not fully realized
before I arrived, soon sealed me off from all but formal or brief
association with the students. This fact became a source of vast
annoyance to me. Students, the chief reason for a university's being,
and for me the paramount appeal and attraction in campus life,

were in danger of becoming numerical figures on forms and passing, unknown faces on campus. Supervising the management of a vast endowment that included one of the largest real estate empires in New York; administrating an economic enterprise that employed more maintenance people, to mention just one category, than most colleges had students; satisfying the demand for speeches, alumni appearances, ceremonial functions; correcting an appalling deficit that threatened academic standards, salary scales, and Columbia's traditional objective of excellence—all these, as ravenous of energy as they were of time, fast became a moat against communication with the young men and women.

In the Army, whenever I became fed up with meetings, protocol, and paper work, I could rehabilitate myself by a visit with the troops. Among them, talking to each other as individuals, and listening to each other's stories, I was refreshed and could return to headquarters reassured that, hidden behind administrative entanglements, the military was an enterprise manned by human beings. As a university president, perhaps less sure of myself, I did not at first permit myself as much freedom as I enjoyed in Army command. The invisible and intangible rules of academic propriety and procedure were partial shackles on my personal inclinations.

With the advantages of hindsight, I know now that I should have tossed the rules into the trash can, abandoning my office and its minutia more frequently.

In one period, I set myself the goal of visiting every classroom, office, and laboratory. Under the guidance of deans and faculty, I spent a morning or an afternoon each week dropping in on lectures, poking into corners, and occasionally getting a chance to chat briefly with students or teachers. Climbing stairs was good exercise, I suppose; at least I was usually a little tired once back in the office, and I did come to know more than I had before. But a guided tour is seldom fun and often profitless; you are apt to see only what the guide deems proper.

There were countless ways, on the other hand, in which I might have enjoyed myself and possibly done some good—if only by a voluntary return to coaching, and looking in over Lou Little's shoulder while he worked out with the squad, or advising married students on the GI bill how to decorate their apartments. I never succeeded in liberating myself from the traditional decorum and occasional pomp of the university president's role although eventually I think

I would have burst my way into thoroughly enjoying life there. But I remained chief officer of everything from ritual to rentals.

During the years as an Army officer, I had met outstanding men; my command in World War II had brought me into association with great men. Columbia was a concentration of outstanding characters and superior intellects. Here and there was a bore, to be sure. But most of the men and women who make up that complex of culture and learning and buildings called Columbia were brilliant in their talk, profound in their thoughts, and enthusiastic about the University and its work. They immensely broadened my horizons. Among them, I felt myself a student who learned more from them than I could ever hope to give in return.

CHAPTER XXII

Professor Ike

AT COLUMBIA, I not only made friends but was fortunate to be able to take several there with me. Certain men were invaluable to me during my time at the Pentagon. One of these was Kevin McCann, whose interest in education was deep and who was sharply sensitive to the rapidly changing conditions of the postwar years. Another was my administrative aide, Major Robert Schulz, who had joined me in the Pentagon shortly after the war. The others were Master Sergeant John Moaney and his wife Delores, who are regular members of our household, and Sergeant Leonard Dry, my principal driver.

Two trusted confidants in University affairs were Albert Jacobs, the provost, and Kevin, who, as Assistant to the President, was tireless in his efforts to help me, a man whose background was completely governmental and military, understand the needs and sensitivities of a faculty and others in our educational institution. Learning how to take a place in academic life was not simple but learning to like the people of Columbia was; I conceived an instant liking for many faculty members and administrators. I had only known one, Lou Little, before my arrival.*

* In the number of friendships made, the Columbia period was one of the richer periods of my life. But an attempt to name each individual who became a friend would be a list marred by omissions, as this note must be. Nevertheless I should mention some of those I saw most often.

Harry Carman, who never walked when he could run, and a scholarly authority in American history, possessed a zest for Columbia College and for living a full life that he communicated to everyone associated with him, including myself. Bob Harron, Columbia's Director of Public Relations, began his professional career as a sports writer—one of his books was Knute Rockne's biography—but he had moved to Morningside Heights because the education of young people became his paramount interest. George Cooper, before World War War I a Columbia great in water polo (when that sport was still organized mayhem), spent much of his time and resources in organizing the University's alumni clubs and in introducing me to them around the country.

When Lou was football coach at Georgetown University, back
in the twenties, I was coaching an Army team that lost to Georgetown by one point. While I was still Chief of Staff, and on the eve
of my departure to take up duties at Columbia, I was given the
mission of saving Lou for the University. He had been offered the
head coaching job at Yale. Columbia alumni panicked. They decided that only I could persuade Lou to stay on. A group of them,
headed by Bill Donovan, of the OSS in World War II, and Frank
Hogan, the New York District Attorney, escorted Lou to Fort Myer

---

In the management and raising of money respectively my chief counselors were
Joseph Campbell and Paul Davis, two men who were masters of their fields. The
former, who knew to the last dollar and the bottom brick the recesses of Columbia
finances and real estate, I later appointed to the Atomic Energy Commission and
then Comptroller General of the United States. Paul Davis was the most vigorous
and informed exponent of voluntary giving for education I have ever encountered.

All the trustees became my close friends. Among them, however, I saw most
frequently, Douglas M. Black, whom I first met in connection with *Crusade in
Europe;* Marcy Dodge, the senior among them in years of service and the youngest
in his enthusiasm about Columbia; George Warren, whose common sense and wisdom
were dependable sources of support; Frank Fackenthal, Acting President between
the death of Dr. Butler and my arrival, who was my chief link with the Columbia
administrative tradition.

To keep me up-to-date in matters as diverse as medicine, literature, science, and
alumni affairs I looked for the latest information to Willard Rappleye, Dean of
the College of Physicians and Surgeons; John Henry Hobart Lyon, who well into
his seventies memorized a new poem every morning and rated all other colleges
and universities on their resemblance to Columbia. George Pegram, a scientist's
scientist, occupied an office immediately above mine and was always ready to drop
in to chat about anything from common fractions to nuclear fission and fusion;
Frank Hogan, the oft-elected New York District Attorney, was as good at solving
alumni problems as in prosecuting criminals.

Two men, dedicated to teaching as a vocation and a profession, gave up their
professional chairs, at my request, for the worries and frustrations and burdens of
administrative duty. They were Lawrence Chamberlain, who became Dean of
Columbia College, and Grayson Kirk, who became Provost, succeeding me as President of the University in 1952. For their willingness to subordinate their preference
to my and Columbia's need, I am indebted to them.

Charles Swift, manager of the Men's Faculty Club, was my host whenever I ate
or attended a University function there. Although he was devoted to Columbia,
I later learned his enduring ambition was to manage the Thayer Hotel at West Point.
Had he lived and had a vacancy occurred there, I would have done everything in my
power to help him fill it.

My personal secretary at Columbia, and an extremely good one, was Marilyn
MacKinnon. Only her decision to become a full-time housewife separated us. Another
in the office, Alice Boyce, did accompany me to France and later to the White House
where she occupied extremely sensitive positions through both terms. Secretaries
like these two multiply a man's official effectiveness.

for a talk. I had no professional or financial arguments to offer. I was reduced to a personal appeal. It was not at all eloquent:

"Lou, you cannot do this to me," I said. "You're one of the reasons I am going to Columbia."

The coach seemed a little flustered. But he recovered quickly and, asking for time to consider his future, we talked football, reminisced, and had a general discussion of the state of the game. For once all the years that I had spent coaching seemed to make sense.

I continued to be uneasy about Lou's decision. And then I learned that immediately on his arrival at his hotel in Washington, he called his wife, Loretta, and said:

"Stop packing. We're not going!"

To the alumni, that success in saving Columbia from depredation by Yale might have been my largest contribution to Columbia's stature. At least I am told that whenever the alumni got together during my time there, my triumph was cited as convincing proof that I had leadership potential. Those of the Columbia family who were less concerned with football may have assessed it with a colder eye. Nevertheless, there was, I think, a substantial academic by-product, one that not everyone could see at the time.

Columbia was pitifully short of ready money. The salary scale, formerly one of the highest in the country, had been static for years. Other universities, with ready cash, were raiding the talent pool of Columbia's faculty and staff. Had Lou Little, a fixture at Columbia, been lured to a rival campus, faculty and staff recruiting by other schools might have hurt the University. Against such raids, the University had, at the time, little protection except appeals to loyalty. More than once, I found such appeals exceeded the bait of dollars.

Some time later, for example, the Nobel Prize winner Isidor Rabi was offered a position at the Institute for Advanced Study in Princeton. There, he would not only enjoy a much larger salary, he would be free from metropolitan pressures and campus schedules, with an opportunity for creative thinking and reflection in an environment of scholarly quiet. He would enjoy daily association with his close friend, Albert Einstein. Such a partnership of brains, I knew, could be highly productive in its contribution to science. As President of Columbia, I had to protect the University against the disastrous effect of faculty morale and academic standards should Dr. Rabi leave.

We were in no position to match Princeton's offer financially. Could I have, it would have been futile, for Dr. Rabi praised intellectual challenge above money. I could only present to him the probabilities of what might happen to Columbia should he leave, in the hope that his concern for the institution and its future would save him for us. I stressed that, to the academic world, he symbolized pure science on Morningside Heights. His departure, I continued, would deprive the University of its chief drawing card—to use layman's language—to bring in brilliant graduate students for whom his presence on our campus meant excellence in science. If their numbers diminished and they were replaced by average or mediocre students, faculty members would soon lose the zest and excitement they knew and they would begin looking for other places. The chain reaction, I pointed out, could do serious damage to the institution.

My arguments were simple. I could not speak as one scientist to another; our conversation was man to man. I was only sorry that I could not find the splendid phrases such an appeal and such a figure deserved.

Then Dr. Rabi delighted me and assured Columbia against sudden deterioration in science by agreeing to stay on.

Although our alumni body was one of the largest in the country and many of its members successful and affluent, alumni support was relatively meager. One reason was the widespread conviction that Columbia was immensely rich. Another was the notion, among those who equated physical growth with quality, that Columbia was stagnant. No new building had been erected since the depression. Some Columbia College graduates pointed out that the gifts they had already made for a field house at Baker Field had been banked by the University. They suspected that Columbia's officers were more concerned with the interest the money earned than in using it for the purpose intended.

This complaint had to be dealt with. I investigated and having learned that the money had in fact been hoarded, I went to the trustees and urged approval of a new field house. The amount of money involved was around $650,000, petty cash by present spending standards in many colleges.

No one could argue that the new building added to the academic stature of the University. Realistically examined, it only made life more convenient for the athletic squads. But as it went up, it brought down the alumni grievances. And it was at least a hint that the

University might be ready for new expansion. I pushed its construction as hard as I could.

More important than bricks and mortar to me was the moral and intellectual strength of Columbia, a power for good throughout the country and the Western World. To extend this strength, to channel it better to serve the nation, new growth—I thought—should be rooted in the chief asset of any university, its faculty.

The Columbia faculty, I believed, was capable of taking the lead in studying and analyzing the national viewpoint on the vast social, political, and economic problems thrust upon us after World War II. With such a venture, they would amplify the University's role so that its influence would not be restricted to campus classrooms or scholarly conferences. Among the nationwide problems that concerned us at the time were:

§ The mental and physical health of our young people. Weakness of mind and body among far too many of them had been startlingly revealed during the war years when hundreds of thousands were rejected from the country's service because they were below minimal educational and physical standards.

§ The role of pressure groups in every area of our social and economic life. I would later make this the subject of my last address as President of the United States but even then the aggressive demands of various groups and special interests, callous or selfish, or even well intentioned, contradicted the American tradition that no part of our country should prosper except as the whole of America prospered. Unless there were changes, I felt that eventually only the promises of the extreme right and the extreme left would be heard in public places.

§ Third—there was a sort of torpor about individual responsibility and a disbelief that an enlightened and dedicated individual could, on his own, accomplish much for the good of all. This seemed to suggest a disregard for the meaning of American citizenship, and its obligations as well as its rights, or an ignorance of the opportunities for self-expression and self-development in our country.

For examining these and other problems, I saw on the Columbia faculty an immense pool of talent, scholarly and humane in its comprehension of human needs and aspirations, above the bias of sect and party. At first I thought of it as a sort of intellectual Supreme Court which could search through the entanglements of the problems before us and by dispassionate study, and with imaginative and profound thought, propose solutions that would win acceptance. I found that when I began to speak out on this point, many—even within the faculty itself—thought my notions were too idealistic. They may well have been right.

In any case, with Dean Philip Young of the Graduate School of Business, I began to elaborate the idea of a truly national assembly where we could mobilize in addition to the University's educational and intellectual resources other experts from every walk of life. Gathered together free from telephone calls and urgent summons to make instant decisions, they might examine the larger problems, find a common ground of agreement about answers, and arrive at working conclusions.

There was little or no co-ordination or joint effort among the schools within the University at that time. The real co-ordination was with the student himself, who picked out courses, and drew on the various disciplines. But the various faculties did little together. Young and I got them working on problems and drafting papers, and then brought in businessmen, encouraging an atmosphere of the free exchange of ideas. My own education at Leavenworth and at the War College had been in the "case method" and I understood its usefulness.

Working toward this idea became an absorbing pursuit for me through most of 1949. I talked about it, wrote about it, thought about it almost incessantly. Till late in the year, I got no farther than a name—the American Assembly. Then, Averell Harriman became interested. He offered the family home, Arden House, with superb surrounding acreage, high on a ridge near the Hudson as a site for the Assembly. I visited the place and found it a mansion of delightful drawing rooms and endless corridors. I was enthusiastic and the property was soon transferred to Columbia.

Now known as the Harriman campus of Columbia University, the old mansion has witnessed scores of meetings concerned with almost every aspect of human society. Throughout the years, its influence, although difficult to measure, has been far reaching beyond my dreams of almost two decades ago. Much of the time I think its beginnings were my principal success as University President. The American Assembly, however, was not the only venture that meant much to me during my short academic career.

Another project undertaken at Columbia, called the Conservation of Human Resources, had its beginnings, too, in my wartime realization that we had seriously neglected the full education and preparation of our young people to be vigorous and productive members of society. This neglect was tragically tabulated, among young men, in those armed forces rejection records of the years 1940–1945. I suspected that a fair study of these records, while they were still easily available, could produce guideposts for our future conduct as a nation. Dr. Eli Ginzberg, whose profound scholarship did not in the slightest blunt an almost boyish enthusiasm about any proposal for the betterment of human living, took over this project with a passion. This support I was able to produce in furthering his research and advancing his proposals is still one of my proudest memories of life at Columbia.

The Institute for the Study of War and Peace, the new Engineering Center headed by Dean John Donning, the Citizenship Education Project were innovations we worked out during my Columbia years. One innovation was less a matter of intellect than of the senses. It reflected the distaste for concrete and macadam of a big-city University President who had started out as a country boy.

Our campus of twenty-six acres or so was, by New York standards, an immense real estate holding. The original planners probably thought they had ample room for buildings and open lawn. They had not foreseen an enrollment of thirty thousand. By the time I arrived, despite a few trees and small patches of lawn, we were a "campus" of buildings and paving.

The factory yard appearance distressed me most of all. Leaving my office by the front entrance of Low Library on a hot day, I looked down the long flight of stone steps, across 116th Street crowded with parked cars and creeping traffic, over the dry gravel and clay of tennis courts to Butler Library, grassless, treeless. This was the physical center and heart of the University. It should be a green oasis. In my eye, I could see the hot and noisy street converted into lawn, with automobiles forever barred.

An improvement would take a little time and only a small expenditure of money. When I first presented the idea to city officials, all of them, including Mayor William O'Dwyer, were sympathetic. I quickly learned that stopping the flow of traffic through a single block of the main artery on Manhattan Island presents the city authorities with problems they think appalling and unsolvable. For one thing, New Yorkers through generations have been accustomed to free movement on 116th Street. To restrict their use of it would provoke an outraged reaction expressed in meetings and at the polls. I countered that most of the traffic was University-centered and our people would adjust their driving patterns for the sake of an attractive park.

The second objection was that fire equipment could not be barred from the street. Although I suspected that such equipment did not use 116th Street once a year, I suggested that the barrier to other traffic would be the flimsiest sort of fencing which, in an emergency, would be no obstacle to any public vehicle. At times it seemed that settling one problem spawned the birth of two or three more. The project that I thought could be accomplished within a very few months dragged on eternally. I was living in the White House, surrounded by lawn, before the dream became reality and 116th Street a pleasant mall.

All the ideas I had for changes, all the projects for advancing Columbia, were so different from the tasks of my earlier years, so novel and fresh in their appeal, that I found the work fun—or would have, if only I could have concentrated without the distraction of other demands.

Instead, I found myself caught up in a whirl of additional duties. My life at the University, exhausting enough for a neophyte in education, was complicated by a presidential summons in the fall of 1948. I was asked to go to Washington regularly to serve as senior adviser to the Secretary of Defense. When these new duties were first presented to me, the usual assurances were made that they could be done in my spare time. Politicians thought the academic life was marked by an abundance of that! I was assured that even if my new task called for long hours occasionally, the work would still be compatible with my University role and even profitable to Columbia.

In the first flush of my arrival on campus, knowing that the trustees would expect me to be an active spokesman for the University, I had accepted numerous invitations to speak during the winter months. On the campus itself, I had become involved in enough developments to consume all my waking hours when I was not in front of the microphone. Now, the "part-time" duty in Washington turned out to be no less than a major role in the reconstruction of the military establishment.

Sometimes I was an umpire between disputing services; sometimes a hatchetman on what Fox Conner use to call Fool Schemes. It was true that both my jobs, at the University and in Defense, were somewhat compatible; each was concerned with the expanding future and security of the nation. Most of the time they were a tolerable load, and frequently inspiring and rewarding.

But commuting by plane and train between Washington and New York ate up a good many hours. Making half a dozen speeches a week was something of a burden although, to be sure, if prepared texts were not required, the speeches were harder on the audience than on the speaker. And the ride between New York and Washington, although a soon-familiar monotonous and dreary process through familiar train yards and past endless billboards, did offer occasional leisure for relaxation, reading, or a nap.

The several kinds of work extended through many months and it was clear that they demanded a tungsten steel constitution. My constitution, although I didn't know it, was being violated.

Before going further, a few words on the subject of health. I have always been generous in doling out counsel on how to stay well or get well. This habit probably had its beginnings years ago when as a company and battalion commander, I knew that the number of men on sick call often decided whether or not a day's work would be done. In an amateurish way, I became a diagnostician who learned to distinguish between the malingering gold-bricker and the seriously ill. My urge to dispense medical advice did not arise out of my own bouts with illness. Until I reached sixty-five, I enjoyed fairly good health. Except for the torn knee which I had suffered in 1912, and the case of blood poisoning in my youth, I had been free from major mishaps. True, sniffles and headcolds hit me with any few degrees change in temperature or a slight shift in the wind.

Stomach aches, however, of sharp intensity were known to me. I made a self-diagnosis and decided that the culprit was my appendix. Whether they agreed with me or not, the doctors were co-operative. They removed my appendix, possibly on the theory that no harm would be done, that it would shut me up, and if a cure was not effective, I might be more hesitant in the future about invading their field. The cure did not take. Three decades would pass before I would learn the cause of my repeated distress, when doctors described it as a "young man's disease," ileitis.

Whenever attacks occurred, I blamed them, like most people, on "something I ate." I began to accumulate a list of foods to which I was undoubtedly sensitive. In time, everything produced on land

and sea was included with the exception of beef and a few of the least inspiring elements in a bland diet. I resigned myself to the attacks.

Apart from these episodes, I was never much concerned with my health. A good constitution, a gift of my forebears, and a reasonably active outdoor life, a requirement of my profession, combined to give me months on end without the slightest ache or pain. I must confess that I was inclined to be careless about my health. For one thing, cigarettes were less a habit with me than an addiction. My immoderate use of tobacco was matched by immoderate working hours whenever a big job was to be done. I was, when working, driven by the need to go at top speed, day after day, starting early and continuing past midnight. This was rough on my staff and several times during the war it might have been fatal to me. But the climax did not come until the peaceful days of 1949.

In early March of that year, I was reasonably certain I could finish my Defense assignment by the end of the month. Heartened by the prospect that I would soon have time to concentrate on my Columbia schedule, I pushed myself to make sure that no delay in winding up the Washington tour would be possible. I pushed too hard.

On the evening of March 21, 1949, I stretched out in my Washington hotel room, and knew that I was sick. General Howard Snyder, my physician, treated me as though I were at the edge of the precipice and teetering a bit. For days, my head was not off the pillow. The doctors transferred me to Key West, Florida, and I remained on the sick list, forbidden solid food and cigarettes. During most of that time, I was so ill that I missed neither. Then I woke one morning and asked for a cigarette.

Howard Snyder was no fanatic about smoking. He could take cigarettes or leave them. When he thought that he was smoking too much, he cut back to a few a day or to none at all. Still, he did insist that, since I had been able to go for some time without a single cigarette, I should reduce my consumption to something less than my customary four packs.

Although I was still sick, my head was clear enough to ponder this advice. Every time I lit a cigarette, I would have to total in my mind the number already smoked and the number of hours left in which to ration my remaining allowance. Inevitably, some afternoon when the pressure would be particularly severe, I'd find that I had already exhausted my day's quota and would have to suffer the agonies of deprivation or start again on the four-pack-a-day road.

Cigarettes, I had known for a long time, were doing me no good whatsoever. Now that I had become a public speaker of sorts, forever on the run from lectern to lectern, cigarettes were as much help as sandpaper on my vocal cords. But I rebelled, as vehemently as I could in my weakened condition, at the prospect of a life in which cigarettes would be counted and smoking regulated by the clock. The doctor was adamant.

I had to agree with him. Moreover, at that moment I wanted above anything else to avoid another collapse. If I had lived for ten days without a cigarette, I could get along without them for another ten days, ten years, or ten decades. "I'll just have to quit," I said. And I did, although I often suspected that Howard Snyder put little faith in the durability of my resolve.

During a month or so of recuperation at Key West, the quiet and leisurely pace there helped me adhere to the decision. But oddly, it was one of the easier ones. The best guard against relapse was a sense of humor, a readiness to laugh at my own weakness whenever I seemed to be on the verge of temptation to smoke just one.

In early May, I returned to Washington. Before I had been taken ill, Defense Secretary Louis Johnson had asked me to continue. I did for a few weeks, but as military budgets were reduced and reduced, I finally had to say, "You don't want me. I can't agree with this." General Alfred Gruenther, head of Joint Planning, and I wanted a $16 billion budget as minimum. Secretary Johnson kept making it less and less and I asked to be relieved. Now, I cleaned up the loose ends of the assignment, and returned to Columbia, convinced that Washington would never see me again except as an occasional visitor.

Columbia was threatened by a strike. While the law provided that eleemosynary institutions were not required to permit their employees to organize, the University, during World War II, had agreed to the unionization of maintenance workers. Now the workers wanted a wage increase. If denied it, they threatened a walkout.

I checked our lawyers to learn what measures were possible. First I found that, although the union was recognized by the University, we could, if the maintenance force quit, enlist the services of students on a part-time basis. But before taking such a step, I had to find out whether the workers' demands were justified.

There was some justice in them and if a compromise could be reached, both sides might be satisfied. The Columbia maintenance workers were part of the New York Transport Workers' Union, headed by Michael Quill. Mike Quill, a tough, blustering fellow that some people described as a "professional Irishman," came to see me. I told him that the University would do its best to meet a reasonable request because I realized that costs had gone up and the workers were entitled to an increase in pay. But I pointed out that Columbia was not making money, we were basing all our budgets on frugality, and were not yet making ends meet. Unless he was prepared to be reasonable, we would have to part right then and there.

Mike Quill grinned and said, "Look, General, I'm not going to have any trouble with you. I've got more sense than to be taking on an opponent who is as popular as you seem to be in this city."

We quickly settled the strike and had no further difficulty.

A new turn of events might well have brought the University crashing down. Louis Hacker, Dean of the School of General Studies, was quite successful in securing distinguished outside lecturers for subjects in which his classes were interested. Then he made a mistake of coming to me one day to ask that I be one of them.

I told Lou Hacker emphatically that this was ridiculous. All I could talk about was military history, military training and operation, the mobilization of a nation for war, or the probems of demobilization. He said that the students, particularly in history and economics, would be interested. With considerable diffidence, I finally agreed to try a talk before an evening group.

I specified that because I always despised long, dreary lectures, I would talk for not more than twenty minutes and would be prepared to answer questions, if any were forthcoming. I said also that I would have to leave no later than 9:30, if we began at 8:00 P.M. I was certain that a longer stay would produce a sleeping student body.

When the time came to deliver the lecture, the room was filled with several hundred students. They listened attentively as I went through a sketch of some of the major aspects of war, from its historical beginnings to the tactics and weapons we employed in World War II. Then I went a little further to speculate about the prospects of future wars now that the atomic bomb existed. I talked about the methods used by government in time of war to keep the fighting forces and the productive capacity of the nation in balance, so that neither should be exhausted. When I finished, I was astonished to find dozens of students on their feet, ready to ask questions. As each was answered, a half dozen more were ready. This went on for an hour, and finally, the professor stood up to say that he had promised to get General Eisenhower out of the lecture room by 9:30, it was already 9:45, and time to adjourn. I got out as gracefully and quickly as possible—and perspiring from every pore. I had really been "through the wringer" and wanted only a quiet corner where I could regain my equilibrium. The questions had been searching. But there were no mean or loaded questions, none designed to trip up the old soldier; these people wanted to learn.

Next morning Dean Hacker called to say that I'd done well. In fact he asked that I sign up on an annual basis for two or three of these lectures. I was complimented but I silently determined that in coming years I'd be unavailable.

It was just as well. At another point, Gabriel Silver, a friend of Columbia University, said that he would endow an annual lecture on the general subject of peace and war, but he made the stipulation that the endowment money would be forthcoming only if I would give the first lecture. Well, I could not allow an opportunity for a contribution of that sort to go by the board, so with the valuable help of Kevin McCann, I set about preparing the lecture. My previous attempt at professorship had been completely extemporaneous. Giving the new lecture was a more studied effort and, being written out, it did not put quite so much strain on me. But it put a tremendous strain on the listeners. It went on for about an hour, which was probably fifty minutes too long, and there were no demands for an encore. Fortunately, the good benefactor provided the promised endowment.

So far as I can recall, these were my only ventures into the realm of the classroom lecturer. All my other talks and addresses were ceremonial or official as the University's chief spokesman. At one point I attended a dinner where there were three previous speakers. Each had gone on at considerable length and as the evening threatened to become morning, I decided to set aside my own text. When the time came to speak, I stood up, said that every speech, written or otherwise, had to have punctuation, "Tonight, I am the punctuation—the period," and sat down. It was one of my most popular addresses.

☆   ☆   ☆   ☆   ☆

Perhaps, as I settled into campus routine, I might have become an occasional visitor to the lecture halls. Both Mamie and I were becoming very comfortable at Columbia, certain that ahead of us lay no sudden summons which would take us away from university life. We were so sure, in fact, that after more than a third of a century of married life, we began to think about buying a house and farm to which we could retire when my campus days were over.

While I was Chief of Staff, Mamie and I frequently discussed the sort of home that would fit us best, if we ever got one. On several occasions, we actually began making specific plans. These never got beyond sketchy scratchings. We knew that years would pass before we could do anything more than dream and talk. Now, after leaving the military and moving into Columbia, we started thinking again about a place of our own. The topic recurred regularly at Morningside Heights. For my part, I wanted an escape from concrete into the countryside. Mamie, who had spent a lifetime adjusting herself to other people's housing designs, or the lack of them, wanted a place that conformed to her notions of what a home should be. In the fall of 1950, we finally did something about it.

George and Mary Allen had recently bought a small farm in the Gettysburg area, a mile or so south of the battlefield. On it was a stone house dating back to the eighteenth century which Mary planned to restore. They urged us to consider the same sort of move. We would be within easy traveling distance of Washington and New York and we could reach any spot in the United States quickly. The idea was attractive. After all, Gettysburg had been significant in the early years of our married life and our sentimental attachments to it were reinforced by its significance in American, as well as our personal, history.

So, one weekend, we left New York with the Allens on a farm hunting expedition. Of all the properties we saw, the one most appealing was a farm of not quite 190 acres. The house, dwarfed by an immense barn, was located at the end of a private dirt lane a half mile long.

The buildings had seen better days. So had the soil. It would take work and money to modernize it. But the view of the mountains to the west was good.

Mamie had found the place she wanted. To complete the story, I must move ahead in time. Shortly after we bought the property, we were ordered back to Europe and once again our plans for the home we had in mind were deferred. And later, entering the White House in 1953, Mamie said, "I still have no home of my own." This had become such a touchy point with her that she had made up her mind, come what may, to build her own.

She started off by deciding to restore the old farmhouse located on the ground we had bought. I had an engineering survey made and found, much to Mamie's dismay, that she could not really rebuild. While the house had a face of brick, much of it was actually a log cabin, with a brick veneer covering its walls. The logs were moldy and worm-eaten, about two hundred years old. There was nothing to do but tear the place down.

So anxious was Mamie to retain even a fragment of the original structure, that when she found one portion of the wall and a Dutch oven in which no logs had been used, she built a complete house around them. We could not enlarge the basement because the house stood on a rocky ridge. This meant that to a certain extent the pattern of the house was already predetermined.

I went to a builder, Charles Tompkins, a friend of ours, and asked whether he would undertake construction of the building on a cost-plus basis. He said that his own work was largely in heavy construction, but he would be delighted to take on the job and would do it without charging anything for overhead.

Because he had no prepared architectural plans, the house had to be built step by step, according to Mamie's ideas. Building this way, work frequently had to be redone. Mamie occasionally forgot a detail or two. For example, when the walls were going up, we discovered that no plans had been made for central air-conditioning. Part of the walls had to be torn down so that air ducts could be installed. We found that electric switches were not in the proper places. Other work had to be done over because of our improvised design. But the work was done well and the house, although not completely convenient, did conform largely to her ideas.

Before the building began, Charlie Tompkins asked me whether I wanted to use union labor or local labor, which was not unionized but which he considered competent. I told him that as President of the United States, I would be dealing with unions and I thought it only proper to use union labor. When the house was finished, he told me that he had kept two sets of books—one of costs actually incurred and the other of what the cost had been if we had used local labor. The additional expense was $65,000.

This involved much more than a mere difference in wages, of course. It was caused by the transport of laborers, in some instances from Washington, requiring us to pay for an eight-hour day for four hours' work, with the other hours spent in traveling to and from the job. The jurisdictional strikes in Pennsylvania delayed the work and finally, when the bill was handed to us, it amounted to $215,000. This did include $45,000 for projects and improvements on other than the house itself.

This was considerably more than Mamie had thought of spending at the outset. But during construction, we began to scrape the barrel. Mamie had some money accumulated through the years and helped by her mother, she willingly participated in meeting the costs. By mid-1955, we had a place that we could call home—and it was paid for.

From that time onward, whenever Mamie saw a piece of furniture or an article that she wanted to own, she had a place to send it rather than depending on storage facilities in Washington or elsewhere. We have now lived in our home for eleven years—counting the time spent in it on weekends during the latter part of my Presidency. While it is beautiful to us, like other home builders, we have found things we would like to change. But we have learned to live with our mistakes.

And we have learned, too, that one room can constitute a home. All the others are hardly more than support or embellishment. At Gettysburg, the important room is a glassed-in porch, not much larger than a modest living room, where we spend hours from early breakfast to late evening. Facing east, with the morning sun brightening it and in shadow through the heat of a summer day, the furnishings casual and designed for comfort, both Mamie and I find it an oasis of relaxation. I don't expect that we will ever again attempt to build a house. Were we to do so, I think it would be built around such a porch.

Naturally, because George Allen was involved, at least at the start, there is a small story to go with this case history. When we first went down to Gettysburg to look at property, there was no place for us to stay and we decided to go to a motel. George made the reservation, signing the ledger "George Allen and party." We waited in the car.

We had dinner, went to a drive-in movie (the only one I have ever been in), and went back to the motel. The man waved the registration book at us. "You can't come in until you *all* register," he said.

For years, ever since my name came to have a certain currency, others have registered for me. And while we were shopping for property, there was reason not to let it be known that I was the prospective purchaser. But he said, "When there are ladies involved, everyone must be registered."

I went in, signed, and when he saw my name, he seemed reassured. It has always amused this pair of old married parties, who have made their temporary homes in all parts of the world, that we had to really measure up for one night in a Pennsylvania motel.

Our purchase of the farm in 1950 was, as I said, a reflection of our confidence that the balance of my working years would be spent at Columbia, followed by retirement to Gettysburg. The ink was not long dry on the papers when new word arrived from Washington. It reached me on a December evening in a rather dismal freight office of a railroad yard in Bucyrus, Ohio. The previous day, Mamie and I had left New York by rail for a Christmas visit with her folks in Denver. En route, I had stopped at Heidelberg College to fulfill a promise made months before to Dean John Krout of Columbia, a Heidelberg alumnus and my friend and fellow worker at the University, to speak at his alma mater. Returning to the railway car, where Mamie awaited me, I learned that President Truman had been trying to reach me by phone.

I made my way to the freight house, got the connection made to the White House, and the President told me that he would like me to return to Europe to command the NATO forces then being assembled.

He said that the other members of the Treaty Organization had unanimously requested him to designate me for the post. He put the message as a request. But he was the President of the United States and I told him that my own convenience had nothing to do with it; I had been a soldier all my life and by law was still an active soldier and I would report at any time he said. Did I have to return immediately to Washington? The President said that I could go ahead with my leave in Denver and he would see me immediately after our return.

The weather in Denver was perfect. On the edge of the Rockies, and at its altitude of 5280 feet, the city was normally frozen at Christmastime. It happened that this was a mild and open season and on Christmas day we played golf at my favorite course, Cherry Hills. The others in the foursome were my friends Governor Dan Thornton, Bill Flannigan, and Rip Arnold. The weather was so beautiful that we played in short-sleeved shirts. Rip had the happy idea of a picture, he ran into his office, got a camera and also a calendar on which December 25 was visible, and so the photograph showed both the weather and the date. It was a pleasant note on which to end another phase of life, and to make another change.

CHAPTER XXIII

The *Shape* of Things to Come

AT FOUR O'CLOCK in the morning, on Washington's Birthday, 1951, Mamie and I were roused from a sound sleep, debarked from an ocean liner, and drank champagne toasts in a warehouse on the Cherbourg docks.

The *Queen Elizabeth*, on which we had sailed from New York, had brought us to the port. Because this was the region where the Allied forces under my command had begun the liberation of Europe, the ship was met by the mayor of the city, his council, and a number of other officials. Sleepy-eyed, and barely presentable, we were conducted to the warehouse. The morning was dark and a cold fog wrapped itself around ship and people.

Inside the warehouse, we were hospitably offered breakfast to accompany the champagne. The circumstances were eerie. The building was dimly lighted and, if heated at all, no furnace could have dispelled the frigid damp of the barnlike structure. But the warmth of the welcome was genuine.

The toasts were frequent, grandiose, and delivered in French. My replies were brief. My French was halting, the sound approximately that of a Kansas threshing machine with gear trouble. For Mamie and me, the greeting was especially charming. It helped to offset the stories we had read about the sentiments plastered on billboards a few weeks earlier in European capitals that expressed resentment at American presence in Europe. *Yanks Go Home* signs were, we felt, the sporadic outburst of a Communist-led minority. But they certainly weren't auspicious, given the job at hand, and so the warehouse champagne breakfast was a good start for our residence in France.

Mamie and I had left Columbia with regret. I was reluctant to end my University career but I felt that an absentee President, at a time when important new projects were getting under way at Columbia, would harm it. Before going to Washington to confer with President Truman, I had told Fred Coykendall, Chairman of the

Columbia Board of Trustees, that I would resign. The terminal date
of my assignment in France was unknown; my tour might last several years. After discussing this with his associates, he said that all
were in favor of giving me an indefinite leave; only in the event that
my absence was prolonged would they consider accepting a resignation. They were insistent that the topic be shelved for two years or so.
I must say I accepted their decision gladly for it permitted me the
hope of eventual return.

At the meeting with President Truman, I had said that I thought
my first task should be to proceed as quickly as possible to each of
the NATO countries. There, talking with the government leaders, I
could find out whether each was ready to go ahead seriously with
the security programs that would now be necessary. It was silly to
attempt a military defense for Western Europe unless every nation
was ready to put its heart and soul into the task. The harsh facts of
the international scene demanded such commitment.

That winter, the world outlook was bleak for those of us who
only five years before had fought a war to eradicate tyranny from the
earth. It now seemed that, at any moment, the arrogance of Communist power might be converted into offensive action against the
West. It had already exploded in the Far East where the United Nations troops on the Korean front that season were suffering tragic
reverses.

Few things were predictable about the supreme command of an
enterprise that required wholehearted co-operation by twelve nations
—nations whose territories were as small as tiny Luxembourg or as
globe-spanning as the United States and Great Britain. We were
attempting to forge a unified organization out of many peoples and
personalities, many languages, diverse cultures and faiths and histo-
ries. Apprehensions about a potential aggressive move against the
West provided the starting point for a common alliance for survival.
But we were not at war. The absence of an imminent threat meant
the absence of strong motivation. It diminished any feeling of ur-
gency—except in those of us who were attempting to build the North
Atlantic Treaty Organization. None of us in this new venture, least
of all I, had any assurance that NATO could win from all its members their complete allegiance.

Then, as now, I thought it a fact that in the British-American
partnership for waging World War II there was less military, economic, or political friction than in any prior coalition known to his-

tory. But achieving that mutual trust, even when our fortunes in war were tightly bound together, was not always easy.

Once, in Africa, in 1943, I received a message from Washington conveying an American suspicion that in establishing our Allied air bases throughout the Mediterranean Theater the British were surreptitiously exerting their influence to see that the bases were located and built with an eye to promoting British postwar commercial interests. The message puzzled me. Most of the fields from which we were operating were of a temporary type, using perforated steel plate for surfacing and shacks for ground facilities. We expected to abandon them, removing every scrap of usable material as our advance permitted the establishment of new bases. But the message reflected a suspicion that was unhealthy, to say the least, and I thought it necessary to clean the air at once.

A thorough investigation revealed no grounds whatever for the ridiculous allegation. In directing two officers, one British and one American, to draft a reply, my only orders were to tell the truth, as they knew it, and to use as the opening words of the answering cable, "This Allied Headquarters believes . . ." In this way I served notice that neither British nor American officials in my theater were concerned in maneuvering for post-war advantage on a nationalistic basis. Our aim was to damage, defeat, and destroy the enemy wherever we could find him.

During the war, some Americans thought that I had become so friendly with the British political and military leaders that the British had more influence with me than their American counterparts. This suspicion was pure fantasy. On the other hand, there were British officers who were sure that I had to subordinate my own judgments to those of my American superiors. After one meeting with Prime Minister Churchill at Chequers, for example, where British and American views were not meshing too well, and I was inclined to favor the American, General Brooke said:

"Naturally, you cannot be expected to oppose violently something that Washington apparently wants."

Although I am sure he did not mean to imply that I was swayed by fear of a reprimand, I explosively set him right. I told him flatly that only the merits of a proposal, not its place of origin or its sponsorship, mattered to me when the fortunes of nations were at stake.

Suspicions of this sort may have provided fodder for small talk or bar gossip. But they never disturbed in the clutch of war the mu-

tual purpose of Allies at the command level. The North Atlantic
Treaty Organization, however, could be marred, possibly wrecked,
unless all in it were prepared to repress prejudice and partisanship,
pooling their talents and energies in a common trust. Because nothing of the sort had ever before been attempted except under pressure of war, no one could be sure of the outcome. A personal reconnaissance was my first job.

On New Year's Day 1951, I'd left Columbia for Washington. The
following afternoon at Arlington Cemetery, I bade farewell to an
old comrade, General Walton Walker, who had been killed in Korea.
Two and a half days were filled with briefings and a final visit to the
White House. Then I left for Europe a little after noon on January
6, arriving at Orly airport in France at nine the following morning.

In Paris, I broadcast to all the peoples of the Atlantic community.
I wanted to explain that an alliance for peace was an entirely practical matter and that the power generated in a venture of such magnitude could bring confidence to the hearts of freedom-loving people
everywhere. In the opening paragraph, I tried to keynote my own
attitude:

I return to Europe as a military commander, but with no miraculous
plans, no display of military force. I return with an unshakable faith in
Europe—this land of our ancestors—in the underlying courage of its
people, in their willingness to live and sacrifice for a secure peace and the
continuance and the progress of civilization.

And then, in eighteen days and in bitter winter weather, a few
staff officers and I visited eleven European capitals.

Except in Portugal, the elements everywhere seemed allied to
make travel disagreeable and at times risky. In Oslo, we landed in a
blinding snowstorm. The press plane following us from Denmark
had to turn back because of the increasing severity of the storm. In
London we ran into a smallpox scare and each of us had to be vaccinated—again. During all my years in the Army I had been repeatedly vaccinated but the last time one had taken effect was when
I was about ten years old. Now, at sixty, I again had a "take"
resulting in a sore and swollen arm for several days. When I got to
Germany, I encountered a virus of a particularly vicious kind. At
Heidelberg the doctors put me to bed where I had to stay for forty-
eight hours.

Despite these souvenirs, the trip was fascinating. I was favorably impressed by the governments with which I conferred. Each was prepared, more or less, to do its part. Of course, each wanted more American strength in Europe than we then had and I agreed to strive to attain reinforcement, but only on a temporary, emergency basis. I had to point out over and over again that the United States would be providing a strong Navy and Air Force for the benefit of all of us and at the same time we would always have to be one of the principal arsenals of democracy in the event we got into trouble. This meant to my mind, and I so told them, that the thickly populated areas of Western Europe should be able to provide the vast bulk of the land and conventional forces needed, even if we had to provide a few divisions to give them confidence as each country achieved a respectable strength of its own.

That period has long since elapsed. I did, and do, believe however that we should keep in Europe, for the foreseeable future a force of reasonable size. In my opinion at this time our own permanent ground strength in Europe should be about the equivalent of two divisions. But their presence there would be clear evidence that in the event of general war, we would be in it from the beginning with all we have.

President Truman had suggested that it might be well for me to report my conclusions in an informal session with the Congress on my return and, perhaps, to the people on a nationwide broadcast. Now I had to get to work on the two speeches. In substance, they presented no difficulty. Even in the short time I had been abroad, I had come to the conclusion that each of the several governments involved in NATO was determined to carry out its responsibilities. The difficulties would be many. All the nations were war weary. None had completely recovered from the damage done in six years of World War II. Nevertheless, I felt it would be entirely possible to establish a collective defense. So, aboard the plane flying from Greenland to Canada, I began writing out my estimate of the situation.

The pilot said that instead of taking the shortest route to Ottawa, we would go west and then south, following the "pressure curve." On the westward leg of the flight, we were so far to the north that for hours during the day we could see the sun almost literally bouncing along the southern horizon. It seemed to be a huge, red ball with its lower edge in the sea. I was then an enthusiastic amateur photographer and snapped at least forty or fifty pictures of the scene during our flight. It was a spectacular sight.

Those of us in the party were rather unspectacular. Everyone was thoroughly tired. Even the plane had grown weary; engine trouble delayed our departure from Ottawa, and we were told that a frigid and sleety welcome awaited us at Stewart Field, West Point. We might not be able to land. Even when we were over the field, the control tower, talking us down to the runway, was tense with fear of a mishap. We landed safely. The appalling weather was offset by Mamie's pleasure. I was back from a mission which she had feared, reading newspaper accounts, might be the death of me.

For the next four days, I kept to the Thayer Hotel at West Point. A center of gaiety every other time I had been there, the place was now almost deserted. This pleased me for in its quiet, no longer under the gun of early starts and late hours, I could review all that I had seen and heard during the trip. Hours on end, I worked over the talk. Few speeches have ever given me so much trouble. On one hand, I had to stress, as forcefully as I could, the weakness, almost the defenselessness, of Western Europe against any possible irruption from the East. (This would be assisted in some sectors of Europe by local Communists.) On the other hand, just as forcefully, I had to stress the spiritual vigor of the European peoples, who for years had labored, with the help of the Marshall Plan, to repair the devastation of war, and having fought the creeping paralysis of Communism now found in the North Atlantic Treaty new hope.

The three principal points I wanted to make were: that the preservation of a free America required our participation in the defense of Western Europe; that success *was* attainable, given unity in spirit and action; and that our own major role should be as a storehouse of munitions and equipment, although initially a fairly heavy commitment of American troops would be required.

On the last day of the month, with the speech shaping up to my satisfaction at last, Mamie and I flew to Washington where I was to lunch with the President at Blair House. The bad weather was still with us. As we approached National Airport, the city and countryside were coated with snow and ice. The Potomac River was frozen over. And apparently traffic conditions were so bad that the President, who had insisted upon meeting us, was late in arriving at the field. The plane's crew had to keep flying, circling the area so as to land just as the President reached the field.

The following morning, I appeared before members of both houses of the Congress. This was not a formal Joint Session, and the meeting was held in Coolidge Auditorium of the Congressional Library. In essence I told them exactly what I had told the President the previous day—that NATO was a feasible military alliance, that if we could unify the forces of the various countries and establish them under a single command we could build an effective defense, and that our nation, for a time, would have to keep in Europe something like six divisions.

Because of the size of the audience, no question-and-answer session could follow. Later that day, however, in a two-hour executive session of the Foreign Relations Committee, and the following morning in a like session with the members of the House Armed Services and Foreign Relations committees, I was questioned almost to the point of cross-examination.

On both occasions, I came to realize that these representatives of the people were sharply divided in their attitude toward the Republic's role in world affairs. A hard core of extreme nationalists seemed to be echoing the isolationist philosophy of more than ten years earlier. Others were extremely skeptical of our Allies' dependability and even their will to defend themselves. Still others, although professing their belief in the interdependence of the Atlantic community, felt our contribution to the new organization should be limited to money and supplies. Fortunately, many shared the conviction that NATO, as a regional expression of the United Nations charter for mutual security among neighbors, could be a success.

Most of the criticism I had foreseen and despite my incorrigible fervor in revising any given talk up to the moment of delivery, nothing new developed in the two executive sessions that required changes of more than a few words in my talk to the nation. Because I had worked and reworked it through so many hours since I first started it over the Greenland icecap, because I had been so carefully questioned by the Congress, I had it now almost committed to heart. It would require almost half an hour to deliver. To expect an audience to sit before their television sets, watching as I read it, would be asking too much. What I was going to say came out of my heart and my head. Instead of reading from a text, I had the entire speech lettered out on large cards. They were held on either side of the camera. As I finished one it was whisked out of the way

and replaced by another. The impression got around that I delivered
the entire thing extemporaneously.

Since the announcement of my appointment to the Supreme Command, I had been pondering what I could do to stop once and for all
the speculation about my possible candidacy for the Presidency. There
was something else on my mind. I felt I should try to persuade, in
person, those opposed to our participation in the military defense of
Europe. I had to make it clear that by going to Europe we were,
curiously enough, only protecting our own frontier. The long-range
plane had moved America's frontier three thousand miles eastward,
to the heart of Europe, as far as military effectiveness was concerned.

At that moment, the debate in Congress centered around two
basic issues. The first was the constitutional power of the President,
without the approval of Congress, to deploy troops abroad in time
of peace as he saw fit. The second was the size of the forces that the
United States should deploy in Europe to fulfill its obligations under
the NATO concept. A noisy argument had developed between those
who, with the President, favored a strong commitment of approximately six divisions and those who argued for considerably less.

All this disturbed me deeply. The United States would be in an
untenable position if it should, as one of the NATO members, provide the commander for whatever joint common forces could be
developed and then, by either minimizing its own commitments or
by a bitter and continuing debate at home, should weaken the whole
structure.

Personally, I thought that the President had complete authority
to deploy troops as he chose and to determine the strength of the
deployment. However, I well knew, as the others did, that troops
could be maintained in Europe only as Congress provided money
for their maintenance and, indeed, for their existence.

The President was a Democrat and it was natural to suppose
that his party would follow his lead, although there might be dis-
sident individuals. Some Republicans had become champions of the
theory that the free world could exist only if we could establish effective co-operation among the principal free nations. One of these
was Senator Arthur Vandenberg, who was joined by others of similar
beliefs.

On the other hand, within the Republican party there was an
important element in opposition to the President on both points. I
felt that before leaving for Europe I should see what I could do to

smooth over the differences. I asked Senator Robert Taft for an appointment to discuss the NATO project. He promptly replied that he would be glad to see me but he suggested that rather than my coming to his office, he would come to the Pentagon, for a private and unannounced talk. This was encouraging.

I thought it might be possible for me to kill two birds with one stone. My first purpose was to be assured that when I got to Europe, the United States government's position would be solid in support of NATO. If such assurance were forthcoming, from the chief spokesman of what seemed to be the opposition, there was also a way to kill off any further speculation about me as a candidate for the Presidency.

Before the conference with the Senator, I called in two staff officers and we wrote out a statement that I would issue that evening, on the assumption that Senator Taft would agree that collective security should be adopted as a definite feature of our foreign policy. My statement was so strong that, if made public, any political future for me thereafter would be impossible. We worked on the statement for a time, and having written it out in pencil, I folded it up and stuck it in my pocket.

When Senator Taft appeared at one of the less obvious entrances to the Pentagon, a staff officer met him and whisked him to an elevator and into my office.

We had a long talk. I think he may have been a bit suspicious of my motives. A good many persons had been urging me publicly to get into politics—in fact to run for the Presidency.

I posed only one request. I explained that it was not my business to talk about the constitutional powers of the President as compared to those of the Congress, nor was I ready to say that we needed six divisions in Europe. My purpose was to study the whole matter seriously, once I was on the ground in Europe; only then could I make final recommendations. My sole question was, "Would you, and your associates in the Congress, agree that collective security is necessary for us in Western Europe—and will you support this idea as a bi-partisan policy?"

 I explained that if the principle were accepted wholeheartedly, if he could answer "yes," I would be completely happy in the new job and would spend my next years attempting to fulfill the great responsibility given me. But if this was going to be a matter of deep and serious division within the Congress, between the Congress and the President, then NATO would be set back, and I would probably be back in the United States.

I used all the persuasion I could but Senator Taft refused to commit himself. He said, several times, "I do not know whether I shall vote for four divisions or six divisions or two divisions."

I assured him again that I had no interest in that detail at the moment. I only wanted to know whether he would support the concept of collective security for the North Atlantic community. Our conversation was friendly but I had no success. This aroused my fears that isolationism was stronger in the Congress than I had previously suspected.

When Senator Taft left my office, I called my assistants in, took the drafted statement from my pocket, and told them to forget about it completely. I tore it up in front of them. In the absence of the assurance I had been seeking, it would be silly for me to throw away whatever political influence I might possess to help keep us on the right track.

My plan of making a dramatic and flat announcement was scrapped. That announcement, as I reconstruct it now in my mind, was:

Having been called back to military duty, I want to announce that my name may not be used by anyone as a candidate for President—and if they do I will repudiate such efforts.

These were two big disappointments, although I said nothing except to one or two good friends. First, now I could not feel the unity of our government behind me and, second, I had lost the chance to settle the political question once and for all.

To produce Allied co-operation for World War II was far easier than developing a military defense for NATO and peace. This was an enterprise without precedent. In wartime, neither Britain nor the United States ever held back in the hope that the other would perform the necessary but nasty chores. In time of peace, and in spite of common danger, the same desire to make maximum contributions did not always prevail. For example, in most European countries the tour of military service required under the draft laws was too short to allow the kind of technical training that had become necessary in modern times, where every service is equipped with highly sophisticated weaponry, effective only when operated by educated personnel.

In Europe, I found that Belgium was the only country that had laws requiring a full two-year tour of military duty. I went to the other countries citing Belgium and urging others to follow her example. Not a single nation, as far as I can remember, increased the term of service. Instead, after the first year, Belgium decided that because other nations were not requiring military training of equal length, it would reduce the tour of service in its Army. This was discouraging, not only because of the deleterious effects upon the NATO establishment itself, but because of the likelihood that each country, in order to avoid political resentment in its own population, was ready to lessen its level of sacrifice for the common good.

NATO was, nevertheless, a necessary mechanism. The Marshall Plan had not yet reached full fruition—self-confidence was lacking both in Western Europe as a whole and in each nation. One of the greatest goals of NATO and the military forces to be assembled was to restore and sustain the confidence so needed throughout Europe. Throughout my tour of duty as Supreme Commander of NATO Military Forces, no objective was more important than this one. The defensive forces that existed at the start could not match, or even scratch, those of the Communist bloc nations. But the knowledge that a unified, progressive effort to mobilize and generate strength was under way had an almost electrifying effect on European thinking.

It is clear that each nation could not be expected to produce a rounded defense, using all kinds of weapons and arms. It would be ridiculous to think that Luxembourg, for instance, could produce satisfactory fighting airplanes or that Holland, Belgium, the Scandinavian countries, or Portugal should each produce a formidable share of a high-seas fleet. It was even more obvious that the smaller nations should not be asked to produce their own nuclear capability.

We studied the types and quantities of contributions that could be made by each of the NATO countries. The United States was carrying the burden of producing the nuclear deterrent, an expensive and difficult task. We were also maintaining an enormous air force and a powerful navy. Each of the larger European countries was improving industrially and we were hopeful that each would produce matériel best suited to its industrial pattern. By and large, the effort was to mobilize troops and weapons of a kind most easily and effectively produced in each nation and so to lighten, to a considerable extent, the burden on each. It was out of this idea that a single operational command for NATO's defense forces was originally conceived.

There was no thought, of course, of amalgamating troops so that each unit would become an international hodge-podge. The differences in languages alone would be enough to defeat any such plan. Each unit of division strength would be homogeneous as to nationality while the larger units, corps and armies, could logically contain within themselves units of different nationalities. The plan to effect this was called the European Defense Community.

From the first, the small countries in NATO agreed with the idea. Originally, Mr. Churchill was opposed. And the plan, largely designed by the French, soon ran into opposition—from the French.

The French government at that time was passionately concerned lest German strength become so powerful that it would take a dominant position in the Allied establishment. Mr. Churchill's reasons were less clear, for he was himself a major influence in achieving a somewhat similar organization in World War II. As for the French worry, the treaties made with Germany forbade certain kinds of munitions manufacture and with that nation divided into East and West it seemed impossible to the rest of us in NATO Headquarters that Germany could become a menace to the peace as a military entity.

For many months, my staff, together with the military officials of all NATO countries, worked hard to get the kind of organization and command system that would give no nation a unilateral advantage—or a position of overweening influence. At the same time, they worked to produce the maximum defensive force.

Our work toward an alliance gave me opportunities to visit the NATO capitals and to meet nearly all the political leaders of Western Europe, as well as those of Greece, Turkey, Canada, and Iceland.* A few figures stood out from the crowd.

During the first ten months of my tour, Clement (now Lord) Attlee was Prime Minister of Great Britain. I knew him from war-

---

* Because of the outspoken antagonism of a number of NATO governments to the Franco regime in Spain, I made no attempt to visit that nation. For similar reasons I did not go to Yugoslavia and, out of respect for the neutrality of Sweden and Switzerland, I refrained from visiting those two countries.

time but though he was in Mr. Churchill's Cabinet, as Deputy Prime Minister, I had never been as closely associated with him as with other British officials of that period. He and I never discussed the domestic policies and politics of Britain, which were, of course, none of my business. But in 1951, as well as earlier, he impressed me as a man of sincerity and earnestness. He had little of Churchill's charm and phrase, but he was a friendly man, decisive in expressing himself, in a rather sharp, high-pitched voice, and he was always ready to examine common problems and to seek solutions. He was a real supporter of NATO which of course endeared him to me.

The political figure I liked best in the British Labor government of the SHAPE period was the Foreign Minister, Mr. Ernest Bevin. Ernie Bevin was a heavy-set, down-to-earth, unpretentious man, full of humor and fun. He was never hesitant in talking about his lack of early educational advantages, he was resolutely self-confident, and he relied upon his energy, natural adaptability, and native common sense to carry him through the mazes of international politics. I felt that had he possessed the early advantages available to Mr. Churchill—and assuming that he would still have chosen to become a member of the Labour party—he would have been a truly formidable opponent for that brilliant Conservative leader.

On the continent, there were a few men in official position who seemed to stand out in any conference. Mr. Joseph Bech, Minister of Foreign Affairs of Luxembourg, representing a tiny country of some four hundred thousand persons, was nevertheless admired by his colleagues. Whenever he spoke, we all listened with great respect.

Another impressive individual was Henri Spaak, a Belgian. From the beginning, I thought of him as an internationalist in the best meaning of that word. Citizens of the smaller but highly civilized nations of the world always seemed to me to be far more aware of the interdependence of peoples than those who lived in more powerful or more extensive countries. I still encounter Americans who are astounded when I say anything about the dependence of America upon other countries.

Spaak was a student and an articulate one. Again, I knew little of his domestic politics but when the subject was Europe and the North Atlantic community he was always worth listening to. (He reminded me of another man I liked and admired—Lord Ismay—Pug to his friends, a British soldier who later became Chairman of the NATO Council. Pug was also a thoughtful student of international affairs but less eloquent in expressing his convictions.)

My own message to the NATO governments never varied—I hammered it home everywhere. If we could make a go of a practical pact permitting common military plans, procurement, organization, and control of the forces of NATO, the security of Western Europe would be assured. The region would then become a complex which would be, militarily, economically, and politically, as powerful as any other in the world.

Beyond the military advantage, there was my conviction that European unity was both possible and necessary to the full achievement of its destiny. In support of such concept, I made a talk on July 3, 1951, before the English Speaking Union in London.

Both the Prime Minister, Mr. Attlee, and Winston Churchill were present. After the talk, each congratulated me on it. The following morning, a letter came from Mr. Churchill, beginning "My dear Ike." It said, in part, that as he was getting rather deaf, he had not been able to hear the speech. But he had located a copy and said that he was arranging for the widest circulation within his powers.

Mr. Churchill's praise was extravagant—he insisted that it was one of the greatest speeches delivered by any American in his lifetime—and he said that he had not "comprehended the splendor" of the speech until he had read the text. But any praise from the master speech maker was heady stuff.

Mr. Churchill's optimism about the future, expressed in the letter, especially about progress toward European unity, was not borne out by events. I had stressed that Europe could never attain the stature possible and inherent in its peoples' skills and spirits so long as it divided itself by patchwork territorial fences, pyramiding every cost with tariffs, taxes, and overstuffed overhead; barred the efficient division of resources and the easy flow of trade; promoted distrust and suspicion; and served vested interests at the expense of people.

Mr. Jean Monnet, whom it was my good fortune to know, carried the cause of the unified Europe as his banner. He has never changed his fundamental convictions on the engrossing prospect of Europe's common good, nor have I. He has had both official and unofficial connections with several organizations devised to secure European unity and I have applauded every word and act of his in support of this. Personally, I have no doubt that one day a kind of political union will eventuate and when it does, Monnet will be rightfully recognized as the father of a united Europe.

The talk before the English Speaking Union was my only formal and public exposition of my convictions on European unity—except militarily. Privately, in my office and visiting around the continent, I was emphatic in the expression of my views. But first things had to come first—and our goal was the establishment of an effective defense force. Toward that goal we progressed slowly, but steadily.

By early spring of 1952, all the governments, except France, were ready to sign the protocol for an international military organization with unified commands. Sometimes the French seemed to believe that only they had any military experience or possessed any real military knowledge. To some of us in NATO Headquarters, this seemed strange in view of recent history. But it was a fact with which we had to deal.

In May of 1952, the French government finally initialed the agreement and with this document unanimously approved by all nations, I felt that the organizational work for which I had been sent to NATO was largely accomplished and I could be released from active duty.

By now Greece and Turkey had joined the organization. We were in constant communication with the authorities of West Germany and we were sure that within a few years that country would become a full-fledged member also, bringing the total of sovereign powers in the alliance to fifteen.

A year and a half before we had started the venture without precedent to guide us. We had surmounted the obstacles of nationalism, provincialism, and outright disbelief that the job could be done. These nations had proved unified in purpose and performance —around the conference table, in the planning councils, on the maneuver fields. Whatever the future might hold for us or for our creation, NATO had become a vital and intercontinental institution, a historic fact. Whatever history might decide, I am glad this mighty force has existed.

Tremendous demands had developed urging me to get into politics. These came from both parties. Men of every kind and class, it seemed, visited my headquarters during all of 1951 and each had his own reasons for asserting that I owed it to the country to become a political candidate. With none of this did I agree.

Nor did I believe that my visitors, despite their political acumen and experience, reflected majority opinion in either party or in the country. Until March I made no personal contribution to the issue other than the statement of Republican affiliation I had felt it necessary to make in January. This, to be sure, reduced by half the partisan pressures. In a way, it also gave me a little peace of mind, for I was sure that the Taft forces within the Republican party were strong enough to deny anyone else the nomination. In this belief I was steadfast until the New Hampshire primary.

The day before it was held, I dictated a letter to Arthur Summerfield declining an invitation to visit Michigan before the national convention. He had asked me, along with other "candidates," to be seen and heard by the Republicans there. I explained that I could not accept because I was not a candidate. The following morning, reading the letter over, I signed it and added a postscript in longhand, saying that before nightfall, the New Hampshire voters might very well eliminate me from the possibility of candidacy any time, anywhere.

They did not. For weeks thereafter I had to wrestle with the facts and arguments so often and so long presented. Finally, I came to the conclusion that with numerous people I deeply respected stressing the need of our country for a change in political control and domestic programs, I should return to the United States. I would abide by the decisions of my party and of the electorate if I were nominated.

We looked around us, said good-bye to Europe, and turned toward home. Once again, Mamie and I began packing.

NOTE 1

LANE UNIVERSITY

STARTED less than twenty years before my parents' arrival there, Lane was a typical venture in higher education before the Morrill Act launched a multitude of tax-supported colleges and universities. Until then practically all colleges west of the Alleghenies were the product of church zeal, faculty sacrifice—and a small amount of money.

In the case of Lane, the founding cash gift amounted to $2000 given by James Lane, first United States Senator from Kansas, whose generosity was recognized in the name of the new school. The state of Kansas contributed thirteen acres in Lecompton, originally intended as the site of the state capital by the pro-slavery group that had been in control of the territory until 1858. Their defeat by the anti-slavery forces and the removal to Topeka had left Lecompton a sort of ghost town with many empty buildings that had been constructed for housing the legislature and state officials.

Among them was the Rowena House, a sizable structure forty-five feet by seventy-five feet, with three stories above the basement. This became the original college building in 1865 when the school opened. According to a description of the time, it contained four recitation rooms, an auditorium, an office, one library, one laboratory room, twenty studios, and a large basement room. A few years before my parents enrolled, a new building, the pride of the campus, had been finished, using the foundation that had been prepared for the state capitol and materials that had been accumulated almost a quarter century earlier for its construction. A third building, with a bell tower, was built for a chapel and additional classrooms. Although this was not much physical plant for a university, it was large enough for an enrollment that seldom exceeded one hundred.

According to a former student, academic standards were hardly at modern university levels. But the literary societies, which were a major activity of Lane as he recalls it, were a center of school life where in discussions and debates the student body covered the realm of knowledge from agriculture to zoology, engaging in what was practically self-education. They were all very poor, he writes, but alert, ambitious, and determined. These qualities, undoubtedly, made up for many deficiencies in facilities and faculty. That they were also young and human is stressed by an anecdote of my parents' time at Lane.

The bell above the chapel used as a signal for college exercises as well as a fire alarm was the subject of study by some students interested in its disturbance-creating possibilities. After some consideration, they procured one evening a hungry mule which they introduced into the small room where the bell rope hung. To the mule's neck, they tied the rope. On the floor before the animal, they placed a box of feed. Then they made themselves scarce.

In no time at all, the campus and the town were aroused by the insistent clamor of the bell as the mule relieved its hunger. One of those awakened was an elderly member of the faculty who crept through the darkness to the chapel door, sure that the offending student was trapped. Quietly opening the door of the room, then listening, the professor launched himself at the culprit and found himself tightly embracing the mule by the neck.

Few, if any, official records survive of Lane University, its faculty, and its students. Throughout its life span as an institution, those who conducted it were engaged as much in a war against debt as in a crusade against ignorance. The United Brethren churches, committed to its support, numbered among their constituents no wealthy people. The students themselves, coming from families where hard money was a scarce commodity, paid little in tuition and fees; some of them managed to board themselves there for $1.25 a week. Eventually, economic considerations compelled the merger of Lane with Campbell College in Holton, Kansas, in 1903. Ten years later, Campbell merged with Kansas City University which, in turn, was a fatality of heavy financial obligations and the 1929 market crash. When this institution closed its doors in 1931, the last visible evidence of Lane University's existence, other than a few buildings in Lecompton, disappeared.

NOTE 2

VEGETABLE SOUP

THE best time to make vegetable soup is a day or so after you have had fried chicken and out of which you have saved the necks, ribs, backs, *un*-cooked. (The chicken is *not* essential, but does add something.)

Procure from the meat market a good beef soup bone—the bigger the better. It is a rather good idea to have it split down the middle so that all the marrow is exposed. I frequently buy, in addition, a couple of pounds of ordinary soup meat, either beef or mutton, or both.

Put all this meat and the bone, early in the morning, in a big kettle. The best kind is heavy aluminum, but a good iron pot will do almost as well. Put in also the bony parts of the chicken you have saved. Cover it with water, something on the order of 5 quarts. Add a teaspoon of salt, a bit of black pepper, and, if you like, a touch of garlic (one small piece). If you don't like garlic put in an onion. Boil all this slowly all day long in the open kettle. Keep on boiling till the meat has literally dropped off the bone. If your stock boils down during the day, add enough water from time to time to keep the meat covered. When the whole thing has practically disintegrated, pour it out into another large kettle through a colander. Make sure that the marrow is out of the bones. I advise you to let this drain through the colander for quite a while as much juice will drain out of the meat. (Shake the colander well to help get out all the juice.)

I usually save a few of the better pieces of meat to be diced and put into the soup after it is done. The rest of it can be given to your dogs or to your neighbor's dog. Put the kettle containing the stock you now have in a very cool place, outdoors in the wintertime or in the icebox; let it stand all night and the next day until you are ready to make your soup.

You will find that a hard layer of fat has formed on top of the stock which can usually be lifted off since the whole kettle full of stock has jelled. Some people like a little bit of the fat left on and I know a few who like their soup very rich and do not remove more than about half of the fat.

Put the stock back into your kettle and you are now ready to make your soup.

In a separate pan, slowly boil in water about a third of a teacupful of barley. This should be cooked separately since it has a habit, in a soup kettle, of settling to the bottom and if your fire should happen to get too hot it is likely to burn. If you cannot get barley use rice, but it is a poor substitute.

One of the secrets of making good vegetable soup is not to cook any of the vegetables too long. However, it is impossible to give you an exact measure of the vegetables you should put in because some people like their vegetable soup almost as thick as stew, others like it much thinner. Moreover, sometimes you can get exactly the vegetables you want; other times you have to substitute. Where you used canned vegetables, put them in only a few minutes before taking the soup off the fire. If you use fresh ones, naturally they must be fully cooked in the soup.

The things I like to put into my soup are about as follows:

1 quart canned tomatoes, ½ cup peas or cut cut green beans, 2 potatoes diced, 3 branches celery, 1 large sliced onion, 3 large carrots diced, 1 turnip diced, ½ cup canned corn, 1 handful raw cabbage chopped.

Your vegetables should not all be dumped in at once. The potatoes, for example, will cook more quickly than the carrots. Your effort must be to have them all nicely cooked but not mushy, at about the same time.

The fire must not be too hot but the soup should keep bubbling.

When you figure the soup is about done, put in your barley which should now be fully cooked, add a tablespoonful of "Kitchen Bouquet" and taste for flavor. (If you cannot get "Kitchen Bouquet," use one teaspoonful of Lee and Perrin's "Worcestershire Sauce.") If necessary add salt and pepper and if you have it, some onion salt, garlic salt, and celery salt.

Cut up the few bits of the meat you have saved and put about a small handful into the soup.

While you are cooking the soup do not allow the liquid to boil down too much. Add a bit of water from time to time. If your stock was good and thick when you started, you can add more water than if it was thin when you started.

As a final touch, in the springtime when nasturtiums are green and tender, you can take a few nasturtium stems, cut them up in small pieces, boil them separately as you did the barley, and add about one tablespoonful of them to your soup.

Originally published in *What's Cooking at Columbia*, 1948.

NOTE 3

A FEW NOTES ON MORALE

THERE is at least one striking difference between the American soldier and numerous other soldiers in history. The Army, however, as far back as the days of Von Steuben, learned that Americans either will not or cannot fight at maximum efficiency unless they understand the why and wherefore of their orders. To Von Steuben, after his professional career in Europe, where troops were only pawns to be moved about the board of war without consideration of them as individual human beings, this was a wonder. To meet it, changing his own practice and attitude completely, he worked to develop in Washington's army an understanding by the individual—down to the last private—of his place in the scheme of battle and of the training drudgery necessary for him to maintain that place honorable.

Von Steuben's fundamental doctrine that the American soldier must know the reason why he must do thus and so has been fundamental United States Army doctrine ever since his day. Before World War I, no extensive records were kept of programs that expressed this doctrine and its recognition was probably a by-product of individual commanders' leadership. The intense loyalty of the Army of the Potomac to George McClellan, despite the frustration of several half-won, half-lost campaigns, may have very well been due to the sustained training program insisted on by him that gave each soldier a thorough understanding of his role in the Army.

In World War I, however, Von Steuben's doctrine became a formal and common element in Army training programs. Among the millions of men volunteering or being drafted, destined for service far from home, engaged in a war whose outcome, in their view, would not instantly menace our own security, using weapons and vehicles that required skills not common in our civilian population, the morale of the troops might be seriously damaged if, in the encampments where they were concentrated, large numbers of men remained obviously unfit for a soldier's duty.

From my report to President Quezon, (Chapter XVII):

Morale is born of loyalty, patriotism, discipline, and efficiency, all of which breed confidence in self and in comrades. Most of all morale is promoted by unity— unity in service to the country and in the determination to attain the objective of national security. Morale is at one and the same time the strongest, and the most delicate of growths. It withstands schocks [sic], even disasters of the battlefield, but can be destroyed utterly by favoritism, neglect, or injustice. To foster a proper morale in the Army is an undertaking worthy of the incessant effort of His Excellency, himself.

The Army should not be coddled or babied, for that does not produce morale, it merely condones and encourages inefficiency. But the Army should be taught to respect itself, and to render a quality of service that will *command* respect throughout the nation. Thus the population will come to look upon the uniform as the badge of loyalty, of duty, and of efficiency, and this feeling will be reflected, inescapably, in still higher performance in the Army.

NOTE 4

HISTORY LESSON IN TRAVEL FOR
EISENHOWER GRANDCHILDREN AND OTHERS

UNTIL the advent of the steam locomotive and the steamship, man's traveling speed was exactly the same as that of Ramses and Alexander. The waterways of the country—rivers, lakes, and canals—had been the most dependable and most used avenues of commerce and travel. To be sure, on the eastern seaboard, a primitive roadnet gradually developed because the rivers—except for the Hudson, the Delaware, and the tidal rivers of Virginia and Maryland— were shallow and short. By the Revolutionary War a horseman could travel at a fairly fast pace from Massachusetts and New Hampshire as far as Savannah, Georgia. Washington and Jefferson, for example, thought nothing of riding sixty miles or more in a day; most other travelers, of course, were more leisurely. But wheeled vehicles were doing well when they averaged twelve to fifteen miles a day on a long trip. And there were long trips undertaken. Two or so generations later, in the early days of western migration from the Mississippi to the Pacific coast, because few rivers flowed in an easterly or westerly direction, tens of thousands crossed the plains and mountains over trails first made by Indians, Spanish, French, or American explorers.

So far as I know, the only formal venture in developing a road route across a large area of the country was the old National Road or Cumberland Pike that approximately paralleled the 40th degree of latitude. Although national in name and in its purpose of tying the Atlantic coast to the Mississippi basin, the maintenance of this road after its blazing by Boone and other pioneers was a local responsibility. Where the citizens were alert and energetic, it was for its day an adequate thoroughfare; where they were few in number or careless about the good of others, this road could be more dangerous and hazardous in its deep ruts and wide washouts than the wilderness around it.

But the waterways, except in time of flood or drought, provided at least a smooth means of travel. The steamboat, dependent on neither current nor wind, enabled its passengers and freight to move at an extraordinary speed compared to all earlier standards. An Army unit in the Mexican War, for example, moving entirely by water, traveled from Fort Detroit to Mexico, a distance of more than 1200 miles, in ten days; until World War II this was not at all bad by the Army standards of any country.

The railroads, built at a feverish pace from the early 1850s onward, year by year reduced American reliance on its water routes until those routes were abandoned, some of them, late in the last century. At the same time, because rails reached practically every community of any size in the United States by the time I was born, only simple roads for local hauling were needed.

Competition between the railroads for passengers and freight became so fierce and rates in consequence so low that no one of good sense would have thought of traveling or transporting freight by any other means. Had your great-great-great-grandparents moved from Pennsylvania to the frontier before the Civil War, almost certainly they would have moved themselves and their goods in wagons. When my grandparents actually did move, they would have been thought very odd indeed if they had not used rail transport. In consequence, the road system of the United States well into this century may have been less usable for transcontinental traffic than it had been fifty or sixty years earlier.

So far as passenger travel was concerned, the automobile and the airplane did to the railroads what the locomotive had done to the waterways. The process, of course, was far from instantaneous. Not until the eve of the First World War was there any organized attempt to develop for the automobile a modern equivalent of what the national road had been for the cart and wagon. The war years, naturally, blunted the efforts of enthusiasts for transcontinental road traffic; too many other things had far higher priority. With the end of war and the explosive expansion of automotive industry, national highways became both an evident need and an outlet for economic energies.

The beginnings of construction on the first modern transcontinental highway were marked by a faith in community initiative that is rare today. Its promoters, a group of private individuals calling themselves the Lincoln Highway Association, to demonstrate the desirability of permanent road surfaces, engaged in the building of what were known as "Seedling Miles." Wherever it was thought that such short construction, to contrast with old-fashioned graded dirt roads that quickly rutted or became mud holes, would inspire local residents to tax themselves for its extension throughout their home area, they were built.

Of its proposal, the Lincoln Highway people said:

"The Association has particularly encouraged the building of Seedling Miles in those districts of the Middle West where no permanent improvement has existed on the route. Any such community along the Lincoln Highway desiring to construct a Seedling Mile can, by making proper application to the Lincoln Highway Association and securing its approval, secure sufficient cement for the construction of a standard sixteen-foot road. The only condition is that satisfactory sub-grade and drainage must be provided at the expense of the community, the labor cost of doing the work financed, and adequate provision made for the maintenance of the road for a reasonable period following its construction."

Were any individual or organization to make such a proposal these days in connection with a national venture of any sort, I am afraid denunciations of both a pinch-penny attitude and the fatuity of faith in local initiative would be loud. Cartoonists could have a field day; columnists might exhaust themselves; and I am afraid millions would think the proposal a stupid and hopeless way of getting things accomplished. To such an extent have we changed in less than half a century; many people in 1919 thought the Seedling Mile rather a good idea and out of it did come a coast-to-coast thoroughfare. I hasten to add that I am making an observation this time, not a complaint.

Within the Army, until 1916 pretty much tied to mule and horse as it had been a century earlier, the new vehicle, whose capacities had been well tested in training and in combat support, offered a speed of movement and a mobility not restricted by rail schedules or routes. In part prodded by the enthusiasts for a transcontinental highway and in part moved, as I have said, to search out the military capabilities of automobile and truck, the War Department committed itself to the venture of a coast-to-coast convoy that was, under the circumstances of the time, a genuine adventure.

NOTE 5

THE GUILDHALL ADDRESS
(*London, June 12, 1945*)

THE high sense of distinction I feel in receiving this great honor from the City of London is inescapably mingled with feelings of profound sadness. All of us must always regret that your great country and mine were ever faced with the tragic situation that compelled the appointment of an Allied Commander-in-Chief, the capacity in which I have just been so extravagantly commended.

Humility must always be the portion of any man who receives acclaim earned in blood of his followers and sacrifices of his friends.

Conceivably a commander may have been professionally superior. He may have given everything of his heart and mind to meet the spiritual and physical needs of his comrades. He may have written a chapter that will glow forever in the pages of military history.

Still, even such a man—if he existed—would sadly face the facts that his honors cannot hide in his memories the crosses marking the resting places of the dead. They cannot soothe the anguish of the widow or the orphan whose husband or father will not return.

The only attitude in which a commander may with satisfaction receive the tributes of his friends is in the humble acknowledgment that no matter how unworthy he may be, his position is the symbol of great human forces that have labored arduously and successfully for a righteous cause. Unless he feels this symbolism and this rightness in what he has tried to do, then he is disregardful of courage, fortitude, and devotion of the vast multitudes he has been honored to command. If all Allied men and women that have served with me in this war can only know that it is they whom this august body is really honoring today, then indeed I will be content.

This feeling of humility cannot erase of course my great pride in being tendered the freedom of London. I am not a native of this land. I come from the very heart of America. In the superficial aspects by which we ordinarily recognize family relationships, the town where I was born and the one where I was reared are far separated from this great city. Abilene, Kansas, and Denison, Texas, would together equal in size, possibly one five-hundredth of a part of great London.

By your standards those towns are young, without your aged traditions that carry the roots of London back into the uncertainties of unrecorded history. To those people I am proud to belong.

But I find myself today five thousand miles from that countryside, the honored guest of a city whose name stands for grandeur and size throughout the world. Hardly would it seem possible for the London Council to have gone farther afield to find a man to honor with its priceless gift of token citizenship.

Yet kinship among nations is not determined in such measurements as proximity, size, and age. Rather we should turn to those inner things—call them what you will—I mean those intangibles that are the real treasures free men possess.

To preserve his freedom of worship, his equality before law, his liberty to speak and act as he sees fit, subject only to provisions that he trespass not upon similar rights of others—a Londoner will fight. So will a citizen of Abilene.

When we consider these things, then the valley of the Thames draws closer to the farms of Kansas and the plains of Texas.

To my mind it is clear that when two peoples will face the tragedies of war to defend the same spiritual values, the same treasured rights, then in the deepest sense those two are truly related. So even as I proclaim my undying Americanism, I am bold enough and exceedingly proud to claim the basis of kinship to you of London.

And what man who has followed the history of this war could fail to experience an inspiration from the example of this city?

When the British Empire stood—alone but unconquered, almost naked but unafraid—to defy the Hitler hordes, it was on this devoted city that the first terroristic blows were launched.

Five years and eight months of war, much of it on the actual battle-line, blitzes big and little, flying V-bombs—all of them you took in your stride. You worked, and from your needed efforts you would not be deterred. You carried on, and from your midst arose no cry for mercy, no wail of defeat. The Battle of Britain will take its place as another of your deathless traditions. And your faith and endurance have finally been rewarded.

You had been more than two years in war when Americans in numbers began swarming into your country. Most were mentally unprepared for the realities of war—especially as waged by the Nazis. Others believed that the tales of British sacrifice had been exaggerated. Still others failed to recognize the difficulties of the task ahead.

All such doubts, questions, and complacencies could not endure a single casual tour through your scarred streets and avenues. With awe our men gazed upon the empty spaces where once had stood buildings erected by the toil and sweat of peaceful folk. Our eyes rounded as we saw your women, serving quietly and efficiently in almost every kind of war effort, even with flak batteries. We became accustomed to the warning sirens which seemed to compel from the native Londoner not even a single hurried step. Gradually we drew closer together until we became true partners in war.

In London my associates and I planned two great expeditions—that to invade the Mediterranean and later that to cross the Channel.

London's hospitality to the Americans, her good-humored acceptance of the added inconvenience we brought, her example of fortitude and quiet confidence in the final outcome—all these helped to make the Supreme Headquarters of the two Allied expeditions the smooth-working organizations they became.

They were composed of chosen representatives of two proud and independent peoples, each noted for its initiative and for its satisfaction with its own customs, manners, and methods. Many feared that those representatives could never combine together in an efficient fashion to solve the complex problems presented by modern war.

I hope you believe we proved the doubters wrong. And, moreover, I hold that we proved this point not only for war—we proved it can always be done by our two peoples, provided only that both show the same good-will, the same forbearance, the same objective attitude that the British and Americans so amply demonstrated in the nearly three years of bitter campaigning.

No man alone could have brought about this result. Had I possessed the military skill of a Marlborough, the wisdom of Solomon, the understanding of Lincoln, I still would have been helpless without the loyalty, vision, and generosity of thousands upon thousands of British and Americans.

Some of them were my companions in the High Command. Many were enlisted men and junior officers carrying the fierce brunt of battle, and many others were back in the United States and here in Great Britain in London.

Moreover, back of us always were our great national war leaders and their civil and military staffs that supported and encouraged us through every trial, every test. The whole was one great team. I know that on this special occasion three million American men and women serving in the Allied Expeditionary Force would want me to pay a tribute of admiration, respect, and affection to their British comrades of this war.

My most cherished hope is that after Japan joins the Nazis in utter defeat, neither my country nor yours need ever again summon its sons and daughters from their peaceful pursuits to face the tragedies of battle. But—a fact important for both of us to remember—neither London nor Abilene, sisters under the skin, will sell her birthright for physical safety, her liberty for mere existence.

No petty differences in the world of trade, traditions, or national pride should ever blind us to our identities in priceless values.

If we keep our eyes on this guidepost, then no difficulties along our path of mutual co-operation can ever be insurmountable. Moreover, when this truth has permeated to the remotest hamlet and heart of all peoples, then indeed may we beat our swords into plowshares and all nations can enjoy the fruitfulness of the earth.

My Lord Mayor, I thank you once again for an honor to me and to the American forces that will remain one of the proudest in my memories.

Index